D0759631

COGNITIVE LINGUISTICS AND LEXICAL CHANGE

CURRENT ISSUES IN LINGUISTIC THEORY

AMSTERDAM STUDIES IN THE THEORY AND HISTORY
OF LINGUISTIC SCIENCE – Series IV

ISSN 0304-0763

General Editor

E.F.K. KOERNER

Zentrum für Allgemeine Sprachwissenschaft, Typologie
und Universalienforschung, Berlin
efk.koerner@rz.hu-berlin.de

Associate Editor

JOSEPH C. SALMONS

University of Wisconsin-Madison

Current Issues in Linguistic Theory (CILT) is a theory-oriented series which welcomes contributions from scholars who have significant proposals to make towards the advancement of our understanding of language, its structure, functioning and development. CILT has been established in order to provide a forum for the presentation and discussion of linguistic opinions of scholars who do not necessarily accept the prevailing mode of thought in linguistic science. It offers an outlet for meaningful contributions to the current linguistic debate, and furnishes the diversity of opinion which a healthy discipline must have.

A complete list of titles in this series can be found on *http://benjamins.com/catalog/cilt*

Volume 331

Natalya I. Stolova

Cognitive Linguistics and Lexical Change. Motion Verbs from Latin to Romance

COGNITIVE LINGUISTICS AND LEXICAL CHANGE

MOTION VERBS FROM LATIN TO ROMANCE

NATALYA I. STOLOVA

Colgate University

JOHN BENJAMINS PUBLISHING COMPANY
AMSTERDAM/PHILADELPHIA

The paper used in this publication meets the minimum requirements of
the American National Standard for Information Sciences – Permanence
of Paper for Printed Library Materials, ANSI z39.48-1984.

DOI 10.1075/cilt.331

Cataloging-in-Publication Data available from Library of Congress:
LCCN 2014015364

ISBN 978 90 272 4850 3 (HB ; alk. paper)
ISBN 978 90 272 6986 7 (E-BOOK)

John Benjamins Publishing Co. · P.O. Box 36224 · 1020 ME Amsterdam · The Netherlands
John Benjamins North America · P.O. Box 27519 · Philadelphia PA 19118-0519 · USA

Table of contents

Preface & Acknowledgments

My interest in the development of motion verbs from Latin to Romance goes back to my doctoral dissertation of 2003 at the University of Pennsylvania under the supervision of Paul M. Lloyd. His passionate interest in historical Romance linguistics and his distinguished scholarship, especially his monumental *From Latin to Spanish* (1987), have been a great source of inspiration for me.

An important point in the writing process of the present monograph was my participation in the 8th International Conference on Late and Vulgar Latin held at St Catherine's College, Oxford in September 2006. It offered me the first opportunity to present some of the study's key findings. I am especially grateful to the conference organizer and editor of its proceedings, Roger Wright (University of Liverpool), for his comments on my paper (Stolova 2008) and for discussing with me on several occasions my progress on this book. I am also thankful to the president of the session at which I gave my paper, Benjamín García-Hernández (Universidad Autónoma de Madrid), for providing me with his publications on Latin preverbation.

Another venue which provided me with helpful feedback on some of the present study's main findings was the session on historical and contrastive description of the Romance languages at the 25th International Congress on Romance Linguistics and Philology held at the University of Innsbruck in September 2007. I am particularly grateful to the session's president, Peter Koch (University of Tübingen), for taking his time to discuss with me at length my presentation which was later published in the Congress' proceedings (Stolova 2010a).[1]

My gratitude also goes to Joel Rini (University of Virginia), Donald Tuten (Emory University), Yanira B. Paz and Haralambos Symeonidis (both at the University of Kentucky), who were the organizers of the sessions on Hispanic and Romance linguistics at the annual Kentucky Foreign Language Conference which I have been attending since 2006. Although at the University of Kentucky I spoke mostly on topics other than the topic of the present book, I always tried to integrate historical Romance data with cognitive linguistics, posing the following questions: (1) How can the cognitive framework help us explain the developments attested from Latin to Romance and (2) How can the developments attested from

---

1. Earlier, in 2004, Prof. Koch had kindly provided me with papers of his on cognitive historical Romance onomasiology and semasiology.

Latin to Romance help us refine and expand the cognitive framework? The fact that my audience found these questions stimulating, gave me the inspiration to advance these questions with regard to lexical change.

Another source of inspiration has been the work of Steven N. Dworkin (University of Michigan) on Spanish and Romance lexical change. I am thankful to him for providing me with his publications and for offering helpful comments and suggestions on earlier versions of parts of the manuscript. I have also greatly benefited from the conversations with David A. Pharies (University of Florida) about Latin and Romance word-formation and with Christopher J. Pountain (Queen Mary, University of London) about the phenomenon of capitalization. I am likewise grateful to Mark Davies (Brigham Young University) for discussing with me the textual composition, architecture, and interface of his *Corpus del Español* (Davies 2007): a number of Spanish examples in Chapters 6 and 7 of the book derive from this 100 million word historical corpus.

I would also like to thank several persons at my home University where I have been working since 2003. I am grateful to the staff at the Inter-Library Loan Department at Colgate library, particularly its Coordinator Ann Ackerson, for patiently helping me access the difficult-to-get multi-volume materials. At the Department of Romance Languages and Literatures I would like to thank my colleagues Frederick Luciani, Fernando Plata Parga, Patrick Riley, and Franziska Merklin for answering my questions about Spanish, French, and Italian. I am also thankful to Oana Patilea, Colgate University Class of 2012 and a native speaker of Romanian, for sharing with me her linguistic insights. My most sincere thanks also go to Patricia Ryan for going over my manuscript with me and making excellent suggestions on its English style. My work with both Ms. Patilea and Ms. Ryan was sponsored by the Colgate University Research Council, whose support I hereby gratefully acknowledge.

I have long admired the Current Issues in Linguistic Theory (CILT) series for combining linguistic data with theoretical advances. Because this book is both data-driven and theory-oriented, I would like to thank the General Editor of the CILT series, E.F.K. Koerner, for taking on this project and for supporting my work throughout all its stages with extraordinary dedication, remarkable patience, and generous help. Special thanks are also due to the three anonymous referees who read my manuscript with great care and offered detailed comments, constructive criticism, and valuable suggestions, all of which allowed me to refine my ideas and improve their presentation. Needless to say, I am the only one responsible for any remaining shortcoming. Last but not least, I would like to express my gratitude to Anke de Looper and Patricia Leplae at John Benjamins for their most professional assistance throughout the production process.

Hamilton, N.Y., March 2014   Natalya I. Stolova

CHAPTER 1

Objectives and key concepts

1.1 Goals of the present study

This book explores the lexical change of motion verbs from Latin to Romance in light of current advances in cognitive linguistics and examines the contribution of Latin and Romance historical data to the cognitive linguistics framework. The research on Latin and Romance verbs of motion (i.e., verbs like 'go', 'enter', 'walk') that has been carried out so far is often scattered in dictionaries, grammars, articles, and monographs that treat the topic incidentally. The few articles and book-length studies that actually do make these verbs their prime concern choose to limit themselves to only one or a few lexical items, one language, and one point in history. Besides that, within the Romance family, the amount of material available to us on verbs that express movement varies from language to language. While Spanish, French, and Italian have received more attention, Portuguese, Romanian, and non-national Romance languages are left neglected. In addition, the existing accounts tend to be atomistic as they treat only one of the two levels at which lexical change takes place (lexicology/onomasiology, semantics/semasiology) without integrating them with one another. Furthermore, the focus of the existing studies has been the description and classification of the developments that took place, but not the analysis of the motivational mechanisms of the changes at hand. Consequently, while these research efforts provide valuable insights, they do not offer a balanced comprehensive picture.

How to see the forest for the trees? In this monograph, I argue that the theoretical approach known as historical cognitive linguistics is particularly well suited to achieve this task. The present study applies the historical cognitive linguistics framework to Latin and Romance verbs of motion in order to provide a unifying and comprehensive perspective on the evolution of the lexical field of motion verbs from Latin to the modern Romance languages. More specifically, the goal is to assess the continuity of Latin verbs of motion and the Romance innovations as far as lexical change is concerned and to examine how similar Pan-Romance tendencies manifest themselves differently in each particular language. In addition, my aim is not only to evaluate the developments that took place from Latin to Romance, but also, through the application of the cognitive framework, to identify the cognitive mechanisms involved and evaluate their role as enabling factors of change. In other words, the objective is not only to establish what happened to the lexical field in question and how it happened, but also to find out why it happened. Furthermore, while interested in the new insights that cognitive linguistics can reveal about Latin and Romance diachronic data, I am at the same time focusing on what Latin and Romance diachronic data can reveal about cognitive linguistics. In other words, another research objective of this study is to illustrate ways in which historical Romance linguistics and the cognitive linguistics framework can mutually benefit each other, and to advance the elaboration of methods for cognitive diachronic lexicology and lexical semantics.

Because this book provides the first in-depth historical lexical and semantic analysis of motion verbs for Romance linguistics and cognitive linguistics alike, its intended audience includes several types of readers: those interested in the language-specific field of historical Romance linguistics, those interested in the field of cognitive linguistics, and those interested in the phenomenon of lexical change.

The study adopts a broad Pan-Romance perspective. It relies on the diachronic data from ten languages: Latin, five national Romance varieties (Spanish, French, Italian, Portuguese, Romanian), and four non-national ones (Catalan, Occitan, Sardinian, Raeto-Romance). Several additional non-national Romance varieties (e.g., Aragonese, Sicilian) are mentioned whenever relevant to highlight similarities and contrasts within the Romance family. Non-Romance languages and language families (e.g., English, Chinese, Amerindian) are referred to when the need arises to place Latin and Romance developments in the cross-linguistic context.

The present work consists of ten chapters. The rest of Chapter 1 defines motion verbs, introduces the phenomena subsumed under lexical change, and identifies points of conversion between the historical and the cognitive approaches to language. Chapters 2 through 4 take up the question of recruitment to the lexical field of motion. Chapter 2 outlines the main principles of cognitive onomasiology and relates them to the cognitive typology of motion encoding. Chapter 3 presents Latin and Romance onomasiological data by providing the biographies of the verbs in question. Chapter 4 employs the theoretical framework outlined in Chapter 2 and the data presented in Chapter 3 to identify patterns of onomasiological change, focusing on such phenomena as degree of continuity, lexical loss, and innovative lexical creation on both Pan-Romance and language-specific levels. Chapters 5 through 7 are devoted to the semantic development of motion verbs. Chapter 5 outlines the main principles of cognitive semasiology and relates them to motion-based conceptual metaphors. Chapter 6 addresses the continuity and loss of the metaphorical extensions of the verbs in question. Chapter 7 examines the Romance innovative metaphorical mappings not attested in Latin. While Chapters 2 through 7 concentrate on how the cognitive framework enables us to account for patterns of lexical change from Latin to Romance, Chapters 8 and 9 turn the tables and focus on how these diachronic patterns inform current theoretical discussions within cognitive linguistics. Chapter 8 illustrates the ways in which my analysis contributes to the cognitive typology of motion encoding. Chapter 9 explores the implications of my results for the conceptual metaphor theory. The concluding Chapter 10 presents the book's main findings and points towards some possible research directions for the future.

1.2 Motion verbs in the Romance language family

The question "What are motion verbs?" has no single correct answer because the answer depends on what we understand as motion (or movement). On the one hand, motion can be construed as a physical state opposed to rest. Charles Bally (1865–1947), for example, classifies as verbs of motion such French verbs as *saisir* "to grab", *casser* "to break", *vibrer* "to tremble", *frotter* "to rub", *ouvrir* "to open", and *mêler* "to mix" (Bally 1951 II: 235–237). In a similar way, in his *Dictionnaire alphabétique et analogique de la langue française*, Paul Robert includes *palpiter* "to beat [of heart]", *plier* "to fold", and *tordre* "to twist" within the section entitled "Mouvement" (Rey, ed. 2001 IV: 1713–1719). One can also conceptualize movement as opposed to displacement (or translocation), as proposed by Lucien Tesnière (1893–1954) in the section "Mouvement et déplacement" of his *Éléments de syntaxe structurale*: a cyclist on a stationary bicycle achieves *mouvement* but not *déplacement* (Tesnière 1959: 308). This criterion, however, presents a problem: a particular verb can refer to both movement and displacement, depending on the context. For example, in *He jumped up and down*, *jumped* refers to movement, while in *He jumped over the fence* the same verb indicates displacement (Selimis 2002: 1). We should also take into consideration whether a movement of the whole body or just that of its parts is involved. For example, when a person puts things with their hand, the hand is moving with regard to the body, but the whole body does not move with regard to its background (ibid., pp. 5–6). In other words, as modern physicists recognize by building upon the revolutionary ideas of their great predecessors, Nicolaus Copernicus (1473–1543), Giordano Bruno (c.1548–1600), and Galileo Galilei (1564–1642), "motion is relative" and is to be studied "from the point of view of an inertial frame of reference" (Landau & Kitajgorodskij 1980: 46, 48).

As a consequence of such a wide choice of criteria, the number of verbs of motion established by linguists differs dramatically. For example, according to Paul Robert (1910–1980), French has more than 228 verbs of motion, while Annibale Elia states that there are around 150 of them in that language (Rey, ed. 2001 IV: 1717; Elia 1982: 352). Thus, it becomes clear that when talking about verbs of motion it is imperative to clarify what is being understood under this term. For the purpose of the present study I adopt the definition formulated by Françoise Létoublon:

> Par 'verbes de mouvement', ou 'verbes sémantiquement apparentés au verbe *aller*', on entend [...] les verbes référant à un *mouvement autonome du sujet, avec déplacement*: ces verbes s'opposent donc à la fois à ceux qui renvoient à une position statique (*être debout/couché/assis* etc.), à ceux qui renvoient a un mouvement sur place, sans déplacement (comme *se lever, se dresser, s'asseoir, tourner* ou *toucher*) – [...] et aux verbes qui renvoient à un mouvement avec déplacement non du sujet, mais de l'objet, qui n'est pas 'autonome'. (Létoublon 1985: 14; original emphasis)

> [By verbs of motion, or verbs that are semantically similar to the verb *to go*, we understand [...] verbs that refer to the subject's autonomous movement with displacement. These verbs contrast at the same time with the ones that refer to static position (*to be standing up, to be laying down, to be seated*, etc.), with the ones that refer to movement on one spot without displacement (like *to get up, to stand up, to sit down, to turn*, or *to touch*), [...] and with the ones that refer to non-autonomous movement not of the subject but rather of the object.]

In other words, when I say 'motion verbs' or 'verbs of motion' I am referring to those verbs that express self-propelled motion of the subject which involves a change of place, i.e., translocation.[1]

It should be stressed that regardless of the method used to identify verbs of movement, these lexemes do not form a homogeneous group. A number of linguists have highlighted the broad and heterogeneous nature of the lexical field of motion verbs, dividing it into subfields based on criteria related to word-formation, semantics, and syntax. These classifications can be found in many places, from Bally (1951) in French to Cuartero Otal (2006, 2010) in Spanish.[2]

The present study focuses on verbs that express the following motion concepts: (1) movement in general without any specification of means or direction (equivalent of English "to go"), (2) movement toward and/or reaching a particular location (equivalent of English "to come", "to arrive"), (3) movement away from a

---

1.   Self-propelled motion is also known as "agentive", "voluntary", "self-caused", and "internally-caused" (Filipović 2007: 18, n.11). Motion that involves a change of location is referred to as "translational" (Talmy 2000 II: 35; 2007: 80–81). For two recent taxonomies of motion, see Pourcel (2010) and Zlatev et al. (2010).

2.   See Meya (1976), Ferrari de Egues (1985), González Aranda (1998), Cifuentes Honrubia (1999), Hidalgo Rodríguez (1999), and Morimoto (2001) for Spanish; Guého (1979), Krassin (1984), Sikora (1985), Laur (1989), Sablayrolles (1991), Montibus (1996), Rossi (1999), Rey ed. (2001), and Lepetit (2004) for French; Ketterer (1971) for 16th- and 17th-century French; Lamiroy (1983) for French and Spanish; Violi (1996) for Italian; Welty (1974) for Italian and French; Rehfeldt (1980) for Portuguese; Ionescu (1963), Reinheimer (1965), and Evseev (1974) for Romanian.

particular location (equivalent of English "to go away", "to leave"), (4) movement inside (equivalent of English "to go in", "to enter"), (5) movement outside (equivalent of English "to go out", "to exit"), (6) movement upward (equivalent of English "to go up", "to ascend"), (7) movement downward (equivalent of English "to go down", "to descend"), (8) movement on foot by taking steps (equivalent of English "to walk"), (9) swift movement on foot (equivalent of English "to run"), and (10) movement by springing off the ground (equivalent of English "to jump"). The first seven categories are selected because they represent some of the main ways in which language organizes motion in terms of space, and the last three categories are included because they represent some of the main ways in which language organizes motion in terms of manner.[3] In other words, the lexical items that express these ten concepts constitute what is commonly referred to as "el núcleo o el centro del campo" (Geckeler 1976: 306), i.e., the core of the lexical field.

In the majority of cases, a single concept is lexicalized not by one but rather by several verbs. For example, in Latin "to go out" corresponds to EXIRE, EGREDI, and EVENIRE. In Spanish, "to go down" is rendered by *bajar* and *descender*, as well as by Old Spanish *abaxar* and *deçir*. Similarly, in Romanian "to go up" is lexicalized as *a urca*, *a sui*, and *a se ridica*. Thus, focusing on the ten core concepts listed above makes the total number of verbs analyzed in detail over two hundred, i.e., high enough to identify patterns of lexical change while manageable enough to be dealt with within a single study.

1.3 Levels of lexical change: Onomasiology and semasiology

Lexical change takes place on two levels: on the level of form and on the level of meaning. Therefore, it is analyzed on two levels: on the level of onomasiology and on the level of semasiology. Onomasiology (< Greek *ónoma* "name") is defined as the study of the different designations (also known as 'forms' or 'signifiers') of a given concept (also known as 'sememe' or 'mental object'); cf. Baldinger (1980: 110, 136). As Traugott & Dasher (2002: 25) put it, onomasiology focuses on "the development or restructuring of coded representations of a particular domain such as COLOR, INTELLECT [etc.]". Semasiology (< Greek *séma* "sign") is concerned with the ways in which a given lexical item acquires new meanings. In the words of Traugott & Dasher (2002: 25), the focus of the semasiological research is on "the

---

3.   For a discussion of ways in which language organizes motion in terms of space and manner, see Kibrik (1970), Vernay (1974), Pick & Acredolo eds. (1983), Menovščikova (1986), Vandeloise (1986), Lý (1989), Violi (1991), Aurnague et al. eds. (1993), Svorou (1994), Bloom et al. eds. (1996), Pütz & Dirven eds. (1996), Wälchli (2001a), Levinson (2003), Shay & Seibert eds. (2003), Berthele (2006), Hickmann & Robert eds. (2006), and Levinson & Wilkins eds. (2006).

development of polysemies (or, where relevant, splits into homonymies)". Schematically speaking, onomasiology departs from the concept analyzing the forms
recruited to lexicalize it (i.e., proceeds from function to form), while semasiology
departs from the lexical item exploring the concepts that it is able to express
(i.e., proceeds from form to function).

When studying lexical change, words are usually not considered by themselves
on a word-by-word basis but rather as part of a larger group known as semantic
(also lexical, or onomasiological) field; cf. Gordon (2001). Such fields are "closely
integrated sectors of the lexicon, in which a certain sphere of experience is divided
up and organized in a particular way which may vary from one language or one
period to another" (Ullmann 1972: 370). Each element that belongs to the field
both influences the rest of the elements and depends upon them: "[it] helps to
delineate and limit its neighbors, and is delineated and limited by them" (Sylvester
1994: 21). Verbs of motion are a classic example of a semantic field. In his article
"Bedeutungssysteme" published in 1910, Richard Moritz Meyer (1860–1914), who
greatly contributed to the genesis of the concept of the semantic field,[4] chooses
verbs of motion as one of his examples. Meyer points out that German verbs which
express the concept of motion include semantic components that differentiate one
verb from another. For example, *schwimmen* "to swim" and *marschieren* "to march"
imply even repetitiveness, while *gehen* "to go" does not; *schwimmen* "to swim" refers to movement in the water, while *fliegen* "to fly" to that in the air. Meyer also
observes that verbs of motion often include not one but a number of such components: *sinken* "to sink" implies 'downwards', 'slowly', and 'evenly'; *fallen* "to fall"
implies 'downwards', 'fast', and 'evenly'; *stürzen* "to hurl, to plunge" implies 'downwards', 'fast', and 'unevenly', etc. (Meyer 1910: 360–363). The interdependence that
exists between the members of this field on the diachronic level can be illustrated
with the contrast between Standard German and the Alemannic dialects of High
German. Among its verbs of motion Standard German has *gehen* "to go, to walk",
laufen "to run", *springen* "to jump", and *hüpfen* "to hop". The Alemannic dialects, on
the other hand, have experienced "the generalization of the basic verb *gehen* to a
general movement verb" (Krifka 2001: 2). This generalization, in turn, produced a
"chain effect", in which "the change in one slot of a semantic field exerts pressure
on the words in other slots", resulting in *gehen* "to go", *laufen* "to walk", *springen* "to
run", and *hüpfen* "to jump" (ibid.).

---

4.   In *Semántica estructural y teoría del campo léxico*, Geckeler (1976: 100) assesses Meyer's
fundamental contribution as follows: "R. M. Meyer [ha sido] [...] el primero que [...] ha
demostrado de forma coherente y bastante detallada la idea de campo, si bien todavía no con la
terminología posterior" ["R. M. Meyer [= Richard Moritz Meyer (1860–1914)] has been the first
one to demonstrate coherently and in a fairly detailed way the notion of the semantic field; although he did not yet use the terminology employed in later studies"].

1.4 The historical cognitive linguistics framework as a new type of diachrony

Until fairly recently, work on lexical change of the Romance lexicon, in general, and work on lexical change of Romance motion verbs, in particular, has followed the long-established tradition of focusing on words' internal and/or external history. Within the internal history approach, attention has been given to the modifications that took place at the level of language as a linguistic system. Within the external history framework, the focus has been placed on the cultural and social realities of the speakers. The theoretical apparatus employed by these traditional approaches has been based largely on two foundational studies: Stephen Ullmann's (1914–1976) *The Principles of Semantics* of 1957 and Eugenio Coseriu's (1921–2002) "Pour une sémantique diachronique structurale" of 1964. Relying on these traditional approaches, linguists have been able to gather a great amount of data on the evolution of the Romance lexicon. However, as pointed out by Dworkin (2006a, b, 2010), most of such studies describe and classify the results or consequences of the changes that took place, but do not deal with broader theoretical issues related to the motivations behind the changes. At the same time, it is widely recognized that historical Romance linguistics has a great potential to answer not only the questions "What happened?" and "How did it happen?", but also the question "Why did it happen?" (see essays assembled in Dworkin 2003 and 2005, as well as Maiden 2004a). The approach known as 'historical cognitive linguistics' aspires to address the motivations of the changes by combining diachronic linguistics with the insights gained within cognitive linguistics.[5]

What makes the combination of historical Romance linguistics and cognitive linguistics so appealing for the study of lexical change? Such a question can be approached through a brief overview of the emergence and the evolution of these two fields with a focus on the goals that they have pursued and the research principles that they have followed.

---

5. It should be clarified that the term 'motivation' is better understood within the cognitively-oriented diachronic research as 'enabling factor', rather than 'cause' or 'explanation', as Hopper and Traugott point out in their study on grammaticalization (1993: 63). Along the same lines, in her study on historical semantics, Eve Sweetser (1990: 3) writes:

> By 'motivated,' I mean an account which appeals to something beyond the linguist's intuition that these senses are related, or that these two senses are more closely related than either is to a third sense. For example, it is possible to crosslinguistically examine meaning changes and to observe what senses frequently historically give rise to what later senses. We would then argue that there is reason to posit a close semantic and cognitive link between two senses if one is regularly a historical source for the other.

For a more detailed discussion of motivation in cognitive linguistics, see Radden & Panther (2004), Panther & Radden (2011), and Panther (2012).

The field of historical Romance linguistics (sometimes referred to as Romance philology)[6] emerged as a scientific discipline in the first half of the 19th century. The birth of this discipline is intrinsically connected to the development of historical-comparative linguistics, particularly the publication of such pioneering studies as Franz Bopp's (1791–1867) *Conjugationssystem* (1816), Rasmus Rask's (1787–1832) *Undersøgelse* (1818 [1814]), and Jacob Grimm's (1785–1863) *Deutsche Grammatik* (1819–1837). In 1816 François Raynouard (1761–1836) published his *Grammaire de la langue romane* that reflected his research on Old Provençal texts. Although Raynouard's work contained a fundamental error (he mistakenly believed that Old Provençal was the intermediate stage between Classical Latin and all of the modern Romance varieties), it was of great importance for the emergence of Romance philology since it provided a text-based grammar of an old Romance language and focused on the commonalities between the members of the Romance family. It is Friedrich Diez's (1794–1876) *Grammatik der romanischen Sprachen* (1836–1844) and *Etymologisches Wörterbuch der romanischen Sprachen* (1853) that are considered as the foundational works of historical Romance linguistics because Diez fully applied the comparative and the historical methods outlined by Bopp and Grimm to the Romance data. As can be inferred from the scope of studies by Raynouard and Diez, the main goal of Romance philology from its very beginning has been the understanding of the earlier stages of the Romance languages and the analysis of ways in which the diachronic patterns found on the way from Latin to Romance manifest themselves in different members of the linguistic family. This objective is firmly embedded in the cultural and intellectual milieu of the late 18th – early 19th centuries with its interest in earlier periods central to the Romantic movement in the humanities and its focus on evolution and comparativism characteristic of the natural sciences.

The importance of the comparative-historical methodological principle, or of the so-called "conscience romaniste" (Ernst et al. 2000: 185) that allowed Romance philology to establish itself as a scientific discipline, has remained until the present day. As can be seen from the articles collected in Dworkin (2003), modern practitioners of this field concur that the comparative-historical methodological principle is the very essence of Romance philology. For example, Koch (2003b: 42) writes: "It has always been the historical-diachronic relationship of the Romance languages to Latin which holds Romance philology together at its innermost core".

---

6.   On the controversy that surrounds the possibility of using the terms 'linguistics' and 'philology' interchangeably, see Koerner (1989) and Swiggers (1998, 2001). There is no complete equivalence between historical Romance linguistics and Romance philology because the latter encompasses both linguistic and literary studies.

Along the same lines, in his reaction to Dworkin (2003), Maiden expresses his position as follows:

> The term "historical Romance linguistics" is arguably tautologous. Romance linguistics is, *by definition*, a comparative subject, where any comparison of genetically related languages inevitably leads to reflection on historical evolution. Romance historical linguistics is at its most powerful, insightful and intellectually demanding when it is most fully comparative, with its practitioners commanding and integrating the great wealth of sources of evidence at our disposal. (Maiden 2004a: 216; original emphasis)

In sum, Romance philologists strongly believe that linguistic development can only be fully understood when considered within both the unity and the diversity of the Romance linguistic family as a whole, i.e., within the Pan-Romance perspective.

In the case of cognitive linguistics, we are dealing with a field defined as "the study of language in its cognitive function, where *cognitive* refers to the crucial role of intermediate informational structures in our encounters with the world" (Geeraerts & Cuyckens 2007: 5). This theoretical approach emerged in the 1970s from dissatisfaction with the focus that formalist theories (e.g., Generative Grammar) placed on form rather than on meaning (Nerlich & Clarke 2007: 590–591). As part of the broader movement of functional linguistics, cognitive linguistics is usage-based and stresses the semantic aspect of linguistic analysis (Geeraerts 2006a: 17–18).

Because cognitive linguistics views language as a cognitive faculty and analyzes it "in its relation to other cognitive domains and faculties such as bodily and mental experiences, image-schemas, perception, attention, memory, viewing frames, categorization, abstract thought, emotion, reasoning, inferencing, etc." (Dirven 2005: 17), the essential characteristic of this approach has been the so-called "cognitive commitment" defined by Lakoff as "a commitment to make one's account of human language accord with what is generally known about the mind and the brain, from other disciplines as well as our own [i.e., linguistics]" (1990: 40). The central part of the cognitive commitment is "to explicitly seek out systematic relations between linguistic structures and conceptual structures" (Gibbs et al. 2004: 1190–1191). In other words, as Kibrik (2003, 2008) explains, language is understood as a manifestation of the underlying cognitive structure. Of course, considering linguistic diversity, we cannot assume that the correspondence between language and other cognitive domains is one-dimensional. At the same time, this linguistic diversity is not chaotic either: it exhibits certain patterns and limits. It is the dynamics between linguistic diversity and linguistic uniformity that serves as a window into the options of cognitive structures available to humans (Kibrik 2003: 44; 2008: 53).

Thus, I would argue, the picture that emerges from the comparison between historical Romance linguistics and cognitive linguistics is the picture of two fields that while conceived apart have benefited from a common intuition: to explore the unity among languages by identifying overarching common patterns, and to explore ways in which languages are different from one another by establishing the limits of linguistic diversity.

At the level of onomasiology, this common intuition manifests itself well in the interest that both Romance philology and cognitive linguistics have had in the study of lexical fields. Exploring the variety of linguistic options available for encoding specific concepts has proven to be of great interest to both disciplines. In the case of historical Romance linguistics, the bibliographies found in Quadri (1952), Baldinger (1964), Heger (1965), de Gorog (1973), Corrà (1981), Hiltbrunner ed. (1981–1992), Heidermanns (2005), and Grzega (2009) clearly illustrate that researching semantic fields has always been extremely popular among Romance philologists. Such diverse fields as terms of kinship (Tappolet 1895), body parts (Zauner 1903, Blank & Koch 2000), seasons and months (Merlo 1904), adjectives of color (Kristol 1978), and verbs of posture (Stengaard 1991) have been studied, to name just a few. In the case of cognitive linguistics, one can think, for example, of Berlin & Kay's seminal work on basic color terms of 1969, Talmy's (1985, 2000) publications on the lexicalization of motion, Newman's (1996) monograph on the lexicalization of the concept 'give', or of the research on the links between semantic fields and frames (Nerlich & Clarke 2000).

At the level of semasiology, the common intuition shared by these two disciplines manifests itself in the way in which both Romance philology (and the historical-philological tradition, in general) and cognitive linguistics have understood meanings as mental/psychological concepts, and in the interest that both disciplines have had in polysemy (Geeraerts 2006c: 367–397; 2010: 9–25, 192–199). Exploring the variety of means that language uses to expand the semantic value of words has repeatedly attracted the attention of linguists working within the two fields in question. In the case of historical Romance linguistics, one might think, for example, of writings by Arsène Darmesteter (1887), Michel Bréal (1897), and Kristoffer Nyrop (1913) on the mechanisms of semantic change that result in polysemous clusters. In the case of cognitive linguistics, a good example would be the research presented in Lakoff & Johnson (1980) on metaphor and in Panther & Radden (1999) on metonymy (see Geeraerts 2002b, 2006c).

In fact, as pointed out by Koch (1997: 240; 2003b: 48; 2004: 79), many years before the birth of cognitive linguistics, Romance philologists already had "proto-cognitive intuitions", as in the case of Adolf Zauner's (1870–1943) study (1903) of body-part terms in Romance, Leo Spitzer's (1887–1960) 1967 [1918] observations on future tense forms in Romance and non-Romance languages, Olaf

Deutschmann's (1912–1989) 1953 publication on quantity designations in Romance, and Carlo Tagliavini's (1903–1983) 1982 [1949] study on the designations of the concept 'pupil' in Romance and other language families. This does not come as a surprise, because, as Koch (2003b) shows, the Romance languages form a microcosm able to illustrate developments attested in other language families, thus exhibiting the fundamental cognitive options. For example, the path LOCATION > EXISTENCE (e.g., Italian cè) is also present in Germanic (e.g., English *there is*); the path POSSESSION > EXISTENCE > LOCATION (e.g., French *il (y) a*, Spanish *ha(y)*, Portuguese *há*, Catalan *(hi) ha*) corresponds to Modern Greek *éçi*, Southern German *es hat*, Bulgarian *ima*, Swahili *-na*, and Nubi *fíi* (Koch 2003b: 45). This microcosmic quality makes Romance historical data particularly useful for studies undertaken within the cognitive framework (Lebsanft 2005: 203–204). Furthermore, Romance historical data are exceptionally valuable for linguistic theory because of the unique nature of the Romance language family as a family that has a documented proto-language (Latin), documented intermediate attestations, and great synchronic spread and diversity (Malkiel 1964: 672–673; Green 2005: 196–197; Maiden et al. 2010: xviii; Sornicola 2010: 3).[7]

I would suggest that seeking common ground between Romance philology and cognitive linguistics is of particular relevance at the present moment because of the future vision that these two disciplines have outlined for themselves. On the one hand, Romanists view Romance diachronic data as valuable material that can both benefit from and contribute to the advances in theoretical linguistics, and therefore call for continuing the intellectual dialogue between historical Romance linguistics and linguistic theory (see essays collected in Smith & Maiden 1994, Dworkin 2003 and 2005, as well as Maiden 2004a and Tornatore 2006). At the same time, cognitive linguists advocate the importance of testing their theories against an enlarged sample of languages and predict that in the future cognitive linguistics "will keep enlarging its cross-linguistic and cross-cultural database" (Hilferty 2005: 9). The integration of Romance philology and cognitive linguistics is still in its infancy and both disciplines can profit from furthering it.

A good illustration of the contribution that historical cognitive linguistics can make when it comes to analyzing the motivation of change on the level of recruitment to the lexical field of motion is the evolution of Spanish *llegar* "to come", Portuguese *chegar* "to come", and Romanian *a pleca* "to go away", all three forms deriving from Latin PLICARE "to fold". A focus on internal history (e.g., Budagov 1963, Rohlfs 1979) can highlight the structural changes that led to the creation of these verbs and the consequences that their formation has had on the rest of the

---

7.   The importance of these factors has also been stressed by Divjak et al. (2007) in their discussion of the relevance of Slavic data for cognitive linguistics.

system. As just mentioned, in Classical Latin PLICARE meant "to fold". However, in Late Latin, PLICARE in addition to its original meaning takes on the new meaning which is a hyponym of "to come". In the *Peregrinatio Aetheriae* (late 4th – early 5th century A.D.) we find the following examples: *et sic plecaremus nos ad montem Dei* "and then we approached the mountain of God", *plicavimus nos ad mare* "we arrived to the sea", *cum iam prope plicarent ciuitati* "when they were just approaching the city" (Buck 1949: 703; Adams 2007: 349–350). The consequences of this change for the modern Romance family vary from language to language. As illustrated in Budagov (1963: 128–130), Romance developments can be grouped into three categories. The first category includes languages such as French and Italian where *ployer/plier* and *piegare* continue the Classical Latin meaning "to fold". In Italian, *piegare* sometimes expresses movement when used in the sense "to retreat" and occasionally designated motion in Old Italian, but in general this verb is not one of motion. The second category is formed by Spanish and Portuguese where Classical Latin PLICARE gave the semi-learned form *plegar* and the learned form *plicar* "to fold", while Late Latin PLICARE gave *llegar* and *chegar* "to come". The third category is represented by Romanian, where Classical Latin and Late Latin PLICARE produced a pair of homonyms, *a pleca* "to droop, to be bent" and *a pleca* "to go away". A similar approach focused on internal history has been applied to Latin SALIRE "to jump" that produced three different types of motion verbs: (1) Romanian *a sări* "to jump", Raeto-Romance *siglir* "to jump"; (2) French *saillir* "to go out", Spanish *salir* "to go out", Portuguese *sair* "to go out"; and (3) Italian *salire* "to go up" (Rohlfs 1979: 175).

Returning to the case of Latin PLICARE "to fold", but now from the external history perspective, we can consider the fact that while the reflexes of this Latin verb in Spanish and Portuguese mean "to come", its reflex in Romanian means "to go away". This contrast has been attributed to the cultural, social, and economic characteristics of the cultures in question. The marine Iberian society surrounded by the sea traces Spanish *llegar* and Portuguese *chegar* to the combination PLICARE VELAM "to fold the sail", i.e., "to come", while the Balkan shepherd society traces Romanian *a pleca* to the expression PLICARE TENTORIA "to fold the tents", i.e., "to go away" (Machado 1977 II: 135; Rohlfs 1979: 178–179).[8]

At the same time, the case of Latin PLICARE "to fold" > Spanish *llegar* "to come", Portuguese *chegar* "to come", Romanian *a pleca* "to go away" can also be analyzed using the advances achieved within the cognitive linguistics framework. As we have seen earlier in this section, one of the main methodological

---

8.   In a parallel way, the evolution of Latin MERGERE "to dip, to plunge" into Romanian *a merge* "to go" has been attributed to the mountain and forest topography of the Balkans (Vidos 1963: 264–265; Pușcariu 1973: 41), but this explanation is unreliable.

principles of cognitive linguistics is the so-called "cognitive commitment", part of which is "to explicitly seek out systematic relations between linguistic structures and conceptual structures" (Gibbs et al. 2004: 1190–1191). Two theoretical notions that emerged from this interest in conceptualization are 'frame' and 'prototype'. The notion of the frame, inspired by work in cognitive psychology and artificial intelligence, was developed by Charles Fillmore. According to Fillmore, who uses the terms 'frame', 'schema', and 'scenario' interchangeably, "people have in memory an inventory of schemata for structuring, classifying, and interpreting experiences, and [...] have various ways of accessing these schemata and various procedures for performing operations on them" (1976: 25). For example, such verbs as *buy, sell, pay, cost, spend*, and *charge* are all part of the "commercial event frame" (ibid.). The concept of the prototype was introduced in the 1970s by Eleanor Rosch in her experimental work in cognitive psychology (e.g., Rosch 1975) and was applied to linguistics in the 1980s and 1990s in studies like Lakoff (1987) and Langacker (1987, 1991). The main tenet of the prototype theory is that not all members of the category are created equal: "prototypical instances are full, central members of the category, whereas other instances form a gradation from central to peripheral depending on how far and in what way they deviate from the prototype" (Langacker 1987: 17). For example, a swallow is more prototypical of the category 'bird' than an ostrich, while an ostrich is more prototypical of the category 'bird' than a penguin (Geeraerts 1994: 3385; 2006b: 151–155). The two notions (i.e., frame and prototype) can be linked to one another, as "in some cases the area of experience on which a linguistic frame imposes order is a prototype" (Fillmore 1975: 123).

As Blank (1999: 74–75) points out, within the frame of approaching the shore, the concept of arrival at one's destination and the concept of folding the sail have a strong and habitual relation between themselves, and as a result become designated with the same word, resulting in Spanish *llegar* "to come", Portuguese *chegar* "to come" < Latin PLICARE (VELAM) "to fold (the sail)". In a similar way, within the frame of leaving the place of lodging, the concept of folding the tents and the concept of going away possess a strong and habitual relation with one another, making possible the evolution of Latin PLICARE (TENTORIA) "to fold (the tents)" into Romanian *a pleca* "to go away". Due to the fact that different frames are employed, the same item, i.e., PLICARE, took two opposite semantic directions "producing a kind of 'interlinguistic antonymy'" (Blank 1999: 75). Furthermore, sailing on a boat could represent the prototypical way of arriving at a destination, and, as a result Spanish *llegar* and Portuguese *chegar* lexicalize arrival in general, rather than just arrival at the shore. Such prototype effect can also be viewed as the driving force behind Latin AD "towards" + RIPA "shore" > Late Latin ADRIPARE "to get on shore"[9] > French *arriver*, Italian *arrivare*, Catalan *arribar* "to come" (Blank 1999: 77–76; Montserrat 2004, Montserrat i Buendia 2007, Dworkin 2006a: 70).

As far as semantic development of motion verbs is concerned, a good illustration of the contribution that cognitive linguistics can make is the case of Spanish *levantar(se), alzar(se)* "to raise, to rise, to get up", and Portuguese *deixar* "to leave, to let". According to Pottier Navarro (1991 [1979]: 162) and Rehfeldt (1980)[10] who approach these lexemes from a more traditional perspective, the development of the verbs' polysemy is understood best in terms of their componential analysis. New advances in cognitive linguistics, especially the work on conceptual metaphors and image schemas, has enabled researchers to gain a new perspective on the evolution of these verbs' meaning. The conceptual metaphor theory holds that "metaphors map structures from a source domain to a target domain" (Evans & Green 2006: 296). For example, English speakers understand the target conceptual domain LOVE in terms of the source conceptual domain JOURNEY, hence the conceptual metaphor LOVE IS A JOURNEY[11] which manifests itself in such expressions as *Look how far we have come*, *We are at a crossroads*, and *We cannot turn back now* (Lakoff & Johnson 1980: 44). Based on this theoretical premise, Santos Domínguez & Espinoza Elorza (1996) were able to analyze Old Spanish combinations of *levantar(se)* "to raise, to rise" with such nouns as *voz* "voice", *grito* "yell, shout", and *ruido* "noise" in terms of the conceptual mapping MORE IS UP, and the combination of Old Spanish *alçar* "to raise" with such noun as *saña* "rage" in terms of the conceptual mapping ANGER IS FIRE (pp. 63–64, 201–206). Image schema is commonly understood in cognitive linguistics as "a mental pattern that recurrently provides structured understanding of various experiences" (Johnson 1987: 2). For example, the 'path' schema emerges from our experience of movement and contains four structural elements: source (starting point), destination (end point), path (a sequence of contiguous locations connecting the source and the destination), and direction (toward a destination) (Johnson 1987: 275). Applying the notions of image schema and prototype to the development of Latin LAXARE "to let go", Soares da Silva (2003) has demonstrated that its Portuguese reflex *deixar* "to leave, to let"

---

9.   For examples of Late Latin ADRIPARE "to get on shore, to land", see Niermeyer & Van De Kieft (2002 I: 29) and Du Cange (1883–1887 I: 92).

10.   *Deixar* is not among the verbs that Rehfeldt analyzes in detail, but the author does recognize its polysemous nature, illustrating it with such examples as *Ela deixou o filho em casa* "She left the son at home", *Ela deixou Porto Alegre* "She left Porto Alegre", and *Ela deixou o menino sair* "She let the boy go out" (Rehfeldt 1980: 87).

11.   I follow the convention established in cognitive linguistics of using small capital letters for representing conceptual metaphors and their components.

has evolved into a polysemous and multifunctional (homonymic) lexical item through reorganizations of prototypes and image-schema transformations.

As can be inferred from the examples provided above, even though historical cognitive linguistics represents a major paradigm shift,[12] it neither rejects nor replaces the traditional internal history and external history approaches. Instead, it aspires to complement them. In a nutshell, the practitioners of historical Romance linguistics who work within the historical cognitive linguistics framework strive to comprehend the cognitive substrate of the changes addressed in the studies on internal and external history: "Y a-t-il des universaux cognitifs suffisamment puissants pour guider, comme une 'main invisible' les innovations [...]?" ["Are there cognitive universals sufficiently powerful to guide linguistic innovations like an invisible hand?"] (Koch 2000b: 80).[13] In other words, Romanists regard historical cognitive linguistics as an approach that should be integrated within the long-standing tradition of diachronic linguistics, not as something that should compete with what has been done in the past. For example, the editors of the volume entitled *La cognition dans le temps: Études cognitives dans le champ historique des langues et des textes* articulate their goal as follows: "Ce projet implique l'espoir que 'l'histoire cognitive' puisse s'avérer être une troisième voie entre l'histoire externe (essentiellement événementielle) et l'histoire interne, tributaire des avatars du modèle structuraliste" ["This project implies the hope that 'cognitive history' could establish itself as the third perspective, side by side with external history (which focuses on historical events) and with internal history, which is based on structural changes"] (Blumenthal & Tyvaert, eds. 2003: back cover text). In a similar way, the opening chapter of *Historische Semantik in den romanischen Sprachen* (Lebsanft & Gleßgen, eds. 2004) entitled "Historische Semantik in den romanischen Sprachen. Kognition, Pragmatik, Geschichte" (pp. 1–28) includes a section "Etymologie, Wortgeschichte, Philologie" (23–25) in which the editors emphasize the connection between (cognitive) historical semantics and such traditional Romance fields as etymology, word-history, and the philological analysis of older texts. Along the same lines, the "Introduction" sections of such collections as *Historical Semantics and Cognition* (Blank & Koch, eds. 1999) and *Lexical Data and Universals of Semantic Change* (Mihatsch & Steinberg, eds. 2004) applaud the fact that cognitive research has been making its way into the manuals of historical

---

12. For a discussion regarding the place of cognitive linguistics within linguistics and within the 'cognitive revolution' (also known as the 'cognitive turn'), see Geeraerts (2007), Geeraerts & Cuyckens (2007), and Nerlich & Clarke (2007). For a discussion regarding the place of diachronic research within the cognitive linguistics enterprise, see Bybee (2007) and Winters (2010).

13. As Koch (2000b: 75) notes, the theoretical construct of the invisible hand was introduced into historical linguistics from the field of economics in Keller (1990, 1994).

linguistics.[14] Romanists working within this novel historical cognitive linguistics framework are highly committed not only to fully taking into consideration the advances made by their predecessors who subscribed to the traditional approaches, but also to maintaining the link between onomasiology and semasiology characteristic of earlier studies on lexical change: "Combining the onomasiological approach with a well-founded semasiological typology of diachronic semantic processes will enable us to understand, in a sort of 'panromanic' perspective, the basic cognitive patterns of how man conceives the world" (Blank & Koch 1999a: 11). A more detailed picture of cognitive onomasiology will be offered in Section 2.1, and cognitive semasiology will be surveyed in a more comprehensive way in Section 5.1 (below).

---

14.   Naturally, the supporters of the cognitive approach do not necessarily agree with all the ideas presented within the traditional frameworks. Such disagreements, however, do not preclude linguists working within historical cognitive linguistics from acknowledging earlier achievements nor from seeking common ground. See, for instance, Taylor (1999) on the confrontation between structural semantics and cognitive semantics and on the possible commonalities between them.

CHAPTER 2

Cognitive onomasiology and cognitive typology of motion encoding

2.1 Cognitive onomasiology

The study of semantic fields and cognitive linguistics have several common de-nominators. In his article "Words and Concepts in Time: Towards diachronic cog-nitive onomasiology", Andreas Blank argues that the main assumptions about lan-guage proper of onomasiology, on the one hand, and the main strategies of cognitive linguistics, on the other hand, are quite similar, as in the case of "the grouping of contiguous elements to domains, the association of similar and op-posite elements, the analysis of complex scenarios into clear-cut smaller scenes, the forming of figure-ground schemas, or the recognition of recurrent elements, etc." (Blank 2003: 43; cf. Geeraerts 2002a). These common denominators conflate into cognitive onomasiology. Cognitive onomasiology benefits from the diachron-ic approach and from an enlarged sample of languages, as demonstrated by Peter Koch and his collaborators in three University of Tübingen (Germany) research projects: (1) DECOLAR (*Dictionnaire Etymologique et Cognitif des Languges Romanes*), (2) LexiType$_{Syn}$ (*Lexical Motivation in French, Italian and German*), (3) LexiType$_{Dia}$ (*Lexical Change – Polygenesis – Cognitive Constants: The Human Body*). DECOLAR focuses on the history of words designating body parts as well as human perception and qualities attributed to man in fourteen Romance lan-guages. LexiType$_{Syn}$ studies and compares the lexical motivation of parts of the lexicon of French, Italian, and German. LexiType$_{Dia}$ investigates the denomination strategies of body-part terms within the domain of HEAD in a representative sam-ple of fifty languages of the world.

In a series of studies,[1] Koch and his colleagues have developed the main prin-ciples of cognitive onomasiology and its central methodological tool: the three-dimensional grid. This three-dimensional grid classifies the three motivational

---

[1]   Koch 1997, 1999, 2000a, b, 2001a, b, c, 2002, 2003a, c, 2004, 2008, Blank & Koch 1997, 1999a, b, 2000, Blank et al. 2000, Gévaudan et al. 2003, Koch & Marzo 2007.

dimensions of lexical change: (1) the cognitive (or cognitive-associative) dimension, (2) the formal dimension, and (3) the stratificational dimension.[2]

Koch and his colleagues point out that the relations that belong to the cognitive dimension "ultimately go back to the three associative relations of 'contiguity', 'similarity', and 'contrast' that have been well established since Aristotle and have been corroborated by Husserl's phenomenology [...], by gestalt psychology [...], and by free association tests" (Koch & Marzo 2007: 269). "By differentiating and combining contiguity, similarity and contrast in various ways, [...] [they] arrive at the universal, closed inventory of seven cognitive relations": (1) conceptual identity, (2) contiguity, (3) metaphorical similarity, (4) co-taxonomic similarity, (5) taxonomic superordination, (6) taxonomic subordination, and (7) conceptual contrast (ibid.). The cognitive relation of conceptual identity is "an extreme case of similarity" (Koch 2004: 80). For example, in the case of French *pur* "pure" → *pureté* "purity" there is no change at all on the conceptual level (Koch 2000b: 82). The cognitive relation of contiguity is "the relation which underlies the 'engynomic' aspect of conceptual hierarchies, i.e., the relationship between frames and their elements or between two or more elements of the same frame, for example that between TREE, FRUIT, WOOD, SHADOW, TO PLANT, etc." (Koch 2004: 80), as in the case of French *pomme* "apple" producing French *pommier* "apple tree" (Koch 2000b: 90). The cognitive relation of metaphorical similarity is the type of similarity "which – deliberately across to frames and taxonomies – maps new concepts onto existing ones" (Koch 2004: 80), as in the case of English *to grasp* "to seize and hold" → *to grasp* "to comprehend" (Koch & Marzo 2007: 270). The cognitive relation of co-taxonomic similarity is the type of similarity "which connects concepts of the same level of hierarchy within a taxonomy, for example OAK, FIR, APPLE-TREE, etc." (Koch 2004: 80), as in the case of French *sapin* "fir" and *hêtre* "beech" (Koch 2000b: 82). In the cognitive relation of taxonomic superordination "the taxonomically superordinate concept emphasizes the similarity [...] between subordinate concepts at the expense of at least some of the contiguities [...] specific to them (part-whole relationships, properties, etc.)" (Koch 2004: 80), as in the case of Sardinian (Logudorese) *póddighe* "finger" deriving from Latin POLLEX "thumb" (Koch 2000b: 86). The cognitive relation of taxonomic subordination is, as the label suggests, the opposite of the cognitive relation of taxonomic superordination: "in relation to the superordinate concept, the taxonomically subordinate concept foregrounds contiguities [...] (part-whole relationships, properties, etc.) specific to the subordinate concepts and background similarity [...] with concepts that are taxonomically at the same level" (Koch 2004: 80), as in the case of Catalan *artell*

---

2.   As discussed in Koch (2002), in the case of verbs an additional fourth level can be added, namely, that of verbal valency.

"finger joint" deriving from Latin ARTICULUS "joint" (Koch 2000b: 86). The cognitive relation of contrast involves entities that are conceptually opposed to one another, as in the case of English *bad* "not good" → English (slang) *bad* "excellent" (Blank 2003: 48).

The relations that belong to the formal dimension constitute an open inventory that accounts for "the great variety of morpholexical devices fulfilling lexical motivation tasks in the world's languages" (Koch & Marzo 2007: 271). In the case of the Indo-European languages, these relations include formal identity, as in the case of French *bois* "woods" (↔ *bois* "wood"); number alternation, as in the case of French *reins* "loin" (↔ *rein* "kidney"); word-class alternation, as in the case of Italian *rimborso* "reimbursement" (↔ *rimborsare* "to reimburse"); suffixation, as in the case of Italian *libraccio* "bad book" (↔ *libro* "book"); prefixation, as in the case of English *impossible* (↔ *possible*); compounding, as in the case of German *Stadtrand* "outskirts" (↔ [a] *Rand* "edge", ↔[b] *Stadt* "town"); voice alternation, as in the case of Ancient Greek *misthoûsthai* "to rent" (↔ *misthoûn* "to let"), etc. (Koch & Marzo 2007: 270).

The stratificational dimension of motivation includes three types of relations: autochthonous words, as in the case of Spanish *corva* "back of the knee" < Latin CURVUS "curved"; lexical borrowings, as in the case of Spanish *talle* "waist" < French *taille* "waist"; and calques, as in the case of Galician *corda do embigo* "umbilical cord" < Galician *corda* "cord" + *embigo* "navel" calqued upon French *cordon ombilical* "umbilical cord" < French *cordon* "cord" + *ombilical* "umbilical" (Koch 2000b: 87–89).

As we will see in Chapter 4 (Section 4.2), these cognitive, formal, and stratificational dimensions of lexical change will allow us to account for the Romance innovative lexicalization patterns within the field of motion verbs.

2.2 Cognitive typology of motion encoding

According to the typology proposed by Leonard Talmy, the lexical field of Latin verbs of motion is typologically different from the Romance one. In his pioneering study "Semantics and Syntax of Motion", Talmy represents the semantic structure of the motion event-schema in terms of four components: "Motion situation: figure + motion + path + ground" (Talmy 1975: 182). The Figure is "the object that is considered as moving or located with respect to another object", the Path is "the respect in which one object is considered as moving or located to another object", and the Ground is "the object with respect to which a first object is considered as moving or located" (p. 181). In his 1985 study Talmy elaborates that "in addition to these internal components a Motion event can have a 'Manner' or a 'Cause', which we analyze as constituting a distinct external event" (p. 61).

Because Talmy (2009: 390) understands path as "criterial to a Motion sentence", a brief clarification is in order regarding the term 'Path' written with the capital 'P' by Talmy but with either the capital 'P' or with the lower case 'p' by others. While the definition of path in Talmy (1975: 181) as "the respect in which one object is considered as moving or located to another object" is akin to that of direction, the definition of path in Talmy (1985: 61) as "the course followed or site occupied by the Figure object with respect to the Ground object" is akin to both that of direction and that of a trajectory. The definition of path in Talmy (2000 II: 25; 2007: 70) also subsumes both direction and trajectory: "The Path (with a capital P) is the path followed or site occupied by the Figure object with respect to the Ground object". Commenting on the difference between his understanding of path, on the one hand, and the 'Location', 'Source', 'Goal', and 'Path' cases presented in Fillmore (1977), on the other hand, Talmy (2000 II: 53–57; 2007: 71) underscores that path is not a simplex constituent and argues in favor of a broad understanding of the concept: "by abstracting away all notions of path into a separate Path component, [it] allows for the representation of semantic complexes with both universal and language-particular portions" (Talmy 2000 II: 27).[3]

Talmy, in fact, proposes a cognitive typology of languages based on the components included in the root of their verbs of motion. He argues that focusing on the verb root is practical because it allows comparison of languages with very different word structure (Talmy 1985: 61). Talmy's typology is particularly interested in the most characteristic way in which each language expresses motion, i.e., in the way that is "*colloquial* in style, rather than literary, stilted, etc.", "*frequent* in occurrence in speech, rather than only occasional", and "*pervasive*, rather than limited,

---

3.   Given the importance and the complexity of the issue, Zlatev (2007: 330–333) dedicates several pages to the discussion of the ways in which the terms 'path' and 'direction' are used in cognitive semantics. He writes (pp. 330–331):

> In its [...] more common usage, which may be called 'elaborated path', it [path] refers to the trajectory of actual or imagined motion of the 'trajector' ['figure'] with respect to the 'landmark' ['ground'] (Talmy 1983; Lakoff 1987). This trajectory may be somewhat schematic, but it has both extension and shape. For example, in Dewell's (1994) analysis of *over*, the basic sense of the preposition profiles, in essence, a circular type of path.

When there are no landmarks (e.g., *Come here!*), translocation is defined in terms of the concept 'direction', "which is specified as a vector along one of the axes provided by a frame of reference" (Zlatev 2007: 332). Zlatev goes on to say that "In most cognitive semantic analyses, particularly in those where 'path' is treated in the elaborated sense [...], the concept of direction is subsumed under the category 'path' and often referred to as 'imperfective path' (as in [...] [*The bird flew toward its nest*]) as opposed to the 'perfective path' (as in [...] [*The bird flew to its nest*]) (Hawkins 1984)" (332–333).

that is, a wide range of semantic notions are expressed in this type" (Talmy 1985: 62; original emphasis). This typology, revisited by Talmy in his highly acclaimed two-volume work entitled *Toward a Cognitive Semantics* (2000), consists of three categories:

1. Chinese and all branches of Indo-European except the Romance languages, but including Latin are of the "Motion + Manner/Cause" conflation type, also known as the "Motion + Co-event" type (Talmy 2007: 72). For example, English *slid* in *The rock slid down the hill* informs us about motion and its manner (sliding), while English *blew* in *The napkin blew off the table* contains information about motion and its cause (the blow [of wind]). The prepositions *off* and *down* are "satellites", i.e., "immediate constituents of a verb root other than inflections, auxiliaries, or nominal arguments [...] [that] relate to the verb root as periphery (or modifiers) to a head" (Talmy 1985: 102). Prefixes in such languages as German, Classical Greek, Russian, or Latin (e.g., Latin IN-IRE "to go in", IN-VOLARE "to fly in") are also satellites. The languages listed above are 'satellite-framed' because in them the satellites carry the information about the path.

2. Such languages as Atsugewi (a Hokan language within the Amerindian family spoken in northern California) and Navajo (an Athabaskan language within the Na-Déné family spoken in northwestern New Mexico and northeastern Arizona) belong to the 'Motion + Figure' conflation type. For example, in Atsugewi the verb root *-lup-* indicates movement of a small shiny spherical object (e.g., a round candy), while the verb root *-caq-* indicates movement of a slimy lumpish object (e.g., a toad). These languages are also 'satellite-framed' because they also encode path with the help of the satellites.

3. Semitic, Polynesian, and Romance languages are of the 'Motion + Path' conflation type. These languages are 'verb-framed' since in them the information about the path is contained within the verb itself (e.g., Spanish *subió* "went up" in *El globo subió por la chimenea* "The balloon went up the chimney").[4]

---

4.   It should be mentioned that even though Talmy was the first one to create the typology of motion encoding, the fact that verbs of motion vary from language to language had been noted by a number of linguists well before him. Strohmeyer (1910), Frauendienst (1935), Bally (1944), Tesnière (1959), and Malblanc (1961), among others, contrast French and German verbs of motion. Bergh (1948) compares French to Swedish. Vinay & Darbelnet (1958), revised as Vinay & Darbelnet (1971) and translated into English as Vinay & Darbelnet (1995), contrast French and English. Gak (1963, 1966) discusses the 'abstract' nature of French verbs of motion when compared to their Russian counterparts. Ducháček (1970) contrasts French and Romanian verbs with Latin verbs, while Evseev (1974) contrasts Romanian and Russian. As Talmy himself states, his own contribution consists in creating an "encompassing theoretical account" of the "phenomena involved" (Ibarretxe-Antuñano 2005: 327). It should also be clarified that although my overview of Talmy's ideas on the lexicalization of motion starts with Talmy (1975), his earlier

Talmy's typology has generated an enormous amount of interest within the linguistic community working with the Romance languages, and has greatly contributed to the creation and advancement of several research initiatives. One major group of studies calls for a more fine-grained classification of motion encoding. Works like Schwarze (1985), Koch (2001b), Wienold & Schwarze (2002), Melka (2003), and Berthele (2004), to name only a few, draw attention to the fact that although the Romance languages are predominantly of the 'Motion + Path' verb-framed type, they also possess verbs that belong to the 'Motion + Manner/Cause' satellite-framed category: e.g., verb-particle constructions (phrasal verbs) such as Spanish *ir adentro* "to go in", Italian *andare fuori* "to go out", and Raeto-Romance (Engadine) *gnir giò* "to go down", as well as manner verbs like French *chevaucher* "to ride (on a horse)". Thus, these studies argue that the satellite-framed vs. verb-framed dichotomy is too rigid and contend that a more accurate typological assessment is in order. Koch (2000a, 2001b), for instance, has classified Italian as a mixed language due to its abundant use of such path particles as *via* "away", *fuori* "outside", and *giù* "below". The conference held in Turin (Italy) in February 2007 entitled "I verbi sintagmatici in italiano e nelle varietà dialettali. Stato dell'arte e prospettive di ricerca"/"Phrasal verbs in Italian and Italian dialects. State of the art and new lines of research" (see Cini, ed. 2008) demonstrates the great importance that Italian and the Italian dialects play in the process of refining Talmy's satellite-framed vs. verb-framed opposition. Another major line of research inspired by Talmy has been the investigation of the inventory of manner-of-motion verbs in different languages; more specifically of the hypothesis that the inventory of such verbs in the verb-framed languages is not as large as in the satellite-framed ones (e.g., Cardini 2008, Cifuentes-Férez 2009, 2010, Iacobini 2010). The research that belongs to the third category has focused its attention on the diatopic variation in motion encoding (e.g., Hijazo-Gascón & Ibarretxe-Antuñano 2010 on the dialects of Aragonese, Ibarretxe-Antuñano & Hijazo-Gascón 2012 on the dialectal variation in Spanish and Aragonese). The fourth major group of studies that uses Talmy's cognitive typology as its springboard are works like Slobin (2004) and Pourcel (2004) which concern themselves with the relationship between Talmy's typology, on the one hand, and narrative styles, language processing, memory, and categorization, on the other. The fifth major group of studies inspired by Talmy's research includes works on the relationship between the typology in question and

---

studies (Talmy 1972a, b, 1973) were also dedicated to the topic in question. Since 2005, Talmy refers to his three-way classification which comprises the 'Motion + Manner/Cause', the 'Motion + Figure', and the 'Motion + Path' conflation types as the 'Motion-actuating typology', and to his two-way classification which comprises the 'satellite-framed' and the 'verb-framed' types as the 'Motion-framing typology', noting that the two classifications are complementary (Ibarretxe-Antuñano 2005, Talmy 2012).

second language acquisition (e.g., Cadierno 2004) and first language acquisition (e.g., Hickmann & Hendriks 2006). Another large group of works (e.g., Pascual Aransáez 1999, Ibarretxe-Antuñano 2003) deals with the ramifications of Talmy's typology for translation studies.

While we find a plethora of synchronic studies from the six groups listed above that apply Talmy's typology to the modern Romance varieties, the diachronic dimension of Talmy's typology, on the other hand, has been addressed to a much lesser extent. Such diachronic work is limited to a handful of studies that focus on the evolution of phrasal verbs,[5] on the development of the role of French preverbs (Buridant 1995, Dufresne et al. 2003, Kopecka 2006, 2009a, 2013), on the changes in the expression of direction and manner from Latin to French (Schøsler 2008), and on the expanding use of manner verbs and post-verbal particles in Italian and French (Iacobini & Fagard 2011, Iacobini 2012). In other words, the diachronic focus so far has been mostly on a specific language and on a specific phenomenon. It is only fairly recently that Baldi (2006), in his study "Towards a history of the manner of motion parameter in Greek and Indo-European", has urged linguists to take a closer look at the place of Latin and of its descendents within the typology in question on a more systematic level.

In my earlier studies (Stolova 2003: 38–39; 2008: 253–254, 260; 2010a: 188), I have spelled out the need for a new line of inquiry: tracing and explaining the transition of motion encoding from predominantly satellite-framed Latin to predominantly verb-framed Romance in light of Talmy's typology. In these studies I have demonstrated that the comparative-historical approach that covers a wide span of languages on the Pan-Romance scale and pays attention to the historical progression through the intermediate stages is essential for this endeavor. I have proposed that the cognitive linguistics framework, with its emphasis on what is known about the language-cognition interface and about spatial cognition, is particularly promising for the task of understanding the motivations behind the changes that have taken place (Stolova 2003: 33–34, 531–534; 2008: 260; 2010a: 190–194). As highlighted in Stolova (2010a: 188), carrying out this task is important for historical Romance linguistics for two reasons: (1) the Romance family is the only Indo-European language family with a predominantly verb-framed system, and (2) understanding the typological shifts between Latin and Romance, such as the reduction of the case system in nominal morphology and the change from the predominantly synthetic to the predominantly analytic system in verbal morphology, has always been at the very heart of Romance philology. At the same

---

5.   See Vicario (1997) on Friulian; Masini (2005, 2006), Iacobini & Masini (2007a, b, 2009), Iacobini (2009), Mosca (2012) on Italian; Amenta (2008) on Sicilian; Burnett & Tremblay (2009), Kopecka (2009a, 2013) on Old French.

time, as pointed out in Stolova (2010a: 194), the significance of the task is not confined to the language-specific discipline of historical Romance linguistics because the wide range of lexicalization patterns attested in Romance diachronic data has potential implications for linguistics at large, and particularly for linguistic typology. I have also illustrated that, when studying the evolution of the lexical field of motion from Latin to Romance, it is not just the predominant types and the patterns of innovation that matter; the less prominent types and the patterns of continuity deserve as much attention (Stolova 2003: 81–88, 522–524; 2008: 259–260; 2010a: 189–190).

As I shall demonstrate in Chapter 4 (Sections 4.1 and 4.2) and Chapter 8, while Talmy's classification of Latin and Romance as belonging to two distinct types does reflect the prevalent patterns, the transition from Latin to Romance is much more complex than just a substitution of one type by another.

CHAPTER 3

Latin and Romance verb biographies

3.1 Generic motion

The main verbs that Latin[1] used to refer to movement in general without any spec-ification of means or direction were IRE "to go" and VADERE "to go". It also had a number of other verbs to express this concept, but they were either used very rare-ly or had "to go" as their secondary meaning. For example, MEARE "to go, to pass" and CEDERE "to go, i.e., to be in motion, to move, to walk, to go along" are practi-cally absent from prose and are found almost exclusively in poetry. Such verbs and idioms as TENDERE "to direct one's self or one's course", GRADI "to take steps, to walk, to go", PERGERE "to go on", INGREDI "to go into, to enter", PROGREDI "to come or go forth", INCEDERE "to go, to step or march along", PROCEDERE "to go forth or before", and PEDEM FERRE "to go or come [by foot]" were common, but their core meaning implied, in addition to the idea of movement, either the means, the man-ner, or the direction of motion.

The *Latin Dictionary* (Lewis & Short 1966: 648) glosses IRE as follows: "to go (of every kind of motion of animate or inanimate things), to walk, ride, sail, fly, move, pass, etc. (very frequent in all periods and sorts of writing)". This verb comes from the prolific Indo-European root *ei-/*i- "to go" and was a part of a great num-ber of compounds. The vast majority of these compounds also belonged to the lexical field of motion.[2] However, some of them, such as INTERIRE "to get lost" and

---

1.   Unless stated otherwise, the definitions of Latin verbs come from Lewis & Short (1966) and Glare ed. (1982), the information about their origin and compounds comes from Walde & Hofmann (1982) and Ernout & Meillet (1985), and the information about the Indo-European roots is based on Pokorny (1959–1969) and Watkins (1993). The sources of information about the etymology of Romance verbs, unless stated otherwise, are the following: Corominas & Pascual (1980–1991) for Spanish; Rey ed. (1994) for French; Cortelazzo & Zolli (1979–1988) and Pfister (1979–) for Italian; Nascentes (1932) and Machado (1977) for Portuguese; Puşcariu (1975), de Cihac (1978), Cioranescu (1966), and Macrea ed. (1958) for Romanian; Alcover & Moll eds. (1930–1962) and Coromines et al. (1980–1991) for Catalan; Alibert (1965) and Lavalade (1999) for Occitan; Wagner (1960–1964) for Sardinian; Bernardi et al. (1994) for Raeto-Romance.

2.   For example, ABIRE "to go away, to exit", ADIRE "to go towards", AMBIRE "to go around", ANT(E)IRE "to go ahead", CIRCUMIRE "to go around", COIRE "to go together", DEIRE "to exit", EXIRE "to exit", INIRE "to enter", INTR(O)IRE "to enter", OBIRE "to go towards", PRA(E)IRE "to go in front/ahead", PRAETERIRE "to pass", PRODIRE "to advance", REDIRE "to return", SUBIRE "to move

PERIRE "to disappear, to get lost", did not directly refer to movement. Latin VADERE, which is defined as "to go, walk; esp[ecially] to go hastily or rapidly, to rush" (Lewis & Short 1966: 1951), was used less frequently than IRE, and, as the definition suggests, could imply the manner in which motion was performed. Apparently this shade of meaning was characteristic of earlier texts (e.g., Q. Ennius 239–169 B.C.), but later disappeared (Ernout & Meillet 1985: 711). As in the case of IRE, VADERE had a number of compounds many of which were motion verbs.[3] Its origin is disputed; it is not clear whether the verb in question came from the Indo-European root *wādh-/*wǝdh- or resulted from the agglutination of the root *wā- "to come" and a suffix (ibid.). In the dictionaries (Glare, ed. 1982, Ernout & Meillet 1985, Dvoreckij 1986) it appears without a hyphen, which suggests that the authors of these dictionaries have reasons to believe that in Classical Latin it was not perceived as a compound, but rather as a simple form. Furthermore, it did not have a prefix, which is significant, as we will see in the next chapter. Therefore, throughout the present study Latin VADERE is referred to as a simple form.

The main Spanish, Portuguese, and Raeto-Romance verb that expresses the concept 'to go' is *ir* < Latin IRE "to go". In some dialects of Old Occitan *ir* < IRE was in use (Bernardi et al. 1994 I: 413) and, according to Meyer-Lübke (1992: 371), *ir* < IRE is found in some varieties of Modern Occitan. The verb *gire* < IRE was used in Old Italian and is still found in some Italian dialects. French also partially retains Latin IRE through suppletion: French *aller* "to go" – first person Singular Future *j'irai*, first person Singular Conditional *j'irais*. According to Maiden, "some French and Occitan dialects not only preserve IRE in the future and conditional, but compound the suppletion by lexicalizing, *just* in future and conditional, certain locative particles derived from Latin IBI or INDE (= French *y* or *en*)" (2004c: 244; original emphasis). This way, in the dialect of Corrèze the first person Future tense form is *n'yirèy* and the first person Conditional form is *n'yiyò* (cf. Present *vaw*, Imperfect *onavo*), while in the dialect of Pierrecourt the first person Future tense form is *j irè* or *j iv irè* and the first person Conditional form is *j iró* or *j iv iró* (cf. Present *i vè*, Imperfect *j'aló*) (ibid.). Another case of suppletion has to do with the Romance reflexes of Latin IRE "to go" that rely on the reflexes of Latin VADERE "to go" in part of or in the entire present tense paradigm: Old Spanish *ir* – *vo(y)*, *vas, va, imos, ides, van*; Modern Spanish *ir* – *voy, vas, va, vamos, vais, van*;

---

underneath, to draw near, to move upward", and TRANSIRE "to pass". This list of compounds and similar lists presented throughout this chapter are of importance because they illustrate the degree to which Latin motion encoding heavily relied on satellite-framed lexical items in which the prefixes carried path information.

3.   For example, EVADERE "to go or come out, to go forth", INVADERE "to go, to come or get into, to enter upon", PERVADERE "to go or come through", SUPERVADERE "to go or climb over", and TRANSVADERE "to cross over".

Portuguese *ir* – *vou, vais, vai, vamos, ides, vão*; Old Tuscan *gire* – *vado, vai, va, gimo, gite, vanno*. While earlier research (Rohlfs 1979: 165) claimed that it is the monosyllabic nature of the Latin present indicative paradigm of IRE[4] that had triggered suppletion, more recent research (Maiden 2004b) has clarified that it is more accurate to speak not of the monosyllabic nature (cf. Latin DO "I give", STO "I am" that did survive), but rather of what Rosén calls "physical feebleness, or to be exact minimal consonantism" (Rosén 2000: 281, quoted in Maiden 2004b: 386).

The main verbs that French, Occitan, Catalan, Italian, and Sardinian use to refer to movement in general are French *aller*, Occitan *anar*, Catalan *anar*, Italian *andare*, Sardinian (Campidanese) *andai*, and Sardinian (Logudorese) *andare*. According to Wagner (1960–1964 I: 87), already in Old Logudorese *andare* was used in the perfect and in the imperfect, but he considers the word in question to be an Italianism. The origin of French *aller*, Occitan *anar*, Catalan *anar*, Italian *andare*, Campidanese *andai*, Logudorese *andare*, as well as the origin of such cognates as Spanish *andar*, Portuguese *andar*, Macedo-Romanian *împnare*, Istro-Romanian *amnà*, and Raeto-Romance (Friulian) *là*, has proven to be one of the most challenging etymological cruxes. Romanists stress over and over again the amount of attention that the problem has received and the obscurity that still surrounds the etymon of the verbs under consideration. As early as 1946, Albert Dauzat states: "l'étymologie des types *andare–aller* est un des problèmes les plus ardus de la linguistique romane" ["the etymology of *andare–aller* is one of the most difficult problems of Romance linguistics"] (p. 176). "To the solution of this narrow problem presumably over one thousand printed pages have so far been devoted", writes Yakov Malkiel in 1954 (p. 267). Witold Mańczak observes that "l'origine de fr. *aller*, esp. *andar*, it. *andare*, prov. *anar* [...], etc. constitue le problème numéro un de l'étymologie romane, étant donné qu'aucun autre mot n'a fait naître autant d'hypothèses que le verbe en question" ["the origin of French *aller*, Spanish *andar*, Italian *andare*, Occitan *anar* [...], etc. constitutes the number one problem of Romance etymology, given that no other word has produced as many hypotheses as the verb in question"] (1974: 89). Coromines et al. (1980–1991 I: 295) claim that at some point the subject matter seemed "un gran problema sense esperances de solució" ["a great problem without hope for solution"]. Jean-Charles Seigneuret begins his article "ADULARE > *aller*" by saying that "there is no lack of etymons [sic] proposed to explain the origin of the French verb *aller*" (1967: 166). A page-long entry dedicated to French *aller* is part of Pierre Guiraud's *Dictionnaire des étymologies obscures* (1982). Migliorini & Duro (1958) claim "etimo incerto" ["unknown etymon"] in the

---

4.   The present indicative paradigm of IRE in Classical Latin was EO, IS, IT, IMUS, ITIS, EUNT, but it is important to bear in mind that "not only IS and IT, but also 1sg. EO and 3pl. EUNT, would have yielded monosyllables in early Romance" (Maiden 2004c: 250, n.12).

entry dedicated to Italian *andare* without even making an attempt to list the multiple theories that have been advanced. Bonfante (1963/1964: 168, n.1) writes about Italian *andare*: "intanto le etimologie proposte, che èrano piú di 27 nel 1907, dovrèbbero ormai passare la cinquantina" ["there were more than 27 etymologies in 1907, and at this point the number would be more than fifty"]. Based on the chronological list of etymologies of the Romance forms in question which spans from 1533 to 1974 offered in Mańczak (1974), Mańczak (1975: 735) states that one can count "une soixantaine d'hypothèses" ["about sixty hypotheses"].

Mańczak himself believes that the Romance forms under consideration come from Latin AMBULARE "to walk": "A notre avis, le problème qui nous intéresse a été résolu, dès 1852, par le grand étymologiste Pott,[5] qui s'est rendu compte que les verbes *aller, andar*, etc. proviennent tous de *ambulāre* et que leurs irrégularités s'expliquent par la fréquence d'emploi" ["We believe that the question that concerns us has been resolved since 1852 by the great etymologist Pott who understood that the verbs *aller, andar*, etc. all come from *ambulāre* and that their irregularities are due to frequency of usage"] (1974: 96). This frequency refers both to the everyday speech and to military usage. Adams (1976: 111) explains: "We know from Vegetius [...] of a common military exercise to which the verb *ambulo* was applied. Three times a month soldiers were compelled to make a round march of about ten miles under full armor". Adams goes on to assess the pragmatic dimension of the term: "There can be no doubt that the exercise owed its name to soldiers' irony, for *ambulo* means literally 'to go for a stroll'" (ibid.).[6] In fact, as Malkiel argues, the military vocabulary of the Romans clarifies a number of Romance developments in all kinds of semantic fields:

> In the wake of those advocating the analysis of *aller/andar(e)* as basically an ingredient of the Roman soldier language, I have since tried to categorize similarly *(re)pedāre* 'to return, wend one's way back' (lit. 'to move one's feet back'), extremely well preserved in Peninsular Spanish dialect speech (*repiar*, etc.), proposing soon thereafter to credit a whole derivational model, namely the postverbal, to the same milieu and lifestyle. At present, I am toying with the idea of similarly interpreting OSp. *(a)matar* 'to kill, slaughter' and of resolving along the same line the semantic paradox of Fr. *tirer* 'to draw' conflicting with (O)Sp. *(a)tirar* 'to throw, fling'. (Malkiel 1989 Section XIII: 2–3)

In addition to the frequency with which AMBULARE was used, suppletion in its paradigm may also have contributed to its irregular development because in those members of the paradigm that relied on AMBULARE the root did not bare stress:

---

5.   See Pott (1852: 314–315).

6.   On the role of *sermo militaris* in the development of the Romance forms of the type *andare*, see also Petersmann (1999) and the bibliography contained therein.

El hecho es que en textos vulgares latinos de la baja época se observa la misma repartición de las formas *vado* y análogas, en el singular y tercera persona del plural de los presentes, junto a las formas de *ambulare* en las demás personas y tiempos, que hoy rige aún en francés, italiano, occitano-catalán, etc., entre *vais* y *aller*, *vado* y *andare*, *vau* o *vaig* y *anar*; esta restricción del uso de AMBULARE a las formas verbales acentuadas en la desinencia fue otro poderoso factor en las fuertes alteraciones fonéticas sufridas por el radical de este verbo, alteraciones que no era posible corregir por medio de las formas acentuadas en el radical, pues éstas no se hallaban en uso. (Corominas & Pascual 1980–1991 I: 16–17)

[In Late Latin texts we observe the same distribution between *vado* and its analogs (in first person singular, second person singular, third person singular, and third person plural of the present tense) and the forms based on *ambulare* (in the rest of the present tense paradigm and in the other tenses) as the distribution that is still in place in French, Italian, Occitan, Catalan, etc. between *vais* and *aller*, *vado* and *andare*, *vau* or *vaig* and *anar*. This restriction of AMBULARE to the forms in which stress falls on the ending was another factor that contributed to the major phonetic changes undergone by this verb's stem. These changes were impossible to avoid with the help of the forms stressed on the stem because such forms were not in use.]

The theory summarized and defended in Mańczak (1974) is widely accepted and many etymological and historical dictionaries present AMBULARE as the most likely etymon.[7] As in the case of the Romance reflexes of Latin IRE "to go", the

---

7.   See, for instance, Corominas & Pascual (1980–1991), Coromines et al. (1980–1991), Gómez de Silva (1985), and Corominas (1990) for Spanish; Wartburg (1936–1970), Gamillscheg (1969), Dauzat et al. (1979), Picoche (1992), Bloch & Wartburg (1994), and Rey ed. (1994) for French; Pfister (1979–) for Italian; Alcover & Moll eds. (1930–1962) and Coromines et al. (1980–1991) for Catalan. It should be stressed once more, however, that there is no consensus: several dictionaries, articles, and monographs give an etymon other than AMBULARE. For example, while Wartburg (1936–1970) and Bloch & Wartburg (1994) trace French *aller* to AMBULARE, they state that Spanish *andar*, Italian *andare*, and Occitan *anar* come from Late Latin *AMBITARE, which in turn is a frequentative of AMBIRE "to go around". This is also the view expressed in Meyer-Lübke (1992) and Picoche (1992). Likewise, Maiden (2004b, 2005) traces Italian *andare* to *AMBITARE and French *aller* to AMBULARE, as do Clackson & Horrocks (2007: 283). By tracing the different members of the group *andar*, *andare*, *aller*, etc. to different etyma, these scholars place themselves in opposition to those who view all these forms as "une série indissociable dans les langues romanes" ["an undivided Romance series"] (Lanly 1996: 31). Although Pfister (1979–) traces Italian *andare* to AMBULARE, several other etymological dictionaries of Italian such as Meini ed. (1995), Rosselli & Eynard (1996), and Devoto & Oli (1997) trace Italian *andare* to Late Latin *AMBITARE < AMBIRE "to go around". Alibert (1965) attributes Occitan *anar* to the combination of AD "towards" and NARE "to swim". Other sources list more than one etymon without indicating which one of them they consider to be the correct one. For example, Cortelazzo &

Romance reflexes of Latin AMBULARE "to walk" also rely through suppletion on the reflexes of Latin VADERE "to go" in part of the present tense paradigm: French *aller* "to go" – *vais, vas, va, allons, allez, vont*; Italian *andare* "to go" – *vado, vai, va, andiamo, andate, vanno*; Catalan *anar* "to go" – *vaig, vas, va, anem, aneu, van*.[8]

The main Romanian verb that expresses the idea 'to go' is *a merge*. It comes from Latin MERGERE "to dip, to plunge, to sink". The change in meaning can schematically be represented as 1. "to dip" > 2. "to disappear" > 3. "to draw away" > 4. "to leave" > 5. "to go" (Budagov 1963: 130), or as 1. "to sink" > 2. "to disappear under water" > 3. "to disappear from view" > 4. "to go away" > 5. "to go" (Maiden 2004c: 240). Another member of the Balkan Sprachbund, namely Albanian, still preserves stage #3 of this change by means of *mërgoig* "I move away" (equivalent of French *j'éloigne*), *mërgonem* "I withdraw" (equivalent of French *je m'éloigne*) (de Cihac 1978 I: 162). In some Transylvanian dialects of Romanian the verb *a se duce* (< Latin DUCERE "to lead") is used as the main lexeme to express the concept 'to go', and in some locations of Transylvania *a merge* "to go" and *a se duce* "to go" are both employed as parts of a suppletive paradigm (Maiden 2004c: 240–244; 2007: 513). For instance, in the locality of Fundătura, the present indicative paradigm is *mə duk, t'e duc, sə 'duce, 'mɛrem, 'mɛrets, sə duk* (ibid.).

3.2 Direction-specific motion

3.2.1 Movement toward and/or reaching a particular location

The main Latin verbs that served as the equivalents of "to come, to arrive"[9] were VENIRE "to come", ADVENIRE "to come to a place, to reach, to arrive at", PERVENIRE

Zolli (1979–1988) mention both *AMBITARE and AMBULARE in their discussion of Italian *andare*, and Machado (1977) gives both AMBULARE and *AMBITARE as the possible etyma of Portuguese *andar*.

8.   On patterns of IRE – VADERE and AMBULARE – VADERE suppletion, see Aski (1995), Lüdtke (1999: 56–57), Juge (2000), Maiden (2004b: 383–387; 2004c: 232–233; 2005: 153–154, 161; 2007: 512–513; 2010: 254–261), Rini (2005), and Veselinova (2006: 106–112).

9.   Although the direction of 'come' and 'arrive' is the same, 'come' highlights movement as such, whereas 'arrive' highlights the final phase of movement. More specifically, in their study of the Gospel according to Mark in one hundred languages carried out by using the method of multidimensional scaling (MDS), Wälchli & Cysouw (2012: 691) establish the following distinction:

> It is not trivial to clarify the distinction between 'arrive' and 'come' descriptively. Quantitatively the MDS plots show that this distinction is less clear-cut than various other distinctions in motion events. What distinguishes contexts where 'arrive' verbs occur most frequently [...] are especially two aspects of perspective which can apply individually or jointly: (a) 'arrive' is used for moving to places which have been previously

"to come to, to arrive at, to reach a place", and DEVENIRE "to go to, to arrive at, to reach". Other verbs, such as ADIRE "to go to or approach a person or thing", OBIRE "to go or come to or towards", SUBIRE "to move underneath, to draw near, to move upward", ACCEDERE "to go or come to or near", ADVENTARE "to come continually nearer to a point", PROCEDERE "to go forth or before", and the expression PEDEM INFERRE "to go or proceed to a place", could also refer to this concept, but their core meaning was other than "to come, to arrive".

According to the *Latin Dictionary* (Lewis & Short 1966: 1969), the main sense of VENIRE was "to come". This verb goes back to the Indo-European root *$g^w\bar{a}$- (also *g^wem-) "to go, come" and was widely used both in the Archaic and in the Classical periods. It had a great number of compounds, most of which expressed motion, including the three compounds (ADVENIRE, PERVENIRE, DEVENIRE) whose basic sense was also "to come, to arrive": ADVENIRE "to come to a place, to reach, to arrive at", ANTEVENIRE "to come before", CIRCUMVENIRE "to come around something", DEVENIRE "to come from somewhere", EVENIRE "to come out, to come forth", INVENIRE "to come or light upon a thing, to find", INTERVENIRE "to come between, to come upon", PERVENIRE "to come to, to arrive at, to reach a place", PROVENIRE "to come forth, to appear", and SUBVENIRE "to come up or advance to one's assistance".

In Spanish and Portuguese the main verbs that express the idea of 'to come, to arrive' are Spanish *venir*, *llegar* and Portuguese *vir*, *chegar*. Spanish *venir* and Portuguese *vir* go back to Latin VENIRE "to come", as also do French *venir*, Italian *venire*, Romanian *a veni*, Catalan *venir*, Occitan *venir*, Sardinian (Campidanese) *benni*, Sardinian (Logudorese) *bènnere*, and Raeto-Romance *vegnir*, *gnir*. It should be stressed, however, that the deictic range of the Latin etymon and the deictic range of the Spanish and Portuguese reflexes do not match. As Corominas & Pascual (1980–1991 V: 770) explain, Latin VENIRE did not necessarily imply movement towards the speaker as do Modern Spanish *venir* and European Portuguese *vir*, but rather "un movimiento a un lugar definido", i.e., "movimiento hacia un lugar cualquiera que fuese la posición que respeto de él ocupase el sujeto hablante" ["movement toward a specific place"], i.e., ["movement toward any place, regardless of the position occupied by the speaker with respect to this place"]. Old and Classical Spanish *venir*, however, still retained the usage range inherited from

established in discourse rather than for introducing new places, and (b) arrival is a nontrivial achievement (i.e. it is beyond the full control of the figure whether or when s/he will arrive). For instance, Mark 5:1 *And they came over unto the other side of the sea* is a typical 'arrive' context because the new place has been introduced already before in 4:35 (*Let us pass over unto the other side*) and there has in fact been an unexpected storm on the sea which is why it was not clear for everybody whether they actually could make it to the other side.

Latin. Based on his analysis of Spanish Golden Age literary texts, Icaza assesses the difference between *venir* in Modern Spanish and in earlier stages of the language as follows:

> El verbo *venir* tuvo por mucho tiempo en castellano la amplitud que trajo de su origen y que aún conserva en otras lenguas, en francés, por ejemplo. *Venir* no sólo significaba antes, como ahora significa, caminar alguno desde la parte de allá acercándose a la de acá, en sentido directo o figurado, sino que en otros varios usos quiso decir también *ir* o *llegar en cualquier sentido*. [...] Es decir que entonces se usaba, como en francés, en la frase *je viendrai chez vous*, que no indica de ninguna manera el sitio donde se habla. (Icaza 1916: 75; original emphasis)

> [The verb *venir* had for a long time in Spanish the breadth that it brought from its etymon and that it still maintains in other languages, like French, for example. In the past, *venir* not only meant, as it does today, to go from there to here in the literal and in the figurative senses, but also to go or to come in general. [...] That is to say that in the past, it could be used, as in the French phrase *je viendrai chez vous* [I will come to your house], which does not in any way refer to the place at which the conversation takes place.]

In "Los demonstrativos y los verbos de movimiento", Badía Margarit (1952) examines the verbs *ir* and *venir* in Spanish and Catalan, and comes to six conclusions regarding the relationship between these verbs' deictic range and the demonstrative system in these languages. Conclusions 2 and 3 (pp. 30–31) affirm the following:

> En la Península Ibérica subsisten los tres demostrativos latinos, como arcaísmo debido a su separación material del resto del Imperio. Se exceptúa de ello la zona oriental en que se forma el catalán, mejor comunicada con el resto de Romania. Sin embargo, la reducción de los tres términos locativos a dos, es aquí, lenta y laboriosa, y el catalán antiguo y dialectal presenta épocas y comarcas vacilantes (hoy en valenciano se conservan los tres términos).

> Los verbos *ir* y *venir* en sus acepciones fundamentales equivalen en castellano y catalán, pero difieren cuando se ha de expresar movimiento hacia el segundo término demostrativo, para lo cual el castellano usa *ir* y el catalán *venir*; esta última construcción no se logra después de superar la etapa del catalán medieval, en que era frecuente el uso de *anar* como en castellano (y lo propio ocurre hoy en catalán dialectal, como en valenciano).

> [In the Iberian Peninsula, three Latin demonstratives remain in use as an archaism which is due to the Penisula's separation from the rest of the Roman Empire. The eastern part, where Catalan was formed, was more connected to the rest of the Empire and constitutes an exception. However, the reduction of the tree-tier locative system into the two-tier system in the Catalan-speaking part was slow. Old Catalan and Catalan dialects offer phases and regions that vacillate between the three-tier and the two-tier systems; Valencian retains the tree-tier one.]

[The core meanings of the verbs *go* and *come* in Spanish and Catalan are the same. However, to express movement toward the second demonstrative Spanish uses *go*, while Catalan uses *come*. This latter usage established itself after the Middle Ages. In Medieval Catalan *go* was commonly used the same way it is used in Spanish. Catalan dialects and Valencian still employ it this way.]

In other words, while in Spanish the opposition *ir – venir* is that of 'motion to the place of the second/third person' vs. 'motion to the place of the first person', in Catalan the opposition *anar – venir* is that of 'motion to the place of the third person' vs. 'motion to the place of the first/second person' (Coseriu 1990: 268; Taylor 1999: 27).

The restricted deictic usage of Modern Spanish *venir* and European Portuguese *vir* sets these languages apart from the linguistic varieties spoken across Europe. In the typology of deictic motion verbs based on twenty European languages (Italian, Spanish, Portuguese, French, German, English, Dutch, Swedish, Danish, Czech, Polish, Russian, Ukrainian, Serbo-Croatian, Slovenian, Lithuanian, Albanian, Modern Greek, Hungarian, Finnish), Ricca (1993) has established that on the linear hierarchy of goals with which the venitive forms in different languages can appear, Spanish and Portuguese are situated on the very left (p. 108). This is to say that while Spanish and Portuguese venitive forms are used with only one type of goal labeled by Ricca as HUC "here", the venitive forms in other European languages are much more versatile. For instance, Finnish employs the same venitive form *tulla* "to come" with three goals (HUC "here", EGO "I", TU "you"): e.g., *Hän tuli tänne eilen* "He came here yesterday", *Hän tuli luokseni eilen* "He came to my place yesterday", and *David tuli luoksesi eilen* "David came to your place yesterday" (p. 109). To offer another example, a number of languages (e.g., German, Slovenian) employ exclusively the venitive form with the goal ISTUC "there" in indirect speech, or, as in the case of English and French, use either the venitive or the andative in such context: e.g., German *Anna hat mich angerufen und mich eingeladen, heute abend zu ihr zu kommen* "Anna phoned me and asked me to come/go to her place" (p. 107).[10]

Spanish *llegar* and Portuguese *chegar* derive from Late Latin PLICARE whose origin has been interpreted in two different ways. As pointed out in Section 1.4, in Classical Latin PLICARE had the meaning "to fold". However, in Late Latin PLICARE, in addition to its original meaning takes on the new meaning which is a hyponym of "to come", as can be seen from the examples from the *Peregrinatio Aetheriae* cited in the same section. It also has been suggested that Late Latin PLICARE "to come" is not directly related to Classical Latin PLICARE "to fold", but rather is a

---

10. In addition to Ricca (1993), for a more detailed discussion of the deictic nature of the Romance reflexes of Latin VENIRE "to come", see Chevalier (1976), Monti (1981), Ibáñez (1983), Ricca (1991, 1992), Vernay (1974), and Bourdin (1992).

back-formation from Classical Latin APPLICARE which meant "to lean against" and, as a nautical technical term, "to drive, to direct, to steer, or bring a ship anywhere, to land, to bring to land". Väänänen (1990: 240) summarizes the difference of opinions as follows: "pour les uns, PLICARE et APPLICARE sont deux verbes distincts et indépendants, bien que sémantiquement approchés; pour les autres, la forme simple provient de la forme composée" ["for some, PLICARE and APPLICARE are two separate independent although semantically similar verbs; for others, the simple form goes back to the compound one"]. For example, Machado (1977 II: 135), Rohlfs (1979: 178–179), and Blank (1999: 74–75) trace Spanish *llegar* and Portuguese *chegar* "to come" to PLICARE VELAM "to fold the sail", that is "to arrive", and Romanian *a pleca* "to go away" to PLICARE TENTORIA "to fold the tents". In contrast, Corominas & Pascual (1980–1991 IV: 729) present Late Latin PLICARE as a result of back-formation. Corominas & Pascual (1980–1991 IV: 729–731) and Corominas (1990: 370) imply that the connection between PLICARE and APPLICARE can be seen if we compare Spanish *llegar*, Portuguese *chegar*, Romanian *a pleca* (< PLICARE), on the one hand, and Valencian *aplegar*, Old Catalan *aplegar*, Sardinian (Campidanese) *appillai* (< APPLICARE), on the other hand. Tagliavini (1952: 180) also draws our attention to Valencian *aplegar*, as well as to Old Portuguese *achegar*. It should likewise be taken into account that Old Spanish alternated between *llegar* and *allegar* (Sánchez-Prieto Borja 1992).

The main French verbs that express the concept 'to come, to arrive' are *venir* < VENIRE and *arriver*. The latter verb comes from Late Latin ADRIPARE "to come to the shore" composed of AD "towards" and RIPA "shore". *Arriver* first meant "to moor" and this meaning (which is now conveyed by *accoster* or *aborder*) coexisted with the meaning "to come" until the 15th century. However, in the 16th century *arriver* started being used mostly in the broader sense "to come" and the meaning connected to navigation began to depend on the context. Occitan *venir*, *arribar*, Catalan *venir*, *arribar*, Italian *venire*, *arrivare*, and Raeto-Romance *vegnir*, *gnir*, *arrivar*, *rivar* have the same etyma as the French cognates. Aragonese relies on both *plegar* < PLICARE and *arribar* < AD + RIPA, combining the two main Romance options (Lüdtke 2004: 16–17). Both Romance options are also employed in Valencian as *aplegar* and *arribar* (Colón 1993: 42–43). In addition to *venire* and *arrivare*, Italian expresses the concept 'to come, to arrive' with *giungere* which is the reflex of Latin JUNGERE "to join, to unite, to connect". As for Catalan, in addition to *venir* and *arribar*, it employs *pervenir* < PERVENIRE "to come, to arrive, to reach", but this verb usually implies that place was reached with effort/difficulty and therefore it is not the core verb for expressing arrival. In French a reflex of PERVENIRE (*parvenir*) also implies that place was reached with effort/difficulty and therefore, as in the case of Catalan *pervenir*, it is not the core verb for expressing arrival either. As Stefenelli (1992: 260–261) notes, the Romance reflexes of Latin PERVENIRE (French *parvenir*, Catalan *pervenir*, as well as Italian *pervenire* and Occitan *pervenir*) are probably learned words.

As for Sardinian, "to come, to arrive" is expressed in Campidanese by *benni* < VENIRE, *tzucai* (of unknown origin), *lompi* (and its variant *krompi*) < COMPLERE "to fill up, to fill out, to complete", and *arribai* < Late Latin ADRIPARE. Logudorese relies on *bènnere* < VENIRE, *arrivare* < ADRIPARE, and *lòmpere* (*cròmpere*) < COMPLERE. As Vernay (1991–1996 III: 113, 126) points out, Sardinian also makes use of the reflexes of Latin ASCENDERE "to go up" (Logudorese *asèndere*, Campidanese *asèndiri*) when expressing arrival, but these verbs mark not so much the arrival to the desired location but rather arrival to some location in general. The main Romanian verbs that refer to the notion 'to come, to arrive' are *a veni* < VENIRE, *a ajunge*, and *a sosi*. The etymon of *a ajunge* is Classical Latin ADJUNGERE "to connect", which in turn is a compound consisting of the prefix AD- "towards" and the root JUNGERE "to join, to unite, to connect". The source of *a sosi* is the subjunctive of the aorist of Modern Greek σώνω "I catch up, I reach, I arrive". Two other languages from the Balkan Sprachbund also have borrowings from this Greek word: Albanian *sos* "to finish, to arrive, to be enough" and Bulgarian *sos'vam* "to be enough" (Du Nay 1977: 78).

3.2.2 Movement away from a particular location

The main Latin verbs that expressed movement away from a particular location were ABIRE and ABSCEDERE. There existed other verbs that also could refer to the concept in question, but whose core meaning was other than "to go away, to leave".[11] The compound ABIRE "to go from a place, to go away, to depart" was created as a combination of IRE "to go" with AB-, a Latin prefix of Indo-European origin whose fundamental meaning is "from, departure from some fixed point". ABSCEDERE "to go off or away, to depart" is also a compound. It is formed by CEDERE "to go, i.e., to be in motion, move, walk, go along" and the prefix ABS-, which is one of the variants of the aforementioned AB-.

The main Spanish verbs that express the concept 'to go away, to leave' are *irse*, *marcharse*, and *partir*. Spanish *irse* goes back to the combination of IRE "to go" and

---

11. Among these verbs we find DISCEDERE "to part asunder, to divide, to separate, to depart from any place or person, to go away from, to leave", EXCEDERE "to go out, to go forth or away, to depart, to retire, to withdraw", FACESSERE "to do eagerly or earnestly, to dispatch, to perform, to execute, to accomplish, to go away, to retire, to depart", DEMIGRARE "to migrate from, to emigrate, to depart, to remove from a place", RELINQUERE "to leave behind, to leave, to go away from, to forsake, to abandon, to desert", DERELINQUERE "to forsake wholly, to abandon, to desert, (in Late Latin) to leave behind, to bequeath", PROFICISCI "to set out, to start, to march, to travel, to depart", EXIRE "to go out or forth, to go away, to depart", DIGREDI "to go apart or asunder, to separate, to part, to go away, to depart", and EGREDI "to go or come out, to come forth".

the reflexive particle SE whose broad functional range will be addressed in Section 4.2 (below). *Marchar* comes into Spanish in the 16th century and the reflexive *marcharse* appears two centuries later. The origin of the Spanish form is French *marcher* which in turn came from Frankish *markôn (Corominas & Pascual 1980–1991 III: 846). Frankish *marka designated a sign that marks a border and *markôn meant "to make or imprint the signs" or "to leave footprints on the soil". Gamillscheg (1969: 598) proposed another etymon, namely "to clear one's way with a hammer" from Latin MARCUS "hammer", but his view is not widely accepted. Spanish *partir* comes from Latin PARTIRI/PARTIRE "to divide". According to Lewis & Short (1966: 1308), both PARTIRI and PARTIRE "to share, to part, to divide, to distribute" were used in Classical Latin, but the deponent form was used more extensively. Ernout & Meillet (1985: 485) also include both verbs. Rey, on the other hand, claims that the Classical Latin verb was PARTIRI, and that PARTIRE is a later form (Rey, ed. 1994 II: 1439). Through the development of the notion of separation implied in the act of dividing something, Spanish *partir* acquired the idea of movement. Relevant examples are already available in the *Poema de mio Cid* (date of composition debated, presumably the 12th century). In Old Spanish, and even in the language of Cervantes' *Quijote* (early 17th century) it appeared as *partirse*. In French, Italian, and Portuguese the situation with the reflexive derivatives of PARTIRI is similar. When French *partir* first appeared (mid-12th century) it was used as a reflexive *se partir* (Rey, ed. 1994 II: 1439), in Old Italian the reflexive form *partirsi* was commonly used (Battaglia, ed. 1961 XII: 685), and Portuguese still employs *partir-se (de alguém)*. However, moving away from a particular location is generally expressed in Portuguese with the non-reflexive *partir* or with the reflexive *ir-se*. In addition to Spanish, Portuguese, French, and Italian, Latin PARTIRI/PARTIRE survives as Campidanese *partiri*, Logudorese *partire*, and Raeto-Romance *partir*.

The main French verbs that express the concept of going away or leaving are *s'en aller* and *partir*. Like *aller*, *s'en aller* probably comes from Latin AMBULARE. The adverbial pronoun *en* derives from the Latin adverb INDE "thence". As Arsène Darmesteter explains, the appearance of *s'en aller* is part of a new type of word-formation with *en* < INDE, unknown in Latin but common in French:

> Latin did not use it [INDE] in composition. French from the earliest times has added it, according to [the] mode [Particle + Verb = Verb][12] to certain verbs of motion, to indicate removal from a place: *emporter, envoyer, enlever, emmener, enfuir, entraîner, envoler – s'en aller, s'en retourner, s'en venir*. (Darmesteter 1899: 424)

---

12. Some examples of this word-formation model are *porter* "to carry" – *apporter* "to bring", *comporter* "to admit, to comprise", *déporter* "to carry away", *reporter* "to carry back", *supporter* "to support"; *faire* "to make" – *défaire* "to demolish, to undo", *refaire* "to remake"; *mettre* "to put, to place" – *admettre* "to admit", *commettre* "to commit", *démettre* "to dislocate, to dismiss", *permettre* "to permit, to allow", *remettre* "to put back", *soumettre* "to subdue" (Darmesteter 1899: 412).

As can be seen from the examples given above, *en* usually turned into a prefix, which is united with the verb even in compound tenses: e.g., *ils se sont enfuis* "they have fled". In the case of *s'en aller*, however, such unification is rejected by prescriptive grammar: "Grammatical laws recommend the separation of the adverb (*je m'en suis allé*) but modern everyday usage tends more and more to complete fusion: *il s'est en allé*" (Rohlfs 1970: 140). As for French *partir* (Old French *se partir*), it goes back to PARTIRI/PARTIRE, as do its Romance cognates, as mentioned above. Occitan *s'enanar* and Catalan *anar-se'n* have the same origin as French *s'en aller*, namely SE + INDE + AMBULARE. In Catalan, *marxar* < French *marcher* "to walk" is also commonly used to express the concept of leaving, but "to go away" is not *marxar*'s main meaning and to use it instead of *anar-se'n* is considered to be a Castilianism.

Italian and Raeto-Romance use the reflexes of PARTIRI/PARTIRE (Modern Italian *partire*, Old Italian *partirsi*, Raeto-Romance *partir*) as the main way to express the idea of leaving, as mentioned above. Italian also employs *andarsene* < AMBULARE + SE + INDE, and the varieties of Raeto-Romance spoken in the Engadine valley can employ *s'inir* < SE + INDE + IRE (Vernay 1991–1996 III: 80, 111). As for Sardinian, Campidanese relies on *partiri* < PARTIRI and *moviri* < MOVERE "to move", and Logudorese relies on *partire* and *mòvere* that have the same etyma as their Campidanese equivalents. According to Wagner (1960–1964 II: 131), in Late Latin SE MOVERE could be used in the sense "to go away, to set out". The same is true for Old Spanish *mover*: e.g., *ca a mover ha mio Cid ante que cante el gallo* "for My Cid has to set out before the rooster crows" (*Poema de mio Cid*, verse 169), *movió con su mesnada* "he set out with his men" (Juan Ruiz, *Libro de buen amor*, verse 1313). Old and Modern Italian *muoversi* offers similar examples: e.g., *la mattina quando si funno per muovere* "the morning when they were about to set out" (Giovanni Sercambi, 1347–1424, *Novelle*). Wagner (1960–1964 II: 131) views Campidanese *moviri* and Logudorese *mòvere* "to go away" as part of this Late Latin/Early Romance tendency.

The main Romanian verbs that refer to the notion 'to go away, to leave' are *a se duce*, *a pleca*, *a se depărta*, *a se îndepărta*, and *a se retrage*. *A se duce* and *a pleca* come from Latin DUCERE "to lead" and PLICARE "to fold", respectively. *A se depărta* and *a se îndepărta* are combinations of Latin DE[13] with PARTIRI/PARTIRE "to divide" and INDE "thence" with PARTIRI/PARTIRE, respectively. *A se retrage*, which is also a combination of Latin elements, namely RE "back, against" and TRAHERE "to draw, to drag, to haul, to drag along, to draw off, forth or away", is calqued upon the French pair *retirer* "to pull, to draw, to take out", *se retirer* "to go away".

---

13. The meaning of Latin DE will be addressed in Section 3.2.6 (below).

3.2.3   Movement inside

The main Latin verbs that referred to movement inside were INIRE "to go into, to enter a place", INTROIRE "to go in or into, to enter", INGREDI "to go into, to enter, to go along, to advance, to proceed, to march", and INTRARE "to go or walk into, to enter". The verb OBIRE, which in Classical Latin prose predominantly meant "to go or come to a thing or place" and in poetry and post-Augustan prose meant "to go or come to or towards, to come in, to go to meet, to go against" could also be used to express movement inside, but, as the definitions suggests, "to enter" was not OBIRE's core meaning. INIRE, INTROIRE, and INGREDI are compounds: they come from IN + IRE, INTRO + IRE, and IN + GREDI, respectively. Both IN "in, within, on, upon, among, at, into, towards" and the derived from it INTRO "inwardly, internally, on the inside, to the inside, within, in" go back to Indo-European *en "in". IRE goes back to the Indo-European *ei-/*i- "to go". As for GREDI, it is a variant of GRADI "to take steps, to walk, to go" which goes back to Indo-European *ghredh- "to walk, to go".

While the sources of INIRE, INTROIRE, and INGREDI are clear, the origin of INTRARE presents a challenge. On the one hand, it might be a combination of the prefix IN- and the verb *TRARE. The *Oxford Latin Dictionary* (Glare, ed. 1982) does not include *TRARE. The *Indogermanisches Etymologisches Wörterbuch* (Pokorny 1959–1969 I: 1076) admits the possibility of Latin *TRARE, stating that Latin TRANS perhaps was its participle. The "Indo-European Roots" inventory (Watkins 1993), based on Pokorny (1959–1969), includes *trā- (variant of *terə-) "to cross over, pass through, overcome", and lists as one of its derivatives Latin TRANS "across, over beyond, through", which "perhaps originally [was] the present participle of a verb *trāre 'to cross over'" (Watkins 1993: 1620). The second, also questionable, hypothesis postulates that Latin INTRARE derives from the adjective *INTERUS "interior" which in turn derives from the preverb IN(-) and the locative form *TER, *TERI. Walde & Hofmann (1982) subscribe to the first theory, while Ernout & Meillet (1985) present both of them as equally questionable. Whether the origin of INTRARE is IN + *TRARE or IN + *TER/*TERI, it seems that in Classical Latin the verb was not perceived as a compound. The Latin dictionaries that follow the practice of separating parts of compound words with a hyphen (e.g., Glare, ed. 1982, Ernout & Meillet 1985, Dvoreckij 1986) list INTRARE without a hyphen. This is significant because, as we will see in the next chapter, the simple or the compound nature of Latin verbs of motion influenced their chances of survival.

In Spanish, French, Italian, Portuguese, Romanian, Catalan, Occitan, Sardinian, and Raeto-Romance the concept 'to enter' is expressed with the reflexes of INTRARE "to enter": Spanish *entrar*, French *entrer*, Italian *entrare*, Portuguese *entrar*, Romanian *a intra*, Catalan *entrar*, Occitan *(d)intrar*, Campidanese *intrai*, Logudorese *intràre*, and Raeto-Romance *entrar*. In Old Catalan such variants of *entrar* as *intrar* and *entrar-se'n* are commonly found: e.g., *entrar-me'n-he en la mia cambra* "I shall enter my room" (Joanot Martorell, 15th century, *Tirant lo Blanc*) (Coromines et al. 1980–1991 III: 395). In both Campidanese and Logudorese the form with *b-* (*bintrai* and *bintrare*) is also in use in some regions (Wagner 1960–1964 I: 640; Lepori 1988: 90). Wagner (1960–1964 I: 494) and Meyer-Lübke (1992: 353) interpret *b-* as deriving from the Latin adverb IBI "there", but more recent research views it as an epenthesis (cf. Sardinian *bok(k)ire* "to kill" < Latin OCCIDERE "to fall, to kill') (Floricic 2004: 74–75). To express the concept 'to enter' all the languages mentioned above (except for Romanian where *a păşi* means "to stride, to march") can also use the reflexes of Late Latin PASSARE[14] < Classical Latin PASSUS "step, pace": Spanish *pasar*, French *passer*, Italian *passare*, Portuguese *passar*, Catalan *passar*, Occitan *passar*, Sardinian (Campidanese) *passai*, Sardinian (Logudorese) *passàre*, and Raeto-Romance *passar*, although their core meaning is not "to enter" but rather "to go along/across".

3.2.4 Movement outside

The main Latin verbs that expressed movement outside were EXIRE "to go out or forth, to go away, to depart, to go or pass beyond a thing", EGREDI "to go or come out, to come forth", and EVENIRE "to come out, to come forth". All three of them were compounds: EX + IRE "to go", EX + GREDI "to take steps, to walk, to go", and EX + VENIRE "to come", respectively. However, as Grandgent (1952: 38) points out, in Late Latin EXIRE seems to have been perceived not as a compound but rather as a simple (monomorphemic) verb. The origin of IRE, GREDI, and VENIRE was discussed earlier in this chapter. As for E- and EX-, they are variants of the same prefix whose meaning is "out from the interior of a thing in opposition to in, out of, from" and whose origin is Indo-European *eghs* "out".

In Spanish and Portuguese the idea 'to exit' is expressed by *salir*, *sair* < SALIRE "to jump". In several Romance languages (Spanish *salir*, Portuguese *sair*, Occitan *sal(h)ir*, French *saillir*, Catalan *sallir*)[15] this Latin verb underwent a semantic evolution and from a vertical jump started referring to a horizontal one and later replaced the verb EXIRE "to exit" (Rohlfs 1979: 175). In Old Spanish *salir* could mean both "to exit" and "to jump", as can be seen from numerous examples from the *Poema de mio Cid*: e.g., *salieron de la eglesia, ya quieren cavalgar* "they exited the

---

14. On Late Latin PASSARE, see Niermeyer & Van De Kieft (2002 II: 1002) and Du Cange (1883–1887 VI: 196).

15. In French, Catalan, and Occitan the meaning of the reflexes of SALIRE are not so much of movement but rather of bubbling or effervescing of water (in a fountain).

church and are ready to ride" (verse 367), *ensiéllanle a Bavieca, [...] myo Çid salió sobrél* "Babieca is saddled [...] My Cid mounted" (verses 1585–1586) (Corominas & Pascual 1980–1991 V: 139). At the same time, *exir* "to go out" < EXIRE is also widely used in the *Cid*: e.g., *gradó exir de la posada* "he [Martín Antolínez] was eager to exit the house" (verse 200) (Cejador y Frauca 1971: 197). However, even though *exir* is still found in 13th-century texts and beyond, already in the Medieval period it is clearly losing ground to *salir* and is disappearing from the language (Šišmarëv 2002: 132). In Portuguese the old form *e(i)xir* was likewise eventually abandoned in favor of *sair*.

In Catalan the main verbs that express movement outside are *sortir* and *eixir* < EXIRE. According to the most widely accepted etymology, *sortir* comes from Latin SORTIRI which meant "to throw lots or to choose by a lot" (Coromines et al. 1980–1991 III: 253). The idea of movement could have started to become attributed to SORTIRI as an extension of the meaning of the past participle SORTITUS "the one who was distinguished by a lot" (Rey, ed. 1994 II: 1980). Etymological dictionaries of Catalan (Alcover & Moll, eds. 1930–1962 X: 23; Coromines et al. 1980–1991 VIII: 100), while listing SORTIRI as the etymon, at the same time assume a connection between Catalan *sortir* and Late Latin *SURCTUS < Classical Latin SURGERE "to get up, to rise". However, etymological and historical dictionaries of French either explicitly reject or do not mention SURGERE in their discussion of French *sortir* (Gamillscheg 1969: 816; Dauzat et al. 1979: 702; Rey, ed. 1994 II: 1980; Picoche 1992: 466; Bloch & Wartburg 1994: 600). In Occitan we also find *sortir* < SORTIRI and *eissir* < EXIRE. In addition to that, Occitan can express the concept 'to go out' with *sal(h)ir* < SALIRE "to jump".

While Catalan and Occitan still have reflexes of both EXIRE and SORTIRI,[16] Modern French uses only the reflex of SORTIRI, namely, *sortir*. Prior to the 16th century the use of *sortir* as a verb of motion was relatively rare in French and the idea of going outside was expressed by Old French *eissir* ((*s'en*) *issir*) (Rey, ed. 1994 II: 1980). However, by the 17th century the French reflex of EXIRE was almost extinct and from that point on it can be used only in reference to lineage, as in *il est issu de telle famille* "he comes from such and such family" (Darmesteter 1887: 191, n.1). In other words, while in Catalan and Occitan the reflexes of EXIRE are still available as motion verbs, in Spanish and French they have disappeared from the lexical field in question. In Italian, Romanian, and Sardinian EXIRE does

---

16. Valencian maintains the reflexes of both EXIRE and SORTIRI as well, as *eixir* and *sortir*, respectively. The former is the default verb to express the concept 'to go out', while the latter is used to refer to an unexpected, violent eruption or outburst (Colón 1993: 99).

survive to refer to movement outside. In Italian it produced *uscire*[17] and in Romanian it resulted in the form *a ieşi*. In the case of Sardinian, the origin of Campidanese *bessiri* and Logudorese *bessìre* has been interpreted as IBI + EXIRE (Wagner 1960–1964 I: 471) or as EXIRE which has undergone epenthesis (Floricic 2004: 74–75). In Northern Logudorese the forms *disessire* and *dessessire* are also in use (Wagner 1960–1964 I: 471). As for Raeto-Romance, to express movement outside this language uses the learned word *ceder* < Latin CEDERE "to go, i.e., to be in motion, move, walk, go along" and the loan-word *sortir* borrowed from Italian *sortire* "to sort, to pick" or from French *sortir* 'to go out'. The Friulian variety of Raeto-Romance employs *išì* which is a reflex of Latin EXIRE "to go out" (Meyer-Lübke 1992: 265).

3.2.5   Movement upward

The main Latin verbs that expressed upward movement were the compounds of SCANDERE/SCENDERE "to ascend, to make one's way uphill or to the top": A-SCENDERE "to ascend, to go up, to mount up, to climb", CON-SCENDERE "to mount, to go up to, to climb to", and E-SCENDERE "to proceed to a place on a higher level, to go up". The origin of these words is the Indo-European root **skand-* (**skend-*) "to leap, to climb". SCANDERE was also in use, but the compounds were much more common, especially in prose, and eventually the compounds replaced the simple form (Ernout & Meillet 1985: 599). Latin SUBIRE "to move underneath, to draw near, to move upward" could also express upward motion, but this function was not the one used most widely.

The main Spanish and Portuguese verbs that express the idea 'to go up' are *subir* and *ascender*. *Subir* comes into both languages from Latin SUBIRE, which is a combination of the prefix SUB- and the root IRE "to go". As García-Hernández (1978, 1995a, 1995b, 1999, 2000, 2003) illustrates, the Latin preverb SUB(-) had three main kinds of spatial usage: (1) "up, upward", (2) "behind", and (3) "below, under". The first of the three functions, i.e., "up, upward", was the earliest one. It was attested in Latin throughout its history, but already by the Classical Latin stage it was no longer productive (García-Hernández 1978: 44). In contrast, the last of the three functions, i.e., "below, under", was the most recent of the three, yet it managed to become the one most widely used (García-Hernández 1999: 224). Given the polysemous nature of Latin SUB-, Latin SUBIRE was also polysemous, and could denote upward motion, motion toward, as well as downward motion.

---

17.   The initial phoneme of Italian *uscire* and the alternation of *u-* and *e-* in its present indicative paradigm (*esco, esci, esce, usciamo, uscite, escono*) are due to the suppletive conflation of Old Italian *escire* with the noun *uscio* "doorway" (Maiden 1995b).

García-Hernández (1999: 226) interprets the survival of SUBIRE in its function "to move upward" as Spanish *subir* and Portuguese *subir* "to go up" as an example *par excellence* of the archaic nature of Ibero-Romance. In Old Spanish *subir* alternated with *sobir* (Corominas & Pascual 1980–1991 V: 322). As illustrated in Pharies (2011), *sobir* belongs to a series of (Old) Spanish lexemes that show the SUB- > *so*-development: e.g., Old Spanish *sohumar, sofumar* (Modern Spanish *sahumar*) "to perfume with incense or aromatic herbs" < Latin SUFFUMARE "to smoke or reek a little"; Old Spanish *sostituir* (Modern Spanish *sustituir*) "to replace" < Latin SUB-STITUERE "to set under or next to"; Spanish *sobornar* "to bribe" < Latin SUBORNARE "to provide, to incite secretly".

Spanish *ascender* comes from Latin ASCENDERE. It is not clear exactly when *ascender* became part of the Spanish language. On the one hand, according to Corominas & Pascual (1980–1991 I: 457), it is a learned word attested for the first time in 1555. It is absent from such dictionaries and word-lists of Medieval Spanish as Oelschläger (1940), Boggs et al. (1946), Cejador y Frauca (1971), Kasten & Cody (2001), and Seco ed. (2003). Dworkin (1995), who studies *ascender* < ASCEN-DERE "to mount, to ascend, to go up" in order to assess its possible role in the demise of Old Spanish *acender* < ACCENDERE "to kindle, to set on fire", finds no examples of the verb in question in the Medieval documents:

> The entry for *ascender* in Cuervo [*Diccionario de construcción y régimen de la lengua castellana*] has no medieval examples of the verb; Martín Alonso's *Diccionario medieval español* contains no entry for *ascender* 'to go up'. The presence in Old Spanish of the religious term *a(s)censión* or of *ascendente* as a technical astronomical term in no way independently confirms the presence or vitality of the related verb. My own survey of glossaries, vocabularies, and concordances to medieval texts has unearthed no examples of *ascender* in Medieval Spanish. Nebrija's Latin–Spanish dictionary turns to *subir* as the gloss for Lat. ASCENDŌ. According to Gili Gaya [*Tesoro lexicográfico (1492–1726)*] (s.v. *ascender*), Covarrubias's *Tesoro* is the first dictionary to record *ascender*. (Dworkin 1995: 537)

On the other hand, in his *Diccionario del español medieval*, Bodo Müller (1987– I: 377–379) lists instances of *ascender* (for *acender*) < ACCENDERE "to kindle, to set on fire" from the *Fuero de Teruel* and the Alfonsine *Primera Partida* preserved in 13th-century codices.[18] The confusion between *ascender* and *acender* in these texts makes Müller imply "the presence of *ascender* < ASCENDERE in at least some

---

18. Müller (1987– I: 377–379) also gives examples of *ascender* for *acender* from other 13th-century texts, but these texts survived only in 15th-century manuscripts and thus, according to Dworkin (1995: 536), "the apparent confusion reflected in these manuscripts between genetically distinct *acender* and *ascender* reflects the linguistic reality of the late fourteenth or early fifteenth centuries rather than that of the thirteenth century".

registers of the Old Spanish lexicon as early as the second half of the thirteenth century" (Dworkin 1995: 536). However, as we have seen above, there is no direct evidence of *ascender* < ASCENDERE before the 16th century. Also, as Dworkin (1995: 535) points out, the popularity of *acender* < ACCENDERE is drastically falling in the 14th and 15th centuries. Thus, the copyists of the *Fuero de Teruel* and the *Primera Partida* who obviously knew Latin were probably unfamiliar with *acender* and therefore confused it with Latin ASCENDERE rather than with its Romance reflex *ascender* (ibid., pp. 535–538).

In Portuguese, on the other hand, *ascender* clearly is present since the Medieval times. In contrast to Old Spanish, Old Portuguese abundantly documents *a(s)cender* "to go up, to raise": "Cunha [*Índice do vocabulário do português medieval*] supplies examples taken from *Leal conselheiro, Vida de Sam Bernardo, Orto do esposo, Livro de Vita Christi,* and *Regra de São Bento*" (Dworkin 1995: 537). In addition to Spanish and Portuguese *ascender*, we also find such Romance reflexes of ASCENDERE as Italian *ascendere* (present in the language since the end of the 13th century), Catalan *ascendir*, Old French *ascendre*, Old Provençal *ascendre*, and Raeto-Romance *ascender*.

The main Catalan verbs that express the idea 'to go up' are *pujar, muntar*, and *ascendir*. The main Occitan ones are *montar* and *pujar (pojar)*. *Pujar, pojar* come from Late Latin *PODIARE < PODIUM "elevated place". Old Spanish could also employ *pujar* as an intransitive motion verb (Brosman 1956: 264–265; Alonso Pedraz 1986 II: 1529–1530), but the most common usage was either transitive, or, when intransitive, then in reference to concepts other than motion: e.g., *Puió en grant riqueza e en grant alavançia* "He grew greatly in wealth and prestige" (Gonzalo de Berceo, *Milagros de Nuestra Señora*, 13th century, verse 661d). Old Aragonese employed *puyar* as well (Colón 1993: 79). Catalan *muntar* and *montar* were created according to a principle similar to the one that produced *pujar*: they come from Late Latin *MONTARE < MONS, MONTIS "mountain", as also do French *monter*, Raeto-Romance *muntar*, and possibly Italian *montare*. Catalan *ascendir* and Old Provençal *ascendre* derive from ASCENDERE.

Going upward is expressed in French with the verb *monter* < Late Latin *MONTARE < MONS, MONTIS, which in Old French coexisted with *ascendre* < ASCENDERE, found mostly in religious and technical texts. French *hausser* < Late Latin *ALTIARE < Classical Latin ALTUS "high" can also indicate going up, but its core sense is "to raise". The relevant Italian verbs are *salire, ascendere*, and *montare*. *Salire*, which is by far the most ordinary of the three synonyms, comes from SALIRE "to jump" and *ascendere* derives from ASCENDERE "to ascend, to mount up, to climb". As far as *montare* is concerned, its origin is somewhat problematic. In the discussion of Spanish *montar* "to mount", Corominas (1954–1957 III: 426) and Corominas & Pascual (1980–1991 IV: 132) state that Spanish *montar* and Italian *montare* are borrowings from French. On the other hand, according to several Italian etymological dictionaries (e.g., Battisti & Alessio 1950–1957, Migliorini & Duro 1958, Cortelazzo & Zolli 1979–1988), *montare* comes from Late Latin *MONTARE "to go up the mountain" < Latin MONS, MONTIS "mountain". *Lexical Borrowing in the Romance Languages* by T. E. Hope (1971) does not list *montare* as a Gallicism. The section "Prestiti galloromanzi (francesi e provenzali)" from the *Grammatica storica dell'italiano* by Pavao Tekavčic (1972 III: 247–249) does not claim *montare* as a Gallicism either, although Tekavčić does state that the list of his examples is not exhaustive. Cortelazzo & Zolli (1979–1988 III: 775) not only claim Latin origin, but also explicitly negate the view expressed in Coromines (1954–1957). Battisti & Alessio (1950–1957 IV: 2503) do acknowledge as a Gallicism one of the meanings of Italian *montare* – namely "mettere in ordine per il funzionamento un meccanismo, un motore" ["to put in order, to assemble a mechanism or an engine"] – but, as was already mentioned, view Late Latin *MONTARE as the etymon.

As for Sardinian, to express movement upward, Campidanese uses *artziai* and *(a)pujai*. The former goes back to Late Latin *ALTIARE < ALTUS "high", and the latter is a Catalanism borrowed from Catalan *pujar* "to go up" < *PODIARE < PODIUM "elevated place". Logudorese uses *alzare, arziàre* < *ALTIARE < ALTUS. In Old Sardinian *koddai (koddare)* < *COLLARE < COLLIS "hill" was used throughout the island in the sense "to go up", but in Modern Sardinian this verb only corresponds to Italian *copire (di animali)* "to cover (of animals)" (Wagner 1960–1964 I: 77, 361). Sardinian also retains a reflex of Latin ASCENDERE – *ašèndere* (Vernay 1991–1996 III: 116). In the case of Raeto-Romance, upward motion is expressed by *ascender* < ASCENDERE (Darms et al. 1989: 310, 398) and *muntar* < *MONTARE. In Romanian the corresponding verbs are *a urca, a sui*, and *a se ridica*. The etymon of *a urca* is probably Latin *ORICARE < ORIRI "to rise, to bestir one's self, to get up", according to Macrea ed. (1958), Cioranescu (1966), and Puşcariu (1975). The Greek etymon defended by Tiktin (1895–1925) and the Slavic one supported by de Cihac (1978) are less likely to be the source of the verb in question (Cioranescu 1966: 876). Romanian *a sui* comes from Latin SUBIRE, and *a se ridica* comes from Latin SE + ERADICARE "to uproot", which in turn is a combination of the prefix EX- "out" and RADICARE "to take roots".

3.2.6   Movement downward

The main Latin verbs that expressed downward movement were DESCENDERE "to come down" (and of inanimate objects "to fall, to sink down, to descend"), DEGREDI "to go down, to march down, to descend", and SUBIRE "to move underneath, to draw near, to move upward". All three were compounds: DE + SCANDERE, DE +

GREDI, SUB + IRE, respectively. There is no agreement about the exact nature of the core meaning of DE in Classical Latin: its original meaning was that of displacement downward, but this sense rapidly became more general and came to be "from there – to here", replacing this way AB "from, departure form some fixed point" and EX "out of, from" (Referovskaja 1961: 39; Ernout & Meillet 1985: 164–165; Adams 2011: 259, 262). For instance, in verbs of stage movement in Latin theater, DE was used in a more general sense marking withdrawal on stage (i.e., moving aside), while AB marked withdrawal from the exterior (i.e., exiting the stage), and EX marked withdrawal from the interior (i.e., entering the stage) (Poduska 1963: 173, 176; González Vázquez 2003: 255). As for SUB, as mentioned earlier in this chapter, it was a polysemous preverb whose main spatial functions were "below, under", "behind", and "up, upward". Latin SCANDERE comes from Indo-European *skand- (*skend-) "to leap, to climb", GREDI goes back to Indo-European *ghredh- "to walk, go", and IRE derives from Indo-European *ei-/*i- "to go".

The main Spanish verbs that refer to downward motion are *bajar* and *descender*. In Portuguese the corresponding verbs are *(a)baixar, descer*, and *descender*. Old Spanish also employed *deçir*, which was used less often than its synonym *(a)baxar* and eventually disappeared from the language. Spanish *bajar* and Portuguese *(a)baixar* come from Late Latin *BASSIARE < Classical Latin BASSUS "low", as does Catalan *(a)baixar*.[19] Modern Spanish regards the prefixed *abajar* as archaic, while in Modern Catalan *abaixar* is the current norm, and the form without the prefix is regarded as the archaic one (Salomonski 1944: 24, n.2). As far as *descender* is concerned, after several unreliable etymologies, such as DECEDERE "to go away, to depart, to withdraw", DESIDERE "to sink, to fall, to settle down", DECIDERE "to fall off, to fall down", and DEJICERE "to throw down", it was established that its etymon is Latin DESCENDERE "to go down". In addition to the Spanish and Portuguese forms, Catalan *descendir*, Old Catalan *dexendre*, French *descendre*, Occitan *descendre*, Italian *discendere, scendere*, and Raeto-Romance *descender* also derive from DESCENDERE.

The origin of Old Spanish *deçir* "to go down" and Portuguese *descer* "to go down" has proven to be one of the most challenging etymological cruxes. Malkiel (1984a) presents a detailed overview of the different theories that have been advanced to explain the source of these verbs. The number of these theories is so great that Malkiel refers to the situation as "caos" ["chaos"] (p. 344) and "laberinto de formas y de opiniones eruditas" ["a labyrinth of forms and learned opinions"]

---

19. According to Malkiel (1993: 158), the etymon of Spanish *bajar* and Portuguese *(a)bajar* is the comparative degree of BASSUS, i.e., BASSIOR, BASSIUS. According to Müller (1987– I: 36), while Old Spanish *abajar*, Old French *abaisser*, Old Occitan *abaissar*, Catalan *abaixar*, and Portuguese *abaixar* go back to Late Latin *BASSIARE, such forms as Italian *abbassare* and Raeto-Romance *abassar, abaser* derive from Late Latin *BASSARE.

(p. 346). Malkiel himself believes that the origin of the verb in question can be found in the blend of Latin DE-/DIS-CEDERE "to depart, to withdraw, to go apart" and DESCENDERE "to go down" (the opposite of SCANDERE "to go up") (1984a: 354; 1989: 54–55). The confusion between these verbs was first noticed by a Latinist named August Engelbrecht (1861–1925), and Leo Spitzer (1887–1960) was the first Romanist who used Engelbrecht's observation to solve the etymology of Old Spanish *deçir* (Malkiel 1984a: 347–348). Malkiel believes that the contrast between Old Spanish *deçir* and Old Portuguese *deçer* (Modern Portuguese *descer*) can possibly be attributed to "the center's stronger exposure than the West's to the effects of lexical polarization, the opposite semantic pole being in this instance *subir*, orig. *sobir* 'to rise'" (1984b: 165). Another problem that Old Spanish *deçir* presents is its disappearance from the language at the end of the 15th century. A number of Romanists (among them Leo Spitzer, Ramón Menéndez-Pidal, and Yakov Malkiel) tried to explain this disappearance as a result of a homonymic clash with Old Spanish *dezir* "to say". Dworkin (1992a, 1992b, 2010) challenges this point of view: "The analyst must exercise caution when invoking homonymy as a cause of linguistic change" (1992b: 493). In Dworkin's opinion, the main reason for the loss of Old Spanish *deçir* "to go down" was its defectiveness, which was brought about by paradigmatic and conjugational difficulties (1992a, 1992b, 2010: 599–560).

The main Catalan verbs that express the idea 'to go downward' are *baixar*, *davallar*, and *descendir*. In Old Catalan *davallar* coexisted with *avallar*; both verbs created based on Latin VALLIS "valley": DE + AD + VALLIS; AD + VALLIS, respectively.[20] Catalan *baixar* derives from Late Latin *BASSIARE < BASSUS "low", as mentioned earlier. As for Catalan *descendir*, it derives from DESCENDERE "to go down". In French movement downwards is expressed with the help of *descendre* < DESCENDERE "to go down". In Old French it coexisted with *avaler* < AD + VALLIS which in Modern French means "to swallow". As Ullmann (1957: 179) points out, in *Pantagruel* François Rabelais (16th century) tried to "rejuvenate" *avaler* as a verb of motion by placing it alongside *monter*: *Si je montasse aussi bien comme je avalle, je feusse désjà au dessus la sphere de la lune avecques Empedocles!* "If I went up as well as I go down, I would already be above the sphere of the moon with Empedocles!". French *dévaler* < DE + VALLIS is still present in the modern language as a motion verb. It can be used to express movement downward, but it usually implies that the action is swift. Parenthetically, it should be noted that Old Aragonese also possessed a reflex of DE + VALLIS, namely, *devallar* (Colón 1993: 78). French *se baisser* < Late Latin *BASSIARE < Classical Latin BASSUS "low" (or its comparative degree BASSIOR, BASSIUS) is also a part of Modern French motion verbs

---

20. See Niermeyer & Van De Kieft (2002 I: 99) and Du Cange (1883–1887 I: 461–462) on Late Latin AVALLARE, AVALARE "to go down a slope".

lexical field, but while it can express movement downward, its core meaning is "to stoop". Occitan refers to downward motion with *descendre* < DESCENDERE and with *davalar* < DE + AD + VALLIS. In Old Occitan *davalar* coexisted with *avalar* < AD + VALLIS (Coromines et al. 1980–1991 IV: 31).

The corresponding Italian verbs are *discendere* and *scendere* from Latin DESCENDERE "to go down" (Vernay 1991–1996 III: 117). Raeto-Romance *descender* is of the same origin (Darms et al. 1989: 398). As far as Sardinian is concerned, Campidanese *calai* and Logudorese *calare* come from Late Latin CALARE[21] "to lower, to let down" < Classical Greek χαλάω "I lower, I let down" (Meyer-Lübke 1992: 139; Corominas 1990: 118). In Old Sardinian and in some modern dialects of the central part of the island the form based on the same etymon is *falare* (Wagner 1960–1964 I: 266). The main Romanian verbs that refer to movement downward are *a coborî*, *a pogorî*, and *a scoborî*, all three related to Old Slavic *pogorĭ* "downwards, down, below", *pogorĭnŭ* "head first", *pod gorije* "valley", *pogorije* "mountain range", and *gora* "mountain". As Cioranescu (1966: 214) explains, out of these three verbs *a coborî* is the most widely used, while *a pogorî* and *a scoborî* are considered to be its variants. *A pogorî*, however, was abundantly used in earlier texts.

3.3 Manner-specific motion

3.3.1 Movement on foot by taking steps

The main Latin verbs that expressed walking were AMBULARE "to go about, to walk", GRADI "to take steps, to walk, to go", and CEDERE "to go, i.e. to be in motion, to move, to walk, to go along". A derivative of CEDERE, namely INCEDERE "to go, to step, or march along at a measured pace" could also be used, but it was likely to have the marked meaning of "walking majestically", as suggested by Seneca the Younger's famous *non ambulamus, sed incedimus* "we do not walk, we parade" (O'Sullivan 2011: 31–33). Latin SPATIARI "to take a walk, to walk about, to promenade" and DEAMBULARE "to walk abroad, to walk much, to take a walk, to promenade" were rare and referred more to the nature of the pastime than to movement. GRADI derives from Indo-European **ghredh-* "to walk, to go" and CEDERE derives from from Indo-European **ked-* (**sed-*) "to go, to yield" (Pokorny 1959–1969 I: 887; Watkins 1993: 1595, 1597–1598). As for AMBULARE, this verb was originally a compound. Etymologically it was a combination of the prefix AMB- "around" and the root **el-* "to go", which in addition to the Italic group can be found in the Celtic languages: e.g., Middle Welsh *el* "he should go" (Ernout &

---

21. On Late Latin CALARE "to lower, to let down", see Niermeyer & Van De Kieft (2002 I: 151) and Du Cange (1883–1887 II: 20).

Meillet 1985: 27). At first, AMBULARE had the sense "to go around", from which the meaning "to walk" eventually developed. In the dictionaries (Glare ed. 1982, Ernout & Meillet 1985, Dvoreckij 1986) it appears without a hyphen, which suggests that the authors of these dictionaries have reasons to believe that in Classical Latin it was perceived not as a compound, but rather as a simple form, which is significant, as we will see in the next chapter.

The main Spanish, Portuguese, and Sardinian verbs that refer to walking come from the same etyma. Spanish *caminar*, Portuguese *caminhar*, Campidanese *caminai*, and Logudorese *caminàre* go back to Late Latin CAMMINUS, which is of Celtic origin (Corominas & Pascual 1980–1991 I: 787). *Caminar* was almost absent from Old Spanish. The *Tentative Dictionary of Medieval Spanish* (Boggs et al. 1946 I: 93) which examines the *Poema de mio Cid*, several works of Berceo, *Libro de Apolonio*, *Conde Lucanor*, and *Libro de buen amor*, finds *caminar* only in Berceo. *Ir* or *andar* (*en piedes*) were used instead. Spanish *andar*, Portuguese *andar*, Campidanese *andai*, and Logudorese *ambulare* probably come from AMBULARE "to walk". In Catalan and Italian the main verbs that express walking come from Late Latin CAMMINUS. In Old Catalan *caminar* coexisted with the form *acaminar*. Raeto-Romance *c(h)aminar* is a loan-word from Italian *camminare*.

In Gallo-Romance the corresponding verbs are French *marcher* and Occitan *marchar*, *marcar* < Late Latin MARCARE[22] < Frankish **markôn* "to make or imprint the signs" or "to leave steps on the soil" < **marka*, as discussed in the case of Spanish *marcharse*. French also has the verb *cheminer* < Late Latin CAMMINUS, but this verb usually implies long, difficult, and slow movement. Already in Classical Latin IRE "to go" and VADERE "to go" had conflated into one suppletive present indicative paradigm (VADO, VADIS, VADIT, IMUS, ITIS, VADUNT), and in Gallic Late Latin (from the 6th century onward) the forms based on AMBULARE "to walk" replaced the IMUS, ITIS forms, resulting in VADO, VADIS, VADIT, AMBULAMUS, AMBULATIS, VADUNT, which, according to Lüdtke (1999: 56–57), might have triggered the appearance of both *marcher* and *cheminer*. Romanian expresses movement on foot with the help of *a umbla* < AMBULARE and *a merge* < MERGERE "to dip, to plunge".

3.3.2   Swift movement on foot

The main Latin verb that expressed running was CURRERE "to run, to move quickly (on foot, on a horse, ship, etc.), to hasten" which goes back to the Indo-European root **kers-* "to run".

---

22.   For examples of Late Latin MARCA "boundary-mark" and MARCARE "to mark", see Niermeyer & Van De Kieft (2002 II: 850–853) and Du Cange (1883–1887 V: 259–264).

The main corresponding verbs in Spanish, French, Italian, Portuguese, Catalan, Occitan, Sardinian, and Raeto-Romance come from the aforementioned Latin CURRERE. Thus we have Spanish *correr*, French *courir*, Italian *correre*, Portuguese *correr*, Catalan *córrer*, Occitan *córrer*, *corrir*, Campidanese *curri*, Logudorese *cùrrere*, and Raeto-Romance *currer*. Old Romanian also had *a cure*, but it is not part of the modern language.

The main verbs used to express the idea of running in Romanian are *a fugi* and *a alerga*. *A fugi* comes from Latin FUGERE "to run away", while the origin of *a alerga* is disputed. De Cihac (1978 II: 475) refers to two possible origins: Hungarian and Italian (*allegro*). Puşcariu (1975: 6) traces the verb in question to *ALLARGARE < Latin LARGUS "ample". Puşcariu (1973: 360–361) presents *a alerga* as a combination of *a* < AD and *larg* < LARGUS and explains in detail his position regarding the origin of the word, the development of its meaning, and its victory over *a cure* < Latin CURRERE, which he attributes to a homonymic clash and a taboo association which resulted from it:

> A alerga "courir", étymologiquement se compose de la préposition *a* (latin *ad*) et de *larg* "large". Son sens primitif a donc dû être analogue à celui de *alunga* "éloigner", fait de *a* et de *lung* "long". La fonction de ce verbe a d'abord été transitive; il a signifié: "obliger quelqu'un à s'éloigner, à prendre le large", puis "chasser, poursuivre quelqu'un": *Uliul se ţine după porumbel şi l-aleargă* "l'épervier vole après le pigeon, et le poursuit". Il devait à l'origine y avoir simplement une nuance entre *alerga* et *alunga*, l'un s'employant, comme dans l'example cité, lorsqu'il s'agissait d'une poursuite à travers un *large* espace, l'autre quand celle-ci avait lieu le *long* d'un chemin. Le sens originel comprenait donc seulement la notion d'"éloignement"; lorsque cet éloignement était forcé, il devenait une "chasse", une "poursuite". C'est le moment où *alerga* commence à se séparer de son ancien compagnon *merge*, qui marque un "éloignement dans les profondeurs"; il lui reste cependant, dans sa forme, une trace de cette société: l'*e* du radical, au lieu de *a*; en effet si on dit *alerg*, et non *alarg*, c'est sous l'influence de *merg*. Lorsque cette idée de "poursuite", d'abord accessoire, s'accentue, l'idée de "fuite" surgit aussi. Ainsi, *alerga* sort de la catégorie des verbes marquant "l'éloignement dans une direction quelconque", pour entrer dans celle des verbes exprimant "un mouvement rapide". La conséquence immédiate a été qu'il a changé de fonction et est devenu *intransitif*. C'est là le carrefour où il s'est separé de son compagnon *alunga* et s'est associé à un autre verbe: *cure*. Ce dernier, en raison du déplaisant équivoque qu'il provoquait (*cur* = "je cours" et "cul") a dû s'effacer devant lui.

> [Etymologically, *a alerga* "to run" is composed of the preposition *a* (Latin *ad*) and *larg* "ample". Its original meaning must have been analogous to that of *alunga* "to remove, to move away", which is made of *a* and *lung* "long". The function of this verb was at first transitive; it meant "to make someone move away, to make someone run away", later "to chase someone, to go after someone": *Uliul se ţine după*

porumbel şi l-aleargă "the hawk flies after the pigeon and chases it". There must have existed at the beginning just a slight difference between *alerga* and *alunga*. The former was used as in the example just mentioned when it referred to pursuit through wide space, and the latter was used when pursuit took place over a long path. The original sense, then, encompassed only the notion of removal; when this removal is forceful it becomes a chase, a pursuit. This is the moment when *alerga* starts separating from its old companion *merge*, which marks disappearance in the depth. But a formal trace of this association between *alerga* and *merge* still exists: *e* instead of *a* in the stem; we say *alerg* rather than *alarg* due to the influence of *merge*. When the idea of a chase which was originally an add-on was emphasized, the idea of a flight or running away also emerged. This way, *alerga* abandons the category of verbs that mark drawing away in any direction and enters the category of verbs that mark fast movement. The immediate consequence of this development is that *alerga* changed its function and became intransitive. At this juncture it separated from its companion *alunga* and became linked to another verb: *cure*. This latter form, due to the awkward confusion that it provoked (*cur* = "I run" and "buttocks") must have become obliterated.]

In contrast, Cioranescu (1966: 19) argues that the analogy with *a merge* could not have taken place because *a alerga* and *a merge* belong to different conjugation types, and proposes that the etymon of the verb in question might have been Latin LEGARE "to send, to depute, to dispatch". He reasonably assigns to *a alerga* the status of "origen dudoso" ["unknown origin"] (ibid.). Stefenelli (1992: 232–233) lists a Romanian reflex of CURRERE "to run", namely, *a curge*. However, Romanian *a curge* is primarily employed not to express running but rather flowing, especially of a liquid: e.g., *un rîu care curge lin* "a river that runs smoothly" (Leviţchi, ed. 1974: 621), the difference in form between *a cure* and *a curge* being a matter of morphological analogy.

3.3.3   Movement by springing off the ground

The main Latin verb which expressed jumping was SALIRE. It goes back to the Indo-European **sel-* "to jump" and in Classical Latin had the meanings "to leap, to spring, to jump". Through the addition of the suffix -TARE, SALIRE produced the so-called *intensivum* form SALTARE "to dance, to represent by dancing and gesticulation, to perform in pantomime".

Spanish, French, Italian, Portuguese, Catalan, Occitan, and Sardinian refer to jumping with the reflexes of the aforementioned Latin SALTARE "to dance": Spanish *saltar*, French *sauter*, Italian *saltare*, Portuguese *saltar*, Catalan *saltar*, Occitan *saltar*, *sautar*, *sauter*, Campidanese *sartiai*, Logudorese *sartiàre*. Campidanese also employs *jumpai* < **JUMPARE* "to jump" (Meyer-Lübke 1992: 377). Old Spanish and even 16th-century Spanish had a reflex of SALTARE with "a more populist pronunciation" (i.e., *sotar* "to dance") which retained the Latin meaning (Malkiel 1988/1989: 13); cf. Old Spanish *sotador* "dancer", Modern Spanish *jota* (Old Spanish *xota*) "*jota*, name of a folk dance" (García de Diego 1989: 948; Dworkin 2012: 124). Raeto-Romance also preserves the Latin meaning of SALTARE by means of *sautar* "to dance" (Meyer-Lübke 1992: 624; Bernardi et al. 1994 II: 690), and to express the notion of jumping it relies on *siglir* which goes back to Latin SALIRE "to jump". Romanian combines the two main Romance options: *a sări* < SALIRE "to jump" and *a sălta* < SALTARE "to dance".

3.4 Biographical overview

Taken together, the data presented in this chapter reveal that both formal continuity and formal change are at work across the semantic field of motion. Neither verbs of generic motion, nor direction-specific verbs, nor manner-specific verbs retained their inventory unaltered. In fact, the lexicalization of every single concept considered above combines stability with innovation. The data also suggest that while the majority of Latin directional verbs are in fact satellite-framed and the majority of Romance directional verbs are in fact verb-framed, as stipulated by Talmy's typology, a number of lexical items, such as Latin VENIRE "to come", Latin SCANDERE "to ascend, to make one's way uphill or to the top", French *s'en aller* "to go away", and Italian *discendere* "to go down", to name just a few, do not correspond to the predominant type. The chapters that follow will demonstrate that the transition from satellite-framed to verb-framed is only one of the multiple layers of lexical change attested on the way from Latin to Romance. We will also see that in contrast with and in spite of the profound transformation in the inventory of motion verbs on the onomasiological level, the range of semantic functions of these verbs on the semasiological level shows remarkable stability.

CHAPTER 4

Patterns of onomasiological continuity and change from Latin to Romance

The verb biographies discussed in Chapter 3 reveal a series of patterns of lexical continuity and lexical loss, on the one hand, and a series of patterns of innovative lexical creation, on the other hand.[1]

4.1 Lexical continuity and lexical loss from Latin to Romance

When it comes to assessing continuity between the Latin vocabulary and the Romance vocabulary, it is practical to distinguish between several types of development. Arnulf Stefenelli (1992: 12–14; 2010) postulates the following five types:

1. Pan-Romance (German 'panromanisch') continuity, which implies that the Latin lexeme survives in all the Romance languages, as in the case of Latin CAELUM "sky" > Romanian *cer*, Italian *cielo*, Sardinian *kélu*, Raeto-Romance *tschêl*, French *ciel*, Occitan *cel*, Catalan *cel*, Spanish *cielo*, Portuguese *céu* "sky".
2. Inter-Romance (German 'interromanisch') continuity, which implies that the Latin lexeme survives in the majority of the Romance languages, as in the case of Latin AMARE "to love", which lives on as Italian *amare*, Sardinian *amare*, Raeto-Romance *amar*, French *aimer*, Occitan *a(i)mar*, Catalan *amar*, Spanish *amar*, Portuguese *amar* "to love", but is lost in Romanian which uses a Slavic loan-word *a iubi* instead.
3. Regional Romance (German 'teilromanisch') continuity, which implies that the Latin lexeme survives in the minority (at least one) of the Romance languages, as in the case of Latin SCIRE "to know", which is retained as Romanian *a şti* and Sardinian *iskíre*, and in the case of Latin METUS "fear", preserved as Spanish *miedo* and Portuguese *medo*.
4. Sporadic continuity marked by Stefenelli as (ø), which implies that the Latin word survives only in a single isolated variety, as in the case of MUNUS "present, gift", which lives on only in Franco-Provençal.

---

1. Some of the results discussed in this chapter are presented in a preliminary form in Stolova (2003, 2008, 2010a).

5.   Zero continuity marked by Stefenelli as ø, which implies that the Latin word has no Romance reflexes, as in the case of DILIGERE "to appreciate".

Stefenelli (1992: 14; 2010) also points out that the meaning of the Romance reflexes does not always match that of the Latin etymon. For example, the Latin adjective FORTIS signified both "strong" as well as "brave", while its Romance reflexes (e.g., Spanish *fuerte*, French *fort*, Italian *forte*) mean only "strong". In contrast, while the Latin noun TEMPUS only signified "time", its Romance reflexes (e.g., Spanish *tiempo*, French *temps*, Italian *tempo*) mean both "time" and "weather". Another type of semantic contrast is illustrated by the development of Latin CAUSA "cause" > e.g., Spanish *cosa*, French *chose* "thing", in which the Latin lexeme has survived but its meaning has shifted. Since the present study deals with motion verbs, the reflexes that do not lexicalize movement (e.g., Spanish *avenir* "to occur" < Latin ADVENIRE "to come", French *devenir* "to become" < Latin DEVENIRE "to come", or French *saillir* "to bubble, to sprout, to cover [of animals]" < Latin SALIRE "to jump") are not counted as cases of continuity.

The biographies of Latin and Romance motion verbs presented in Chapter 3 reveal several groups of Latin verbs that exhibit continuity. The first group is comprised of the members of the deictic pair IRE "to go" – VENIRE, PERVENIRE "to come". IRE survives on the Inter-Romance level, VENIRE is preserved on the Pan-Romance level, and PERVENIRE is retained on the Regional Romance level:

> Latin IRE "to go" > Spanish *ir*, French (part of the paradigm of *aller* < AMBU-LARE) *j'irai* (Future), *j'irais* (Conditional), Old Italian (and some Modern Italian dialects) *gire*, Portuguese *ir*, Occitan (some Old and some Modern dialects) *ir*, Raeto-Romance *ir* "to go"; Spanish *irse*, Portuguese *ir-se*, Raeto-Romance *s'inir* "to go away"

> Latin VENIRE "to come" > Spanish *venir*, French *venir*, Italian *venire*, Portuguese *vir*, Romanian *a veni*, Catalan *venir*, Occitan *venir*, Sardinian (Campidanese) *benni*, Sardinian (Logudorese) *bènnere*, Raeto-Romance *vegnir*, *gnir* "to come"

> Latin PERVENIRE "to come" > French *parvenir*, Catalan *parvenir*, Italian *parvenire*, Occitan *parvenir* "to come (with effort/difficulty)"

It should be remembered that even though VENIRE is retained on the Pan-Romance level, the deictic value of the Latin etymon and that of the Spanish and European Portuguese reflexes is not the same, as we have seen in Chapter 3.

The second group that exhibits continuity is comprised of the manner-of-motion verbs such as Latin AMBULARE "to walk" and CURRERE "to run", both retained on the Pan-Romance level, as well as SALIRE "to jump" and CEDERE "to go, i.e., to be in motion, move, walk, go along" that survive on the Regional Romance level:

> Latin AMBULARE "to walk" > French *aller*, Italian *andare*, Catalan *anar*, Occitan *anar*, Sardinian (Campidanese) *andai*, Sardinian (Logudorese) *andare*, Raeto-Romance (Friulian) *lâ* "to go"; French *s'en aller*, Italian *andarsene*, Catalan *anar-se'n*, Occitan *s'enanar* "to go away"; Spanish *andar*, Portuguese *andar*, Romanian *a umbla* "to walk"

> Latin CURRERE "to run" > Spanish *correr*, French *courir*, Italian *correre*, Portuguese *correr*, Old Romanian *a cure*, Catalan *córrer*, Occitan *córrer, corrir*, Sardinian (Campidanese) *curri*, Sardinian (Logudorese) *cùrrere*, Raeto-Romance *currer* "to run"

> Latin SALIRE "to jump" > Romanian *a sări*, Raeto-Romance *siglir* "to jump"; Italian *salire* "to go up"; Spanish *salir*, Portuguese *sair*, Occitan *sal(h)ir* "to go out"

> Latin CEDERE "to go, i.e., to be in motion, move, walk, go along" > Raeto-Romance *ceder* "to go out"

As mentioned in Chapter 3, Raeto-Romance *ceder* "to go out" is a Latinism and Sardinian (Logudorese) *andare* "to go" is an Italianism.

The third group that exhibits continuity is comprised of such verbs of directed movement as Latin INTRARE "to go in" retained on the Pan-Romance level, EXIRE "to go out" preserved on the Pan-Romance level, ASCENDERE "to go up" maintained on the Inter-Romance level, DESCENDERE "to go down" kept on the Inter-Romance level, as well as SUBIRE "to move underneath, to draw near, to move upward" retained on the Regional Romance level:

> Latin INTRARE "to go in" > Spanish *entrar*, French *entrer*, Italian *entrare*, Portuguese *entrar*, Romanian *a intra*, Catalan *entrar*, Old Catalan *intrar, entrar-se'n*, Occitan *(d)intrar*, Sardinian (Campidanese) *(b)intrai*, Sardinian (Logudorese) *(b)intràre*, Raeto-Romance *entrar* "to enter"

> Latin EXIRE "to go out" > Old Spanish *exir*, Old French *eissir, (s'en) issir*, Italian *uscire*, Old Portuguese *e(i)xir*, Romanian *a ieşi*, Catalan *eixir*, Valencian *eixir*, Occitan *eissir*, Sardinian (Campidanese) *bessiri*, Sardinian (Logudorese) *bessire*, Sardinian (Northern Logudorese) *disessire, dessessire*, Raeto-Romance (Friulian) *iší* "to go out"

> Latin ASCENDERE "to go up" > Spanish *ascender*, Old French *ascendre*, Italian *ascendere*, Portuguese *ascender*, Catalan *ascendir*, Old Occitan *ascendre*, Sardinian (Logudorese) *ašèndere*, Raeto-Romance *ascender* "to go up"

> Latin DESCENDERE "to go down" > Spanish *descender*, French *descendre*, Italian *discendere, scendere*, Portuguese *descender*, Catalan *descendir*, Old Catalan *dexendre*, Occitan *descendre*, Raeto-Romance *descender* "to go down"

> Latin SUBIRE "to move upward" > Spanish *subir*, Portuguese *subir*, Romanian *a sui* "to go up"

As mentioned in Chapter 3, Spanish *ascender* "to go up" is not attested in Old Spanish and therefore is likely to be a Latinism.

The fourth group that exhibits continuity is comprised of the Latin verb VADERE "to go" which, in spite of its disappearance as an infinitive, is retained through suppletion as part of the present indicative and the present subjunctive paradigms of the Romance reflexes of Latin IRE "to go" and of the Romance reflexes of Latin AMBULARE "to walk":

> Old Spanish *ir* "to go" – Pres. Ind. *vo(y), vas, va, imos, ides, van*
> Modern Spanish *ir* "to go" – Pres. Ind. *voy, vas, va, vamos, vais, van*
> Portuguese *ir* "to go" – Pres. Ind. *vou, vais, vai, vamos, ides, vão*
> Old Tuscan *gire* "to go" – Pres. Ind. *vado, vai, va, gimo, gite, vanno*
>
> Old French *aler* "to go" – Pres. Ind. *vois, vas, va(t) (vet, vait), alon, alez, vont*
> French *aller* "to go" – Pres. Ind. *vais, vas, va, allons, allez, vont*
> Italian *andare* "to go" – Pres. Ind. *vado, vai, va, andiamo, andate, vanno*
> Catalan *anar* "to go" – Pres. Ind. *vaig, vas, va, anem, aneu, van*

The rest of the Latin verbs considered in Chapter 3 did not survive on their way from Latin to Romance. These obsolete lexemes are ADVENIRE "to come", DEVENIRE "to come", ABIRE "to go away", ABSCEDERE "to go away", INIRE "to go in", INTROIRE "to go in", INGREDI "to go in", EGREDI "to go out", EVENIRE "to go out", CONSCENDERE "to go up", ESCENDERE "to go up", SCANDERE "to go up", DEGREDI "to go down", and GRADI "to walk". The disappearance of INGREDI, EGREDI, and GRADI can be viewed as part of a larger pattern of lexical loss, that of the deponent verbs that vanished as a class. The rest of the disappeared motion verbs, except for SCANDERE, are all compounds.[2]

The developments outlined above reveal that the relatively high degree of continuity of Latin simple verbs contrasts with the relatively high degree of loss of Latin compound forms. All the simple lexemes except SCANDERE "to go up" and the deponent GRADI "to walk" (i.e., IRE, VENIRE, CURRERE, SALIRE, CEDERE, and VADERE) show some degree of continuity. In contrast, of the nineteen compounds which include three deponent verbs (i.e., ADVENIRE, PERVENIRE, DEVENIRE, ABIRE, ABSCENDERE, INIRE, INTROIRE, INGREDI, INTRARE, EXIRE, EGREDI, EVENIRE, ASCENDERE, CONSCENDERE, ESCENDERE, DESCENDERE, DEGREDI, SUBIRE, and

---

2. It has been argued that INGREDI "to go in" survived as Spanish *engreírse* "to become conceited, vain" (Dworkin 1977), but the meaning of this Spanish verb is not that of movement. The learned reflexes of Latin SCANDERE "to go up, to scan (of a verse)", such as Spanish *escandir* "to scan a verse", do not belong to the field of motion verbs either. Neither are cases such as Spanish *ingresar* "to join" < *ingreso* "joining, entrance", which goes back to Latin INGRESSUS "arrival, entrance", counted as cases of continuity.

AMBULARE) only seven lexemes are retained. Furthermore, these seven compounds that did survive (i.e., PERVENIRE, INTRARE, EXIRE, ASCENDERE, DESCENDERE, SUBIRE, and AMBULARE) do so in a rather peculiar way. Latin PERVENIRE "to come" is retained only on the Regional Romance level as a Latinism whose connotation of effort/difficulty excludes it from the list of core motion verbs. Latin INTRARE "to go in" and AMBULARE "to walk" are retained on the Pan-Romance level, but as we have seen in Chapter 3, in Classical Latin they were already perceived as simple forms. Latin EXIRE "to go out" is also preserved on the Pan-Romance level, but as discussed in Chapter 3, in Late Latin it was also likely to be interpreted as a simple form. In the case of ASCENDERE "to go up" and DESCENDERE "to go down" the value of the prefix seems to be attenuated as well, since the form without the prefix exists only in Italian (*scendere*) and has the same meaning as the prefixed *discendere*. The prefix of SUBIRE "to move underneath, to draw near, to move upward" also lacked transparency, given the polysemous and changing nature of SUB- discussed in Chapter 3. In other words, the Latin verbs that exhibit continuity are either simple (i.e., monomorphemic) forms or lexemes whose compound (i.e., polymorphemic) nature has been reduced as their prefix became nontransparent through fusion with the stem and/or semantic bleaching.[3]

I believe that the motivation behind the patterns of lexical continuity and loss that I have identified can be understood in terms of the cognitive centrality of direction and path within the domain of human motion.

A number of linguistic studies (e.g., Nagucka 1980, Svorou 1994, Koch 2001b) have argued that motion and direction and path are closely related on the conceptual level and that direction and path are among the most conceptually salient features of the motion event schema. For instance, Svorou (1994: 25) writes: "Directionality is inherent in movement. [...] Conceptually, motion and direction are very closely related, being dependent on the way we understand them, which

---

3.   Verbs of motion are not the only Latin verbs whose prefixes could become opaque by fusing with the stem. Consider, for instance, the compounds of FERRE "to carry" listed in Vicario (1997: 202): AF-FERRE (< AD + FERRE) "to bring into contact, to convey", AU-FERRE (< AB + FERRE) "to fetch away, to separate", CON-FERRE (< CUM + FERRE) "to gather", DIF-FERRE (< DIS + FERRE) "to scatter, to disperse, to differ", EF-FERRE (< EX + FERRE) "to bring out or away, to utter". Such verbs as CLAMARE "to call, to cry out, to shout aloud" and RIDERE "to laugh" offer similar examples: CON-CLAMARE (< CUM + CLAMARE) "to cry or call out together", DE-CLAMARE (< DE + CLAMARE) "to exercise one's self in rhetorical delivery", RE-CLAMARE (< RE + CLAMARE) "to cry out against", DE-RIDERE (< DE + RIDERE) "to scoff at", IR-RIDERE (< IN + RIDERE) "to laugh at", SUB-RIDERE (SUR-RIDERE) (< SUB + RIDERE) "to smile" (ibid.). In fact, the 'preverb + verb > (relexified) lexical unit' pattern is pervasive in the evolution of Latin, as demonstrated in Baldi (1979), Lehmann (1983), Haim Rosén (1992), Rousseau ed. (1995), Hannah Rosén (1999), and Vincent (1999), among others. This is significant because it illustrates that the development of motion verbs is fully entrenched within the development of the lexicon at large.

is via our perception of asymmetries created by the change of location and orientation of entities". Along the same lines, Koch (2001b: 1171) observes that "on the cognitive level PATH is indispensable for a MOTION event-frame (except for a few very general verbs like E[nglish] *to go*)".

The importance of path in human cognitive organization of spatial networks is evident from an analysis of elicited narratives. Linde & Labov (1975) studied the responses given by speakers of American English to the question "Could you tell me the lay-out of your apartment?". Only 3% of the respondents provided a verbal map of the kind reproduced below:

> If you were looking down at this apartment from a height, it would be like – like I said before, a huge square with two lines drawn through the center to make like four smaller squares. Now, on the ends – uh – in two boxes facing out in the street you have the living room and a bedroom. In between these two boxes you have a bathroom. (p. 929)

The rest of the respondents (97%) provided a verbal tour such as the following one:

> As you open the door, you are in a small five-by-five room which is a small closet. When you get past there, you're in what we call the foyer [...]. If you keep walking in that same direction, you're confronted by two rooms in front of you ... large living room which is about twelve by twenty on the left side. [...] Now, if you turn right before you went into the dinette or the living room, you, you would see a bedroom which is the small bedroom going into – going in on the right ... And if you kept walking straight ahead, directly ahead of you, you would find a bathroom. (pp. 929–930)

Linde and Labov summarize and evaluate their results in terms of the type of information that the subjects provided and in terms of the role of path in it:

> If the aim of the lay-outs were to instruct us how to make drawings of the outer shape of the apartment and the configuration of its rooms, then we would have to say that almost every speaker has failed. But as we examine the actual structure of the discourse which the speakers use in the tours, we find that each speaker has succeeded in showing us something else: how to enter each of his rooms. More precisely, a tour is a speech act WHICH PROVIDES A MINIMAL SET OF PATHS BY WHICH EACH ROOM COULD BE ENTERED. The path is presented as a series of units of the form DIRECTION (or VECTOR) and ROOM. There are two basic kinds of vectors: the static type (*to the right, straight ahead of you, off of the X*) and the mobile type (*you keep walking straight ahead, now if you turn right*). [...] The task of the speaker, then, is to traverse for this imaginary visitor the spatial network formed by these vectors and rooms. (p. 930; original emphasis)

Attention to path is observed not only in adults but also in other age groups. It is evident early in life, as pointed out by Mandler:

> Infants pay much more attention to some kinds of information than others. Although learning will change what is attended, examples of innately salient information are paths of object motion that change spatial relations, such as into or out of containers, objects going into or out of sight, and contingencies between paths, such as one object chasing another. (Mandler 2012: 426)

Mandler (2004, 2008, 2010, 2012) has shown that during the first year of life pre-verbal infants form approximately twenty-five spatial primitives, including PATH, START PATH, END OF PATH, UP, DOWN, and BEHIND.

Several recent experimental similarity judgment task studies on non-linguistic categorization also point towards identifying path as conceptually salient. For example, in the experiment reported in Pourcel (2004), the subjects (English and French native speakers) were presented with fifteen silent video-clip triads (e.g., a man running up the hill, a man running down the hill, a man walking up the hill) and were asked to perform the similarity judgment task. Pourcel (2004: 508) reports that "in 55.5% of choices in the English sample, and in 53.5% in the French sample" the clips sharing path type were identified as similar, which suggests that "Path may be slightly more cognitively salient than Manner in human motion conceptualization". In a similar way, in the experiment reported in Cardini (2010), English and Italian native speakers presented with twenty-six video-clip triads also showed path bias: same-path clips were selected in 55.1% of the judgments carried out by English subjects and in 54.7% of the judgments carried out by Italian subjects.[4]

Experimental research on attention carried out by using the eye-tracking paradigm also points toward the cognitive salience of path. In one of the non-linguistic experiments reported in Papafragou et al. (2008), native speakers of Greek and English watched animated clips that depicted animate agents (humans or animals) performing instrumental motion such as skating, sailing, and skiing. The researchers recorded participants' eye movements and analyzed them in terms of the regions at which they were directed. For example, in the stimulus

---

4. "The percentage of same-manner variants chosen by the English participants as most similar to the targets was nearly identical to that displayed by the Italian participants (44.9% for the former; 45.3% for the latter)" (Cardini 2010: 1455). It should be clarified, however, that some but not all experimental similarity judgment task studies report path bias. A comparison of different studies (e.g., Finkbeiner et al. 2002, Gennari et al. 2002, Papafragou et al. 2002, Pourcel 2004, 2009, Blomberg & Zlatev 2009, Cardini 2010, Zlatev et al. 2010) indicates that the results of the experiments vary depending on a series of variables. Such variables can be related to the stimuli (e.g., human vs. artificial moving object; intentional vs. forced motion; telic vs. atelic motion) as well as to the way in which the stimuli are presented (e.g., as a static picture vs. as a dynamic video-clip; simultaneously vs. sequentially, possibly prompting the subjects to encode what they saw linguistically). Path is conceptually salient in human (animate) motion, as opposed to artificial object motion (Pourcel 2004: 510; 2009: 378).

that consisted of a person skating towards a snowman, participants' eye movements could be directed at the skater's feet/skates (i.e., the instrument region), at the rest of the skater's body (i.e., the agent), at the snowmen (i.e., the path-endpoint region), or at the empty area between the skater and the snowmen (i.e., the trajectory). While the meaning of looks directed at the empty area and at the rest of the skater's body might be ambiguous, the meaning of looks directed at the skates and at the snowmen is more straightforward. When the subjects look at the skates, they are interested in the manner of motion, and when they look at the snowman, which is the goal reference point, they are interested in the path of motion (Papafragou et al. 2008: 166). The researchers report: "Pilot work revealed that one common eye movement around the start of animation was to 'project the path' of motion to the goal (where the moving character was heading)" (pp. 165–166). During the experiment itself, "both language groups exhibited an overall preference for path-endpoints over instrument regions" (p. 169). In other words, regardless of their native language, the participants were likely to allocate attention to the path of motion.

Category-discrimination task experiments offer additional evidence. Monolingual English speakers and bilingual Spanish/English speakers tested in an English-speaking context and monolingual Spanish speakers and bilingual Spanish/English speakers tested in a Spanish-speaking context in the experiments reported in Kersten et al. (2010) viewed animated motion events that involved bug-like creatures and were asked to sort these events on the basis of manner of motion and on the basis of path of motion. The performance on the manner-discrimination task was influenced by the language of the subjects and by the language of the setting. The path-discrimination task, in contrast, was performed equally well regardless of the language of the subjects and regardless of the language of the setting. The researchers attribute this result to "the primacy of path as an organizer of motion event conceptualizations" (p. 650).

Experimental studies on memory provide further evidence. The moving dots experiment reported in Blake et al. (1997) has demonstrated that "memory for the direction and the degree of coherence of motion is almost as accurate as the ability to discriminate differences in direction and coherence" (p. 368). Price & Gilden (2000) have also shown that humans have highly veridical memory for the direction of motion that involves displacement. The researchers believe that their results support the idea advanced in Glenberg (1997) that "memory evolved in the service of perception and action" (Price & Gilden 2000: 28):

> From a practical point of view, it is a good thing that people can remember the direction of motion when the motion signifies that the object will occupy a new location. New locations require adaptive behavior; it would be disruptive if people could not remember where things went. (ibid.)

This observation is substantiated by ethnographic research on the Ongee hunters and gatherers of the island of Little Andaman (Bay of Bengal) reported in Pandya (1990, 1993). The Ongee tribe lives in an environment where the topographical features are not permanent. For example, a creek or a forest may exist for only part of the year or may have a very different shape depending on the season; the coastline may be in constant flux because of tides and storms. For this reason, when the Ongee create a map they start by drawing lines that correspond to paths that should be taken in order to reach a desired location, and only after that they add landmarks (Pandya 1990: 784). At the beginning of his fieldwork, Pandya could not understand the discrepancy between the official map and the map he created himself, on the one hand, and what looked like constantly changing routes by which the locals took him to specific locations on the island, on the other hand. He received the following explanation from his informant:

> Why do you hope to see the same space while moving? One only hopes to reach the place at the end. [...] Your map tells lies. Places change. Does you map say this? Does your map say when the stream is dry and gone or when it comes and overflows? We remember how to go and come back, not the places which are on the way of going and coming. (ibid., pp. 792–793)

The ethnographer goes on to say that the physical map that an Ongee draws "is not of places in space but of movements in space" and suggests that the mental map that an Ongee develops does not consist of images of places but rather of images of patterns of movement (ibid., p. 793).

In sum, the analysis of the elicited narratives, the experimental studies on non-linguistic categorization and non-linguistic attention, the developmental studies on preverbal infants, the research on memory, and the ethnographic research suggest that path plays a key role in human spatial cognition. Humans attend to path and direction subsumed under path in everyday life and in experimental settings.

Thus, Latin monomorphemic generic and manner-of-motion verbs that did not express path (IRE "to go", CURRERE "to run", SALIRE "to jump", CEDERE "to go, i.e. to be in motion, move, walk, go along", VADERE "to go") were affected the least on the way from Latin to Romance: their ability to lexicalize path was never jeopardized as they never had possessed such ability to begin with. The retention rate of AMBULARE "to walk" which was reinterpreted as a simple manner-of-motion non-directional verb is high as well. The monomorphemic form that did express path, such as VENIRE "to come", was also affected very little: due to its monomorphemic nature it contained the information regarding the path within the stem, that is to say, within the salient core of the word that serves as the basis for lexical access.[5] Of the polymorphemic verbs that expressed path through their prefix the only ones that managed to survive as core motion verbs across the Romance family were those reinterpreted in either Classical Latin or Late Latin as monomorphemic through the prefix's fusion with the stem and/or semantic bleaching: INTRARE "to go in", EXIRE "to go out", SUBIRE "to move underneath, to draw near, to move upward", ASCENDERE "to go up", DESCENDERE "to go down".[6] Such reanalysis allowed these verbs not only to retain the information about the path but also to put such information in the foreground by incorporating it into the verbal stem. The compound Latin verbs that failed to be reanalyzed in such a way disappeared: ADVENIRE "to come", DEVENIRE "to come", ABIRE "to go away", ABSCEDERE "to go away", INIRE "to go in", INTROIRE "to go in", EVENIRE "to go out", CONSCENDERE "to go up", ESCENDERE "to go up".

My postulation of the connection between cognitive centrality of path and patterns of lexical continuity and loss of motion verbs from Latin to Romance, originally formulated in Stolova (2008: 260–261), is in line with the findings from other language families.

Over the course of history, English verbs of motion shifted from a predominantly 'prefix + verb' model (e.g., Old English *utgan*, *in(n)gan*) to a predominantly 'verb + preposition' model (e.g., Modern English *go out*, *go in*) (Ogura 2002: vii). However, as Imbert (2008b) stresses, this does not mean that prefixation in English has lost its productivity in other lexical fields (cf. *undertake*, *overdo*). It is particularly the space-related path-coding function that was transferred to the prepositions. Imbert (ibid.) interprets this fact in functional terms, claiming that Old English motion verbs were the ones affected because the path-coding capacity of the prefixes that tended to fuse with the stem was lower than

---

5.   Over the years, a number of experimental studies have offered psycholinguistic evidence that points towards the key role of stems in providing lexical access. For instance, in their work with English adverbs of the type 'adjective + *ly*' (e.g., *brightly*), Rosenberg et al. (1966) discovered that "the ease of recall of derived low-frequency adverbs is influenced by the frequency of their adjective roots" (p. 75). The experiments on memory representation of English verbs with inflectional suffixes (*-s*, *-ed*, *-ing*), irregular past tense verbs, and adjective and nominal derivatives of verbs carried out by Stanners et al. (1979) suggest "that accessing the variation results in activation of the representation for the base verb and that this activation is a necessary step in the processing of the variation" (p. 399). In a more recent study, Taft & Ardasinski (2006) have examined "the impact of stem frequency on lexical decision responses to prefixed words" and have found "that a whole-word representation exists for prefixed words, but that activation of this representation is always mediated by a representation of the stem" (p. 183).

6.   Latin PERVENIRE "to come" is not listed here because, as mentioned earlier, the semantic connotation of its reflexes (that are Latinisms) excludes these reflexes from the inventory of core motion verbs.

that of the prepositions.[7] In essence, I would suggest, the members of the Romance family and English (a Germanic language) appear to have done the same thing: as their prefixed motion verbs were losing the ability to convey the information about the path, these languages abandoned these verbs in favor of new strategies to encode such information more clearly.[8]

Another piece of evidence that supports my hypothesis comes from the languages of Native North America. As discussed in Mithun (1999), many of these linguistic varieties are polysynthetic, i.e., their words have a high number of meaningful parts or morphemes. For example, Yup'ik (an Eskimoan language within the Eskimo-Aleut family spoken in Alaska) can use the polysynthetic word *kaipiallrulliniuk* which translates as "the two of them were apparently really hungry". This word consists of six morphemes *kaig-piar-llru-llini-u-k* and is glossed as "be.hungry-really-PAST-apparently-INDICATIVE-they.two" (p. 38). However, individual parts can blend together, making the contribution of each morpheme less distinct (pp. 38, 52). Thus, if speakers need to emphasize certain information of special importance, they use the analytic alternatives. For instance, if speakers want to draw attention to the intensity of the hunger, instead of using the suffix *-piar* "really" (the second morpheme in the string of the six morphemes above), they can use a separate word *cakneq* "very (much)", producing the sentence *cakneq kaillrulliniuk* (glossed as "very they.were.apparently. hungry") (pp. 38–39). Mithun proposes the following connection – if the information is critical to the speakers, if it is worthy of special attention, it is likely to be rendered as a full word:

> Does it matter whether information is expressed in a single word or a series of words? Polysynthetic languages like Yup'ik show that it can. [...] Separate words can be given special auditory prominence with intonation, high pitch, volume, and length, an option not available for suffixes. (p. 39)

As Mithun (p. 144) illustrates, motion path is the type of information that is often highlighted by full words. For example, Karuk (a Hokan language within the Amerindian family spoken in northern California) has a full word *'ú·θ* "toward

---

7.   On the attrition of the phonological structure of Old English prefixes, see Lutz (1997).

8.   As mentioned in Section 1.4, cognitive linguistics is usage-based. It understands language change as driven by speaker–listener interactions: "languages don't change; instead, people change language through their actions. In other words, language is changed by the way people use language" (Evans & Green 2006: 123, based on Croft 2000). Therefore, when I say that the language or the verb did something I use this wording as a shorthand for "the speakers used the language or the verb in a certain way and this usage had certain historical outcomes". I include this clarification in order not to perpetuate the misconception challenged in Milroy (2003, 2006) that language changes through its own agency not through the agency of its users.

center of water" that can be used in addition to the routinely employed directional suffixes. For instance, *pí·v-kara* "step over (a creek)" (glossed as "step-horizontally. away.from.the.center.of.a.body.of.water") contains just the directional suffix *-kara* "horizontally away from the center of a body of water". In contrast, in the sentence *Vássihkam 'ú·θ 'úkyi·m-kar* "He fell backwards into the river" (glossed as "back-wards toward.center.of.water he.fell-horizontally.away.from.center.of.water") a special point about the path of motion is made by using both the directional suffix *-kara* and the full word *'ú·θ* (p. 144). In a similar way, in the word *ikre·myá·h-rupu* "north wind to blow" (glossed as "blow-hence.downriverward"), only the directional suffix *-rupu* "hence downriverward" is employed, while in the sentence *Kári xás yúruk 'uθívru·h-rup* "And he floated downriver" (glossed as "then and far.down-river he.floated-hence.downriverward") a special point about the path of motion is made through the use of both the directional suffix *-rupu* and the separate word *yúruk* "far downriver" (p. 144).[9] What the case of the polysynthetic languages of Native North America illustrates is that when it comes to such important information as the path, speakers can strategize to effectively foreground it, to bring it into focus, and to express it as transparently as possible with a separate word. I believe that the loss of the compound Latin motion verbs and the survival of the simple verbs and of the verbs reanalyzed as simple ones may be interpreted as the historical outcome of such communicative strategies of expressing path more transparently.

As we will see in Chapter 8, the patterns of lexical continuity and lexical loss from Latin to Romance established in this section have ramifications for cognitive linguistics, more specifically for the cognitive typology of motion encoding.

4.2 Romance innovative lexical creation

While, as we have just seen in Section 4.1, many Latin motion verbs eventually became obsolete, a number of new lexical items emerged in their place. The principles

---

9.   This brings to mind the fluctuation in Latin between the bare-case forms and prepositional phrases. As discussed in Adams (2011), Plautus tends to use plain accusative and ablative directional expressions with place names familiar to his audience, such as ATHENAE, ATHENARUM "Athens", SYRACUSAE, SYRACUSARUM "Syracuse", and CARTHAGO, CARTHAGINIS "Carthage", yet he tends to use prepositional phrases of the type 'preposition + inflected place name' with place names that are less familiar, such as ELATEA (ELATIA), ELATIAE "Elatia" and CALYDON, CALYDO-NIS "Calydon". Thus, we find bare-case forms ATHENAS "to Athens", SYRACUSAS "to Syracuse", and CARTHAGINEM "to Carthage", as opposed to prepositional phrases IN ELATIAM "to Elatia" and IN CALYDONEM "to Calydon" (p. 264). The same tendency is attested in the Late Latin text *Peregrinatio Aetheriae* (late 4th century – early 5th century A.D.) which by virtue of its subject matter contains a number of exotic place names (ibid.).

of cognitive onomasiology and the three-dimensional grid described in Section 2.1 allow us to establish a series of recurring motivational patterns that account for the novel Romance developments. In the systematics that follows, each developmental step may be accounted for up to three times: once for the cognitive, once for the formal, and once for the stratificational dimension. For example, Raeto-Romance *c(h)aminar* "to walk" which goes back to Italian *camminare* "to walk" is listed as a case of conceptual identity (cognitive dimension), as a case of formal identity (formal dimension), and as a case of borrowing within the Romance family (stratificational dimension). When more than one step in the historical evolution is mentioned, the step relevant to the respective classification is marked with the sign "<<". For example, the just mentioned Italian *camminare* goes back to Late Latin CAMMINUS "way" of Celtic origin. When this development is listed as a case of contiguity (cognitive dimension) and as a case of word-class alternation (formal dimension), it appears as Italian *camminare* << Late Latin CAMMINUS < Celtic. When the same development is listed as a case of borrowing from Celtic (stratificational dimension), it appears as Italian *camminare* < Late Latin CAMMINUS << Celtic. While the majority of developments presented in the systematics that follows are absolute innovations, some developments are more accurately described as innovations with elements of continuity. For example, French *s'en aller* "to go away" < Latin SE + INDE + AMBULARE is innovative in two ways: it employs the new strategy of relying on the reflexive particle SE and on the adverb INDE "thence" detailed later in this Section, and it abandons the manner specification of AMBULARE "to walk". At the same time, this development exhibits an element of continuity because it contributes to the survival of AMBULARE, as seen in Section 4.1 (above).

Within the cognitive dimension, the Romance languages rely on the following relations:

Conceptual identity:

Romanian *a sosi* "to come" < subjunctive of the aorist of Modern Greek σώνω "I catch up, I reach, I arrive"

Sardinian (Logudorese) *andare* "to go" << Italian *andare* "to go" < Latin AMBULARE "to walk"

Old Spanish *deçir*, Old Portuguese *deçer*, Portuguese *descer* "to go down" < Latin DE-/DIS-CEDERE "to depart, to withdraw, to go apart" & DESCENDERE "to go down"

Sardinian (Campidanese) *calai*, Sardinian (Logudorese) *calare* "to go down" < Late Latin CALARE "to lower, to let down" << Classical Greek χαλάω "I lower, I let down"

Sardinian (Campidanese) *jumpai* "to jump" < Late Latin *JUMPARE "to jump"

Raeto-Romance *c(h)aminar* "to walk" << Italian *camminare* "to walk" < Late Latin CAMMINUS "way" < Celtic

Spanish *subir*, Portuguese *subir*, Romanian *a sui* "to go up" < Latin SUBIRE "to move upward"

Sardinian (Campidanese) *(a)pujai* "to go up" < Catalan *pujar* "to go up"

Contiguity:

Spanish *llegar*, Portuguese *chegar* "to come" < Late Latin PLICARE "to come, to arrive" << Classical Latin PLICARE (VELAM) "to fold (the sail)"

Romanian *a pleca* "to go away" < Late Latin PLICARE "to leave" << Classical Latin PLICARE (TENTORIA) "to fold (the tents)"

Italian *salire* "to go up" < Latin SALIRE "to jump"

Spanish *salir*, Portuguese *sair*, Occitan *sal(h)ir* "to go out" < Latin SALIRE "to jump"

French *monter*, Italian *montare*, Catalan *muntar*, Occitan *montar*, Raeto-Romance *muntar* "to go up" < Late Latin *MONTARE "to go up" << Classical Latin MONS, MONTIS "mountain"

Old French *puier*, Catalan *pujar*, Occitan *pujar* (*pojar*) "to go up" < Late Latin *PODIARE "to go up" << Classical Latin PODIUM "elevated place"

Sardinian (Campidanese) *lompi* (*krompi*), Sardinian (Logudorese) *lòmpere* (*cròmpere*) "to come" < Latin COMPLERE "to fill up, to fill out, to complete"

Spanish *partir*, Old Spanish *partirse*, French *partir*, Old French *se partir*, Italian *partire*, Old Italian *partirsi*, Portuguese *partir(-se)*, Romanian *a se depărta*, *a se îndepărta*, Sardinian (Campidanese) *partiri*, Sardinian (Logudorese) *partìre*, Raeto-Romance *partir* "to go away" < Latin PARTIRI/PARTIRE "to divide"

Romanian *a merge* "to go" < "to leave" << "to draw away" << "to disappear" << Latin MERGERE "to dip, to plunge"

Spanish *pasar*, French *passer*, Italian *passare*, Portuguese *passar*, Catalan *passar*, Occitan *passar*, Sardinian (Campidanese) *passai*, Sardinian (Logudorese) *passàre*, Raeto-Romance *passar* "to go in" < Late Latin PASSARE << Classical Latin PASSUS "step, pace"

French *sortir*, Catalan *sortir*, Occitan *sortir* "to go out" < Latin SORTIRI "to throw lots or to choose by a lot"

Raeto-Romance *sortir* "to go out" < Italian *sortire* "to sort, to pick" or French *sortir* "to go out" << Latin SORTIRI "to throw lots or to choose by a lot"

French *arriver*, Italian *arrivare*, Catalan *arribar*, Occitan *arribar*, Sardinian (Campidanese) *arribai*, Sardinian (Logudorese) *arrivare*, Raeto-Romance *arrivar* "to come" < Late Latin ADRIPARE "to come to shore" << Classical Latin AD "towards" + RIPA "shore"

Romanian *a urca* "to go up" < Late Latin *ORICARE << Classical Latin ORIRI "to rise, to bestir one's self, to get up"

Sardinian (Campidanese) *artziai*, Sardinian (Logudorese) *alzare*, *arziàre* "to go up" < Late Latin *ALTIARE << Classical Latin ALTUS "high"

Old Sardinian (Campidanese) *koddai*, Old Sardinian (Logudorese) *koddare* "to go up" < Late Latin *COLLARE << Classical Latin COLLIS "hill"

Spanish *bajar*, Old Spanish *(a)baxar*, Portuguese *(a)baixar*, Catalan *(a)baixar* "to go down" < (AD "towards") + Late Latin *BASSIARE << Classical Latin BASSUS "low" (or BASSIOR, BASSIUS)

Old French *avaler*, Old Catalan *avallar*, Old Occitan *avalar* "to go down" < Latin AD "towards" + VALLIS "valley"

French *dévaler* "to go down (swiftly)" < Latin DE "from" + VALLIS "valley"

Catalan *davallar*, Occitan *davalar* "to go down" < Latin DE "from" + AD "towards" + VALLIS "valley"

Romanian *a coborî*, *a pogorî*, *a scoborî* "to go down" < Old Slavic *pogorĭ* "downwards, down, below", *pod gorije* "valley", *pogorije* "mountain range", *gora* "mountain"

Spanish *caminar*, Italian *camminare*, Portuguese *caminhar*, Old Catalan *acaminar*, Catalan *caminar*, Sardinian (Campidanese) *caminai*, Sardinian (Logudorese) *caminàre* "to walk"; French *cheminer* "to walk slowly with difficulty" << Late Latin CAMMINUS "way" < Celtic

French *marcher*, Occitan *marchar*, *marcar* "to walk" << Frankish *markôn* "to make or imprint a sign" < Frankish *marka* "sign that marks the border"

Spanish *saltar*, French *sauter*, Italian *saltare*, Portuguese *saltar*, Romanian *a sălta*, Catalan *saltar*, Occitan *saltar*, *sautar*, *sauter*, Sardinian (Campidanese) *sartiai*, Sardinian (Logudorese) *sartiàre* "to jump" < Latin SALTARE "to dance"

Romanian *a se ridica* "to go up" << SE + ERADICARE "to uproot" < Latin EX "out" + RADICARE "to take roots"

Romanian *a se retrage* "to go away" < Latin SE + RETRAHERE "to pull back"

Sardinian (Campidanese) *calai*, Sardinian (Logudorese) *calare* "to go down" << Late Latin CALARE "to lower, to let down" < Classical Greek χαλάω "I lower, I let down"

Metaphorical similarity:

Romanian *a ajunge* "to come" << Classical Latin ADJUNGERE "to join, to unite, to connect" < Classical Latin AD "towards" + JUNGERE "to join, to unite, to connect"

Italian *giungere* "to come, to arrive" < Latin JUNGERE "to join, to unite, to connect"

Taxonomic superordination:

French *aller*, Italian *andare*, Catalan *anar*, Occitan *anar* "to go" < Latin AMBULARE "to walk"

French *arriver*, Italian *arrivare*, Catalan *arribar*, Occitan *arribar*, Sardinian (Campidanese) *arribai*, Sardinian (Logudorese) *arrivare*, Raeto-Romance *arrivar* "to come" << Late Latin ADRIPARE "to come to shore" < Classical Latin AD "towards" + RIPA "shore"

Romanian *a fugi* "to run" < Latin FUGERE "to run away"

Spanish *marcharse*, Catalan *marxar* "to go away" << "to walk away" < French *marcher* "to walk" < Frankish *markôn* "to make or imprint a sign" < Frankish *marka* "sign that marks the border"

Romanian *a merge* "to go" << "to leave" < "to draw away" < "to disappear" < Latin MERGERE "to dip, to plunge"

Taxonomic subordination:

Spanish *irse*, Portuguese *ir-se* "to go away" < Latin IRE "to go" + SE

Raeto-Romance (Engadine valley) *s'inir* "to go away" < SE + INDE "thence" + IRE "to go"

French *s'en aller*, Italian *andarsene*, Catalan *anar-se'n*, Occitan *s'enanar* "to go away" < Latin AMBULARE "to walk" + SE + INDE "thence"

Spanish *marcharse*, Catalan *marxar* "to go away" < "to walk away" << French *marcher* "to walk" < Frankish **markôn* "to make or imprint a sign" < Frankish **marka* "sign that marks the border"

Sardinian (Campidanese) *moviri*, Sardinian (Logudorese) *mòvere* "to go away" < Latin MOVERE "to move"

Romanian *a merge* "to walk" << Romanian *a merge* "to go" < "to leave" < "to draw away" < "to disappear" < Latin MERGERE "to dip, to plunge"

Raeto-Romance *ceder* "to go out" < Latin CEDERE "to go, i.e., to be in motion, move, walk, go along"

Within the formal dimension, the Romance languages rely on the following possibilities:

Formal identity:

Spanish *llegar*, Portuguese *chegar* "to come" << Late Latin PLICARE < Classical Latin PLICARE (VELAM) "to fold (the sail)"

Sardinian (Campidanese) *lompi* (*krompi*), Sardinian (Logudorese) *lòmpere* (*cròmpere*) "to come" < Latin COMPLERE "to fill up, to fill out, to complete"

Romanian *a sosi* "to come" < subjunctive of the aorist of Modern Greek σώνω "I catch up, I reach, I arrive"

Catalan *marxar* "to go away" << French *marcher* "to walk" < Frankish **markôn* "to make or imprint a sign" < Frankish **marka* "sign that marks the border"

Romanian *a pleca* "to go away" << Late Latin PLICARE < Classical Latin PLICARE (TENTORIA) "to fold (the tents)"

Sardinian (Campidanese) *moviri*, Sardinian (Logudorese) *mòvere* "to go away" < Latin MOVERE "to move"

Spanish *partir*, Portuguese *partir*, French *partir*, Italian *partire*, Sardinian (Campidanese) *partiri*, Sardinian (Logudorese) *partire*, Raeto-Romance *partir* "to go away" < Latin PARTIRI/PARTIRE "to divide"

Sardinian (Logudorese) *andare* "to go" << Italian *andare* "to go" < Latin AMBULARE "to walk"

French *aller*, Italian *andare*, Catalan *anar*, Occitan *anar*, Sardinian (Campidanese) *andai* "to go" < Latin AMBULARE "to walk"

Romanian *a merge* "to go" < Latin MERGERE "to dip, to plunge"

Romanian *a ajunge* "to come" << Classical Latin ADJUNGERE "to join, to unite, to connect" < Classical Latin AD "towards" + JUNGERE "to join, to unite, to connect"

Spanish *salir*, Portuguese *sair*, Occitan *sal(h)ir* "to go out" < Latin SALIRE "to jump"

French *sortir*, Catalan *sortir*, Occitan *sortir* "to go out" < Latin SORTIRI "to throw lots or to choose by a lot"

Raeto-Romance *sortir* "to go out" << Italian *sortire* "to sort, to pick" or French *sortir* "to go out" < Latin SORTIRI "to throw lots or to choose by a lot"

Raeto-Romance *ceder* "to go out" < Latin CEDERE "to go, i.e., to be in motion, move, walk, go along"

Italian *salire* "to go up" < Latin SALIRE "to jump"

Romanian *a urca* "to go up" << Late Latin *ORICARE < Classical Latin ORIRI "to rise, to bestir one's self, to get up"

Romanian *a merge* "to walk" < Latin MERGERE "to dip, to plunge"

Raeto-Romance *c(h)aminar* "to walk" << Italian *camminare* "to walk" < Late Latin CAMMINUS "way" < Celtic

Romanian *a fugi* "to run" < Latin FUGERE "to run away"

Spanish *saltar*, French *sauter*, Italian *saltare*, Portuguese *saltar*, Romanian *a sălta*, Catalan *saltar*, Occitan *saltar*, *sautar*, *sauter*, Sardinian (Campidanese) *sartiai*, Sardinian (Logudorese) *sartiàre* "to jump" < Latin SALTARE "to dance"

Spanish *subir*, Portuguese *subir*, Romanian *a sui* "to go up" < Latin SUBIRE "to move upward"

Sardinian (Campidanese) *jumpai* "to jump" < Late Latin *JUMPARE "to jump"

Sardinian (Campidanese) *calai*, Sardinian (Logudorese) *calare* "to go down" < Late Latin CALARE "to lower, to let down" < Classical Greek χαλάω "I lower, I let down"

Italian *giungere* "to come, to arrive" < Latin JUNGERE "to join, to unite, to connect"

Sardinian (Campidanese) *(a)pujai* "to go up" < Catalan *pujar* "to go up"

Word-class alternation:

Spanish *pasar*, French *passer*, Italian *passare*, Portuguese *passar*, Catalan *passar*, Occitan *passar*, Sardinian (Campidanese) *passai*, Sardinian (Logudorese) *passàre*, Raeto-Romance *passar* "to go in" < Late Latin PASSARE << Classical Latin PASSUS "step, pace"

Old French *puier*, Catalan *pujar*, Occitan *pujar* (*pojar*) "to go up" < Late Latin *PODIARE << Classical Latin PODIUM "elevated place"

French *monter*, Italian *montare*, Catalan *muntar*, Occitan *montar*, Raeto-Romance *muntar* "to go up" < Late Latin *MONTARE << Classical Latin MONS, MONTIS "mountain"

Sardinian (Campidanese) *artziai*, Sardinian (Logudorese) *alzare, arziàre* "to go up" < Late Latin *ALTIARE << Classical Latin ALTUS "high"

Old Sardinian (Campidanese) *koddai*, Old Sardinian (Logudorese) *koddare* "to go up" < Late Latin *COLLARE << Classical Latin COLLIS "hill"

Spanish *bajar* "to go down" < Late Latin *BASSIARE << Classical Latin BASSUS "low" (or BASSIOR, BASSIUS)

Old Spanish *(a)baxar*, Portuguese *(a)baixar*, Catalan *(a)baixar* "to go down" < (AD "towards") + Late Latin *BASSIARE << Classical Latin BASSUS "low" (or BASSIOR, BASSIUS)

French *marcher*, Occitan *marchar, marcar* "to walk" < Frankish *markôn "to make or imprint a sign" << Frankish *marka "sign that marks the border"

Spanish *caminar*, Italian *camminare*, Portuguese *caminhar*, Catalan *caminar*, Sardinian (Campidanese) *caminai*, Sardinian (Logudorese) *caminàre* "to walk"; French *cheminer* "to walk slowly with difficulty" << Late Latin CAMMINUS "way" < Celtic

Romanian *a coborî, a pogorî, a scoborî* "to go down" < Old Slavic *pogorĭ* "downwards, down, below", *pod gorije* "valley", *pogorije* "mountain range", *gora* "mountain"

Word-class alternation and prefixation:

French *arriver*, Italian *arrivare*, Catalan *arribar*, Occitan *arribar*, Sardinian (Campidanese) *arribai*, Sardinian (Logudorese) *arrivare*, Raeto-Romance *arrivar* "to come" < Late Latin ADRIPARE "to come to shore" << Classical Latin AD "towards" + RIPA "shore"

Old French *avaler*, Old Catalan *avallar*, Old Occitan *avalar* "to go down" < Latin AD "towards" + VALLIS "valley"

French *dévaler* "to go down (swiftly)" < Latin DE "from" + VALLIS "valley"

Catalan *davallar*, Occitan *davalar* "to go down" < Latin DE "from" + AD "towards" + VALLIS "valley"

Old Catalan *acaminar* "to walk" << AD "towards" + Late Latin CAMMINUS "way" < Celtic

Prefixation:

Old Spanish *(a)baxar*, Portuguese *(a)baixar*, Catalan *(a)baixar* "to go down" << (AD "towards") + Late Latin *BASSIARE < Classical Latin BASSUS "low" (or BASSIOR, BASSIUS)

Romanian *a ajunge* "to come" < Classical Latin ADJUNGERE "to join, to unite, to connect" << Classical Latin AD "towards" + JUNGERE "to join, to unite, to connect"

Sardinian (Campidanese) *(a)pujai* "to go up" < *a* "towards" + Catalan *pujar* "to go up"

Voice alternation:

Italian *andarsene*, Catalan *anar-se'n* "to go away" < Latin AMBULARE "to walk" + SE + INDE "thence"

Spanish *irse*, Portuguese *ir-se* "to go away" < Latin IRE "to go" + SE

Spanish *marcharse* "to go away" << French *marcher* "to walk" + *se* < Frankish *markôn* "to make or imprint a sign" < Frankish *marka* "sign that marks the border"

Old Spanish *partirse*, Old French *se partir*, Old Italian *partirsi*, Portuguese *partir(-se)* "to go away" < Latin PARTIRI/PARTIRE "to divide" + SE

French *s'en aller*, Occitan *s'enanar* "to go away" < Latin SE + INDE "thence" + AMBULARE "to walk"

Romanian *a se depărta* < Latin SE + DE "from" + PARTIRI/PARTIRE "to divide"

Romanian *a se îndepărta* "to go away" < Latin SE + INDE "thence" + PARTIRI/PARTIRE "to divide"

Raeto-Romance (Engadine valley) *s'inir* "to go away" < Latin SE + INDE "thence" + IRE "to go"

Romanian *a se ridica* "to go up" < Latin SE + ERADICARE "to uproot"

Romanian *a se retrage* "to go away" < Latin SE + RETRAHERE "to pull back"

Blend:

Old Spanish *deçir*, Old Portuguese *deçer*, Portuguese *descer* "to go down" < Latin DE-/DIS-CEDERE "to depart, to withdraw, to go apart" & DESCENDERE "to go down"

Within the stratificational dimension, the Romance languages rely both on autochthonous words, as well as on lexical borrowings and calques. The lexical borrowings and calques are listed below:

Borrowings within the Romance language family:

Sardinian (Logudorese) *andare* "to go" << Italian *andare* "to go" < Latin AMBULARE "to walk"

Raeto-Romance *sortir* "to go out" << Italian *sortire* "to sort, to pick" or French *sortir* "to go out" < Latin SORTIRI "to throw lots or to choose by a lot"

Raeto-Romance *c(h)aminar* "to walk" << Italian *camminare* "to walk" < Late Latin CAMMINUS "way" < Celtic

Spanish *marcharse*, Catalan *marxar* "to go away" << French *marcher* "to walk" < Frankish *markôn* "to make or imprint a sign" < Frankish *marka* "sign that marks the border"

Sardinian (Campidanese) *(a)pujai* "to go up" << Catalan *pujar* "to go up" < Late Latin *PODIARE "to go up" < Classical Latin PODIUM "elevated place"

Borrowings from Latin (i.e., learned words):

Raeto-Romance *ceder* "to go out" < Latin CEDERE "to go, i.e., to be in motion, move, walk, go along"

Spanish *ascender* "to go up" < Latin ASCENDERE "to go up"

Calques within the Romance family:

Romanian *a se retrage* "to go away" < Latin SE + RETRAHERE "to pull back" (calqued upon French *retirer* "to pull, to draw, take out" and *se retirer* "to go away, to retire, to withdraw")

Borrowings from Greek:

> Romanian *a sosi* "to come" < subjunctive of the aorist of Modern Greek σώνω "I catch up, I reach, I arrive"

> Sardinian (Campidanese) *calai*, Sardinian (Logudorese) *calare* "to go down" < Late Latin CALARE "to lower, to let down" << Classical Greek χαλάω "I lower, I let down"

Borrowings from Slavic:

> Romanian *a coborî, a pogorî, a scoborî* "to go down" < Old Slavic *pogorĭ* "downwards, down, below", *pod gorije* "valley", *pogorije* "mountain range", *gora* "mountain"

Borrowings from Germanic:

> French *marcher*, Occitan *marchar, marcar* "to walk" << Frankish **markôn* "to make or imprint a sign" < Frankish **marka* "sign that marks the border"

Borrowings from Celtic:

> Spanish *caminar*, Italian *camminare*, Portuguese *caminhar*, Old Catalan *acaminar*, Catalan *caminar*, Sardinian (Campidanese) *caminai*, Sardinian (Logudorese) *caminàre* "to walk"; French *cheminer* "to walk slowly with difficulty" < Late Latin CAMMINUS "way" << Celtic

The new Romance signifiers presented above are not isolated occurrences. They are a part of broader word-formation trends attested on the way from Latin to Romance.

Let us consider the 'adjective > verb' pattern. We have seen that the Latin adjective BASSUS "low" (or its comparative forms BASSIOR, BASSIUS) produced Spanish *bajar*, Old Spanish *(a)baxar*, Portuguese *(a)baixar*, and Catalan *(a)baixar* "to go down", as well as French *se baisser* "to stoop, to bend down" via Late Latin **BASSIARE. We also have observed that in a similar fashion Latin ALTUS "high" created Sardinian (Campidanese) *artziai* and Sardinian (Logudorese) *alzare, arziàre* "to go up", as well as Spanish *alzar* and French *hausser* "to raise" via Late Latin **ALTIARE. However, such 'adjective (or past participle) > verb' formations with the suffix -IARE were not limited to the lexical field of motion verbs. They were pervasive in Late Latin, and their effect can be detected in a gamut of semantic fields. Although originally the suffix -IARE could be added only to the adjectives ending in -IS, it soon became productive with all sorts of adjectives regardless of their declension. For instance, we find verbs like Spanish *aguzar*, French *aiguiser*, Italian *aguzzare*, and Portuguese *aguçar* "to sharpen" which go back to Classical Latin ACUTUS "sharp" via Late Latin **ACUTIARE. Likewise, we find French *dresser* and Italian *dirizzare* "to raise, to put up" which go back to Classical Latin DIRECTUS "straight" via Late Latin *DIRECTIARE. In fact, the 'adjective > verb' pattern that relied on the suffix -IARE was already in existence before the Late Latin stage: e.g., Spanish *humillar*, French *humilier*, Italian *umiliare*, and Portuguese *humilhar* "to humiliate" which go back to post-Classical Latin HUMILIARE (attested in Tertullian c.160–230 A.D.) which derives from Classical Latin HUMILIS "low" (Grandgent 1962: 17; Bourciez 1967: 65; Coromines et al. 1980–1991 I: 556; Meyer-Lübke 1992: 11, 241; Dynnikov & Lopatina 1998: 98; Väänänen 2003: 155).

The 'preposition + adjective > verb' pattern, which in the case of motion verbs manifests itself in Old Spanish *(a)baxar*, Portuguese *(a)baixar*, and Catalan *(a)baixar* "to go down", is attested across different semantic fields as well. For instance, the combination of Classical Latin EX "out" and CALIDUS "warm, hot" produced Late Latin EXCALDARE which in turn served as the etymon for Spanish *escaldar*, Portuguese *escaldar*, French *échauder* "to scald, to burn with hot liquid", Italian *scaldare* "to warm", and Romanian *a (se) scălda* "to bathe, to wet" (Bourciez 1967: 69; Meyer-Lübke 1992: 261).

The 'noun > verb' pattern is equally pervasive. In the case of motion verbs, the lexical field of vertical movement is the one affected to a great degree. We have seen that Classical Latin MONS, MONTIS "mountain" produced Late Latin *MONTARE which resulted in French *monter*, Italian *montare*, Catalan *muntar*, Occitan *montar*, and Raeto-Romance *muntar* "to go up". We have also observed that Classical Latin PODIUM "elevated place" created Late Latin *PODIARE which served as the source of Catalan *pujar*, Occitan *pujar* (*pojar*), and Sardinian (Campidanese) *(a)pujai* "to go up". Likewise, we have seen that Classical Latin COLLIS "hill" gave Late Latin *COLLARE, which is the etymon of Old Sardinian *koddai* (*koddare*) "to go up". However, these denominal examples from the field of motion verbs are by no means exceptional. For instance, in the *Peregrinatio Aetheriae* (late 4th – early 5th century A.D.) in the reference to the break of dawn we find the verb LUCERNARE derived from the noun LUCERNA "candle". In a similar way, in the dietetics treatise *De observatione ciborum* composed in Latin by the Greek Anthimus (first half of the 6th century A.D.), we encounter the passive infinitive GYPSARI "to be covered with cast, to be whitened with gypsum" derived from the Latin (of Greek origin) noun GYPSUM "cast, gypsum". In fact, the pattern existed already in Classical Latin: e.g., Classical Latin CALCEUS "shoe" > Classical Latin CALCEARE "to put on shoes" > Spanish *calzar*, French *chausser*, Italian *calzare*, Portuguese *calçar* "to put on shoes" (Grandgent 1962: 16; Bourciez 1967: 202; Guryčeva 2008: 61).

The 'preposition + noun > verb' pattern offers examples from a variety of lexical fields as well. In the case of motion verbs, we find Latin AD "towards" + RIPA "shore" producing French *arriver*, Italian *arrivare*, Catalan *arribar*, Occitan *arribar*, Sardinian (Campidanese) *arribai*, Sardinian (Logudorese) *arrivare*, and Raeto-Romance *arrivar* "to come"; Latin DE "from" + VALLIS "valley" producing French *dévaler* "to go down swiftly"; Latin AD + VALLIS producing Old French *avaler*, Old Catalan *avallar*, and Old Occitan *avalar* "to go down"; and Latin DE + AD + VALLIS producing Catalan *davallar* and Occitan *davalar* "to go down". While being compound etymologically, these new lexical creations were probably perceived as simple (monomorphemic) forms since the counterpart without the prefix did not exist. In the case of other semantic fields, we can think of Classical Latin IN "in" + ODIUM "hate" > Late Latin INODIARE "to inspire hate" (attested in the Latin inscriptions as INODIARI in *Corpus Inscriptionum Latinarum* VIII 13134); cf. Spanish *enojar*, French *ennuyer*, Italian *annoiare*, as well as Portuguese *enojar* and *enjoar* "to annoy". Other examples include Classical Latin DIS- + RAMUS "branch" producing Late Latin *DISRAMARE and DERAMARE that resulted in Spanish *derramar*, Portuguese *derramar*, and Italian *diramare* "to pour out, to distribute"; and Classical Latin IN "in" + PEDICA "trap" > Late Latin IMPEDICARE (attested in Ammianus Marcellinus c.330–400 A.D.); cf. Spanish *empachar*, French *empêcher*, Italian *impacciare*, Portuguese *empachar*, and Romanian *a împiedica* "to impede" (Bourciez 1967: 204–206; Meyer-Lübke 1992: 236, 357, 364–365; Dynnikov & Lopatina 1998: 98; Guryčeva 2008: 61; Väänänen 2003: 163).[10] As in the case of 'adjective > verb', 'preposition + adjective > verb', and 'noun > verb' patterns, the 'preposition + noun > verb' pattern was already attested in Classical Latin: e.g., DE "from" + SUBULA "awl" > DESUBULARE "to make holes with an awl" (Crocco Galèas & Iacobini 1993: 179), EX "out" + PECTUS "heart" > EXPECTORARE "to banish from one's affections", EX "out" + HERES "heir" > EXHEREDARE "to disinherit", and IN "in" + OCULUS "eye, bud" > INOCULARE "to graft (trees) by budding" (Fruyt 2011: 171–172).

The fact that the creation of new motion verbs was a part of broader trends in word-formation is significant because it helps to shed light on the mechanism of the typological shift that was taking place. As we have seen in Section 2.2, according to Leonard Talmy, Latin and Romance exhibit two typologically different lexicalization patterns. Latin, on the one hand, belonged to the 'Motion + Manner/Cause' satellite-framed type in which the prefixes played the role of the satellites that carried the information about the path, while the Romance languages, on the other hand, are of the 'Motion + Path' verb-framed type in which the verbal roots themselves inform us about the path. Reflecting on the differences between the Romance and the Germanic lexicalization patterns in the section entitled "Typological shift and maintenance", Talmy (2007) states that "the factors that may have tilted one language toward reestablishing its typological category and another

---

10.   It should be clarified that some of these Romance forms do not go back directly to Latin, but rather are borrowings within the Romance family. For instance, both Spanish *empachar* "to impede" and Spanish *enojar* "to annoy" are loan-words that entered Spanish from Old Occitan (Corominas & Pascual 1980–1991 II: 568, 653; Dworkin 2012: 125). Likewise, Sardinian (Campidanese) *(a)pujai* "to go up" is a Catalanism, as mentioned in Chapter 3.

language toward shifting to another category must yet be discerned" (p. 155). In other words, Talmy points out that it is necessary for historical and cognitive linguists to address the question of why in the place of the prefixed satellite-framed Old English verbs (like *in(n)gan* and *utgan*) we find the satellite-framed Modern English verbs (like *go in* and *go out*), while the prefixed satellite-framed Latin verbs (like CONSCENDERE and ESCENDERE "to go up") were replaced by the verb-framed Romance verbs (like French *monter* and Catalan *pujar* "to go up").

I believe that the answer to this important question lies in the pervasiveness of the word-formation patterns described in the preceding paragraphs. In Classical Latin and in Late Latin new verbs were being created within all sort of lexical fields following the 'adjective (past participle) > verb' and the 'noun > verb' patterns. As these word-formation patterns were at work in the lexicon at large, nouns and adjectives that had a certain connotation of direction present within them (e.g., MONS, MONTIS "mountain", BASSUS "low") could produce in Late Latin a number of verbs of motion that already belonged not to the Latin 'Motion + Manner/Cause' satellite-framed type, but rather to the Romance 'Motion + Path' verb-framed type. In cases like RIPA "shore" and VALLIS "valley" (i.e., important landmarks that do not necessarily signal a particular direction), another pervasive pattern, namely 'preposition + noun > verb', was used, the preposition making up for the lack of explicit directionality in the noun. The new formations that relied on the 'preposition + noun' combinations, though, were likely to be perceived as simple (mono-morphemic) forms, that is, also belonging to the Romance 'Motion + Path' verb-framed type.

The cognitive salience of path, as argued in Stolova (2008: 260–261), is the driving force behind these new developments. Based on the centrality of path in human conceptualization of motion events and on the cognitive relation of contiguity, the speakers, in their attempt to place path information in the foreground by incorporating it into the verbal stem, began to lexicalize directed movement in terms of the lexemes with spatial and deictic reference. The creation of new simple verb-framed forms (e.g., *MONTARE) and the creation of new forms perceived as simple ones (e.g., ADRIPARE), combined with the loss of compound satellite-framed forms (e.g., ABIRE), with the survival of simple forms (e.g., VENIRE), with the recruitment of simple lexical items from other semantic fields (e.g., PLICARE), and with the survival of compound forms that were reanalyzed as simple ones (e.g., EXIRE) all had a combined effect: the Romance family was gradually moving toward becoming predominantly verb-framed. Late Latin, as shown in Stolova (2003, 2008, 2010a), is of particular importance in this transition. As the title "From Satellite-Framed Latin to Verb-Framed Romance: Late Latin as an intermediate stage" (Stolova 2008) suggests, it is the Late Latin stage at which the developments outlined above were gaining momentum.

In the history of English, on the other hand, one of the dominant word-formation patterns was the creation of the multi-word verbs. The multi-word verbs include phrasal verbs (Hiltunen 1983, Brinton & Traugott 2005: 123–125) and prepositional verbs (Brinton & Traugott 2005: 126). The phrasal verbs are comprised of a verb (typically a monosyllabic one of the Germanic stock) and a limited set of particles that function as markers of verbal aspect, as in *nod off* "fall asleep", *fall down* "collapse", *shoot up* "increase sharply", and *write* N[oun] P[hrase] *up* "give a full written account" (Brinton & Traugott 2005: 122). Although it was earlier assumed that a phrasal verb is a replacement for a lost prefixed verb, more recent research has established that "the phrasal verb exhibits a direct line of development from O[ld] E[nglish] to the present and is more appropriately understood as a continuation of O[ld] E[nglish] verbs accompanied by adverbial particles in preposition or postposition" (ibid., p. 124). In the case of the prepositional verbs, these combinations are composed of verbs (either Romance or Germanic) and a larger set of prepositions, as in *frown on* "disapprove", *look after* "attend", *get at* "reach", and *look into* "examine" (ibid., p. 122). The contribution of the prepositions in the prepositional verbs is not grammatical (as in the case of the phrasal verbs) but lexical: e.g., *take* vs. *take after* "resemble", *come* vs. *come between* "interfere" (ibid., p. 128). The prepositional verbs "represent the functional replacement for prefixed verbs, which already in O[ld] E[nglish] could be highly idiomaticized" (ibid., p. 127). The development of the new multi-word verbs was a part of broader trends in the history of the English language: a shift in the word-formation strategy from stem-based word-formation based on vowel alternations toward derivational morphology, an increasing use of prepositions, and a morphosyntactic typological shift from object-verb to verb-object and from adverb-verb to verb-adverb word order (ibid., pp. 154–156). The periphrastic auxiliaries (e.g., *ought to, need to, dare to*) also developed within this context (ibid., p. 155). In other words, in the history of English we observe the development of several kinds of multi-word verbs. I would suggest that the development of English satellite-framed motion verbs like *go out* could have been a part of this more general word-formation trend.[11]

---

11.   Another kind of parallel between the word-formation trends attested across the lexicon and the word-formation trends found within the lexical field of motion is reported in Fanego (2012): conversion, also known as zero-derivation, was on the rise in late Middle English and Early Modern English and during these time periods English acquired a large number of new manner-of-motion verbs created by means of conversion (e.g., *barge* "a freight boat" > *barge* "to journey by barge"). Further evidence of the connection between the development of motion verbs and the evolution of word-formation at large comes from Slavic. Nichols (2010) has demonstrated that the creation of Slavic indeterminate motion verbs (e.g., Common Slavic **xoditi* "to walk") reflects the shift that the Slavic lexicon underwent from the verb-based derivational type to the noun-based one.

Researchers working with synchronic data (Beavers et al. 2010) have argued that it is the language's inventory of motion-independent morpholexical (word-formation) and morphosyntactic resources that determines the way in which its motion verbs are shaped. For example, the morphological inventory of Klamath (a Penutian language within the Amerindian family spoken in south central Oregon) includes bipartite verb stems. In fact, a substantial majority of Klamath verb stems are bipartite (DeLancey 2009). As DeLancey (2003) illustrates, this allows Klamath to have motion verbs like *bambaata* "wade to the shore" formed by the manner-of-motion stem *ban* "wade" and the locative-directional stem *abaatn* "to the shore, edge", and *honneega* "run into a hole" formed by the manner-of-motion stem *hod* "run" and the locative-directional stem *oneeg* "into a hole". The availability of bipartite verb stems also allows Klamath to create sentences of the type *Coy sdaynas hok nowalGa* "Then the heart flew up [into the sky]". In this sentence the form *nowalGa*, morphologically analyzable as *n-wal-l'G-a* and glossed as "round.obj-on.top-finish-INDICATIVE", incorporates the stem *l*ⁿ "round/rock-like object", which indicates the figure that is moving, and the locative-directional stem *wal* "above, on top", which indicates direction (DeLancey 2003: 70, 73–76). In contrast, French and Japanese morphology does not have bipartite verb stems like those in Klamath and therefore these languages have to resort to other means when expressing the same concepts (Beavers et al. 2010: 360). It is reasonable to assume that if on the synchronic level the word-formation resources available in the language influence the type of motion verbs that this language tends to have, then the same connection is likely to apply on the diachronic level as well.

Although the general tendency on the way from Latin to Romance was to become verb-framed, new satellite-framed verbs continued to make their way into the language. However, what distinguishes these new Romance satellite-framed verbs from the old Latin satellite-framed ones is that rather than relying on the Classical Latin 'spatial preposition + verb' pattern (e.g., EX "out" + IRE "go" > EXIRE "go out"),[12] the new developments followed the patterns that involved the reflexive pronoun SE and the deictic adverb INDE "thence": 'SE + verb' (e.g., SE + PARTIRI/ PARTIRE "to divide" > Old French *se partir* "to go away"), 'SE + INDE + verb' (e.g., SE + INDE + AMBULARE "to walk" > French *s'en aller* "to go away"), 'verb + SE' (e.g., IRE "to go" + SE > Portuguese *ir-se* "to go away"), and 'verb + SE + INDE' (e.g., AM-BULARE "to walk" + SE + INDE > Catalan *anar-se'n* "to go away"). These patterns

---

12. Late Latin texts contain a number of motion verbs with multiple prefixes, as in the case of PER-SUB-IRE in *persubissemus in ipsa summitate* "we had gone up to the mountain summit" from the *Peregrinatio Aetheriae* (Dynnikov & Lopatina 1998: 232), but these do not have Romance motion reflexes. Furthermore, the majority of such forms start with PER- (Noblejas Ruiz Escribano 2004: 579–580), i.e., with a prefix whose function can be interpreted as aspectual rather than spatial; cf. FACERE "to make" vs. PERFICERE "to achieve, to complete" < PER + FACERE.

need to be viewed within broader trends attested in Late Latin, namely the proliferation of the functions of the reflexive pronoun SE, and the recruitment of adverbs into word-formation.

As discussed in such studies as Maiden (1995a), Parry (1998), Cennamo
(1999), and Pountain (2000b), among others, in Classical Latin the pronoun SE
had several canonical functions and the range of its functions expanded over time.
One of the canonical functions was the reflexive usage in which the subject was
coreferential with the object: e.g., *istae veteres, quae se unguentis unctitant* "these
old ladies, who smear themselves with ointments" (Plautus, *Mostellaria*, quoted in
Cennamo 1999: 114). Another prototypical function was the reciprocal one, with
the agent and the patient acting on each other: e.g., *cum angusto exitu portarum se
ipsi premerent* "as they crowded one another at the narrow passages of the gates"
(Caesar, *De Bello Gallico*, quoted in Cennamo 1999: 114). Occasionally, in Classical Latin the reflexive pronoun was used with the middle function, i.e., in structures that "signal not an action carried out by the subject on itself, but an event
originating, as it were, from within the subject, and in which the subject plays a
more or less active role" (Maiden 1995a: 163). This usage became more common
in Late Latin: e.g., *si quod iumentum caudam parietibus fricat, et exulcerat se, sic
curato* "if the donkey rubs its tail against the walls, and gets wounded, you will
treat it in this way" (*Mulomedicina Chironis*, second half of the 4th century A.D.,
quoted in Cennamo 1999: 127); *cum male sibi senserint, ustulant se foco in stoma-
cho* "when they fall ill, they burn with fire in their stomach" (Anthimus, *De observatione ciborum*, first half of the 6th century A.D., quoted in Cennamo 1999: 128).
The middle usage of SE made possible a further extension of the pronoun's functional range:

> The fact that, in middle verbs, the subject is only secondarily involved in the ac-
> tion facilitates the extension of the 'middle' reflexive [...] structure to verbs whose
> grammatical subjects are inert or 'patients'. In other words, the reflexive comes to
> function rather like the passive. (Maiden 1995a: 164)

The passive usage of SE was already attested in Classical Latin and proliferated in
Late Latin: e.g., *clamor se tollit in auras* "the cry is carried up into the air" (Virgil,
Aeneid, quoted in Bourciez 1967: 116); *Myrina quae Sebastopolim se vocat* "Myrna,
which is called Sebastopol" (Pliny the Elder, *Naturalis Historia*, quoted in Bourciez
1967: 116); *mala rotunda toto anno servare se possunt* "round apples can be kept for
the whole year" (Palladius, *De Agricultura*, first half of the 5th century A.D., quoted in Parry 1998: 93, n.40). Since, similar to passives and middles, some intransitive verbs have subjects that do not perform the action but rather undergo it, the
use of the reflexive pronoun extended to a number of intransitives (Maiden 1995a:
151–152, 164). As demonstrated in Cennamo (1999: 134–135), already at the

earlier stage of Late Latin (by the 3rd–4th centuries A.D.), among the verbs appearing with the accusative reflexive SE we find intransitive mental process/emotion verbs, intransitive speech act verbs, and intransitive state verbs: e.g., *et tunc lamentabunt se omnes tribus terrae* "and then all the people of the earth will moan" (*Itala*, second half of the 2nd century A.D., quoted in Cennamo 1999: 128); *hic humor sudoris in ventrem se desidet* "the beads of perspiration settle in his abdomen" (*Mulomedicina Chironis*, second half of the 4th century A.D., quoted in Cennamo 1999: 128). The intransitive verbs that denoted change of state, as well as the intransitive motion verbs that denoted directed change of location, originally took the dative reflexive SIBI: e.g., *statim fugiet sibi* "it will immediately flee/slip away" (*Mulomedicina Chironis*, second half of the 4th century A.D., quoted in Cennamo 1999: 125); *revertatur sibi ad parentes suos* "that he go back to his parents" (*Edictus Rothari*, mid-7th century A.D., quoted in Cennamo 1999: 125). Non-directed change-of-location motion verbs like AMBULARE, VAGARI, and PEREGRINARE also could appear with SIBI, although they are attested with SIBI later than the directed ones: e.g., *ille solemniter sibi ambulabat* "he walked solemnly" (*Formulae Turonensis*, first half of the 8th century A.D., quoted in Cennamo 1999: 125). With time, the difference between the accusative SE and the dative SIBI became neutralized: the neutralization is already well established by the 4th century A.D., and affects the whole paradigm in some texts by the 8th century (Cennamo 1999: 132–134). In the *Peregrinatio Aetheriae*, we find an example of the motion verb VADERE employed with SE: *recipit se episcopus et vadent se unusquisque ad hospitium suum* "the bishop retired and let everybody go to his lodging" (quoted in Vincent 1988: 58). While the form VADENT SE in this latter example might have been triggered in part by RECIPIT SE that precedes it (Claflin 1948: 112), it is lack of any "referential semantic import" on the part of the pronoun that is particularly relevant: "the reflexive pronoun has ceased to have any obvious semantic referentiality, as a consequence of which it cannot be construed as a verbal argument; it is therefore most readily construable as a part of the verb itself" (Pountain 2000b: 19). Other lexical items that could be accompanied by SE in Late Latin are IRE "to go", ABIRE "to go away", OBVIARE "to go towards", and PROGREDI "to come forth" (Bassols de Climent 1948: 49–51; Bastardas Parera 1953: 112–113).

In sum, Latin SE underwent what Christopher Pountain calls "capitalization" – "a continuous history of addition, without loss, of function" (2000b: 5) or "the historical process by which a linguistic feature which already exists in a language comes to be substantially exploited for wider purposes" (2000a: 295). Thus, the development of the Romance motion verbs with SE, i.e., Spanish *irse*, French *s'en aller*, Italian *andarsene*, Portuguese *ir-se*, Catalan *anar-se'n*, etc., is fully entrenched within the expansion of the usage of SE from Latin to Romance. The clitics (French *en*, Italian *ne*, Catalan *en* < Latin INDE "thence") are also a part of a broader

Romance tendency (albeit not as prominent as the proliferation of SE) to incorporate the deictic adverbs IBI "there" and INDE "thence" into word-formation: e.g., French *y avoir* "to exist, there to be" (*y* < IBI), Catalan *haver-hi* "to exist, there to be" (*hi* < IBI) (Badía Margarit 1947, Pinchon 1972).

At this point it is important to address the following question: what are the reasons for classifying the Romance forms with SE and INDE like Spanish *irse*, French *s'en aller*, Italian *andarsene*, etc. as satellite-framed compounds? In other words, what are the reasons for classifying Spanish *-se*, French *s'en*, Italian *-sene*, etc. as satellites?

As we have seen in Chapter 2 (Section 2.2), Talmy defines satellites as "immediate constituents of a verb root other than inflections, auxiliaries, or nominal arguments [...] [that] relate to the verb root as periphery (or modifiers) to a head" (1985: 102). In his more recent scholarship, Talmy offers the following two definitions of a satellite: "It is the grammatical category of any constituent other than a noun-phrase or prepositional-phrase complement that is in a sister relation to the verb root" (2000 II: 102); "A satellite is a constituent in construction with the main verb (root) and syntactically subordinate to it as a dependent to a head" (2009: 390). Talmy clarifies that a satellite "can be either a bound affix or a free word" (2000 II: 102). He further notes that "A verb root together with its satellites forms a constituent in its own right, the verb complex" (ibid., p. 103), and includes a detailed disclaimer that the difference between what constitutes a satellite and what does not is not always clear-cut:

> There is some indeterminacy as to exactly which kinds of constituents found in construction with a verb root merit satellite designation. Clearest are the forms [...] such as English verb particles, Latin verb prefixes, Chinese resultative complements, and the noninflectional affixes in the Atsugewi polysynthetic verb. Seemingly also deserving satellite status are such compounding forms as the first element of English *(to) test-drive*. Probably meriting satellite status are incorporated nouns, like those in the Caddo polysynthetic verb, while pronominal clitics like those in French[13] may merit the designation less, and full noun phrases are entirely excluded. It is uncertain what status should be accorded such verb-phrase forms as inflections, an auxiliary, a negative element, a closed-class particle like English *only* or *even*, or a free adverb semantically related to the verb root. It is further not clear whether this indeterminacy is due to the preset theory's early stage of development or to the cline-like character for the satellite category. (ibid., p. 102)

Talmy (ibid., pp. 103–128) goes on to survey seven types of semantic material encoded by satellites: 'path', 'path + ground', 'patient: (figure/)ground', 'manner', 'cause', 'aspect', and 'valence'. His examples of 'path' satellites include English *forth* and *free* in *She came forth* and *The coin melted free (from the ice)*, as well as German,

---

13.   In this context, the term 'pronominal clitic' refers to the pronoun in French reflexive verbs of the type *se laver* "to wash oneself".

Latin, and Russian verb prefixes (p. 105). Among the 'path + ground' satellites he lists English *home* and *shut* in *She drove home (to her cottage in the suburbs)* and *The gate swung shut (across the entryway)*, as well as a series of Atsugewi directional suffixes, including *-cis* "into a fire", *-wam* "down into a gravitic container (e.g., a basket)", and *-wamm* "into an areal enclosure (e.g., a corral)" (pp. 110–111). In the discussion of the 'patient: (figure/)ground' satellites Talmy focuses on the Amerindian language Caddo and lists a number of its incorporated nouns, including *nisah* "house" in *nisah-nt-káy-watak-ah* glossed as "house-penetrate/traverse-PAST", literally translated as "He-house-traversed" (i.e., "He went through the house") (p. 113). He uses another Amerindian language, namely Nez Perce, to illustrate the 'manner' satellites: e.g., the prefix *ququ--* "(animal) galloping/(human) galloping (on animal)", as in *hi-ququ-- láhsa -e* glossed as "3rd person galloping go-up PAST", literally translated as "He/she ascended galloping" (i.e., "He/she galloped uphill") (p. 113). In the case of the 'cause' satellites, Talmy turns to the Atsugewi short prefixes that immediately precede the verb root that expresses the action: e.g., *ca-* "from the wind blowing on the Patient" (p. 115). As examples of the 'aspect' satellites, he lists English particles such as *up* which encodes the telic aspect in *The dog chewed the mat up in 20 minutes* and *on* which encodes the continuous aspect in *We talked on into the night* (pp. 120–121). Other elements that qualify as aspectual satellites are Russian prefixes such as *za-* which encodes the ingressive aspect in *Kapli doždja zapadali odna za drugoj* "Drops of rain began to fall one after another" (p. 122). Russian aspectual satellites can also be combinations of prefixes and the reflexive particle *-sa* (*-s'*). For instance, in *Ona rasplakalas'* "She burst out crying" the ingressive aspect satellite is the combination of the prefix *raz-* and the reflexive particle *-s'*. Likewise, in *On naelsa* "He ate his fill" the telic aspect is encoded through the combination of the prefix *na-* and the reflexive particle *-sa* (p. 122).[14] The aspectual satellites also include Atsugewi affixes that encode "how the action of the verb root is distributed with respect to the general flow of time" and "how the action is distributed with respect to another ongoing event, namely of one of moving along" (pp. 121–122): e.g., the Atsugewi secondary aspect suffix *-iks* "to a position blocking passage", hence "in going to meet (and give to) someone approaching", which is similar to German *entgegen-* "in going to meet" in *entgegenlaufen* "to run to meet" and to Latin OB- in OCCURRERE "to run to meet" and OBSTRUERE "to build so as to block off" (pp. 123, 145). As for the 'valence' satellites, these "refer to other notions, such as Path, but themselves incorporate valence requirements", i.e., "determine the grammatical relations of the surrounding nominals" (p. 124). For instance, the Russian path prefix *pere-* "across"

---

14. The examples *Ona rasplakalas'* and *On naelsa* are particularly significant because they illustrate that reflexive particles can qualify as satellites.

requires a direct object that encodes the ground: e.g., *On perebežal ulicu (za 5 sekund)* "He ran across the street in five seconds" (p. 127).

Based on the overview of Talmy's understanding of satellites provided above, I would argue that the Romance forms based on Latin SE and INDE like Spanish -*se*, French *s'en*, Italian -*sene*, etc. in Spanish *irse*, French *s'en aller*, Italian *andarsene*, etc. also qualify as satellites for several reasons. First, these forms are constituents of the verbal complex, while at the same time they are neither the verb root nor a part of the verb root. This is to say that Spanish *irse*, French *s'en aller*, Italian *andarsene*, etc. are compounds in a sense that they are composed of two elements: the verb which includes the root (*ir, aller, andare*) and the constituent subordinate to the verb (-*se, s'en, -sene*). Second, the forms like Spanish -*se*, French *s'en*, Italian -*sene*, etc. do not belong to any of the categories excluded by Talmy from the list of satellites, i.e., they are neither noun phrase arguments, nor prepositional phrase arguments, nor auxiliaries, nor inflections.[15] In other words, they fit Talmy's definitions of a satellite. The third reason for classifying these forms as satellites is their function: they encode the first one of the seven satellite categories specified by Talmy, namely path. Lexemes such as Spanish *ir*, French *aller*, and Italian *andare* "to go" are generic verbs that do not convey any information about the path of movement. In contrast, Spanish *irse*, French *s'en aller*, and Italian *andarsene* "to go away" are verbs of directed motion that encode path information, and it is the presence of -*se, s'en*, and -*sene*, respectively, that enables such encoding. The same applies to the whole paradigm, e.g., Spanish *me voy, te vas, se va*, etc. In fact, expressions like Spanish (*yo*) *voy* "I go", (*tú*) *vas* "you go", (*él*) *va* "he goes", (*nosotros*) *vamos* "we go", (*vosotros*) *vais* "you go", (*ellos*) *van* "they go" not only do not provide any path information, but are also ungrammatical.[16] It is the *me, te, se* in (*yo*) *me voy* "I am going away", (*tú*) *te vas* "you are going away", (*él*) *se va* "he is going away", respectively, that both encode path and make the verbal complex complete.

---

15. The entities under consideration form a paradigm: e.g., Spanish (*yo*) *me voy* "I go away", (*tú*) *te vas* "you go away", (*él*) *se va* "he goes away", etc.; (*yo*) *tengo que irme* "I have to go away", (*tú*) *tienes que irte* "you have to go away", (*él*) *tiene que irse* "he has to go away", etc. However, the inflections in this paradigm are not the reflexive pronouns but rather the verbal endings: -*o* in *voy*, -*as* in *vas*, -*a* in *va*, -*o* in *tengo*, -*es* in *tienes*, -*e* in *tiene*. This is particularly clear if we compare the forms that share the reflexive pronoun such as *se va* "he/she goes away" in which -*a* marks third person singular and *se van* "they go away" in which -*an* marks third person plural, while *se* is the same for both forms.

16. Spanish *voy* in the speech act comprised of a request *ven aquí* "come here" and a reply *voy* "I am coming" is grammatical; however, it does not appear by itself, but rather in anaphoric reference to *ven aquí*. Spanish *vamos* is grammatical, but not as expression of motion, but as a discourse marker similar to English *come on!* and *well*.

As we will see in Chapter 8, the patterns of innovative lexical creation established in this section have ramifications for cognitive linguistics, more specifically for the cognitive typology of motion encoding.

4.3 Latin and Romance motion verbs as part of constructions

The expression of motion takes place in different languages, as Talmy (2000 II: 119) points out, through "the cross-linguistic range of meaning-form patterns". In cognitive linguistics and outside of it, such "phrasal *patterns* with identifiable and definable generalizations" or "conventional pairing[s] of form and function" of varying degrees of compositionality are known as "constructions" (Goldberg & Casenhiser 2006: 344, 349; original emphasis). As far as lexicalization of motion events is concerned, the importance of phrasal patterns is evident from a comparison of the following two German sentences with *laufen* "to run, to go, to walk": *Der Hund läuft in den Park* "The dog walks into the park" (glossed as "The dog walks in the + ACCUSATIVE park") and *Der Hund läuft in dem Park* "The dog walks around in the park" (glossed as "The dog walks in the + DATIVE park") (Slack & van der Zee 2003: 3). Therefore, the study of the evolution of motion verbs leads to the study of the evolution of the constructions formed by these verbs.

In the case of Latin, as Baldi (2006) has illustrated, the path of movement can be expressed with the help of several types of constructions. One of the options is the verb itself, more specifically the verbal stem, as in the case of FUGERE which is "primarily separative in its meaning, namely 'flee from, flee away'" (Baldi 2006: 28): e.g., *quo fugiamus?* "where should we flee?" (Plautus, *Captiui*, quoted in Baldi 2006: 28). Another option is a combination of a motion verb with a bare-case form: e.g., *ire domum* "to go home", *ire Romam* "to go to Rome" (Baldi 2006: 15). An additional alternative is a combination of a verb with a preverb governing a nominal: e.g., *quanam Alpes transierit* "by which route he had crossed the Alps" (Livy, *Ab Urbe Condita*, quoted in Baldi 2006: 16). In the next example, in addition to the preverb governing a nominal, we find an adverb: *cum prope moenibus accessiset* "but when he had come quite close to the walls" (Livy, *Ab Urbe Condita*, quoted in Baldi 2006, 16). A verb can also be accompanied by a pre-/postposition governing a nominal: e.g., *nare per aestatem liquidam* "to float through the summer air" (Virgil, *Georgica*, quoted in Baldi 2006: 20). The combination of a verb with both a preverb and a pre-/postposition is yet another alternative: e.g., *at in villam intro involant columbae* "and the doves fly into the villa, inside" (Varro, *Res Rusticae*, quoted in Baldi 2006: 27). Several options are also attested in Latin for the expression of manner. For instance, in *ad quos adnatant* "to which they swim" from Pliny the Elder's *Naturalis Historia* (quoted in Baldi 2006: 23) manner is encoded in the verbal stem. In contrast, in the passage from Q. Curtius Rufus' *Historiae Alexandri Magni* (quoted in Baldi 2006: 23) manner is encoded in the participle: *in quas et Indi et Macedones nantes [...] transibant* "which both the Indians and the Macedonians crossed [...] [by] swimming".

The Romance languages also exhibit a wide range of path and manner constructions. For example, based on a corpus of task-oriented dialogues, Mosca (2010: 52–53) identifies the following eight path types for Italian: (1) the verbal stem (e.g., *esci!* "go out"), (2) combination of the verb and the noun phrase (e.g., *attraversare un ponte* "to cross a bridge"), (3) combination of the verb and the prepositional phrase (e.g., *uscire dalla casa* "to go out of the house"), (4) path verbs that require a satellite (e.g., *girare intorno alla piazza* "to go in circles around the plaza"), (5) path verbs that accept a satellite (e.g., *svoltare a sinistra* "to turn left"), (6) path verbs accompanied by a satellite that expresses part of the trajectory (e.g., *dirigiti verso la piazza* "head toward the plaza", *dirigersi verso nord* "to head north"), (7) generic verbs accompanied by a satellite (e.g., *ti sposti verso la stazione* "move toward the station"), and (8) combination of *fare* "to make" and a noun phrase (e.g., *fai una salita* "make an exit"). In addition, Mosca (ibid., p. 62) identifies as a separate category the combinations of two path elements, the main verb and the subordinate gerund, as in *gira zigzagando intorno al palo* "it rotates around the pole while making zigzags". Manner in the Romance languages can also be encoded with the help of several types of constructions. One of the options is to package manner into the gerund that accompanies the path verb, as in the case of *corriendo* in Spanish *Los de la procesión que los vieron venir corriendo* "The ones participating in the procession who saw them running towards them" from Cervantes' *Quijote* (quoted in Cuervo 1992–1994 II: 551). Another possibility is to place manner into the verbal stem, as in *Corrieron escaleras abajo* "They ran downstairs" from the (1979) Spanish translation of Doris Lessing's (1952) novel *A Proper Marriage* (quoted in Slobin 1996: 213). Another alternative is to package manner into the adverbial clause, as in the following example from the novel *La tía Julia y el escribidor* (1977) by the Peruvian writer Mario Vargas Llosa: *Don Federico avanzó sin apresurarse* "Don Federico walked unhurriedly towards her" (quoted in Slobin 1996: 213). To offer one more example, the Romance languages can encode manner through sound symbolism, as in the case of the ideophone *zas* "boom" in Spanish *¡Zas! Se cayeron al suelo* "Boom! They fell to the ground" (Slobin 2004: 233) from an elicited narrative based on the picture story book *Frog, Where Are You?* (Mayer 1969).

The transition from the construction types attested in Latin to the construction types attested in Romance did not take place in a linear fashion (Luraghi 2010, Adams 2011). For instance, as Adams (2011) points out, throughout the history of Latin the proliferation of the prepositional expressions with motion verbs (i.e., the proliferation of the option widely used in the Romance languages) has a multifaceted motivation and a complex chronology:

> First, [...] the shift to prepositions cannot be explained simply as a move to resolve the potential ambiguities of the Classical case system where, for example, the ablative combines the functions of three earlier cases, ablative, instrumental and locative, such that a form like *Athenis* might express two different ideas, "at Athens" or "from Athens". The prepositional usages [...] are far from forming a neat system with ambiguities or polysemy eliminated. A single preposition might take on several different case functions, just as the old case endings were multifunctional. [...] Nor was there a single preposition for a single case function. [...] Second, the adoption of prepositions where an unaccompanied case form might have carried the same function cannot be put down straightforwardly to phonetic changes, such as the loss of various final consonants. Prepositions were encroaching on case forms long before phonetic developments might have played any part in undermining the Classical case system. (p. 270)

> The language as a whole had moved over to the prepositional construction by the earliest recorded Latin. One should not expect a uniform distinction between the plain case as educated form and the preposition as substandard, and equally one should not expect the prepositional expression to be uniformly, or mainly, late. The shift to prepositional expressions has a variable chronology. (p. 266)

Cognitive linguistics has a rich tradition of emphasizing the study of constructions as conventionalized pairings between form and meaning; cf. Croft & Cruse 2004: 257–290; Janda 2010: 20–21; Dirven & Ruiz de Mendoza Ibáñez 2010: 19–34; Barcelona & Valenzuela 2011: 23–25. Therefore, I share the hope expressed by one of the anonymous referees that the findings of the present study could serve as a starting point for exploration of constructional changes, building on synchronic work on constructional morphology (e.g., Booij 2010) and on diachronic research on lexical and grammatical constructionalization (e.g., Trousdale 2008a, b, Traugott & Trousdale 2013).

CHAPTER 5

Cognitive semasiology and conceptual metaphor theory

5.1 Conceptual metaphor and MOTION source domain

While cognitive onomasiology discussed in Chapters 2 through 4 focuses on the cognitive mechanisms behind the evolution of the designations of the concept 'motion', cognitive semasiology is concerned with the cognitive mechanisms behind the development of the multiple meanings (or polysemy) of such designations. One of the central interests of cognitive semasiology are the metaphorical meanings which are a type of figurative or transferred meanings. This interest is due to metaphor's recognized role as a "vehicle for expanding the range of meanings of a given word" (Hock & Joseph 1996: 222).

Motion verbs are famous for the high number of figurative meanings (i.e., those senses that express domains of experience other than motion) that they take on. As these verbs refer to such common actions as 'to go', 'to come', and 'to enter', they are used frequently. This frequency is relevant since there exists a correlation between the word's frequency and the number of its meanings: "one can observe that the more frequent a word is in literal use, the more often it will be found in combinations which then take on a specialized nonpredictable meaning" (Makkai 1978: 421). In addition to their frequency, verbs of motion possess another characteristic that enables them to take on metaphorical meanings: they are "conceptually dominant" (Miller & Johnson-Laird 1977: 527). Günter Radden explains:

> From a purely descriptive point of view, motion, i.e., change of location, might best be subcategorized as a particular type of change along with change of state, change in time, etc. From the experientialist point of view, however, motional changes are seen as more basic and salient than other types of changes, which are metaphorically understood in terms of physical motion. (Radden 1996: 425)

This idea is widely shared (e.g., Létoublon 1985: 200, 266; Langacker 1987: 168–173; Schwarze 1993: 7; Kustova 2000: 86). It is also important to remember that movement expressed by verbs of motion is movement in space, and space is a renowned source of metaphor across languages.[1] As is widely known, the localist hypothesis (e.g., Anderson 1971) and the embodiment hypothesis (e.g., Lakoff & Johnson 1999) attribute great importance to space as the source domain for expressing non-spatial concepts. Latin and Romance motion verbs are no exception to the general trend: they possess a high number of metaphorical meanings, as has been shown in many studies from Mood (1907) on Latin IRE and VENIRE to Soto Andión (2011) on Galician *pasar*.[2]

The studies in cognitive linguistics carried out within the field of semantics have postulated that metaphorical meanings reflect cognitive patterns. The pivotal point in this development was the publication of the book *Metaphors We Live By* (Lakoff & Johnson 1980) that put forward the conceptual metaphor theory.[3] Lakoff and Johnson understand metaphor as a conceptual mapping that "is pervasive in everyday language and thought, [and whose] essence [...] is understanding and experiencing one kind of thing in terms of another" (1980: ix, 5). As they write in a later work (Lakoff & Johnson 1999: 47), "conceptual metaphors are mappings across conceptual domains that structure our reasoning, our experience, and our everyday language". What is key about these definitions is that "the locus of metaphor is thought, not language" (Lakoff 2006: 186), that is to say, "Conceptual metaphors apply to concepts [...] not to words in a sentence" (Lakoff 2012: 777). Thus, Lakoff and Johnson's metaphor theory is usually referred to as cognitive or

---

1.   On space as source of metaphor, see Whorf (1956 [1939]), Greenberg (1966), Givón (1973), Comrie (1976), Lakoff & Johnson (1980), Traugott (1985a, 1985b), Dirven (1985), Langacker (1987, 1991), Lamiroy (1987), Kalisz (1990), Suxačev (1990), Bierwisch (1996), Haspelmath (1997), Blank (1997a), and Zlatev (2007).

2.   See Collitz (1928/1929, 1931) on Indo-European (including Latin, French, Italian, Spanish) motion-based metaphorical meanings of propriety, fitness, and suitability; Galán Rodríguez (1993) and Pedersen (1999) on Spanish motion verbs; Pottier Navarro (1991) on Spanish *levantar(se)*, *alzar(se)*, and *elevar(se)*; Alarcón Hernández (2004) and Paz Afonso (2009) on Spanish *pasar*; Schlyter (1978, 1979), Lamiroy (1987), and Cadiot et al. (2004, 2006) on French motion verbs; Brosman (1951) on motion verbs in Old French; Picoche (1986) on French *marcher*; Schwarze & Schepping (1995) on French *venir* and *arriver*; Pause et al. (1995) on French *partir*; Bouchard (1995) on French *aller* and *venir*; Schepping (1996) on French *aller*; McLure & Reed (1997) on French *passer*; Fillmore & Atkins (2000) on French *ramper* contrasted with English *crawl*; Stein (1999) on Italian *abbandonare*; Di Meola (2003) on Italian *andare* and *venire*; Rehfeldt (1980) on motion verbs in Brazilian Portuguese.

3.   Lakoff & Johnson (1980: xi-xiii) have acknowledged the link between their thinking and various earlier and contemporary intellectual traditions: those of Edward Sapir (1884–1939), Bronislaw Malinowski (1884–1942), Ludwig Wittgenstein (1889–1951), Benjamin Lee Whorf (1897–1941), Claude Lévi-Strauss (1908–2009), Charles Fillmore (1929–2014), and Eleanor Rosch (b.1938), among others. Lakoff has repeatedly credited the now classic study "The Conduit Metaphor – A case of frame conflict in our language about language" by Michael J. Reddy (1979) as a catalyst for his own ideas (e.g., Ruiz de Mendoza Ibáñez 1997: 40; Lakoff 2006: 186–187).

conceptual. English, for example, as mentioned in Section 1.4, has the conceptual metaphor LOVE IS A JOURNEY, which manifests itself in a number of expressions or instances such as "Look *how far we have come*", "We are *at a crossroads*", "We will just have to *go our separate ways*", "We cannot *turn back now*", "I do not think this relationship is *going anywhere*" (Lakoff & Johnson 1980: 44; original emphasis). The concept that is being understood (in this case, LOVE) is the target conceptual domain of the metaphor (also known in earlier terminology as the 'tenor'), while the concept in terms of which it is being understood (in this case, JOURNEY) is the metaphor's source conceptual domain (also known in earlier terminology as the 'vehicle') (Lakoff 1992: 418). Schematically speaking, a conceptual metaphor consists of "a source domain, a target domain, and a source-to-target mapping" (Lakoff 1987: 276). As can be inferred from LOVE IS A JOURNEY, concepts that function as source domains tend to be more concrete while concepts that function as target domains tend to be more abstract (Lakoff & Johnson 1980: 112).

Another important point in the development of the conceptual metaphor theory was the realization that a distinction should be made between primary experientially based metaphors and complex metaphors that result from unification of primary ones (Grady 1997a, Lakoff & Johnson 1999: 45–73; 2003: 254–255). For instance, LOVE IS A JOURNEY is a complex mapping that combines such primary mappings as RELATIONSHIPS ARE ENCLOSURES, INTIMACY IS CLOSENESS, PURPOSES ARE DESTINATIONS, and ACTIONS ARE SELF-PROPELLED MOTIONS (Lakoff & Johnson 1999: 60–65).[4] Experimental studies have provided support for the assumption that primary conceptual metaphors are psychologically real (e.g., Gentner et al. 2002, Casasanto & Boroditsky 2008, Casasanto 2010 on TIME IS SPACE). Researchers have also been able to offer evidence for the neural basis of primary conceptual mappings (e.g., Feldman & Narayanan 2004, Feldman 2006, Lakoff 2008, 2012). The neural perspective views primary conceptual metaphor as a "neural mechanism that enables networks used in sensorimotor activity also to serve as the substrates that make abstract reason possible" (Gibbs 2005b: 118). In other words, metaphorical thought, like other aspects of cognition, is "grounded in embodiment" (Gibbs 2005b: 3).[5]

---

4.   The distinction between primary and complex metaphors will be addressed in more detail in Chapters 7 and 9 (below).

5.   For the discussion of the embodiment hypothesis and of the meaning of the term 'embodiment' in cognitive linguistics, see Gibbs (2005a, b), Rohrer (2007), and Lakoff (2012). As Rohrer (2007: 28–31) explains, within the cognitively-oriented research, 'embodiment' has been used with at least twelve different senses which can be grouped into two categories. The first category is "embodiment as broadly experiential" (p. 31). It emphasizes the role that human experience (i.e., bodily sensations, experiences, social and cultural contexts, etc.) plays in shaping our conceptualization. The second category is "embodiment is the bodily substrate" (p. 31), which underscores the role of the physiological and neurophysiological bodily substrate. Rohrer points

A large number of metaphors identified within the conceptual metaphor theory have motion (and concepts related to motion, such as location, direction, destination, path, and distance) as their source domains. In addition to the LOVE IS A JOURNEY mapping discussed above, these metaphors[6] include, among others:

STATES ARE LOCATIONS (Lakoff & Johnson 1999: 180)
I'm in love.

A STAGE IN ACTION IS A LOCATION ALONG A PATH (Lakoff et al. 1991: 28)
She has sung her way through the anthem to the point where the really high note is.

CHANGES ARE MOVEMENTS (Lakoff & Johnson 1999: 183)
In the sun, the clothes went from wet to dry in an hour.

ACTIONS ARE SELF-PROPELLED MOTIONS (ibid., p. 52)
I'm moving right along on the project.

MANNER OF ACTION IS MANNER OF MOVEMENT (ibid., p. 188)
We slogged through it.

CAREFUL ACTION IS CAREFUL MOVEMENT (ibid., p. 188)
He is treading on thin ice.

SPEED OF ACTION IS SPEED OF MOVEMENT (ibid., p. 188)
He flew through his work.

PURPOSES ARE DESTINATIONS (ibid., pp. 52–53)
He'll ultimately be successful, but he isn't there yet.

LACK OF PURPOSE IS LACK OF DIRECTION (ibid., p. 190)
He is just floating around.

---

out that it is necessary to "acknowledge both the experiential and bodily substrate senses of 'embodiment'" (p. 31), and offers a broad definition of the embodiment hypothesis as "the claim that human physical, cognitive, and social embodiment ground our conceptual and linguistic systems" (p. 27). The importance of embodiment will come into focus in Chapter 7 (below).

6.   Within the conceptual metaphor theory some metaphors have alternate names. For instance, TIME IS A LANDSCAPE WE MOVE THROUGH is also known as TIME IS A LANDSCAPE IN WHICH EVENTS ARE LOCATED (Lakoff et al. 1991: 77). The same mapping has also been labeled TIME IS STATIONARY AND WE MOVE THROUGH IT (Lakoff & Johnson 1980: 43) and MOVING OBSERVER (Lakoff & Johnson 1999: 145–147). Some metaphors are special cases of more general mappings. For example, BEING BORN IS COMING HERE is a special case of BECOMING IS COMING HERE (Lakoff & Johnson 1999: 205–206). Besides, some linguistic realizations belong to several different mappings. For example, *You go by your beliefs* can be understood as BELIEFS ARE PATHS and BELIEFS ARE GUIDES (Lakoff et al. 1991: 110).

MAKING PROGRESS IS FORWARD MOVEMENT (ibid., p. 191)
Let's keep moving forward.

AN ARGUMENT IS A JOURNEY (Lakoff & Johnson 1980: 90)
We will proceed in a step-by-step fashion.

MORE IS UP, LESS IS DOWN (ibid., pp. 15–16)
The number of books printed each year keeps going up. Turn the heat down.

AMOUNT IS VERTICALITY (Lakoff et al. 1991: 14)
Can you please decrease the number of assignments?

LINEAR SCALES ARE PATHS (Lakoff & Johnson 1999: 51)
John's intelligence goes way beyond Bill's.

SIMILARITY IS CLOSENESS (ibid., p. 51)
These colors aren't quite the same, but they're close.

BECOMING IS COMING HERE (ibid., pp. 205–206)
things coming into existence

BEING BORN IS COMING HERE (ibid., p. 206)
the child's arrival

SUBSTANCE GOES INTO THE OBJECT (Lakoff & Johnson 1980: 73–74)
The water turned into ice.

OBJECT COMES OUT OF THE SUBSTANCE (ibid., p. 74)
Mammals developed out of reptiles.

GOOD IS UP, VIRTUE IS UP, HAPPY IS UP (ibid., pp. 15–16)
Things are looking up. She is upright. You're in high spirits.

BAD IS DOWN, DEPRAVITY IS DOWN, SAD IS DOWN (ibid., pp. 15–16)
Things are at an all-time low. I wouldn't stoop to that. He's really low these days.

CAREER PROGRESS IS VERTICAL MOVEMENT (Lakoff et al. 1991: 38)
He's half-way up the corporate ladder.

FORM IS MOTION (ibid., p. 167)
The roof slopes down before it drops off steeply.

TIME IS A MOVING OBJECT (Lakoff & Johnson 1980: 42)
Time flies.

TIME IS A LANDSCAPE WE MOVE THROUGH (Lakoff et al. 1991: 77)
We're coming up on Christmas.

THINKING IS MOVING (Lakoff & Johnson 1999: 236)
My mind wandered for a moment.

BELIEFS ARE PATHS (Lakoff et al. 1991: 110)
You go by your beliefs.

IDEAS ARE LOCATIONS (Lakoff & Johnson 1999: 236)
How did you reach that conclusion?

5.2   Conceptual metaphor and the evolution of the Romance languages

Originally, the conceptual metaphor theory focused on the English language as the source of its data. However, subsequent research has demonstrated that while it might not be possible to apply every metaphor found in English to the Romance languages, some of these metaphors, and most importantly the conceptual metaphor theory behind them, carry over to the Romance language family (e.g., Galán Rodríguez 1993, Rivano Fischer 1997, Iñesta Mena & Pamies Bertrán 2002, Llamas Saíz 2005, MetaNet[7] in progress). In fact, it has been established that certain metaphorical transfers are shared across language families, which has led linguists to advocate the creation of an inventory of such developments (Schröpfer 1956, Trubačëv 1964, Zalizniak 2001).

While Lakoff and Johnson are mostly concerned with metaphor as a synchronic phenomenon, metaphorical mapping is equally relevant for the study of language change (Traugott 1985b, 2000, Sweetser 1990, Blank 1997b, Traugott & Dasher 2002). Taking Lakoff and Johnson's research as their stepping stone, linguists working within the field of historical semasiology have placed the insights provided by the conceptual metaphor theory within the diachronic perspective. As a theoretical approach, historical cognitive semasiology highlights the importance of viewing meaning change as structured by cognition. In Olaf Jäkel's words, "in the historical development of languages, most metaphorical meaning extensions are not a matter of isolated expressions, but provide evidence of systematic metaphorical projections between whole conceptual domains" (2002: 21). Although, as pointed out by Dworkin (2010: 589), "the application of the insights provided by cognitive semantics to Romance historical semantics is still very much in its infancy", historical Romance linguistics already has amassed a

---

7.   The MetaNet is currently being developed at the University of California at Berkeley International Computer Science Institute in collaboration with researchers from other institutions. It is "a computer system capable of understanding metaphors used in English, Persian, Russian, and Spanish" which is based on "a multi-lingual metaphor repository that represents the network of conceptual metaphors and includes links to linguistic realizations" (ICSI 2012: 1, 4).

considerable amount of evidence that points towards a series of metaphorical mappings that have operated on the diachronic level within the Romance language family. For example, Blank (1997a, 2000: 67) shows the existence of the mapping TIME IS SPACE in the evolution of Romance temporal adjectives that go back to Latin spatial terms, e.g., Latin CURTUS "short (in spatial sense)" > French *court* "short (in temporal sense)". Dworkin (1997, 1998, 2002: 113; 2006a: 74; 2010: 594) identifies parallel SPACE > TIME developments in the case of Spanish *largo* ("wide, ample, generous" > "ample temporal duration"), Old French *viste* (Modern French *vite*), Old Spanish *aína*, and Spanish *rápido* ("rapid, quick in physical speed" > "rapid, quick in passage of time"). Koch (1997: 236) offers numerous diachronic examples of the mapping TO TAKE (GRASP) IS TO UNDERSTAND: Latin COMPRAEHENDERE "to take firmly, seize, grasp" > French *comprendre*, Italian *comprendere*, Spanish *comprender* "to understand"; French *saisir* "to grasp" > French *saisir* "to understand"; French *piger* "to grasp" > French (colloquial) *piger* "to understand"; Latin CAPERE "to grasp" > Italian *capire* "to understand"; Italian *afferrare* "to grasp" > Italian *afferrare* "to quickly achieve a complete understanding". Contemporary colloquial Spanish *pillar* "to seize, to grasp" shows the same development (Dworkin 2006b: 52; 2010: 588). The metaphorical mapping CONTAINER > HEAD manifests itself in such developments as Latin TESTA "pot" producing French *tête*, Italian *testa*, Old Spanish *tiesta* "head"; Latin CONCHA "shell" creating Sardinian *konka* "head" (cf. German *Kopf* "head" < Latin CUPPA "bowl", German *Haupt* "head" < Old Indo-European **kapâila* "bowl, skull"); as well as in the development of such slang terms for 'head' as French *carafe* "carafe, water-bottle", *carafon* "small carafe", *terrine* "bowl", Spanish *casco* "helmet", Argentine Spanish *mate* (of Amerindian origin) "gourd", and Peruvian Spanish *tutuma* (of Amerindian origin) "gourd" (Koch 2003b: 47; Dworkin 2006b: 53; 2010: 590–591). Santos Domínguez & Espinoza Elorza (1996) provide a great number of examples from the history of Spanish to illustrate conceptual metaphors that developed to express such target domains as TIME, UNDERSTANDING, VISION, and SMELL, among others. Dworkin (2006a) illustrates ways in which the conceptual source domain COLOR has evolved in the Romance languages to express such target domains as EMOTIONS and PHYSICAL STATES.

Furthermore, metaphor has been recognized as one of the processes underlying grammaticalization, i.e., the creation of new grammatical markers. Traugott & König (1991: 209) in their discussion of the "strengthening of informativeness and conventionalizing of conversational inferences", Hopper & Traugott (1993: 84, 87; 2003: 90, 94) in their discussion of the "semanticization of conventional inferences" and of "pragmatic enrichment", as well as Bybee et al. (1994: 285) in their discussion of "inference and implicature" have argued that the historical precursor of metaphor involved in grammaticalization is metonymy. This is to say that metaphor is regarded as resulting from metonymic changes:

> While the result of grammaticalization is often synchronically metaphorical, textual evidence for the development of many grammatical formatives out of lexical and constructional material is metonymic in the sense that it is highly context-bound and arises out of the implicatures in the speaker–hearer communicative situation. (Brinton & Traugott 2005: 28)

In other words, the approach that addresses grammaticalization in terms of the "use of lexical item in discourse > grammatical item" model highlights metonymy, while the approach that addresses grammaticalization in terms of the "lexical item > grammatical item" model highlights metaphor (Hopper & Traugott 1993: 81; 2003: 87).

According to the metaphorical extension hypothesis, the process of grammaticalization takes place through a metaphorical extension in which "the concrete meaning of an expression is applied to a more abstract context" (Heine et al. 1991: 21). Heine et al. (1991) illustrate this hypothesis with the following two sentences: *Henry is going to town* and *The rain is going to come* because sentences like the second one historically grow out of sentences like the first one. They convincingly argue (pp. 46–47) that the transition attested in these two phrases, i.e. the transition from *to be going to* as physical movement to *to be going to* as future tense, can be understood as a metaphorical transition SPACE > TIME for the following reasons: (1) both a literal and a transferred meaning are involved, (2) one domain (spatial movement) is used to refer to another domain (future), (3) the concept of spatial movement is "more easily grasped" than the concept of tense, (4) when the sentences like the second one were first introduced they probably seemed like an anomaly, (5) *to go* is usually associated with the human world, but in the second sentence we are faced with an inanimate concept, and (6) in certain contexts sentences of the type *The rain is going to come* also can be understood literally, creating ambiguity, as in *I am going to work*. In fact, some scholars have gone as far as equating grammaticalization with metaphor, defining grammaticalization as "a metaphorical shift towards the abstract" (Matisoff 1991: 384).

Although grammaticalization belongs to morphosyntactic rather than to lexical change, and therefore will not concern us in detail, it is relevant to point out that the Romance languages have created a high number of motion-based grammaticalized periphrases that did not exist in Latin. These new Romance developments have parallels in other language families. For instance, the go-future, found in Spanish, French, Portuguese, Occitan, as well as marginally in Catalan as a calque from Spanish (e.g., Spanish *Voy a leer esto mañana* "I am going to read this tomorrow"), is also a part of the grammatical inventory of Cuna, Igbo, Kishamba,

Krio, Hebrew, and Palestinian Arabic, among others (Traugott 1978: 377; Fleischman 1982: 323; Maisak 2005: 154–162). The come-future that within the Romance family is attested in Raeto-Romance (e.g., Surselvan *Nus vegním a cantar* "We are going to sing") is also found in the languages of Northern Europe (e.g., Swedish) and Africa (e.g., Akan) (Traugott 1978: 377; Maisak 2005: 193). To offer one more example, in Italian, in addition to the passive auxiliary *essere* "to be", the verbs *andare* "to go" and *venire* "to come" have been deployed as passive auxiliaries with particular semantic nuances. For instance, *andare* is commonly used with past participles of verbs that indicate loss, destruction, or disappearance, partially retaining its lexical meaning of "going (away)": e.g., *Nel 1966 a Firenze andarono distrutti capolavori inestimabili* "In 1966 priceless masterpieces were/got destroyed in Florence" (Maiden & Robustelli 2007: 282–283). The combination of *andare* with past participles of other verbs marks obligation: e.g., *Le fragole vanno lavate accuratamente, una a una* "Strawberries should be washed carefully, one by one" (ibid., p. 283). In the case of *venire*, its combination with past participles encodes passive dynamic actions: cf. *La porta viene aperta* "The door gets opened" and *La porta è aperta* "The door is open" or "The door is/gets opened" (ibid., p. 284). The go- and come-passives attested in Italian have a number of parallels in the linguistic varieties outside of the Romance family, particularly in the Indo-Iranian languages. For instance, similar to Italian, Ossetic (an Iranian language spoken in Ossetia in the central Caucasus), has three passive auxiliaries: 'be', 'go', and 'come' (Maisak 2005: 179–180). The cross-linguistic nature of Romance motion-based grammaticalization pathways is important because it provides evidence that the "cognitively natural [...] metaphorical bridges" (to use Koch 2003b: 45 terminology) postulated by the conceptual metaphor theory within semantics are also at work in historical morphosyntax. As I have discussed elsewhere, the diachronic analysis of such Romance developments from the typological perspective also has implications for the study of tense-aspect-mood (TAM) categories (Stolova 2005a), for the identification of typological universals (Stolova 2005b), and for the classification of the Romance languages (Stolova 2009a).

Similar to the case of Talmy's cognitive typology of motion encoding, Lakoff and Johnson's postulation of MOTION and SPACE conceptual source domains has also inspired a number of studies that deal with Romance data. Most of such studies, however, are synchronic. The bulk of the attention has been devoted to a better understanding of which motion-based metaphors are attested cross-linguistically and which ones are language-specific: e.g., Rivano Fischer (1997), Barcelona (2001), Iñesta Mena & Pamies Bertrán (2002), Rojo & Valenzuela (2003) in the case of Spanish. Diachronic Romance-based studies, such as Santos Domínguez & Espinoza Elorza (1996), Blank (1997a), and Dworkin (2006a) mentioned earlier in this section, constitute a clear minority. As we will see in the chapters that follow, the conceptual metaphor theory's perspective on the concept 'motion' is fully relevant for the diachronic work and vice versa.

In fact, I would argue, the principles of cognitive semasiology are particularly useful for the study of the semantic evolution of the Romance lexical field of motion verbs, as they allow to overcome important methodological challenges created by the unstable nature of this lexical field on the formal level. Inevitably, in the attempt to diachronically approach the metaphorical meanings of the semantic field of motion verbs, we are faced with the following question: how to carry out this task in a systematic way? One of the ways in which a research endeavor of this sort could be organized is by comparing the metaphorical extensions of Latin motion verbs to the metaphorical meanings of the corresponding Romance reflexes. For example, the figurative senses of Latin IRE "to go" can be compared with those of Spanish *ir*, Old Italian *gire*, Portuguese *ir*, Occitan *ir*, and Raeto-Romance *ir* "to go". However, such method, even though very logical, poses several major problems. As we have seen in Chapter 4, the vast majority of Latin prefixed verbs of motion did not survive. Neither did the deponent verbs. The infinitive of VADERE also disappeared. Furthermore, a number of verbs that did survive did so only in one single language (CEDERE in Raeto-Romance and SCANDERE/SCENDERE in Italian) or in just a few languages (SUBIRE in Spanish, Portuguese, and Romanian). Out of the twenty-six Latin verbs discussed in detail in Chapter 3 (IRE, VADERE, VENIRE, ADVENIRE, PERVENIRE, DEVENIRE, ABIRE, ABSCEDERE, INIRE, INTROIRE, INGREDI, INTRARE, EXIRE, EGREDI, EVENIRE, CONSCENDERE, ESCENDERE, SCANDERE/SCENDERE, DESCENDERE, DEGREDI, SUBIRE, AMBULARE, GRADI, CEDERE, CURRERE, SALIRE) only eight (IRE, VENIRE, AMBULARE, CURRERE, INTRARE, EXIRE, ASCENDERE, DESCENDERE) survived on the Pan-Romance or on the Inter-Romance level. Therefore, if we were to compare the metaphorical meanings of Latin motion verbs to the metaphorical meanings of these verbs' reflexes we would have to omit or to consider only partially the majority of the Latin verbs that we wanted to include. With this method of comparison we also would be unable to include the Romance motion verbs that emerged in the place of the Latin lexemes that had disappeared. More specifically, we would be unable to incorporate the Romance verbs that are not of Latin origin (e.g., Romanian *a sosi*, *a coborî*, *a pogorî*, *a scobori*). Nor would we be able to consider the numerous Romance motion verbs whose etymon did not express motion, i.e., did not refer to self-propelled movement involving translocation: Romanian *a merge* "to go" < MERGERE "to dip"; Spanish *llegar*, Portuguese *chegar* "to come", Romanian *a pleca* "to go away" < PLICARE "to fold"; Sardinian (Campidanese) *lompi* (*krompi*), Sardinian (Logudorese) *lòmpere* (*cròmpere*) "to come" < COMPLERE "to fill up, to fill out, to complete"; Spanish *partir*, French *partir*, Italian *partire*, Portuguese *partir*, Romanian *a se depărta*, Sardinian (Campidanese) *partiri*, Sardinian (Logudorese) *partìre*, Raeto-Romance *partir* "to go away" < PARTIRI/PARTIRE "to divide"; French *sortir*, Catalan *sortir*, Occitan *sortir*, Raeto-Romance *sortir* "to go out" < SORTIRI "to throw lots or to choose by a lot"; Sardinian (Campidanese) *calai* and Sardinian (Logudorese) *calare* "to go down" < Late Latin (of Greek origin) CALARE "to lower, to let down"; Spanish *saltar*, French *sauter*, Italian *saltare*, Portuguese *saltar*, Romanian *a sălta*, Catalan *saltar*, Occitan *saltar, sautar, sauter*, Sardinian (Campidanese) *sartiai*, Sardinian (Logudorese) *sartiàre* "to jump" < SALTARE "to dance".

Another potential approach could be a comparison of the figurative meanings within each one of the ten motion concepts delineated in Section 1.2. For example, the metaphorical senses of Latin IRE and VADERE "to go" could be compared to those of Spanish *ir* "to go", French *aller* "to go", Romanian *a merge* "to go", etc. However, in a number of cases this method would preclude us from comparing similar metaphorical meanings of verbs from different categories. For example, Latin AMBULARE "to walk" shares several metaphorical senses with its reflexes: French *aller*, Italian *andare*, Catalan *anar*, Occitan *anar*, Campidanese *andai*, and Logudorese *andare*. However, since the etymon belongs to the category 'movement on foot by taking steps (equivalent of *to walk*)', while the reflexes are of the category 'movement in general without any specification of means or direction (equivalent of *to go*)', this method would not allow us to consider the figurative meanings shared by these verbs.

Grouping the figurative meanings of Latin and Romance verbs according to the principles of the conceptual metaphor theory allows us to avoid the methodological problems created by the unstable nature of the semantic field of motion verbs in these languages. For instance, let us consider the following three examples. The first one is the Latin sentence from Valerius Maximus' *Facta et Dicta Memorabilia* Book III Part 4 "*De humili loco natis qui clari evaserunt*" ["Of those born in a humble situation who became illustrious"]: *Miro gradu Varro quoque ad consulatum <e> macellaria patris taberna conscendit* "It was a remarkable stride too by which Varro ascended from his father's butcher's shop to the Consulate" (Shackleton Bailey, ed. 2000: 284–285). In this example, the Latin verb CONSCENDERE "to go up" is employed metaphorically to encode social and career advancement. The second example comes from the 14-century Old Lombard (Northern Italo-Romance) paraphrase of St John Chrysostom: *O ti chi e peccaor te per questa uia e in un passo tu saltere in gloria* "Oh you who are a sinner, along this way and in one step you ascend to glory" (Foerster, ed. 1880/1883: 96). In this example, the Old Lombard verb *saltere* "to jump" metaphorically refers to improvement of one's condition such as attaining salvation.[8] The third example is a series of Modern

---

8.   The *Grande dizionario della lingua italiana* (Battaglia, ed. 1961–2009 XVII: 437) lists this example under Italian *saltare* and glosses it as "pervenire a una condizione migliore una persona" ["(of a person) to attain a better condition"].

Italian expressions *salire di grado* "to rise in rank", *salire nella gerarchia* "to rise in the hierarchy", and *salire in classifica* "to improve one's ranking" (Rubery, ed. 2010: 2361). In this series, the Modern Italian verb *salire* "to go up" metaphorically expresses success. Taken together, these Latin, Old Lombard, and Modern Italian examples can be grouped under the category 'social, career, intellectual, or moral growth expressed as moving upwards or jumping' which roughly corresponds to the conceptual metaphor theory mapping PROGRESS IS VERTICAL MOVEMENT. Such an approach allows us to circumvent the drawback of the first method by permitting us to include those Latin verbs that have disappeared (e.g., CONSCEN-DERE "to go up") and those Romance verbs whose etymon was not that of motion (e.g., Italian *saltare* "to jump" < Latin SALTARE "to dance"). It also enables us to avoid the shortcoming of the second method by allowing us to place together the metaphorical meanings of verbs whose core senses are different (e.g., Italian *salire* "to go up", Italian *saltare* "to jump").

CHAPTER 6

Semantic continuity and loss from Latin to Romance

In contrast with the prominent formal change uncovered in Chapters 3 and 4, the inventory of the metaphorical extensions, in which Latin and Romance motion verbs serve as source domains for concepts other than movement, shows remarkable continuity. In other words, when we compare the figurative meanings of Latin and Romance lexemes analyzed in Chapters 3 and 4, we observe that the conceptual associations attested in Latin are also available in Romance.[1]

6.1 Motion-based mappings shared by Latin and Romance

6.1.1 CHANGE IS MOTION

One of the mappings shared by Latin and Romance is the mapping between change and motion. Since 'change' is understood as 'change of state' and 'motion' is understood as 'change of location', this metaphor is also known as CHANGE OF STATE IS CHANGE OF LOCATION. Latin verbs that can express reaching a specified state or condition and attaining a specified stage of development are IRE "to go", INIRE "to

---

1. This chapter (and Chapters 7 and 9) contain a large number of definitions and examples from dictionaries, as well as examples from primary sources. In the case of definitions and examples from the following dictionaries, I rely on the English translations provided therein: Mansion ed. (1939), Macchi ed. (1970), Bantaş et al. (1981), Reynolds ed. (1981), Galimberti Jarman & Russell eds. (1994), and Rubery ed. (2010). In the case of Glare ed. (1982), I follow the definitions provided therein, but provide my own translation of literary passages. English translations of definitions and examples from the following dictionaries are my own: Puşcariu et al. eds. (1907–), Aulete et al. eds. (1925), Planta et al. eds. (1939–), Macrea & Petrovici eds. (1955–1957), Macrea ed. (1958), Battaglia ed. (1961–2009), Godefroy (1969), Gabrielli (1971), Guilbert et al. eds. (1971–1978), Imbs ed. (1971–1994), Fernandes (1972), Pfister (1979–), Torras i Rodergas ed. (1985), Alonso Pedraz (1986), Dvoreckij (1986), Rey ed. (1989), Rey ed. (1994), Álvar Ezquerra ed. (1990), Rapin (1991–2006), Smith (1992), Cuervo (1992–1994), Coupier (1995), Coteanu & Mareş eds. (1996), Domingo ed. (1997), Sagristà i Artigas ed. (1998), Espa (1999), De Mauro ed. (1999–2003), Puddu (2000), Decurtins (2001), Schonthal ed. (2001), Seco ed. (2003), and Geiger ed. (2008). In the case of English translations of primary sources, translations not identified with a parenthetical reference are my own as well.

go in", INTRARE "to go in", and the equivalents of "to come", i.e., VENIRE, ADVENIRE, PERVENIRE, and DEVENIRE. In the case of IRE, the combination with the preposition IN "in" and the accusative of the noun that specifies the state is widely used: e.g., *ire in matrimonium* "to marry, to get married", *ire in rixam* "to get in a quarrel", *ire in lacrimas* "to break into tears", *in possessionem ire* "to assume possession", *in obliui-onem ire* "to become forgotten, to fall into oblivion" (Glare, ed. 1982: 611; Dvorec-kij 1986: 284). The passage from Plautus' *Trinummus* Act III Scene 3 lines 729–734 serves as an illustration of *ire in matrimonium* "to marry, to get married":

(1) *Meg[aronides]: Vt mihi rem narras, Callicles, nullo modo*
     potest fieri prosus quin dos detur virgini.

     Call[icles]: Namque hercle honeste fieri ferme non potest,
     ut eam perpetiar ire in matrimonium
     sine dote, quom eius rem penes me habeam
     domi.   (Nixon, ed. 1999: 168)

     "Meg[aronides]: From what you tell me, Callicles, it is absolutely impera-
     tive, quite, that the girl be given a dowry.

     Call[icles]: Of course she must. I can hardly in common decency permit
     her to marry without one, when I have [...] that money of hers in my pos-
     session at home." (ibid., p. 169)

Another relevant example, that of *in obliuionem ire* "to fall into oblivion, to be-come forgotten", comes from Seneca the Younger's essay "*De Brevitate Vitae*", more specifically from the passage in which Seneca the Younger, writing in the 1st cen-tury A.D., argues that it is not wise to keep the record of Pompey's elephant fight of 55 B.C. in which men were put up against animals, because keeping it might prompt others to imitate such cruelty:

(2) *Depugnant? Parum est. Lancinantur? Parum est: ingenti mole animalium*
     exterantur! Satis erat ista in oblivionem ire, ne quis postea potens disceret
     invideretque rei minime humanae.   (Basore, ed. 1979: 330)
     "Do they fight to the death? That is not enough! Are they torn to pieces?
     That is not enough! Let them be crushed by animals of monstrous bulk!
     Better would it be that these things pass into oblivion lest hereafter some
     all-powerful man should learn them and be jealous of an act that was no-
     wise human." (ibid., p. 331)

In a similar way, in Virgil's *Aeneid* Book VI verse 758 uttered to Aeneas by his fa-ther Anchises, ITURAS, i.e., the future active participle of IRE "to go", is accompa-nied by the preposition IN and by the accusative NOMEN to indicate entering into possession of the name or inheriting it: *inlustris animas nostrumque in nomen ituras* "souls illustrious and heirs of our name" (Rushton Fairclough, ed. 1974: 558–559). One more case in point is Julius Caesar's use of PERVENIRE "to come" in *De Bello Gallico* Book VI Section 11 to announce that a specific point in his narrative has been reached:

(3) *Quoniam ad hunc locum perventum est, non alienum esse videtur de Galliae Germaniaeque moribus et quo differant hae nationes inter sese proponere.* (Edwards, ed. 1919: 332)
"Since I have arrived at this point, it would seem to be not inappropriate to set forth the customs of Gaul and of Germany, and the difference between these nations." (ibid., p. 333)

In the same manner as reaching a specific state, condition, or stage could be expressed with the equivalents of "to go", "to go in", and "to come", stopping being in a specific state, condition, or stage could also be expressed with motion verbs as part of a sub-metaphor of CHANGE IS MOTION known as STOPPING BEING IN A STATE IS LEAVING A LOCATION. Latin lexemes that participated in this mapping are ABIRE "to go away", ABSCEDERE "to go away", and EXIRE "to go out". For instance, in Varro's *De Lingua Latina* Book VI Section 71, EXIRE accompanied by the preposition DE "from" and the ablative of *SPONS,[2] SPONTIS "will, inclination" marks the abandonment of one's power or control:

(4) *Qui spoponderat filiam, despondisse dicebant, quod de sponte eius, id est de voluntate, exierat: non enim si volebat, dabat, quod sponsu erat alligatus: nam ut in com<o>ediis vides dici: Sponde<n> tuam gnatam filio uxorem meo?* (Kent, ed. 1999: 238)
"He who *spoponderat* 'had promised' his daughter, they said, *despondisse* 'had promised her away', because she had gone out of the power of his *sponte* 'inclination', that is, from the control of his *voluntas* 'desire': for even if he wished not to give her, still he gave her, because he was bound by his *sponsus* 'formal promise': for you see it said, as in comedies: Do you now promise your daughter to my son as wife?" (ibid., p. 239)

In addition, Latin motion verbs such as ABIRE "to go away", ABSCEDERE "to go away", INIRE "to enter", INTROIRE "to enter", INGREDI "to enter", INTRARE "to enter", EXIRE "to go out", and DESCENDERE "to go down" could encode starting or stopping doing something, starting or stopping being something, and starting or stopping being in a certain situation. For instance, in the passage from Livy's *Ab Urbe*

---

2. The nominative case was not used.

Condita Book III Part 8, INIRE expresses the process of entering the interregnum and taking on the political function of the interrex:[3]

(5) *Inde paulatim seu pace deum impetrata seu graviore tempore anni iam circumacto defuncta morbis corpora salubriora esse incipere; versisque animis iam ad publicam curam, cum aliquot interregna exissent, P. Valerius Publicola tertio die quam interregnum inierat consules creat L. Lucretium Tricipitinum et T. Veturium Geminum, sive ille Vetusius fuit.*   (Foster, ed. 1997: 26)
"After that, little by little, whether it was that the gods had been persuaded to forgive or that the sickly season was now past, those whose disease had run its course began to regain their health; and men's thoughts now turned to the commonwealth. Several interregna had expired, when Publius Valerius Publicola, three days after being made interrex, declared the election to the consulship of Lucius Lucretius Tricipitinus and Titus Veturius Geminus – or Vetusius, if that was his name." (ibid., p. 27)

Both CHANGE IS MOTION and STOPPING BEING IN A STATE IS LEAVING A LOCATION conceptual metaphors discussed above with regard to Latin are widely attested in the Romance languages. In Spanish, verbs that are recruited as the source domains of these mappings are *llegar* "to come", *entrar* "to enter", and *salir* "to go out". In the case of *llegar*, a typical expression that serves as illustration is *las cosas han llegado a tal punto, que ya no se hablan* "things have reached such a point that they are not speaking to each other now" (Galimberti Jarman & Russell, eds. 1994: 462). Another common context for the use of *llegar* is arrival at a specific point in the narrative, as in the passage from *Los tónicos de la voluntad* (1923) by Santiago Ramón y Cajal (1852–1934):

(6) *Llegados a este punto, deseará acaso el lector que, abandonando el terreno de las generalidades, definamos el tipo de mujer más adecuado al hombre de ciencia.*   (quoted in Cuervo 1992–1994 VI: 195)
"As this point in our narrative has been reached, the reader would probably prefer that we abandon the discussion of general themes and define the type of woman compatible with a man dedicated to scientific pursuit."

Relevant collocations with Spanish *entrar* "to go in" and *salir* "to go out" are *al entrar en la pubertad* "on reaching puberty", *salir del apuro* "to get out of an awkward situation" (Galimberti Jarman & Russell, eds. 1994: 307, 684), and *salir de dudas* "to no longer be in doubt" (Álvar Ezquerra, ed. 1990: 983). Earlier Old Spanish instances with *entrar* and *salir* include *entrar en la heredad* "to inherit"

---

3.   This passage also contains the verb EXIRE in reference to the conclusion of the interregna, thus illustrating the metaphor TIME IS MOTION discussed in 6.1.21 and 6.1.22 (below).

and *salir del poder* "to stop depending on" exemplified by the 13th-century passages in (7) and (8), respectively:

(7) *Otrosi dezimos que si alguno que fuese deseredado callase & no querellase*
    fasta çinco años despues que el heredero <u>ouiese entrado</u> enla heredad del
    testador que delos çinco años en adelante no se podia querellar [...].

    (Alfonso X, *Estoria de España*, accessed through Davies 2007)
    "In addition, we say that if someone who was left without the inheritance
    did not speak up and did not appeal for five years after the heir assumed
    the inheritance from the testator, then it is not possible to appeal after five
    years [...]."

(8) *Porhijar pueden todo onbre libre que <u>es sallido</u>[4] de poder de su padre.*

    (Alfonso X, *Siete partidas*, accessed through Davies 2007)
    "Any free man who has stopped being dependent upon his father can
    adopt."

French equivalents of "to come", "to go in", and "to go out" are also well suited to
encode the metaphorical functions in question. As far as *venir* and *sortir* are concerned, it is pertinent to mention such expressions as *venir à résipiscence* "to reach
repentance", *venir à la démocratie* "to reach democracy" (Rey, ed. 1989 IX: 674), and
aider quelqu'un à sortir d'une difficulté "to help someone to get out of a difficult
situation" (Mansion, ed. 1939 I: 793). The phrase from *Les Contemporains* (1885) by
Jules Lemaître (1853–1914) illustrates how reaching a specific point in the narrative
can be rendered by French *arriver: Nous arrivons ainsi à la troisième idée de M. de
Banville, à sa théorie de la rime* "This way we reach Banville's third idea, his theory
of rhyme" (quoted in Imbs, ed. 1971–1994 XVI: 570). In the case of *entrer*, relevant
collocations include *entrer en colère* "to lose one's temper, to become angry", *entrer
en fureur* "to become enraged", *entrer en guerre* "to enter the war", and *entrer en
pourparlers* "to start negotiations" (Guilbert et al., eds. 1971–1978 II: 1664).

    Parallel types of usage are available for Italian *andare* "to go", *venire* "to come",
arrivare "to come", *giungere* "to come", *entrare* "to go in", *uscire* "to go out", *salire* "to
go up", *montare* "to go up", and *saltare* "to jump". Examples from Reynolds ed. (1981
I: 39, 854) offer a representative range for *andare* and *venire: andare in collera* "to
lose one's temper", *andare in aceto* "to turn to vinegar", *venire in fama* "to become

---

4. *Salir* in (8) is conjugated with the auxiliary *ser* "to be" rather than with the auxiliary *haber*
"to have" – cf. *entrar* conjugated with *haber* in (7) – because in contrast with Modern Spanish
which relies exclusively on *haber*, Old Spanish had two perfective auxiliaries. For the discussion
of cognitive factors that play a role in the auxiliary selection between 'be' and 'have' in 13th-
century Spanish and other Romance varieties, see Stolova (2006, 2007). On the survival of the
remnants of the perfective auxiliary *ser* in post-Classical Spanish, see Stolova (2009b).

famous", *venire alle strette* "to come to the point, to touch on the heart of the matter". In the case of *arrivare, entrare, uscire,* and *giungere,* pertinent expressions include *a che punto sono arrivati col lavoro?* "how far have they got with the work?", *entrare in guerra* "to enter the war", *uscire dalla depressione* "to come out of depression" (Rubery, ed. 2010: 1517, 1805, 2575), and *sono giunto al capitolo terzo* "I have got as far as chapter three" (Macchi, ed. 1970 I: 588). A number of relevant collocations with *montare* and *salire* are found in Battaglia ed. (1961–2009 X: 847; XVII: 409, 437): *montare in orgoglio* "to become snobbish", *salire in collera, salire in furore, salire sulle furie* "to become furious", *saltare in superbia* "to become arrogant".

In Portuguese, *vir* "to come", *chegar* "to come", *entrar* "to go out", *sair* "to go out", and *descer* "to go down" form similar expressions: e.g., *entrar em uma desordem* "to get into chaos", *sair da adolescência* "to leave adolescence behind" (Fernandes 1972: 291, 538). In the case of Catalan *arribar* "to come", *venir* "to come", *entrar* "to go in", and *sortir* "to go out", parallel examples include *encara no hem arribat a la meitat de l'assignatura* "we have not yet reached the midpoint of the course" (Torras i Rodergas, ed. 1985: 834–835), *venir a madurament un gra* "to ripen (of grain)", *entrar en convalescència* "to start recuperation", *entrar en activitat un volcà* "to become active (of a volcano)", *sortir de dubtes* "to stop being in doubt", and *sortir d'una dificultat* "to get out of a difficult situation" (Sagristà i Artigas, ed. 1998: 1726, 640, 1570). Analogous patterns are available in Occitan, Sardinian, and Raeto-Romance. In the case of Occitan, it is pertinent to mention such expressions with *intrar* "to enter" and *sortir* "to go out" as *intra au service de quaucun* "to enter into someone's service" and *sourti de l'enfantuegno* "to leave childhood behind" (Coupier 1995: 508, 1315). In the case of Sardinian, applicable examples are Logudorese *bènnere* "to come" in *bènner mama* "to become a mother" and *bènner reína* "to become a queen" (Espa 1999: 212), as well as Campidanese *lompi* "to come" and its Logudorese equivalent *lòmpere* (*cròmpere*) used in reference to fruit that has turned ripe (Puddu 2000: 1085): e.g., *sa castanza daghi est lómpida nde falat sola* "when the chestnut is ripe it falls by itself" (Espa 1999: 810). As for Raeto-Romance, relevant collocations with *ir* "to go", *gnir* "to come", *vegnir* "to come", and *entrar* "to enter" include *ir en emblidonza* "to go into oblivion", *gnir da grass* "to become greasy", *vegnir da meffa* "to become moldy, to molder", *entrar en parentella cun enzatgi* "to become related to somebody by marriage", *entrar en matrimoni* "to marry", and *entrar en la tentaziun* "to become tempted" (Planta et al., eds. 1939– VII: 571; VIII: 605, 603; X: 33).

In Romanian, the lexemes that have the metaphorical extensions in question are *a veni* "to come", *a sosi* "to come", *a intra* "to enter", and *a ieşi* "to go out". For instance, the passage from the religious text "*Învăţătură asupra pocăinţii*" by Antim Ivireanul (c.1650–1716) contains the expression *a veni în viaţă* "to come to life":[5]

---

5.   This expression is marked as archaic and rare (Puşcariu et al., eds. 1907– XIII: I: 308).

(9) *În dată ce s-au atins trupul mortului de oasele prorocului, au înviat și au venit iară în viață.* (quoted in Pușcariu et al., eds. 1907– XIII: I: 308)
"As soon as the dead body touched the prophet's bones, it resurrected and came back to life."

In the next example, Romanian *a sosi* "to come" accompanies the noun *situație* in the description of having reached a specified situation:[6]

(10) *Și am sosit unde sîntem astăzi; într-o situație pe care nu o poate îngădui oată lumea.* (August Scriban, *Dicționaru limbii românești*, 1939, quoted in Pușcariu et al., eds. 1907– X: A 4-A: 1258)
"And we arrived at a situation where we are today; a situation that not everyone can allow."

In a similar way, Romanian *a intra* "to enter" can combine with a range of nouns to announce the beginning of a new state or stage: e.g., *a intra în vorbă cu cineva* "to enter into a conversation with somebody", *a intra de serviciu* "to begin one's duty or shift", *a intra în război* "to enter the war", *a intra în luptă* "to enter a fight", *a intra în acțiune* "to go into action, to start operating", *a intra în vigoare* "to go into effect, to become effective" (Coteanu & Mareș, eds. 1996: 502). Along the same lines, in a passage from the historical novella *Alexandru Lăpușneanu* (1840) by Costache Negruzzi (1808–1868), *a intra* combines with the noun *favor* "benevolence" to encode the fact that the subject had gained someone's good will; cf. Latin *gratiam inire* "to win favor in a person's eyes" (Glare, ed. 1982: 891):

(11) *[Domnul] avusese o lungă vorbă cu Moțoc, care intrase iar în favor.* (quoted in Pușcariu et al., eds. 1907– II: I: 818)
"[The ruler] had had a long talk with Moțoc, who again had gained benevolence."

In another earlier Romanian example which comes from the *Minei* (church book) for October 1776 published by Chesarie, bishop of Rîmnic 1773–1780, abandoning the state of composure is rendered by combining the reflexive form of *a ieși* "to go out" and *fire* "reason": *Își eși din fire* "He lost his temper" (quoted in Pușcariu et al., eds. 1907– II: I: 459).

6.1.2   A STAGE IN AN ACTION IS A LOCATION ALONG THE PATH

States and stages in CHANGE IS MOTION can occur in succession, and Latin and Romance motion verbs are equally well suited to express sequential actions that take place in particular order as part of A STAGE IN AN ACTION IS A LOCATION

---

6.   This type of usage is marked as archaic (Pușcariu et al., eds. 1907– X: A 4-A: 1258).

ALONG THE PATH mapping. A comparison between Italian *scendere* "to go down" from a 17th-century text and Latin DESCENDERE "to go down" from a text composed in the 1st century B.C. serves as illustration. In the Italian example from writings by Secondo Lancellotti (1583–1643), *scendere* encodes a succession of different subject matters in a narrative:

(12)   *Non avendo altro che dire della matematica in generale, scendo alla geometria.*   (quoted in Battaglia, ed. 1961–2009 XVII: 935)
       "Not having anything more to say about mathematics in general, I proceed to geometry."

In the Latin example from Book II Part 1 Section 3 of Varro's *Res Rusticae*, DESCENDERE, which appears four times (twice as DESCENDISSE, once as DESCENDERUNT, and once as DESCENDERANT), makes reference to the stages of human evolution:

(13)   *Igitur, inquam, et homines et pecudes cum semper fuisse sit necesse natura [...] necesse est humanae vitae ab summa memoria gradatim descendisse ad hanc aetatem, ut scribit Dicaearchus, et summum gradum fuisse naturalem, cum viverent homines ex his rebus, quae inviolata ultro ferret terra, ex hac vita in secundam descendisse pastoriciam, e feris atque agrestibus ut arboribus ac virgultis decarpendo glandem, arbutum, mora, poma colligerent ad usum, sic ex animalibus cum propter eandem utilitatem, quae possent, silvestria dependerent ac concluderent at manusuescerent. [...] Tertio denique gradu a vita pastorali ad agri culturam descenderunt, in qua ex duobus gradibus superioribus retinuerunt multa, et quo descenderant, ibi processerunt longe, dum ad nos perveniret.*   (Hooper, ed. 1999: 312)
       "I began: 'As it is a necessity of nature that people and flocks have always existed [...] it is a necessity that from the remotest antiquity of human life they have come down, as Dicaearchus teaches, step by step to our age, and that the most distant stage was that state of nature in which man lived on those products which the virgin earth brought forth on her own accord; they descended from this stage into the second, the pastoral, in which they gathered for their use acorns, arbutus berries, mulberries, and other fruits by plucking them from wild and uncultivated trees and bushes, and likewise caught, shut up, and tamed such wild animals as they could for the like advantage. [...] Then by a third stage man came from the pastoral life to that of the tiller of the soil; in this they retained much of the former two stages, and after reaching it they went far before reaching our stage[']."
       (ibid., pp. 313, 315)

6.1.3 PURPOSES ARE DESTINATIONS

Since reaching a specific state, condition, or stage is often the result of conscious and purposeful effort, another metaphorical mapping closely related to CHANGE IS MOTION and widely attested in both Latin and Romance is PURPOSES ARE DESTINATIONS, also known as DESIRED STATES ARE DESIRED LOCATIONS. For instance, in the passage from Book V Part 5 of Livy's *Ab Urbe Condita*, PERVENIRE "to come" marks the completion by the soldiers of the challenging task of building fortifications:

(14)   *Vallum fossamque, ingentis utrumque operis, per tantum spatii duxerunt: castella primo pauca, postea exercitu aucto creberrima fecerunt; munitiones non in urbem modo sed in Etruriam etiam spectantes, si qua inde auxilia veniant, opposuere; quid turres, quid vineas testudinesque et alium oppugnandarum urbium apparatum loquar? Cum tantum laboris exhaustum sit et ad finem iam operis tandem perventum, relinquendane haec censetis, ut ad aestatem rursus novus de integro his instituendis exsudetur labor?*

(Foster, ed. 2002: 16)

"The rampart and the trench, each involving prodigious toil, they have carried all that distance; forts they erected only a few at first, but since then, with the growth of the army, they have built very many; they have thrown up earthworks, not only against the city, but also facing Etruria, if any aid should come from that side; what need to speak of towers, mantlets, penthouses, and the rest of the equipment for storming towns? When they have expended all this labour, and the end of their task is at last at sight, do you vote for abandoning these things, that when summer comes they may sweat and toil again to produce them afresh?" (ibid., p. 17)

Likewise, in Book VI Part 6 of Celsus' *De Medicina*, PERVENIRE is used in the context of accomplishing a cure: *nam melius eodem ratione victus et idoneis medicamentis pervenitur* "for the same result is better attained by dieting and proper medicaments" (Spencer, ed. 1989: 216–217).

The Romance equivalents of "to come, to arrive" are equally well suited to serve as the source domain in the mapping in question. In the case of Spanish *llegar*, relevant examples include *por ambos métodos llegamos al mismo resultado* "we reach the same result by both methods", *nunca llegó a (ser) director* "he never made it to director", and *no se llegó a ningún acuerdo* "no agreement was reached" (Galimberti Jarman & Russell, eds. 1994: 461–462). For French *arriver*, it is pertinent to mention the famous saying *avec du courage on arrive à tout* "with courage one can achieve anything" (Mansion, ed. 1939 I: 54). Italian *arrivare*, *venire*, and *giungere* can appear in such contexts as *arrivare a fare* "to succeed in doing" (Rubery, ed. 2010: 1517), *venire alla verità* "to arrive at the truth" (Reynolds, ed. 1981 I: 854), and *giunse a scoprire il ladro* "he succeeded in discovering the thief" (Macchi, ed. 1970 I: 589). Similar Portuguese expressions with *chegar* and *vir* include *chegou a ministro* "he made it to minister" and *vir a (um) acordo* "to come to an agreement" (Fernandes 1972: 143, 598). Romanian *a ajunge* and *a veni* offer comparable collocations: *a ajunge la un acord* "to come to an agreement", *a ajunge la un compromis* "to reach a compromise, to come to terms", *a ajunge la perfecțiune* "to attain perfection", *a veni la putere* "to come (in) to power, to rise to power" (Bantaș et al. 1981: 18, 633). In the case of Catalan *arribar* and Sardinian (Logudorese) *arrivare*, relevant examples include *després de discutir arribaren a un acord* "after the argument they came to an agreement" (Torras i Rodergas, ed. 1985: 1304) and *arrivare a cumprèndere* "to achieve understanding" (Espa 1999: 141). Parallel Raeto-Romance instances with *arrivar* and *vegnir* are *arrivar alla perschuasiun* "to become convinced" and *vegnir mistral* "to become the cantonal president" (Decurtins 2001: 36, 1187). As we will see in Chapter 9, it is significant that such Romance innovative equivalents of "to come, to arrive" as Spanish *llegar*, Portuguese *chegar*, French *arriver*, Italian *arrivare*, Catalan *arribar*, Sardinian (Logudorese) *arrivare*, Raeto-Romance *arrivar*, Italian *giungere*, and Romanian *a ajunge* share the mapping under investigation with their Latin counterpart PERVENIRE.

6.1.4   ORIGINATING IS MOTION

Latin and Romance motion verbs are frequently recruited to express provenance. The metaphorical extension in question works for a wide range of subjects: animate beings, natural phenomena, concrete nouns, and abstract nouns. For instance, in Varro's *Res Rusticae* Book II Part 6 Section 2, we find EXIRE "to go out" in reference to the origin of the livestock selected for breeding: *ex his locis, unde optimi (asini) exeunt* "from those places from which the best (donkeys) originate" (quoted in Glare, ed. 1982: 640). In a similar way, in Book XVIII Section 278 of his *Naturalis Historia*, Pliny the Elder relies on EXIRE when talking about the source of tempests: *haec ab horridis sideribus exeunt* "these originate from harmful constellations" (quoted in Glare, ed. 1982: 640). The excerpt with Portuguese *venir de* "to come from" used as an equivalent of *resultar de* "to result from, to originate from" shows that the metaphorical extension available in Latin is attested in the Romance languages as well:

(15)   *Divide [Bacon] ele os erros em quatro categorias, a saber, idola tribus, ou erros da natureza humana, idola specus, ou erros individuais, idola fori, ou erros de linguagem, e finalmente idola theatri, ou erros dos sistemas. <u>Resultam</u> eles, no primeiro caso, <u>da</u> imperfeição dos sentidos [...]. No segundo caso, a fonte dos errores <u>vem da</u> diferença entre os espíritos, uns que*

*se perdem nos pormenores, outros em vastas generalizações, e também da
predilecção que temos por certas ciências, o que nos inclina a tudo querer
reduzir a elas.*   (Saramago 1989, accessed through COMPARA)
"He [Bacon] divides errors into four categories, as follows, *idola tribus*, or
the errors of human nature, *idola specus*, or the errors of individuals, *idola
fori*, or linguistic errors, and finally, *idola theatri*, or errors of systems. In the
first instance, these result from the imperfection of the senses [...]. In the
second instance, the source of errors comes from the difference between
minds, some that lose themselves in details, others in vast generalizations,
as well as from our preference for certain sciences to which we are inclined
to reduce everything."   (Saramago 1996, accessed through COMPARA)

Relevant Gallo-Romance examples include French *la confiance vient du savoir*
"confidence is born of knowledge" (Mansion, ed. 1939 I: 881) as well as Occitan *tè
que vèn de Ceilan* "tea that comes from Ceylon", *mot que vèn dóu latin* "word that
comes from Latin", and *lou poudé vèn dóu pople* "power comes from people"
(Coupier 1995: 1468). Similarly, in Raeto-Romance *quella dispetta ei vagnida en-
tras tei* "this quarrel has come from you" (Planta et al., eds. 1939– VII: 566), *gnir*
"to come" indicates the source of the conflict. Likewise, in the Raeto-Romance
excerpt from the legal text *Cudisch civil svizzer* (1907), *descender* "to go down"
encodes origin: *Duas persunas ein parentads en lingia directa, sch'ina descenda da
l'autra* "Two people are directly related to one another when one person descends
from another" (quoted in Planta et al., eds. 1939– V: 177). Along the same lines, in
the passage from *Călătorii în Palestina și Egipt* (1856) by Dimitrie Bolintineanu
(c.1819–1872), Romanian *a veni* "to come" refers to the origin of the river: *La
umbra acestor arbori, cură un rîuleț ce vine din muntele Carantania* "In the shadow
of these trees flows a little river that comes from the mountain Carantania" (quoted
in Pușcariu et al., eds. 1907– XIII: I: 309).

6.1.5   EXISTENCE IS MOTION

Coming into existence, appearing, occurring, and happening is another set of concepts commonly rendered by motion verbs in both Latin and its daughter languages. For instance, the passage from Part 157 Section 13 of Catos' *De Agri
Cultura* employs VENIRE "to come" in combination with the noun MORBUS "sickness" in the discussion of ways to prevent sickness from taking place:

(16)   *Brassica erratica maximam vim habet. Eam arfacere et conterere oportet bene
minutam. Siquem purgare voles, pridie ne cenet, mane ieiuno dato brassicam
tritam, aquae cyatos iiii. [...] Qui sic purgatus erit, diutina valetudine utetur,
neque ullus morbus veniet nisi sea culpa.*   (Hooper, ed. 1999: 148, 150)

"Wild cabbage has the greatest strengths; it should be dried and macerated very fine. When it is used as a purge, let the patient refrain from food the previous night, and in the morning, still fasting, take macerated cabbage with four cyathi of water. [...] One so purged will enjoy good health for a long time, and no sickness will attack him except by his own fault." (ibid., pp. 149, 151)

Likewise, in the passage from writings by Ioan Alexandru Brătescu-Voinești (1868–1946), Romanian *a veni* "to come" accompanies the noun *pandalii* "whim, craze", making reference to the psychic state that overcomes the person:

(17)   *Cel mai de căpetenie lucru pe care-l face Finuleţ cînd îi <u>vin</u> pandaliile e că aprinde douăsprezece lumînări pe pridvorul casei şi cîntă cîntece bisericeşti.*
                    (quoted in Puşcariu et al., eds. 1907– XIII: I: 319)
"The very first thing that Finuleţ does when crazed impulses come to him, is to light twelve candles on the balcony of the house and sing church songs."

Along the same lines, in the passage from *Convorbiri literare* IX, Romanian *a veni* is used with the noun *lacrimi* "tears" in the description of their appearance: *Bietul cîne! [...] zise ea înduioşată [...], simţind că lacrimile îi vin în ochi* "Poor dog! [...] she said heartfelt [...], feeling tears come to her eyes" (quoted in Puşcariu et al., eds. 1907– XIII: I: 318). Other relevant expressions with equivalents of "to come, to arrive" include French *cela arrive tous les jours* "it happens every day" (Mansion, ed. 1939 I: 54) and Raeto-Romance *que po arriver* "this can happen" (Planta et al., eds. 1939– I: 416). Equivalents of "to go out" also participate in the mapping in question, as in the case of French *sortir*, Italian *uscire*, and Spanish *salir*: e.g., *les collections de printemps sont sorties* "the spring collections came out" (Rey, ed. 1989 VIII: 859), *questo giornale esce di martedì* "this magazine comes out on Tuesdays" (Rubery, ed. 2010: 2575), and *la noticia salió en primera página* "the news appeared on the front page" (Galimberti Jarman & Russell, eds. 1994: 684).

6.1.6   DISAPPEARING IS MOTION

Similarly to the metaphorical mapping between appearing or coming into existence and motion discussed in Section 6.1.5, disappearing or stopping to exist can also be rendered by motion verbs. For instance, in the passage from Pliny the Elder's *Naturalis Historia* Book XXI Section 67, we find ABIRE "to go away" in reference to the fact that with change of seasons summer flowers no longer remain in the state of bloom and end their existence:

(18) *Florum prima ver nuntiantium viola alba – tepidioribus vero locis etiam*
      hieme emicat – post ea quae ion appellatur et purpurea, proxime flamme-
      um, quod phlox vocatur, silvestre dumtaxat. [...] Succedunt illis aestivi,
      lychnis et Iovis flos et alterum genus lilii, item iphyon et amaracus quem
      Phrygium cognominant. [...] et iris aestate floret. <u>abeunt</u> et hi marcescuntque.
                                                          (Jones, ed. 1951: 206, 208)
      "The first flower to herald the approach of spring is the white violet, which
      moreover in the warmer spots peeps out even in winter. Afterwards comes
      the violet which is called ion, and the mauve one, followed closely by the
      flame-coloured flower called phlox, but only the wild variety. [...] After
      them come the summer flowers, lychnis, Jupiter's flower, a second kind of
      lily, the iphyon also and the amaracus surnamed Phrygian. [...] The iris
      also blooms in summer. But these too wither and pass away [...]." (ibid.,
      pp. 207, 209)

A parallel example with an inanimate subject is Cato's use of ABIRE in *De Agri*
Cultura Part 135: *in conmissura abibit p. iii* "three feet will disappear in the fasten-
ing [of the rope]" (quoted in Glare, ed. 1982: 5). In the case of French *s'en aller* "to
go away", relevant instances include *Sa volonté s'en va peu à peu* "His resolve disappears little by little" and *Les taches d'encre s'en vont avec ce produit* "Ink stains disappear with this product" (Rey, ed. 1989 I: 262). This latter expression brings to mind
similar patterns with Romanian *a ieși* "to go out" such as *Petele n'au vrut să iasă*
nici cu săpun, nici cu benzină "The spots did not want to disappear neither with
soap nor with gasoline" and *Iese la spălat* "Fades when washed" (Pușcariu et al.,
eds. 1907– II: I: 459). A comparable earlier Romance example with Spanish *salir*
"to go out" comes from the 15th-century translation by Fray Vicente de Burgos of
Bartholomew Anglicus' 13th-century *Liber de proprietatibus rerum*:

(19) *El azeyte mancha las ropas que toca & agrand pena puede su mancha <u>salir</u>*
      & dexa ende su olor & quando es esparzido en agua se va por vnas pequeñas
      gotas sin se mezclar con el agua.   (accessed through Davies 2007)
      "Oil stains the clothes that it touches. Its stain can disappear with great
      difficulty, and it leaves behind its smell. When it is spread in water it does
      not mix with it and creates little drops."

6.1.7 LINEAR SCALES ARE PATHS

Latin and the Romance languages also share the ability to map between horizontal
motion and quantity. For instance, in Julius Caesar's *De Bello Ciuili* Book I Section
52, Latin PERVENIRE "to come" combines with the noun ANNONA "price of provisions": *iam [...] ad x l in singulos modios annona pervenerat* "the price of provisions

had already reached fifty denarii a peck" (quoted in Glare, ed. 1982: 1363). This usage of Latin PERVENIRE is analogous to the function of Romanian *a sosi* "to come" in the 17th-century *Cronica lui Mihail Moxa*:

(20)   *În foamete mare în Ţarigrad de sosi chila de grîu cîte un galben.*
                    (quoted in Puşcariu et al., eds. 1907– X: 4A: 1258)
       "During the great famine in Ţarigrad the price for a kilo of wheat reached a gold coin."

Italian *arrivare* "to come" offers a comparable example form the 16th-century *I trattati dell'oreficeria e della scultura* by Benvenuto Cellini (1500–1571):

(21)   *Al suo tesauriere comandò che mi dessi un diamante che arrivassi a trecento scudi.*   (quoted in Battaglia, ed. 1961–2009 I: 691)
       "He ordered his treasurer to give me a diamond whose value would reach three hundred escudos."

In the case of French *arriver* "to come", a typical similar pattern is *Le dollar est arrivé à x francs* "The exchange rate reached ten francs for one dollar" (Rey, ed. 1989 I: 562). Spanish *llegar* "to come" and Portuguese *chegar* "to come" can appear in a comparable context: *El gasto llegó a diez mil pesetas* "The amount spent reached ten thousand pesetas" (Álvar Ezquerra, ed. 1990: 674) and *As despesas não chegam a 200$* "The expenses do not reach two hundred dollars" (Fernandes 1972: 143). A subtype of this usage is employing equivalents of "to come" in reference to reaching the amount required for everybody, that is, to being enough, as in Catalan *el menjar no arriba per a tothom* "there is not enough food for everyone" (Torras i Rodergas, ed. 1985: 834), Spanish *con un kilo llega para todos* "a kilo will do for all of us" (Galimberti Jarman & Russell, eds. 1994: 461), and Raeto-Romance *que nu riva par tuots* "this is not enough for everyone" (Planta et al., eds. 1939– I: 416). As we will see in Chapter 9, it is significant that although none of the Romance lexemes analyzed in this subsection go back to Latin PERVENIRE, they are nevertheless able to share its metaphorical function.

6.1.8   AMOUNT IS VERTICALITY, MORE IS UP, LESS IS DOWN

While the mapping discussed in 6.1.7 projects between quantities and horizontal motion, metaphorical associations are also possible between quantities and vertical movement. For instance, in Book I Section 24 of Varro's *Res Rusticae*, DESCENDERE "to go down" marks a decrease in quantity: *ut ad cxx (modios) descendat (hostus)* "so that (the amount of expressed olive oil) decreases to 120 (modii)" (quoted in Glare, ed. 1982: 523). In the example from Book VI Part 1 Section 29 of Quintilian's *Institutio Oratoria*, DESCENDERE makes reference to the reduction in intensity of an emotion: *facile deficit adfectus qui descendit* "the emotion that declines easily disappears" (quoted in Glare, ed. 1982: 523). The same verb is able to express a decrease in intensity of color. In the passage from Book XXXVII Sections 121–123 and 125 of Pliny the Elder's *Naturalis Historia*, it appears four times (once as DESCENDUNT, twice as DESCENDIT, and once as DESCENDENS) in the comparison of the purple Indian amethyst with stones whose color is not as prominent, such as other kinds of amethyst and the hyacinth, i.e., the blue sapphire:

(22) *Alius ex hoc ordo purpureis dabitur aut quae ab iis <u>descendunt</u>. principatum amethysti tenent Indicae [...]. Indica absolutum Phoeniciae purpurae colorem habet. [...] alterum earum genus <u>descendit</u> ad hyacinthos; hunc colorem Indi socon vocant, talemque gemmam socondion. dilutior ex eodem sapenos vocatur, eademque pharanitis in contermino Arabiae, gentis nomine. quartum genus colorem vini habet. quintum ad vicina crystalli <u>descendit</u> albicante purpurae defectu. [...] Multum ab hac distat hyacinthos, ab vicino tamen colore <u>descendens</u>. differentia haec est, quod ille emicans in amethysto fulgor violaceus diluitur hyacintho primoque aspectu gratus evanescit antequam satiet, adeoque non inplet oculos ut paene non attingat, marcescens celerius nominis sui flore.*   (Eichholz, ed. 1962: 262, 264, 266)

"Next, we shall assign to another category purple stones or those varieties that deviate from them. Here the first rank is held by the amethysts of India [...]. The Indian amethyst has the perfect shade of Tyrian purple at its best [...]. A second kind of amethyst deviates towards the sapphire. Its color is known to the Indians as 'socos,' and the variety of gem as 'socondios.' A fainter variety of the same stone is called 'sapenos' and also, in the districts adjacent to Arabia, 'pharanitis' after the name of a tribe. A fourth kind has the colour of red wine, while a fifth degenerates nearly into rock-crystal, since its purple fades away towards colourlessness. [...] There is a considerable difference between the amethyst and the 'hyacinthus,' which, however, shows only a slight deviation from a closely related tint. The difference lies in the fact that the brilliant violet radiance that is characteristic of the amethyst is here diluted with the tint of the 'hyacinth flower'; and although at first sight the colour is agreeable, it loses its power before we can take our fill of it and, indeed, is so far from satisfying the eye that it almost fails to strike it and droops more rapidly that the flower of the same name." (ibid., pp. 263, 265, 267)

Another case in point is the use of Latin DESCENDERE in reference to lowering the pitch of one's voice, i.e., going from a pitch corresponding to a higher number of sound wave cycles per second to a pitch corresponding to a lower frequency of such cycles. The excerpt from Book I Preface 16 of Seneca the Elder's *Controuersiae*, in which the author remembers his friend Porcius Latro, serves as illustration:

(23)   *Vox robusta, sed surda, lucubrationibus et neglegentia, non natura infuscata; beneficio tamen laterum extollebatur, et, quamvis inter initia parum attulisse virium videretur, ipsa actione adcrescebat. Nulla umquam illi cura vocis exercendae fuit; illum fortem et agrestem et hispanae consuetudinis morem non poterat dediscere: utcumque res tulerat, ita vivere, nihil vocis causa facere, non illam per gradus paulatim ab imo ad summum perducere, non rursus a summa contentione paribus intervallis descendere, [...].*

(Winterbottom, ed. 1974a: 16)

"His voice was strong but dull, thickened not by nature but by over-work and lack of care. But it was capable of being raised, thanks to the strength of his lungs, and though at the start of a speech it might be thought to have too little power in reserve it grew with the impetus of the speech itself. He never took any trouble to exercise his voice; he could not put off his steadfast, rustic, Spanish character: his motto was to live as circumstances suggested, without doing anything for the sake of his voice (such as gradually taking it up from low to high, and then going down again from the highest pitch by equal intervals), [...]." (ibid., p. 17)

The Romance equivalents of "to go up" and "to go down" offer comparable examples. In the case of Spanish *subir* and *bajar*, it is pertinent to mention such expressions as *sube el volumen* "turn the volume up", *sube el tono* "speak up", *sube un poco la calefacción* "turn the heat up a little", and *nuestro volumen de ventas no ha bajado* "our turnover has not decreased" (Galimberti Jarman & Russell, eds. 1994: 716, 83). In the case of French *monter* and *descendre*, relevant examples are *Les enchères ont monté à dix mille francs* "The bidding went up to ten thousand francs" and *Le thermomètre a descendu de deux degrés* "The thermometer has fallen two degrees" (Mansion, ed. 1939 I: 549, 256). Similar expressions with Italian *salire* and *scendere* include *È salito il prezzo della benzina* "Petrol has gone up (in price)", *Le auto stanno scendendo di prezzo* "Cars are coming down in price", and *Scese al terzo posto* "She dropped to third place" (Rubery, ed. 2010: 2361, 2381). The passage from writings by the contemporary Angolan writer José Eduardo Agualusa illustrates the use of Portuguese *subir* in the context of raising the person's voice to command the attention of his audience:

(24)   *O fenómeno que irão testemunhar, digníssimo público, não é obra de demiurgos nem de magos; é fruto de muitos anos de estudos científicos, de canseiras e trabalhos inumeráveis sobre a química do clorofórmio – a voz do*

químico <u>subiu</u> de tom. – Excelentíssimas senhoras, ilustres cavalheiros, aquilo que vos vou mostrar nunca mais o haveis de esquecer.

(Agualusa 1990, accessed through COMPARA)

"'The phenomenon you are about to witness, my esteemed audience, is not the work of demiurges or of sorcerers; it is the fruit of many years of scientific study, of exhaustive research involving countless experiments dealing with the chemical properties of chloroform.' The voice of the chemist rose a step. 'Most excellent ladies, illustrious gentlemen, what I am about to show you is something you will never forget.'"

(Agualusa 1995, accessed through COMPARA)

Similar Romanian collocations include *a ridica glasul* "to raise one's voice", *a coborî drapelul* "to lower the colors", and *a (-și) coborî vocea* "to lower one's voice" (Bantaș et al. 1981: 482, 77). In the case of Catalan *pujar* and *descendir*, it is pertinent to mention such sentences as *El franc francès ha pujat* "The French franc has risen" and *La febre ha descendit bruscament* "The fever dropped rapidly" (Sagristà i Artigas, ed. 1998: 1372, 507). Likewise, in Occitan we find expressions with *montar* like *Lis acioun mounton* "The stock prices go up" and *mounta la gamo* "to go from a lower musical scale to a higher one" (Coupier 1995: 906). As we will see in Chapter 9, it is significant that Latin and the Romance languages share the AMOUNT IS VERTICALITY, MORE IS UP, and LESS IS DOWN metaphors despite the fact that on the formal level verbs of vertical movement show little stability.

6.1.9   PROGRESS IS VERTICAL MOVEMENT, GOOD IS UP, BAD IS DOWN

Verticality also serves as the source domain in metaphors that encode improvement and deterioration. For instance, in the sentence from Valerius Maximus' *Facta et Dicta Memorabilia* Book III Part 4 "*De humili loco natis qui clari evaserunt*" ["Of those born in a humble situation who became illustrious"], Latin CON-SCENDERE "to go up" refers to social and career advancement:

(25)   *Miro gradu Varro quoque ad consulatum <e> macellaria patris taberna conscendit.*   (Shackleton Bailey, ed. 2000: 284)
   "It was a remarkable stride too by which Varro ascended from his father's butcher's shop to the Consulate." (ibid., p. 285)

This Latin sentence brings to mind a parallel Old French example with *monter* "to go up" from Jean Molinet's (1435–1507) chronicle published in the 19th century: *Pierre Lauchast, issu de petite maison, [...], s'estoit tellement monté, que le roi l'avoit fait chevalier* "Pierre Lauchast, of humble origin, [...] had advanced so much that the king had knighted him" (quoted in Godefroy 1969 V: 399). Likewise, in Book II verse 369 of Statius' *Thebaid*, DESCENDERE "to go down" describes the process of stepping down from a position of eminence: *laetum descendere regno* "gladly descend from royalty" (quoted in Glare, ed. 1982: 523). In the passage from Book X Part 1 Section 126 of his *Institutio Oratoria*, Quintilian employs DESCENDERE to criticize the quality of Seneca's writing style:

(26)   *Ex industria Senecam in omni genere eloquentiae distuli, propter vulgatam falso de me opinionem qua damnare eum et invisum quoque habere sum creditus. Quod accidit mihi dum corruptum et omnibus vitiis fractum dicendi genus revocare ad severiora iudicia contendo; tum autem solus hic fere in manibus adulescentium fuit. Quem non equidem omnino conabar excutere, sed potioribus praeferri non sinebam, quos ille non destiterat incessere, cum diversi sibi conscius generis placere se in dicendo posse quibus illi placerent diffideret. Amabant autem eum magis quam imitabantur, tantumque ab illo defluebant quantum ille ab antiquis descenderat.*

(Russell, ed. 2001b: 318, 320)

"I have deliberately postponed Seneca in my discussion of the various genres, because there was a general, though false, impression that I condemned him and even regarded him as an enemy. This came about when I was trying to recall a decadent manner of writing, enfeebled by all kinds of errors, to a severer standard. Now at that time Seneca was almost the only author in young men's hands. I did not try to make them drop him altogether, but I was not prepared to see him preferred to the better writers whom he had never stopped criticizing, because he knew that his own style was quite different and did not feel confident of pleasing those who were pleased by them. The young loved him more than they imitated him, and fell as far below him as he had fallen below the ancients." (ibid., pp. 319, 321)

Along the same lines, in Book VI Section 16 of Caesar's *De Bello Gallico*, DESCENDERE appears in the discussion of alleged human sacrifice by the inhabitants of Gaul as an equivalent of "to demean oneself by resorting to unethical behavior": *ad innocentium supplicia descendunt* "they demean themselves by resorting to the execution of the innocent" (quoted in Glare, ed. 1982: 523). In another passage from Caesar's writings, namely in the description of his enemies in Book I Section 81 of *De Bello Ciuili*, SUBIRE appears with the noun DEDITIO, DEDITIONIS "surrender" in the sense "to submit to a surrender, to endure a surrender":

(27)   *Tum vero neque ad explorandum idoneum locum castris neque ad progrediendum data facultate consistunt necessario et procul ab aqua et natura iniquo loco castra ponunt. [...] Prima nocte aquandi causa nemo egreditur ex castris; proximo die praesidio in castris relicto universas ad aquam copias*

educunt, pabulatum emittitur nemo. His eos suppliciis male haberi Caesar
et necessariam <u>subire</u> deditionem quam proelio decertare malebat.

(Peskett, ed. 1990: 110)

"Then, indeed, having no opportunities of searching for a suitable place for their camp nor of advancing, they are obliged to halt and pitch their camp far from water and in a place unfavourable by nature. [...] On the approach of night no one goes out of camp for watering; on the following day, leaving a guard in the camp, they lead out all their forces for water, but no one is sent out for fodder. Caesar preferred that they should be harassed by such suffering and submit to a compulsory surrender rather than fight a pitched battle." (ibid., p. 111)

In Section 139 of *Pro Sestio*, Cicero also uses SUBIRE with the meaning "to endure", although in a more positive context: *subeundae saepe pro re publica tempestates* "difficulties that often have to be endured for the good of the State" (quoted in Glare, ed. 1982: 1838).

The Romance equivalents of "to go up" and "to go down" are widely recruited into the mappings in question. In the case of Spanish *subir* "to go up" and *bajar* "to go down" relevant examples include *ha subido en el escalafón* "he has been promoted", *han subido a primera división* "they have gone up to the first division", *ha subido mucho en mi estima* "she has risen greatly in my estimation", *ha bajado mucho la calidad del producto* "the quality of the product has deteriorated badly", and *su popularidad ha bajado últimamente* "her popularity has diminished recently" (Galimberti Jarman & Russell, eds. 1994: 715, 83). An earlier example with Spanish *descender* "to go down" comes from writings by Gaspar Melchor de Jovellanos (1744–1811):

(28)   *El estilo de la comedia debe ser puro, elegante, animado – sin <u>descender</u>*
       jamás á expresiones vulgares, bajas y groseras.

(quoted in Cuervo 1992–1994 II: 999)

"Comedy's style must be pure, elegant, and animated – without lowering itself through the use of vulgar, rude, and offensive expressions."

Similar representative expressions with French *monter* "to go up" and *descendre* "to go down" are *monter au grade de colonel* "to rise to be a colonel" and *descendre jusqu'au mensonge* "to descend to lying" (Mansion, ed. 1939 I: 549, 256). Italian relevant collocations with *salire* "to go up" include *salire di grado* "to rise in rank", *salire nella gerarchia* "to rise in the hierarchy", and *salire in classifica* "to improve one's ranking" (Rubery, ed. 2010: 2361). The writings by Baldassare Castiglione (1478–1529) offer an earlier example with Italian *discendere* "to go down":

(29) *Bisogna esser prudente ed aver molto rispetto al loco, al tempo, ed alle per-*
      sone con le quai si parla e non <u>*descendere*</u> *alla buffoneria.*

                              (quoted in Battaglia, ed. 1961–2009 IV: 591)
      "It is necessary to be wise and to take into consideration the place, the
      time, and the people with whom one is speaking, and not to lower oneself
      to comicality."

Portuguese verbs of vertical motion also participate in the mappings in question:
e.g., *subir na vida* "to advance in life", *ascender socialmente* "to advance socially",
descer à infâmia "to lower oneself by acting badly" (Geiger, ed. 2008, s.v. *subir, as-*
cender, descer). Romanian *a urca* "to go up", *a se ridica* "to go up", and *a coborî* "to
go down" offer similar patterns: e.g., *a urca o treaptă în ierarhia socială* "to get a lift
up in the world", *a urca pe treptele societăţii* "to rise in the world/in life", *a se ridica
deasupra tentaţiei* "to rise superior to temptation", *a se ridica la înălţimea cuiva* "to
rise to the level of somebody", and *a coborî pe scara socială* "to sink in the social
scale" (Bantaş et al. 1981: 621, 482–483, 77). Catalan *pujar* "to go up" and *descendir*
"to go down" are equally pertinent: e.g., *Ha pujat a alcalde* "He attained the mayor's
position" and *descendir de categoria* "to drop in ranking" (Sagristà i Artigas, ed.
1998: 1372, 507). In the case of Occitan *montar* "to go up" and *davalar* "to go
down", similar expressions include *A mounta en grado* "He has gone up in rank"
and *A davala dóu cade* "He has morally fallen" (Coupier 1995: 906, 393). As we will
see in Chapter 9, it is significant that both Latin and Romance verbs of vertical
movement serve as the source domain in the PROGRESS IS VERTICAL MOVEMENT,
GOOD IS UP, and BAD IS DOWN mappings despite the fact that on the formal level
this subfield has experienced a profound change.

6.1.10   MANNER OF ACTION IS MANNER OF MOTION

Latin and its daughter languages commonly employ motion verbs to encode such
concepts as acting in a certain way, following a certain line of conduct, and devel-
oping in a certain manner. For example, in Seneca the Younger's *Thyestes* lines
219–220, IRE "to go" appears in the sense "to conduct oneself": *pietas fides priuata
bona sunt, qua iuuat reges eant* "goodness, loyalty are private values, kings should
conduct themselves the way it pleases them" (quoted in Glare, ed. 1982: 611). Likewise, in Virgil's *Aeneid* Book VII verse 592, IRE is used with the subject RES "things"
as an equivalent of "to develop": *nutu Iunonis eunt res* "things develop according to
Juno's will" (quoted in Glare, ed. 1982: 611). Romance motion verbs offer comparable examples. For instance, Portuguese *ir* "to go", in *O negócio vai bem* "Business
is going well" (Fernandes 1972: 393), combines with the adverb *bem* "well" to express satisfactory functioning of business. Parallel collocations are available for

French *aller* "to go" and *marcher* "to walk": *ainsi va le monde* "such is the way of the world", *les affaires marchent* "business is brisk", and *ça va comme sur des roulettes* "everything is working smoothly" (Mansion, ed. 1939 I: 28, 520, 754); cf. Occitan *marchar sus de ròdas nòvas* "to develop smoothly" (Rapin 1991–2006 IV: 35). In the next example, Raeto-Romance *gnir* "to come" combines with the adverb *bain* "well" in reference to adequate development of crops: *ils gra(u)ns vegnan bain* "the grains develop well" (Planta et al., eds. 1939– VII: 565); cf. Spanish *la cebada viene bien en este campo* "barley grows well on this field" (Álvar Ezquerra, ed. 1990: 1119) and Catalan *com va la verema?* "how is the grape harvesting going?" (Torras i Rodergas, ed. 1985: 775). In the case of Spanish *ir* "to go" and *andar* "to walk", relevant expressions include *¿cómo va el nuevo trabajo?* "how's the new job going?" and *siempre anda con prisas* "he is always in a hurry" (Galimberti Jarman & Russell, eds. 1994: 432, 42). Similar patterns are available for Italian *andare* "to go" and *venire* "to come": e.g., *tutto è andato secondo i piani* "everything went according to plan" (Rubery, ed. 2010: 1492) and *il tuo ricamo vien bene* "your embroidery is coming on nicely" (Reynolds, ed. 1981 I: 854). Likewise, in the passage from writings by Mihail Sadoveanu (1880–1961), Romanian *a umbla* "to walk" appears with the subject *război* "war", describing its development:

(30) *Îmi mai spune el cum <u>umblă</u> războiul, căci [...], oricât am întoarce noi gazetele [...], nu prea ajungem la un capăt și la o înțelegere.*
                              (quoted in Pușcariu et al., eds. 1907– X: 5-A: 98)
      "And he tells me how the war unfolds, because [...], no matter how we might interpret the newspapers [...] we do not really reach an end or an agreement."

Along the same lines, in the next example Romanian *a umbla* combines with the noun phrase *cu blîndeță* "with kindness", advising a specific type of behavior: *Umblă cu copiii cu blîndeță* "Act toward children with kindness" (*Atlasul lingvistic român*, quoted in Pușcariu et al., eds. 1907– X: 5-A: 97).

6.1.11   SPEED OF ACTION IS SPEED OF MOTION

One of the subtypes of MANNER OF ACTION IS MANNER OF MOTION is the mapping between speed of action and speed of motion. Latin and Romance equivalents of "to run" and "to jump" are commonly recruited to express actions characterized by swiftness, ease, zeal, or similar characteristics. For instance, in Horace's *Sermones* Book I Part 10, CURRERE "to run" accompanies the noun SENTENTIA "thought" in reference to the unencumbered flow of ideas: *est brevitate opus, ut currat sententia* "there is need of conciseness, as the thought may run on" (quoted in Stone 2005:

248).[7] The Spanish passages that employ *correr* "to run" with the noun phrase *plan de la acción* "plot, story line" in (31) and with the noun *pies* "verses, metrical feet" in (32) show that the mapping in question is also available in Romance:

(31)   *El plan de la acción está en general bien dispuesto; y especialmente en los tres primeros actos se desarrolla y* corre *con facilidad y soltura.* (Francisco Martínez de la Rosa, 1787–1862, *Apéndice sobre la poesía didáctica, la tragedia y la comedia española*, quoted in Cuervo 1992–1994 II: 561)
"The plot is overall well organized, and particularly in the first three acts it develops and proceeds effortlessly and smoothly."

(32)   *Reprendido es Lucilio porque no es poeta muy terso, ni sus pies* corren *con suavidad, mas sus donaires y agudezas loadas son de todos.* (José de Sigüenza, 1544–1606, *Vida de San Jerónimo*, quoted in Cuervo 1992–1994 II: 561)
"Lucilius is criticized because he is not a very elegant poet, and his verses do not run smoothly, but his sense of humor and wit are praised by everyone."

Along the same lines, in the example from Cervantes' *Novelas ejemplares* published in 1613, Spanish *correr* appears with the expression *a rienda suelta* "without restraint" in the description of the unstoppable development of strong emotions:

(33)   *A mi parecer los ímpetus amorosos* corren *á rienda suelta hasta que encuentran con la razón ó con el desengaño.* (quoted in Cuervo 1992–1994 II: 552)
"In my opinion, love impulses run without restraint until they meet with reason or with disillusion."

As far as equivalents of "to jump" are concerned, it is pertinent to mention Plautus' *Cistellaria* Act II line 551 in which Latin SALIRE makes reference to the racing beat of the heart prompted by strong emotions: *Iam horret corpus, cor salit* "Oh, I'm all of a tremble! My heart's jumping up and down!" (Nixon, ed. 1988: 156–157); cf. Romanian *îmi saltă inima de bucurie* "my heart leaps with joy" (Bantaş et al. 1981: 491).

6.1.12   OMITTING IS JUMPING

The second subtype of MANNER OF ACTION IS MANNER OF MOTION is the mapping between omitting and jumping. In the case of Latin, it is relevant to mention the ability on the part of SALTARE "to dance" – which is the 'intensivum' of SALIRE "to jump" – to describe a disorganized action, such as an orator speaking abruptly using incomplete phrases. For instance, in Part 67 Section 226 of *Orator*, Cicero uses SALTARE in his criticism of Hegesias' mincing rhetoric:

---

7.   Phrases of this type can also be interpreted as IDEAS ARE MOVING OBJECTS discussed in 6.1.25 (below).

(34) *Nec ullum genus est dicendi aut melius aut fortius quam binis aut ternis*
    ferire verbis, nonnunquam singulis, paulo alias pluribus, inter quae variis
    clausulis interponit se raro numerosa comprehensio; quam perverse fugiens
    Hegesias, dum ille quoque imitari Lysiam volt, alterum paene Demosthe-
    nem, <u>saltat</u> incidens particulas. (Hendrickson & Hubbell, eds. 1999: 496)
    "There is no style better or stronger than to strike with phrases of two or
    three words, sometimes with single words, and at other times with several,
    in the midst of which comes sparingly the rhythmical period with varying
    cadences. Hegesias perversely avoids this, and while, he, too, tries to imi-
    tate Lysias, who is almost the equal of Demosthenes, he hops about, cut-
    ting his style into little fragments." (ibid., p. 497)

Parallel Spanish examples include *saltaba de una idea a otra* "she was skipping
from one idea to the next" and *el disco ha saltado del cuarto al primer puesto* "the
record has jumped from number four to number one" (Galimberti Jarman &
Russell, eds. 1994: 685). French *sauter* offers similar expressions: *sauter de sujet en
sujet* "to jump from one subject to another", *sauter du rire aux larmes* "to pass suddenly from laughter to tears" (Mansion, ed. 1939 I: 767), and *sauter vinght feuillets*
"to skip twenty pages" (Rey, ed. 1989 VIII: 604). Relevant Italian collocations include *saltare da un argomento all'altro* "to skip from one subject to another" and
saltare il (proprio) turno "to miss one's turn [in games]" (Rubery, ed. 2010: 2361–
2362). Likewise, Portuguese employs expressions such as *saltou de alferes a major*
"he jumped in rank from lieutenant junior to major" (Aulete et al., eds. 1925 II:
823), *saltou da matéria em que estava para outra* "he jumped from the subject matter with which he was dealing to another one", and *saltou duas páginas na leitura*
"he skipped two pages in his reading" (Fernandes 1972: 539). Along the same lines,
Romanian uses *a sări* in such collocations as *a sări un cuvînt* "to skip a word", *a sări
un pasaj* "to skip a passage", and *a sări un rînd* "to skip a line" (Bantaș et al. 1981:
493). Similar Romance expressions also include Catalan *saltar d'una cosa a l'altra*
"to jump from one activity to another" (Torras i Rodergas, ed. 1985: 1167), Occitan
sauta de la cabro au perié "to jump from one idea to another" (Coupier 1995: 1270),
and Raeto-Romance *siglir d'ina caussa all'autra* "to jump from one subject to another" (Decurtins 2001: 980).

6.1.13 DEVIATION IS MOTION

The third subtype of MANNER OF ACTION IS MANNER OF MOTION is the mapping
between deviation and motion. Latin and Romance verbs that express movement
commonly make reference to inconsistent, incoherent, unpredictable, sudden, or
unacceptable things or actions, that is to say, to things or actions that do not fit the

mold or the previously established pattern. For instance, in the passage from Book XXI Part 46 Section 6 of Livy's *Ab Urbe Condita*, we find VENIRE "to come" used in the expression *ad pedes pugna venerat* "the battle had turned to fighting on foot", which makes reference to the fact that the battle had adopted a new strategy by shifting away from the old one:

(35)   *Inde equitum certamen erat aliquamdiu anceps, dein quia turbabant equos pedites intermixti, multis labentibus ex equis aut desilientibus, ubi suos premi circumventos vidissent, iam magna ex parte ad pedes pugna venerat, donec Numidae, qui in cornibus erant, circumvecti paulum ab tergo se ostenderunt.*   (Foster, ed. 1996: 136)[8]
"Then followed a cavalry fight of which the issue was for a time in doubt; but by and by the horses became excited by the presence of the foot-soldiers who were mingled with them, and many riders lost their seats or dismounted on seeing their fellows in distress, and the battle was now fought chiefly on foot; until the Numidians, who were posted on the flanks, rode round in a little circuit and showed themselves on the rear." (ibid., p. 137)

The fragment from Cervantes' *Quijote* which contains Spanish *salir* "to go out" in the expression *salió del temor* "he turned away from fear" offers a Romance analog:

(36)   *Acudió Lotario con mucha presteza, despavorido y sin aliento, a sacar la daga, y en ver la pequeña herida salió del temor que hasta entonces tenía y de nuevo se admiró de la sagacidad, prudencia y mucha discreción de la hermosa Camila [...].*   (Cervantes 1998 I: 412)
"Breathless with terror, Lotario ran to pull the dagger out, but when he saw how slight the wound was the fear that till then has possessed him was dispelled, and he was struck anew with amazement at the lovely Camila's cunning, prudence and quick wits [...]."   (Cervantes Saavedra 2001: 327)

In another relevant example from Book IV Part 3 Sections 15–16 of *Instituto Oratoria*, Quintilian uses Latin EGREDI "to go out" in his discussion of the remarks that can potentially take the orator away from the subject matter:

(37)   *Quae cum sunt argumentis subiecta similium rerum, quia cohaerent egredi non videntur; sed plurima sunt quae rebus nihil secum cohaerentibus inseruntur, quibus iudex reficitur admonetur placatur rogatur laudatur.*
                                         (Russell, ed. 2001a: 290)

---

8.   Glare ed. (1982: 5) lists this passage in the entry for ABIRE "to go away" as *ad pedes pugna abierat* and glosses the meaning of the verb in it as "(of an action) to pass (from its original condition or method)". As we have seen at the beginning of this chapter, expressions of this type can also be interpreted as CHANGE IS MOTION.

"When these are subordinate to Arguments involving similar subjects, they are not felt as Digressions, because they cohere with the whole; but many such passages are inserted with no such coherence with the context, and serve to refresh, admonish, placate, plead with, or praise the judge." (ibid., p. 291)

The following sentence from writings by Ion Creangă (1837–1889) provides a counterpart with Romanian *a se depărta* "to go away": *Dar ia, să nu ne depărtăm cu vorba și să încep a depăna firul poveștii* "But hey, let us not deviate and let me start telling the story" (quoted in Macrea & Petrovici, eds. 1955–1957 II: 52). Italian *uscire* "to go out" offers another relevant example: *questo incarico esce della mie competenze* "this assignment falls outside my competence" (De Mauro, ed. 1999–2003 VI: 923). Along the same lines, in Pliny the Younger's *Epistulae* Book VII Letter 33 Section 10, Latin EGREDI "to go out" makes reference to the necessity on the part of history to accurately adhere to the facts and not deviate from them: *nec historia debet egredi veritatem* "history should not go outside of the realm of truth" (quoted in Glare, ed. 1982: 595). A letter written in 1580 by Santa Teresa de Jesús (1515–1582) to María de San José, prioress of Seville, contains a similar example with Spanish *salir* "to go out" in the description of a member of the religious order who adheres to her superiors' demands: *Al menos es obediente, que no saldrá de lo que vuestra reverencia quisiere* "At least she is obedient and will not deviate from what your majesty wishes" (quoted in Cuervo 1992–1994 VIII: 378).

6.1.14 FORM IS MOTION

Latin and Romance also share the ability to employ motion verbs in descriptions of stationary objects. One of the subtypes of this metaphor is the so-called 'fictive motion' which is a projection between motion and extended static scenes.[9] For instance, in Book XVIII Part 76 Section 326 of Pliny the Elder's *Naturalis Historia*,

---

9. Cognitive linguists employ a number of terms in their discussion of phrases with motion verbs that refer to extended static scenes such as *The mountain range goes from Canada to Mexico* and *The cord runs from the TV to the wall* (Talmy 2000 I: 104): "virtual motion" (Talmy 1983), "abstract motion" (Langacker 1987, Matlock 2010), "subjective motion" (Matsumoto 1996), and "fictive motion" (Talmy 2000, 2003, Rojo & Valenzuela 2003, Matlock 2004a, b, Lakoff 2012). These terms reflect the fact that, as established by psycholinguistic experiments, the language user (or the conceptualizer) "mentally scan[s] or 'move[s]' along the path associated with the subject noun phrase [...] [and] in doing so [...] experiences something akin to actual motion" (Matlock 2004b: 225). Mental scanning of this sort is not an isolated phenomenon. For instance, a related type of mental scanning motivates phrases like *There is a cottage every now and then through the valley*, in which a static situation (cottages) appears with a path phrase (through the valley) (Langacker 2010: 36–37).

CURRERE "to run" combines with the noun LIMES "boundary path" in reference to its extension:

(38) *Observato solis ortu quocumque die libeat stantibus hora diei sexta sic ut ortum eum a sinistro umero habeant, contra mediam faciem meridies et a vertice septentrio erit; qui ita limes per agrum <u>curret</u> cardo appellabitur.*

(Rackham, ed. 1950: 394)

"After observing the position of sunrise on any given day, let people stand at midday so as to have the point of sunrise at their left shoulder: then they will have the south directly in front of them and the north directly behind them; a path running through a field in this way will be called a cardinal line." (ibid., p. 395)

In a similar way, in Book V verses 249–251 of the *Aeneid*, Virgil uses CURRERE when depicting a thread on a piece of clothing:

(39) *ipsis praecipuos ductoribus addit honores:*
victori chlamydem auratam, quam plurima circum
purpura Maeandro duplici Meliboea <u>cucurrit</u>

(Rushton Fairclough, ed. 1999: 488)

"For the captains themselves he adds special honours; to the winner, a cloak wrought with gold, about which ran deep Meliboean purple in double waving line [...]." (ibid., p. 489)

Likewise, Book V verses 558–559 of the *Aeneid* contain IRE "to go" in the description of the shape of a piece of jewelry that extends over the body: *it pectore summo flexilis obtorti per collum circulus auri* "high on the breast around the neck passes a pliant circlet of twisted gold" (Rushton Fairclough, ed. 1999: 508–509). The mapping in question is also available for DESCENDERE "to go down", as can be seen in the passage from Book II Part 51 Section 136 of Pliny the Elder's *Naturalis Historia*:

(40) *sunt in Italiae quoque partibus iis quae a septentrione <u>descendunt</u> ad teporem, qualis est urbis et Campaniae tractus, iuxta hieme et aestate fulgurat, quod non in alio situ evenit.*   (Rackham, ed. 1938: 272, 274)[10]

"Also in the parts of Italy that slope down from the north towards the warmth, such as the district of Rome and the Campagna, lightning occurs in winter just as in summer, which does not happen in any other locality." (ibid., pp. 273, 275)

---

10. This passage also contains the verb EVENIRE in reference to the occurrence of a natural phenomenon, thus illustrating the metaphor EXISTENCE IS MOTION discussed in 6.1.5 (above).

Extension of stationary objects reflected in their measurements is another case in point. For instance, in the passage from Book II Part 112 Section 243 of his *Naturalis Historia* dedicated to the dimensions of inhabited earth from East to West, Pliny the Elder employs CURRERE "to run" in reference to two types of measurement, the one taken by water and the one taken by land: *Mensura currit duplici via* "The measurement runs by a double route" (Rackham, ed. 1938: 366–367).

The metaphorical projection between motion and extension of static scenes is widely attested across the Romance languages. The following Gallo-Romance examples with French *descendre* "to go down", French *courir* "to run", and Occitan *montar* "to go up" serve as illustration: *Le chemin descend jusqu'à la vallée* "The road slopes down to the valley", *Le chemin court au bord du lac* "The road lies along the lake-side" (Mansion, ed. 1939 I: 256, 206), and *Aqui ounte la routo mounto* "Over there where the road climbs up" (Coupier 1995: 906). Italian *correre* "to run", *giungere* "to arrive", *salire* "to go up", *scendere* "to go down", and *discendere* "to go down" form similar expressions: *un fregio corre lungo la facciata* "a frieze runs along the façade", *La pineta giunge fino al mare* "The pine wood stretches down to the sea" (Macchi, ed. 1970 I: 323, 588), *La strada sale verso la montagna* "The road goes up the mountain", *vestito che scende fino alle caviglie* "dress that comes down to the ankles", and *La collina discende fino al fiume* "The hill slopes down to the river" (Rubery, ed. 2010: 2361, 2381, 1762). A comparable Spanish example with *ir* "to go" is *La autopista va desde Madrid hasta Valencia* "The highway stretches from Madrid to Valencia" (Galimberti Jarman & Russell, eds. 1994: 432). Along the same lines, Romanian *a merge* "to go" and Raeto-Romance *ir* "to go" describe static scenes in writings by Nicolae Bălcescu (1819–1852), as in (41), and by Andri Peer (1921–1985), as in (42):

(41) *Mergea atunci podul [...] de la capul cel de lîngă oraşul Giurgiului [...] pînă la poalele castelului.*   (quoted in Puşcariu et al., eds. 1907– VI: 407)
      "Back then the bridge was extending [...] from the cape next to the city Giurgiu [...] up to the edges of the castle."

(42) *La via nun es largia, i va a dretta, a schnestra, bod sur ün muot, bod in üna foppa.*   (quoted in Planta et al., eds. 1939– X: 34)
      "The road is not wide, it goes to the right, to the left, sometimes over a hill, sometimes in a lowland."

6.1.15 CHANGE IN SIZE IS MOTION

The second subtype of FORM IS MOTION is the mapping between motion and change in size of static objects that are solid yet capable of expansion, or between motion and change in contours of non-solid amorphous substances. Trees and their branches are a typical example of solid static objects undergoing expansion. For Latin, it is relevant to cite Book II Part 1 verses 101–102 of Statius' *Silvae* that contain IRE "to go" accompanied by ALTIUS "higher" in reference to the growth of a tree's branches: *vidi ego transertos alieno in robore ramos altius ire suis* "I have seen branches grafted on an alien tree grow higher than its own" (Shackleton Bailey, ed. 2003a: 110–111). In a similar Romance phrase French *monter* "to go up" combines with the noun *arbres* "trees": *Ces arbres montent trop, il faut les étêter* "These trees grow a lot, it is necessary to trim them" (Rey, ed. 1989 VI: 559). In the case of amorphous substances undergoing expansion, liquids constitute a typical example. For instance, in the passage from Book III Part 16 Section 27 of Varro's *Res Rusticae*, ESCENDERE "to go up" specifies the requirement that water should not rise beyond a certain mark:

(43)   *Cibi pars quod potio et ea iis aqua liquida, unde bibant esse oportet, eamque propinquam, quae praeterfluat aut in aliquem lacum influat, ita ut ne altitudine* <u>*escendat*</u> *duo aut tres digitos; in qua aqua iaceant testae aut lapilli, ita ut extent paulum, ubi adsidere et bibere possint.*   (Hooper, ed. 1999: 514)
"As drink is a component of food, and as this, in the case of bees, is clear water, they should have a place from which to drink, and this close by; it should flow past their hives, or run into a pool in such a way that it will not rise higher than two or three fingers, and in this water there should lie tiles or small stones in such a way, that they project a little from the water, so that the bees can settle on them and drink." (ibid., p. 515)

Similar Romance patterns include Catalan *arribar* "to come" in *L'aigua va arribar al tercer esglaó* "The water reached the third stair" (Sagristà i Artigas, ed. 1998: 148) and Occitan *montar* "to go up" in *Rose a mounta d'un mètre* "The level of water in Rhône has gone up one meter" (Coupier 1995: 906). The reflexive form of "to go out" is commonly used with liquids (and metonymically with objects that contain them) as an equivalent of "to overflow, to spill, to leak": e.g., Spanish *el río se salió de su cauce* "the river overflowed its banks" (Galimberti Jarman & Russell, eds. 1994: 684), *la leche se ha salido* "the milk has spilled by boiling over", *el cántaro se sale* "the jar leaks" (Álvar Ezquerra, ed. 1990: 983).

6.1.16   SHAPE IS MOTION

The third subtype of FORM IS MOTION encompasses the capability on the part of motion verbs to encode the subject's correspondence to a specific shape or contour and the subject's fit or lack of fit within established physical boundaries. For instance, in Gellius' *Noctes Atticae* Book XI Part 15 Section 8, Latin EXIRE "to go out" appears in the description of the word-final suffix -BUNDUS in which present participles of the type LAETABUNDUS "cheerful" end:

(44) *Sed inquirentibus nobis quaenam ratio et origo esset huiuscemodi figurae "populabundus" et "errabundus" et "laetabundus" et "ludibundus" multorumque aliorum id genus verborum, [...] Apollinaris noster videri sibi ait particulam istam postremam in quam verba talia <u>exeunt</u> vim et copiam et quasi abundantiam rei cuius id verbum esset demonstrare, ut "laetabundus" is dicatur qui abunde laetus sit, et "errabundus," qui longo atque abundanti errore sit, ceteraque omnia ex ea figura ita dici ostendit, ut productio haec et extremitas largam et fluentem vim et copiam declararet.*

(Rolfe, ed. 1968: 334, 336)

"But when I was inquiring about the signification and origin of such forms as *populabundus, errabundus, laetabundus, ludibundus,* and many other words of that kind, our friend Apollinaris – [...] – remarked that it seemed to him that the final syllable of such words indicated force and abundance, and as it were, an excess of the quality belonging to the primitive word. Thus *laetabundus* is used of one who is excessively joyful, and *errabundus* of one who has wandered long and far, and he showed that all other words of that form are so used that this addition and ending indicates a great and overflowing force and abundance." (ibid., pp. 335, 337)

This Latin passage brings to mind collocations with Italian *uscire* "to go out" of the type *una parola che esce in consonante* "a word ending in a consonant" (Reynolds, ed. 1981 I: 843). Along the same lines, the equivalents of "to go out" can describe the endpoint of topographic features, as in Italian *Questa strada esce in piazza Castello* "This street comes out on piazza Castello" (Rubery, ed. 2010: 2575) and in Spanish *¿esta calle sale al Paseo Colón?* "does this street come out onto the Paseo Colón?" (Galimberti Jarman & Russell, eds. 1994: 683).

The use of motion verbs to depict protrusion is another case in point. For instance, in Statius' *Thebaid* Book VII verses 291–293, EXIRE "to go out" appears with the noun phrase CASSIDIS APEX "helmet top" in reference to the helmet's projection above the horseman's head:

(45) *illi autem, quanam iunguntur origine fratres?*
sic certe paria arma viris, sic <u>exit</u> in auras
cassidis aequus apex (Shackleton Bailey, ed. 2003b: 420)
"Those brothers now, what origin unites them? Thus surely their arms match and equal helmet crests rise into the air." (ibid., p. 421)

The excerpt from the novel *La busca* (1904) by Pío Baroja (1872–1956) offers a comparable example with Spanish *salir* "to go out" which comically describes an oversized *sombrero* "hat":

(46)   *El señor Custodio llevaba las prendas de toda gala; el sombrero hongo nue-*
        vo, nuevo aunque tenía más de treinta años; su chaqueta de pana forrada,
        excelente para las regiones boreales, y un bastón con puño de cuerno com-
        prado en el Rastro; la mujer del trapero llevaba un traje antiguo y un pañuelo
        alfombrado, y Manuel estaba ridículo con un sombrero sacado del almacén,
        que le salía un palmo por delante de los ojos, un traje de invierno que le so-
        focaba y unas botas estrechas.   (Baroja 1904: 299–300)
        "Señor Custodio took out his finest apparel: the new fedora, new although
        it was more than thirty years old; his coat of doubled cloth, excellent for
        the boreal regions, and a cane with a horn handle, bought in El Rastro; the
        ragdealer's wife wore a flowered kerchief, while Manuel made a most ri-
        diculous appearance in a hat that was taken from the shop and protruded
        about a palm's length before his eyes, a winter suit that suffocated him and
        a pair of tight shoes."   (Baroja 1922: 274–275)

Latin and Romance equivalents of "to go out" also share the ability to express the subject's visibility outside of a given limit. For instance, in *Metamorphoses* Book I verses 343–345, Ovid employs Latin EXIRE in the description of hills that are visible above the water after the world has recovered from the flood:

(47)   *iam mare litus habet, plenos capit alveus amnes,*
        flumina subsidunt collesque exire videntur;
        surgit humus, crescunt sola decrescentibus undis   (Miller, ed. 1994: 26)
        "Now the sea has shores, the rivers, bank full, keep within their channels;
        the floods subside, and hill-tops spring into view; land rises up, the ground
        increasing as the waves decrease [...]." (ibid., p. 27)

In a similar passage from Gustave Flaubert's *Madame Bovary* (1857), French *sortir* refers to the visibility of the child's feet partially covered by her clothes:

(48)   *L'enfant arriva sur le bras de sa bonne, dans sa longue chemise de nuit, d'où*
        sortaient ses pieds nus, sérieuse et presque rêvant encore.
                                        (Flaubert 1971: 325)
        "The child arrived in the nurse's arms, her bare feet peeping out from be-
        neath her long nightgown, her expression serious, only half awake."
                                        (Flaubert 2004: 283)

6.1.17 PLACEMENT IS MOTION

A metaphor closely related to SHAPE IS MOTION discussed above is the mapping between movement and the object's placement into or inclusion in a specified entity. For instance, in the following passage from Part 21 Section 3 of *De Agri Cultura*, Cato uses IRE "to go" twice with the noun CLAVUS "bolt" in his discussion of proper positioning of the bolt in the construction of a mill:

(49) *Supra imbrices extrinsecus cupam pertundito, qua clavus <u>eat</u>, qui orbem cludat. Insuper foramen librarium ferreum digitos sex latum indito, pertusum utrimque secus, qua clavus <u>eat</u>.*   (Hooper, ed. 1999: 38)
"Above these plates pierce the bar on the outside for the bolt to fasten the stone. On top of the opening place a one-pound iron collar, 6 fingers wide, pierced on both sides to allow the bolt to enter." (ibid., p. 39)

In the case of Spanish *ir* "to go", Italian *andare* "to go", Catalan *anar* "to go", and Portuguese *entrar* "to go in", relevant expressions include *¿dónde van las toallas?* "where do the towels go?" (Galimberti Jarman & Russell, eds. 1994: 433), *il piatto non va in forno* "the dish is not ovenproof" (Rubery, ed. 2010: 1492), *Aquestes fitxes van al primer calaix* "These cards go into the first drawer" (Sagristà i Artigas, ed. 1998: 96), and *Essa palavra não entrou no dicionário* "This word was not included in the dictionary" (Geiger, ed. 2008, s.v. *entrar*). The equivalents of "to go" and "to enter" commonly encode placement or inclusion by necessity, as in the case of Italian *andare*, Catalan *entrar*, and Romanian *a intra*: *in questa giacca ci vanno cinque bottoni* "there are five buttons to this jacket" (Reynolds, ed. 1981 I: 39), *En aquest vestit, hi entraran tres metres de roba* "Three meters of material will go into this dress" (Sagristà i Artigas, ed. 1998: 640), and *La acest palton intră stofă multă* "A lot of fabric goes into this coat" (Macrea, ed. 1958: 392). This pattern applies not only to concrete nouns but also to abstract ones, as in Spanish *todo esto va para el examen* "all of this will be included on the exam" (Galimberti Jarman & Russell, eds. 1994: 433).

6.1.18 SIMILARITY IS MOTION

Using motion verbs to express resemblance is another option available in both Latin and Romance. For instance, in Book XXXVII Part 20 Section 76 of his *Naturalis Historia*, Pliny the Elder employs EXEUNTE(s), which is the present participle of EXIRE "to go out", when comparing the color of precious stones to the color of a precious metal:

(50) *Eandem multis naturam aut certe similem habere berulli videntur. India eos gignit, raro alibi repertos. poliuntur omnes sexangula figura artificum ingeniis, quoniam hebes unitate surda color repercussu angulorum excitetur.*

aliter politi non habent fulgorem. probatissimi ex iis sunt qui viriditatem maris puri imitantur, proximi qui vocantur chrysoberulli, paulo pallidiores, sed in aureum colorem <u>exeunte(s) fulgore.</u> (Eichholz, ed. 1962: 224) "Many people consider the nature of beryls to be similar to, if not identical with, that of emeralds. Beryls are produced in India and are rarely found elsewhere. All of them are cut by skilled craftsmen to a smooth hexagonal shape, since their colour, which is deadened by the dullness of an unbroken surface, is enhanced by the reflection from the facets. If they are cut in any other way they lack brilliance. The most highly esteemed beryls are those that reproduce the pure green of the sea, while next in value are the so-called 'chrysoberyls.' These are slightly paler, but have a vivid colour approaching that of gold." (ibid., p. 225)

Along the same lines, in the earlier stages of Italian, *ascendere* "to go up" could be employed as an equivalent of *tendere a riprodurre una qualità* "to resemble a quality", *accostarsi* "to approach", and *somigliare (parlando di un colore)* "to be alike (of color)" (Battaglia, ed. 1961–2009 I: 721; Pfister 1979– III: 1535). In this way, in his dialogue *Delle bellezze delle donne* written in 1542, Agnolo Firenzuola (1493– 1543) uses *ascendere* side by side with *pendere* "to tend toward" and *somigliare* "to resemble" in the discussion of different shades of color required for painting:

(51)   *E voi sapete, che de' capegli il proprio e vero colore è esser biondi. Il lionato è di due ragioni; delle quali una ne <u>pende</u> nel giallo, e questo non è per noi; l' altra all' oscuro, e chiamasi tanè, e di questo ce ne basterà due pennellate. Il nero non ha bisogno di molta dichiarazione, perciocchè ognuno il conosce; e quella Fiorentina, che da voi è stata ben ricevuta, se ne vale assai: il qual colore, quanto più è chiuso, e più <u>ascende</u> all' oscuro, tanto più è fino, tanto più è bello. [...] Il vermiglio è quasi una spezie di rosso, ma meno aperto; ed è quello finalmente che <u>somiglia</u> le guance della bella Francolina di Palazzuolo quando l' ha stizza [...].* (Firenzuola 1848 I: 283)
"You know that the proper and true color of hair should be blonde. There are two types of tawny: one tending toward yellow (and this is not for me) and another, called tan, tending toward a darker hue, and two brushstrokes of this will be enough for us. Black does not need much of an explanation because everyone is familiar with it. That Florentine lady whom you welcomed so well takes very good advantage of it. The darker and deeper this color is, the finer and more beautiful it is. [...] Vermillion is almost a kind of red, but less vivid. In short, it resembles the cheeks of beautiful Francolina from via di Palazzuolo when she is in a temper."
(Firenzuola 1992: 45)

6.1.19 DIFFUSION IS MOTION

Latin and Romance motion verbs are frequently recruited to express diffusion, dissemination, spreading, or circulation of things that cannot participate in self-propelled motion, including inanimate, abstract, and non-material entities. For instance, Latin IRE "to go" could collocate with the noun MORBUS "sickness" in reference to spreading of disease, as in Lucretius' *De Rerum Natura* Book VI verses 1205–1207: *profluvium porro qui taetri sanguinis acre exierat, tamen in nervos huic morbus et artus ibat* "Moreover, he who survived this cruel flux of foul blood, yet found the disease passing into his sinews and limbs" (Rouse, ed. 1992: 582–583). The use of Latin CURRERE "to run" with the meaning in question was particularly common. For instance, in Book IV verses 804–805 of Statius' *Thebaid*, we find CURRERE employed with the noun CLAMOR "cry, shout, clamor": *longusque uirum super ora cucurrit clamor, 'aquae!'* "And over the warriors' mouths ran the long clamour: 'Water'" (Shackleton Bailey, ed. 2003b: 264–265). Book XI verses 296–297 of Virgil's *Aeneid* contains an analogous example with CURRERE accompanying the noun FREMOR "clatter, murmur": *Vix ea legati, variusque per ora cucurrit Ausonidum turbata fremor* "Scarce thus the envoys, when a various murmur ran along the troubled lips of Ausonia's sons" (Rushton Fairclough, ed. 1996: 254–255). Along the same lines, in *Aeneid* Book II verses 120–121, CURRERE collocates with the noun TREMOR "shake, shudder, tremble": *gelidusque per ima cucurrit ossa tremor* "and a cold shudder ran through their inmost marrow" (Rushton Fairclough, ed. 1999: 324–325). Likewise, in *Aeneid* Book XII verses 64–66, CURRERE collocates with RUBOR "blush", making reference to its expansion:

(52) *accepit vocem lacrimis Lavinia matris*
      flagrantis perfusa genas, cui plurimus ignem
      subiecit rubor et calefacta per ora <u>cucurrit</u>.

                                    (Rushton Fairclough, ed. 1996: 302)
      "Lavina heard her mother's words, her burning cheeks steeped in tears, while a deep blush kindled its fire, and mantled o'er her glowing face."
      (ibid., p. 303)

The mapping in question is widely attested across the Romance varieties. In the case of Spanish, it is relevant to mention such expressions with *subir* "to go up", *correr* "to run", and *llegar* "to come" as *subir la epidemia* "to spread (of an epidemic)" (Álvar Ezquerra, ed. 1990: 1028), *corre el rumor de que* "there is a rumor going around that", and *su voz llegaba al fondo del teatro* "his voice carried to the back of the theater" (Galimberti Jarman & Russell, eds. 1994: 199, 461). In addition, the reflexive form of Spanish *correr* can encode diffusion of materials that create visual images or effects. Domingo ed. (1997: 290) lists this function as "esparcirse la tinta, pintura, etc., por el papel o lienzo, dejando los trazos borrosos" ["to spread (of ink, paint, etc.) over paper or canvas, leaving blurry marks"], and Galimberti Jarman & Russell eds. (1994: 199) illustrate it with such expressions as *correrse la tinta* "to run (of paint)", *correrse el maquillaje* "to smudge (about makeup)", and *correrse el rímel* "to smudge (about mascara)". Similarly, Spanish *correr(se)* can appear with nouns that refer to heat-sensitive substances that spread while melting, and metonymically with nouns that refer to items made of these substances, as in *la vela (se) corría poco a poco* "the candle melted slowly" (Schonthal, ed. 2001: 145).

In the case of French, representative examples with *arriver* "to come", *courir* "to run", and *monter* "to go up" include *Le bruit est arrivé jusqu'à ses oreilles* "The noise reached their ears", *Il court un préjugé contre cette théorie* "There is a prejudice circulating against this theory", *Une chanson qui court par le pays* "The song that is going around the country", *La mode qui court* "The fashion that is widespread", and *D'adorables senteurs montent de la plaine* "Pleasant scents spread from the plain" (Rey, ed. 1989 I: 562; II: 1010; VI: 559). In similar Italian expressions, *correre* "to run" accompanies the nouns *voce* "rumor", *mormorio* "whisper", and *brivido* "shiver": *un mormorio corse tra la folla* "a whisper ran through the crowd", *è una voce che corre* "it is a rumor that is going around" (Rubery, ed. 2010: 1704), and *un brivido gli corse lungo la schiena* "a shiver ran down his spine" (Macchi, ed. 1970 I: 323). Portuguese, Catalan, and Occitan equivalents of "to run" are just as relevant: *Corre que vais embarcar* "It is rumored that you are going to leave on a trip" (Fernandes 1972: 171), *Una notícia que ha corregut tot Tarragona* "A piece of news that spread through Tarragona" (Sagristà i Artigas, ed. 1998: 445), and *faire courre uno novo* "to spread the news" (Coupier 1995: 318). Raeto-Romance *ir* "to go" forms parallel patterns: *ei va la curella che, ei va la fama che, ei va la tuna che* "it is rumored that" (Planta et al., eds. 1939– X: 29). In the case of Romanian, *a merge* "to go" can accompany such nouns as *vorbă* "word" and *sun* "echo", as in *merge vorba* "the word is going around" and *Marsă sun (= ecou) pîm pădure* "The echo had spread through the forest" (Puşcariu et al., eds. 1907– VI: 407). Along the same lines, in the following late 18th-century example from the collection of chronicles *Letopisiţile ţării Moldovii* published in the mid-19th century, *a merge* collocates with the noun *cuvînt* "word": *Mersăse cuvîntul din om în om [...] până [...] la urechile celor mari* "The word had gone from man to man [...] until [...] [it reached] the ears of the rulers" (quoted in Puşcariu et al., eds. 1907– VI: 407).

A subtype of the mapping in question is the use of motion verbs in reference to circulation of goods, including to their circulation at a certain price as the equivalent of "to sell" and "to cost": e.g., Italian *andare* "to go" in *il nuovo modello va (bene)* "the new model is selling (well)" and Italian *venire* "to come" in *quanto viene la sciarpa?* "How much is the scarf?" (Rubery, ed. 2010: 1492, 2589).[11] Analogous examples include Catalan *anar* "to go" and Spanish *salir* "to go out", as in *Anar a baix preu* "To cost little" (Sagristà i Artigas, ed. 1998: 96) and *me sale a (por) veinte pesetas* "it costs me twenty pesetas" (Álvar Ezquerra, ed. 1990: 983). Spanish *correr* "to run" is equally relevant: e.g., *el aceite corre a (por) tantas pesetas litro* "the oil costs x pesetas a liter" (Álvar Ezquerra, ed. 1990: 305); cf. Late Latin *currebat in ipsis diebus illo cafiz in duabus solidos de argentu* "in those days the kayis cost two silver solidi" (Seco, ed. 2003: 169).[12]

6.1.20 POSSESSION IS MOTION

'To be destined to a particular addressee' and 'to become someone's possession' is another set of concepts commonly expressed by Latin and Romance motion verbs. For instance, in the excerpt from Book XL Part 17 Section 4 of Livy's *Ab Urbe Condita*, PERVENIRE "to come" refers to transfer of land from the Numidian king Syphax to the Carthaginians:

(53) *Eodem anno inter populum Carthaginiensem et regem Masinissam in re praesenti disceptatores Romani de agro fuerunt. Ceperat eum ab Carthaginiensibus pater Masinissae Gala; Galam Syphax inde expulerat, postea in gratiam soceri Hasdrubalis Carthaginiensibus dono dederat; Carthaginienses eo anno Masinissa expulerat. Haud minore certamine animorum quam cum ferro et acie dimicarunt res acta apud Romanos. Carthaginienses, quod maiorum suorum fuisset, deinde ab Syphace ad se pervenisset, repetebant.*

(Sage & Schlesinger, eds. 2000: 54, 56)

"In the same year Roman arbitrators who were on the ground took part in a dispute about land-ownership between the Carthaginian people and King Masinissa. Gala, the father of Masinissa had taken it from the Carthaginians; Syphax had driven Gala out of it and later, as a favour to his father-in-law Hasdrubal, had presented it as a gift to the Carthaginians; Masinissa had that year expelled the Carthaginians. The case was argued before the Romans with no less ardour of temper than when they fought with arms in the line of battle. The Carthaginians were reclaiming it

---

11. The use of Italian *venire* as the equivalent of "to cost" is marked as informal (Rubery, ed. 2010: 2589).

12. This passage is dated 1067. It uses Late Latin as the written mode of Early Ibero-Romance, a practice analyzed in Wright (1982, 1994, 2002). Seco ed. (2003) quotes it from the *Colección de documentos para el estudio de la historia de Aragón* (Salarrullana y de Dios & Ibarra y Rodríguez, eds. 1907, 1913). *Cafiz* "kayis" is a unit of capacity for grains. On the exact meaning of *solidos de argentu [kaçimi]*, see Gil Farrés (1978) and Chalmeta (1981).

because it had belonged to their forefathers and had then come again to them from Syphax." (ibid., pp. 55, 57)

The passage from Guy de Maupassant's *Un million* (1882) illustrates a parallel Romance usage of French *aller* "to go":

(54)   *La tante, fidèle à l'idée fixe de toute sa vie, laissait son million à leur premier né, avec la jouissance de la rente aux parents jusqu'à leur mort. Si le jeune ménage n'avait pas d'héritier avant trois ans, cette fortune irait aux pauvres.*
(quoted in Imbs, ed. 1971–1994 II: 554)
"The aunt, faithful to her life-long obsession, left her million to their first-born, with the parents having the right to a pension for life. If the young couple did not have an heir within three years, that fortune would go to the poor."

Comparable instances also include Spanish *ir* "to go" in *Va para usted* "This is for you", Spanish *venir* "to come" in *Le vendrá de su padre una hacienda* "He will receive a farm from his father" (Álvar Ezquerra, ed. 1990: 626, 1119), and Catalan *pervenir* "to come" in *li eren pervingudes aquelles terres* "he had inherited those lands" (Sagristà i Artigas, ed. 1998: 1272). Italian *andare* "to go" forms similar patterns, as in the case of *I soldi andranno in beneficenza* "The money will go to charity", *La casa andrà al miglior offerente* "The house will go to the highest bidder", and *La maggior parte del merito dovrebbe andare all'autore* "Most of the credit should go to the author" (Rubery, ed. 2010: 1492). Likewise, Nicola Nicolau's 1819 Romanian translation of Pierre Blanchard's (1772–1856*) Le Plutarque de la jeunesse* offers a relevant example with Romanian *a veni* "to come": *Acesta scrise 97 tragedii, [...] dintre care numai 7 veniră la noi*" "He wrote ninety-seven tragedies, [...] of which only seven had come down to us" (quoted in Puşcariu et al., eds. 1907– XIII: I: 318).

6.1.21   TIME IS MOTION: TIME IS SOMETHING MOVING

Temporal metaphors constitute another well-represented category in both Latin and Romance. In one of the subtypes of the TIME IS MOTION mapping, time and units in which it is measured, such as years, months, and days, are encoded as being in motion (TIME IS SOMETHING MOVING). A very common context in which this metaphor is used is the expression of dismay at how fast time goes by. For example, in *Carmina* Book II ode 5 verses 13–14, Horace employs Latin CURRERE "to run" with the subject AETAS, AETATIS "time" when describing time's fleeting nature: *currit [...] ferox aetas* "unrestrained time runs on" (quoted in Glare, ed. 1982: 476). In the case of the Romance languages, it is commonplace to depict the fleeting nature of time with the equivalents of "to go along/across, to enter", such as Spanish *pasar*, French *passer*, Italian *passare*, Portuguese *passar*, Catalan *passar*, Occitan *passar*, and Raeto-Romance *passar*. The following list provides a representative range: Spanish *¡cómo pasa el tiempo!* "how time passes!" (Smith 1992: 536), French *L'été a passé sans qu'on s'en aperçoive* "summer has gone without our noticing it" (Mansion, ed. 1939 I: 611), Italian *la serata era passata fin troppo in fretta* "the evening had passed all too quickly" (Rubery, ed. 2010: 2177), Catalan *Una hora que ha passat volant* "An hour that went by quickly" (Sagristà i Artigas, ed. 1998: 1239), Occitan *Li jour passon* "days go by" (Coupier 1995: 1007), and Raeto-Romance *il temps passa* "time flies" (Decurtins 2001: 721). The fragment from José Saramago's novel *História do cerco de Lisboa* (1989), which in addition to Portuguese *passar* contains *correr* "to run" and *ir* "to go", is particularly eloquent:

(55)　*É o que tem o tempo, <u>corre</u> e não damos por ele, está uma pessoa por aí ocupada nos seus quotidianos, subitamente cai em si e exclama, meu Deus como o tempo <u>passa</u>, ainda agora estava o rei Salomão vivo e já lá <u>vão</u> três mil anos [...].*　　　　(Saramago 1989, accessed through COMPARA)
"That's time for you, it races past without our noticing, a person is taken up with his daily life when he suddenly comes to his senses and exclaims, dear God, how time flies, only a moment ago King Solomon was still alive and now three thousand years have passed [...]."
(Saramago 1996, accessed through COMPARA)

Another common context is making reference to temporal endpoints. For instance, in the passage from Book II Part 76 of Tacitus' *Historiae*, Latin ABIRE "to go away" combines with TEMPUS "time" indicating that a specified phase has come to its conclusion:

(56)　*Ego te, Vespasiane, ad imperium voco, quam salutare rei publicae, quam tibi magnificum, iuxta deos in tua manu positum est. [...] <u>Abiit</u> iam et transvectum est tempus quo posses videri non cupisse: confugiendum est ad imperium.*　　　　(Moore, ed. 1968: 280)
"I call you, Vespasian, to the throne. How advantageous to the state, how glorious for you this may prove, are questions which depend, after the gods, on your own acts. [...] The time is already past and gone when you could seem to have no desires for supreme power. Your only refuge is the throne." (ibid., p. 281)

The following excerpt with Romanian *a veni* "to come" accompanying the noun *an* "year" offers a Romance analog:

(57) *Dau trei galbini pe an. Acuma cînd a venit anu [...] śică "stăpîne să-n dai ai trei galbeni".* (Cornelia Cohuţ & Magdalena Vulpe, *Graiul din zona "Porţile de Fier".* I. *Texte. Sintaxă,* 1973, quoted in Puşcariu et al., eds. 1907– XIII: I: 318)[13]

"I pay three gold coins a year. Now that the year has come to an end, [...] he says 'master, you have to give me three gold coins.'"

The metaphor in question is also frequent in background descriptions. For instance, in Ovid's *Fasti* Book III verses 559 and 573–576, Latin IRE "to go" collocates with ANNUS "year" in the identification of the time frame within which events take place; cf. Spanish *corría el año 1939 cuando* "it was in 1939 that" (Galimberti Jarman & Russell, eds. 1994: 199) and Italian *correva l'anno 1960* "it was 1960" (Macchi, ed. 1970 I: 323):

(58) *pellitur Anna domo [...].*
[...]
tertia nudandas acceperat area messes,
inque cavos ierant tertia musta lacus;
signa recensuerat bis sol sua, tertius ibat
annus, et exilio terra paranda nova est.   (Frazer, ed. 1996: 160, 162)
"Anna was driven from home [...]. [...] For the third time the reaped corn had been carried to the threshing-floor to be stripped of the husk, and for the third time the new wine had poured into the hollow vats. Twice had the sun traversed the signs of the zodiac, and a third year was passing, when Anna was compelled to seek a new land of exile." (ibid., pp. 161, 163)

6.1.22   TIME IS MOTION: TIME IS A LANDSCAPE WE MOVE THROUGH, TIME IS A LANDSCAPE IN WHICH EVENTS ARE LOCATED

In the second subtype of temporal metaphors, it is not time that moves, but rather people move along the timeline (TIME IS A LANDSCAPE WE MOVE THROUGH) and events are placed on the timeline or extend along it (TIME IS A LANDSCAPE IN WHICH EVENTS ARE LOCATED). For instance, in Book VI verses 65–66 of Virgil's *Aeneid*, Latin VENTURI, i.e., the future active participle of VENIRE "to come", encodes future events: *sanctissima vates, praescia venturi* "most holy prophetess, who foreknow the future" (Rushton Fairclough, ed. 1999: 536–537). The Spanish adverbial phrase *en lo por venir* "in what follows, in the future" (Álvar Ezquerra, ed.

---

13. The use of Romanian *a veni* with units of time as an equivalent of *a se încheia* "to end" and of *a se împlini* "to come to an end" is marked as archaic and informal (Puşcariu et al., eds. 1907– XIII: I: 318).

1990: 1119) constitutes a Romance analog. Likewise, in Ovid's *Fasti* Book IV verse 947, Latin EXIRE "to go out" marks duration of events: *exit et in Maias sacrum Florale Kalendas* "The rites of Flora also extend into the Kalends of May" (Frazer, ed. 1996: 258–259). Along the same lines, in the fragment from the *Introducción al símbolo de la fe* by Fray Luis de Granada (1504–1588), Spanish *correr* "to run" makes reference to extension of beliefs through time:

(59) *La misma fe y los mismas dogmas que los santos tuvieron desde el principio del mundo, ésos <u>han corrido</u> por todas las edades siguientes hasta la nuestra, y <u>correrán</u> hasta la fin del mundo.* (quoted in Cuervo 1992–1994 II: 563) "The same faith and the same dogmas that the saints had from the beginning of the world have extended through all the subsequent epochs up to our times, and they will last until the end of the world."

In the next quotation, which belongs to Ulpian who composed numerous texts on Roman law in the early 3rd century A.D., Latin CURRERE "to run" collocates with the noun USUCAPIO "usucapion" with the meaning "to be reckoned (from a date)": *ut usucapio currat* "so that the usucapion may be computed" (quoted in Glare, ed. 1982: 476).[14] This latter example brings to mind such modern expressions with Catalan *córrer* and Spanish *correr* as *El lloguer corre des de primer d'any* and *El alquiler corre desde primero de año* "Rent starts to compute from the first day of the year" (Sagristà i Artigas, ed. 1998: 445).

6.1.23 SELECTION IS MOTION

Latin and Romance motion verbs also share the ability to take on the senses "to be selected", "to fall by lot", "to be elected", and "to be determined by vote". The lexemes recruited into this mapping are the equivalents of "to go out". For instance, in the passage from Book VIII Part 22 Sections 9–10 of Livy's *Ab Urbe Condita*, Latin EVENIRE refers to the fact that particular military obligations were allotted to a specific consul:

(60) *Inter consules provinciis comparatis bello Graeci persequendi Publilio <u>evenerunt</u>; Cornelius altero exercitu Samnitibus, si qua se moverent, oppositus – fama autem erat defectioni Campanorum imminentes admoturos castra – ibi optimum visum Cornelio stativa habere.* (Foster, ed. 1999: 86) "By the division of the commands between the consuls, the war with the Greeks fell to Publilius; Cornelius, with another army, was ordered to be ready for the Samnites, in case they should take the field; and since it was

---

14. Latin USUCAPIO "usucapion" is a legal term defined as "acquisition of the ownership of something by virtue of uninterrupted possession" (Glare, ed. 1982: 2110).

rumoured that they were only waiting to bring up their army the moment the Campanians began a revolt, that seemed to be the best place for the permanent encampment of Cornelius." (ibid., p. 87)

Portuguese *sair* offers a Romance analog: *Saiu-lhe o melhor prêmio das corridas* "The highest prize in the races was awarded to him" (Fernandes 1972: 538). The equivalents of "to go out" can also make reference to people elected or appointed to political office, as in the case of Romanian *a ieşi* in *A ieşit deputat* "He was elected deputy" (Puşcariu et al., eds. 1907– II: I: 459). The passage with Spanish *salir* from *Historia de la conquista de México* by Antonio de Solís y Rivadeneira (1610–1686) offers an earlier Romance example:

(61)   *salieron por alcaldes Alonso Hernández Portocarrero y Francisco de Montejo; por regidores Alonso Dávila, Pedro y Alonso de Alvarado, y Gonzalo de Sandoval; y por alguacil mayor y procurador general Juan de Escalante y Francisco Álvarez Chico.*   (accessed through Davies 2007)
"Alonso Hernández Portocarrero and Francisco de Montejo were appointed magistrates; Alonso Dávila, Pedro and Alonso de Alvarado, and Gonzalo de Sandoval, aldermen; Juan de Escalante, chief constable; and Francisco Álvarez Chico, chief of legal council."

The mapping in question is also widely used in the description of exam topics drawn by students at random: e.g., Spanish *salir*, as in *me salió un tema que no había estudiado* "I got a subject I hadn't studied" (Galimberti Jarman & Russell, eds. 1994: 684). Games based on chance, such as lottery, roulette, and cards provide another common context: e.g., Italian *uscire* in *è uscito per primo il (numero) 23* "number 23 was drawn first" (Rubery, ed. 2010: 2575) and Spanish *salir* in *el as de diamantes todavía no ha salido* "the ace of diamonds hasn't come up yet" (Galimberti Jarman & Russell, eds. 1994: 683).

French *sortir*, Catalan *sortir*, and Occitan *sortir* are also able to function as equivalents of "to be selected", "to fall by lot", and "to be elected". A pertinent French example with *sortir* comes from the description of the gambling house in the novel *Le Père Goriot* by Honoré de Balzac (1799–1850):

(62)   *Eugène, suivi de tous les spectateurs, demande sans vergogne où il faut mettre l'enjeu. – Si vous placez un louis sur un seul de ces trente-six numéros, et qu'il sorte, vous aurez trente-six louis, lui dit un vieillard respectable, à cheveux blancs. Eugène jeta ses cent francs sur le chiffre de son âge, vingt et un. Un cri d'étonnement part sans qu'il ait eu le temps de se reconnaître. Il avait gagné sans le savoir.*   (Balzac 1835: 173)
"Eugène, who was followed by the whole company, asked, without the least embarrassment, where he was to place his money. 'If you put one

louis on any of these thirty-six numbers and it comes up, you will win thirty-six *louis*,' said a respectable-looking old man with white hair. Eugène placed the whole hundred francs on the number of his own age, – twenty-one. A cry of astonishment broke from every one before he knew himself what had happened. He had won." (Balzac 1894: 179)

Similar Catalan instances include *Va sortir elegit el nostre candidat* "Our candidate was elected" and *A la rifa d'avui ha sortit premiat el número x* "Number x won to-day's lottery" (Sagristà i Artigas, ed. 1998: 1570). In the case of Occitan, comparable expressions are *Lou sujèt que sort à-n-un eisamen* "The topic that is drawn on the exam" and *Lou numerò que vèn de sourti* "The number that was just drawn" (Coupier 1995: 1315). However, as we have seen in Chapters 3 and 4, the etymon of French, Catalan, and Occitan *sortir* is Latin SORTIRI "to throw lots or to choose by a lot". Hence, in the case of these languages, the examples above represent not the metaphorical meaning, but rather the original one from which the motion sense later developed. At the same time, according to the *Dictionnaire historique de la langue française*, modern French speakers seem to perceive these expressions with *sortir* as figurative extensions:

> *sortir* est employé pour 'être tiré' en parlant d'un numéro (de loterie, etc.) que désigne le hasard [...], d'où par analogie à propos d'un sujet d'examen [...], mais le verbe est alors senti comme rattaché au sens moderne 'aller au dehors', par une spécialisation ou une extension. (Rey, ed. 1994 II: 1980)

> [*sortir* is used as an equivalent of "to be drawn" when talking about a number (in a lottery, etc.) which designates a chance [...], and by analogy when talking about an exam topic [...], but this usage is perceived as connected to the modern sense "to go out" through specialization or extension.]

This is noteworthy because it serves as a reminder of the importance of the diachronic approach for the accurate identification of what constitutes a metaphorical mapping and what does not.[15]

---

15. In her discussion of English *dull* and *keen*, Allan (2008: 186) makes a similar point about the role of diachrony in avoiding preconceptions:

> Folk etymology seems to attribute the meaning 'stupid' to a source meaning connected with sharp/piercing, but the evidence of the *OED* [*Oxford English Dictionary*] suggests that in fact the opposite transfer of meaning has occurred. The earliest meaning for *dull* is defined as 'Not quick in intelligence or mental perception; slow of understanding; not sharp of wit; obtuse, stupid, inapprehensive. In early use, sometimes: Wanting wit, fatuous, foolish'. This is supported by quotations as early as the tenth century, and has a cognate in Germanic. The concrete meaning of the term, 'Not sharp or keen; blunt (in *lit.* sense)', seems to be much later, and the earliest supporting quotation for this dates to c.1400 [...]. *Keen* appears to develop in a similar way, with the abstract sense evidenced earlier than the concrete [...].

6.1.24   THINKING IS MOVING IN THE IDEASCAPE: REASONING IS FOLLOWING A PATH

Another metaphor available in both Latin and Romance projects between moving and thinking. One of the subtypes of this mapping encodes the thinking person as the person in motion (REASONING IS FOLLOWING A PATH). For instance, Latin PER-VENIRE "to come" could function in the sense "to arrive (at) by mental process" (Glare, ed. 1982: 1363). In Book III Part 6 Section 55 of Quintilian's *Institutio Oratoria*, this verb combines with AD OCTO "to eight", making reference to the number of bases, such as competence, quality, and quantity, that writers come up with by using their thought: *Alii pervenerunt usque ad octo, translatione ad septem superiores adiecta* "Others again make eight by the addition of *competence* to the above-mentioned seven" (Butler, ed. 1969: 436–437). Another relevant projection available in Latin is the use of INIRE "to go in" as part of the expression *rationem inire* defined as "to go into (a calculation, assessment); to arrive at, determine (a figure, quantity, etc., by calculation)" (Glare, ed. 1982: 891). The fragment from Caesar's *De Bello Gallico* Book VII Part 71 Section 4 serves as illustration: *ratione inita exigue dierum se habere xxx frumentum* "According to the calculation, there was barely enough grain for thirty days" (quoted in Glare, ed. 1982: 891). Likewise, Latin INTRARE "to go in" could take on the meaning "to enter into with the mind, study, look into" (Glare, ed. 1982: 954). For instance, in the passage from Cicero's *De Finibus Bonorum et Malorum* Book V Part 16 Section 44, it is used in the context of studying nature:

(63)   *Intrandum igitur est in rerum naturam et penitus quid ea postulet perviden-dum; aliter enim nosmet ipsos nosse non possumus.* (Rackham, ed. 1967: 442) "We must therefore penetrate into the nature of things, and come to un-derstand thoroughly its requirements; otherwise we cannot know our-selves." (ibid., p. 443)

Latin SUBIRE, whose literal function included upward and downward motion, par-ticipated in the mapping in question as well as an equivalent of "(of a mental im-age, object of thought, etc.) to suggest itself (to a person, his mind, etc.)" (Glare, ed. 1982: 1839). For instance, Ovid laments from exile in *Tristia* Book V poem 7 verses 53–60:

(64)   *unus in hoc nemo est populo, qui forte Latine*
        quamlibet e medio reddere verba queat.
        ille ego Romanus vates – ignoscite, Musae! –
        Sarmatico cogor plurima more loqui.
        et pudet et fateor, iam desuetudine longa
        vix subeunt ipsi verba Latina mihi.

nec dubito quin sint et in hoc non pauca libello
barbara: non hominis culpa, sed ista loci.   (Wheeler, ed. 1996: 238)
"There is not a single man among these people who perchance might express in Latin any words however common. I, the Roman bard – pardon, ye Muses! – am forced to utter most things in Sarmatian fashion. I admit it, though it shames me: now from long disuse Latin words with difficulty occur even to me! And I doubt not there are even in this book not a few barbarisms, not the fault of the man but of the place." (ibid., p. 239)

As far as the Romance languages are concerned, one common collocational pattern is the expression "to reach the conclusion", as in a passage from the novel *Helena* (1876) by the Brazilian writer Joaquim Machado de Assis:

(65) *Refleti muito durante estas duas horas, dizia ele, e <u>cheguei a uma conclusão</u>*
       única.   (Machado de Assis 2004, accessed through COMPARA)
       "I have reflected deeply during these two hours, he wrote, and I have arrived at one conclusion."
                        (Machado de Assis 1984, accessed through COMPARA)

Corresponding Romance analogs include Spanish *llegar a la conclusión* (Galimberti Jarman & Russell, eds. 1994: 461), Italian *arrivare a conclusione* (Rubery, ed. 2010: 1517), and Romanian *a ajunge la o concluzie* (Bantaş et al. 1981: 18). Attaining a specific level of expertise rendered by the equivalents of "to come, to arrive" is another option, as in the case of Spanish *llegar* in *sé algo de electrónica, pero a tanto no llego* "I know something about electronics but not that much" (Galimberti Jarman & Russell, eds. 1994: 461). The projection between motion inside and accepting ideas is relevant as well, as illustrated by the following Romanian sentence with *a intra* from writings by Ion Luca Caragiale (1852–1912): *Ştii că eu nu intru la idee cu una cu două* "You should know that I do not believe ideas very easily" (quoted in Puşcariu et al., eds. 1907– II: I: 819). French *entrer* and Italian *entrare* offer similar patterns: *entrer dans les idées de quelqu'un* "to agree with someone" (Mansion, ed. 1939 I: 324), *entrare in pensiero di qualcosa* "to become convinced of something" (Battaglia, ed. 1961–2009 V: 173). The Romance equivalents of "to enter" can likewise express one's ability to look into the subject matter and comprehend it: e.g., Catalan *El llatí és molt difícil: m'ha costat molt d'entrar-hi* "Latin is very difficult: it has cost me a lot of effort to understand it" (Sagristà i Artigas, ed. 1998: 640).

6.1.25 THINKING IS MOVING IN THE IDEASCAPE: IDEAS ARE MOVING OBJECTS

The second subtype of projection between moving and thinking maps between motion and the process of generating, learning, remembering, understanding, embracing, or abandoning thoughts, ideas, beliefs, information, knowledge, and similar concepts, by encoding these concepts as moving objects (IDEAS ARE MOVING OBJECTS). In the case of Latin, one common combination is *in mentem venire* "to come to one's mind" (Glare, ed. 1982: 2030). For instance, in Plautus' *Bacchides* Act V Scene 3 lines 1993–1994 we read:

(66)   *Non tibi venit in mentem, amabo,*
       si dum vivas tibi bene facias
       tam pol id quidem esse haud perlonginquom [...].   (Nixon, ed. 1966: 452)
       "My dear man, doesn't it occur to you that, supposing you do enjoy yourself all your life, this life is very, very short, after all [...]." (ibid., p. 453)

Another common Latin collocation is *in buccam venire* defined as "to come to one's lips" (Glare, ed. 1982: 2030), i.e., to come to one's mind. Cicero concludes one of his letters to Atticus (*Epistulae ad Atticum* Book I Letter 12) by saying:

(67)   *Tu velim saepe ad nos scribas. Si rem nullam habebis, quod in buccam venerit, scribito.*   (Winstedt, ed. 1944: 32)
       "Please write frequently. If you've no news, write the first thing that comes into your head." (ibid., pp. 31, 33)

The use of Latin DESCENDERE "to go down" as an equivalent of "to penetrate, sink (into the mind, etc.)" (Glare, ed. 1982: 523) was also widespread. Sallust's *Iugurtha* Part 11 Section 7 offers a pertinent example:

(68)   *Tum idem Hiempsal placere sibi respondit; nam ipsum illum tribus proxumis annis adoptatione in regnum pervenisse. Quod verbum in pectus Iugurthae altius quam quisquam ratus erat descendit. Itaque ex eo tempore ira et metu anxius moliri, parare atque ea modo cum animo habere, quibus Hiempsal per dolum caperetur.*   (Rolfe, ed. 1965: 150, 152)
       "Thereupon Hiempsal again spoke up and declared that he approved the suggestion; for it was within the last three years, he said that Jugurtha himself had been adopted and thus given a share in the kingdom. This remark sank more deeply into Jugurtha's mind than anyone would have supposed. So, from that moment he was a prey to resentment and fear, planned and schemed, and thought of nothing except some means by which he might outwit and ensnare Hiempsal." (ibid., pp. 151, 153)

Likewise, in Part 18 Section 8 of Seneca the Younger's essay "*De Consolatione ad Helviam*" we read: *altius praecepta descendunt, quae teneris imprimuntur aetatibus* "instruction that is stamped upon the plastic years leaves a deeper mark" (Basore, ed. 1979: 480–481).

As far as the Romance examples are concerned, it is relevant to mention the equivalents of "to go" accompanied by prepositional phrases in reference to the thinking process. The sentence with Romanian *a merge* from writings by Nicolae Gane (1835–1916) serves as illustration: *Îi mergeau și gîndurile prin cap* "The thoughts were going through his head" (quoted in Pușcariu et al., eds. 1907– VI: 402). A parallel Raeto-Romance example with *ir* comes from writings by Andri Peer (1921–1985): *El [...] disch tuot quai ch'el 'pensa', o plüchöntsch chi til va per cheu* "He [...] says everything that he 'thinks', or rather that goes through his head" (quoted in Planta et al., eds. 1939– X: 30). Another common pattern is to employ the equivalents of "to come" in reference to ideas that occur to the person or in reference to information to which the person gains access, as in the sentence with Spanish *venir* from Cervantes' *Quijote*: *Apenas hubo salido de la venta, cuando le vino al Cura el pensamiento* "Right after the priest had left the inn, a thought occurred to him" (quoted in Cuervo 1992–1994 VIII: 898). While ideas and information can become accessible, they can also become inaccessible, i.e., forgotten, as in the passage with French *sortir* "to go out" from *La scène capitale* (1935) by Pierre-Jean Jouve (1887–1976):

(69) *Ce que nous avons dit dès l'abord devait être insignifiant – ou alors singu-*
      lièrement grave et plein d'importance – car cela est sorti *de ma mémoire.*
                                        (quoted in Imbs, ed. 1971–1994 XV: 704)
      "What we said initially must be of little significance – or extremely serious
      and full of importance – because it escaped my memory."

Occitan *sortir* "to go out" shows the same figurative extension: *Acò m'a sourti de la tèsto* "This slipped my mind" (Coupier 1995: 1315). The equivalents of "to come" and "to go in" can also encode the results of focused thinking, studying, or any other type of intellectual engagement. Expressions with Italian *entrare* "to go in" and *venire* "to come" serve as illustration: *questa poesia non mi entra (in testa)* "I can't get this poem into my head", *che risultato ti è venuto?* "what answer did you get?", *ho fatto la somma e mi viene 60* "I did the sum and got 60 as an answer" (Rubery, ed. 2010: 1805, 2589). Expressions with Catalan *entrar* "to go in", Spanish *entrar* "to go in", and Spanish *llegar* "to come" are equally relevant: *El que ha fet no m'entra al cap* "I can't comprehend what he has done" (Sagristà i Artigas, ed. 1998: 640), *ya se lo he explicado varias veces, pero no le entra* "I've explained it to him several times but he just doesn't understand", *emplea un lenguaje que llega a la juventud* "he uses language that gets through to young people" (Galimberti Jarman & Russell, eds. 1994: 307, 462).

6.2 Motion-based semantic continuity and loss within a wider context

Taken collectively, the data presented in Section 6.1 suggest that continuity between Latin and Romance motion-based metaphors is prominent. Metaphorical
patterns attested in Latin are not lost even though many Latin lexemes have disappeared. This is the case because new Romance forms created in the place of Latin
verbs that became obsolete are equally capable of taking on the metaphorical functions available in Latin. Latin motion-based figurative meanings that do not have
a Romance motion-based counterpart are limited to specialized technical terms,
such as SCANDERE "to go up" in reference to poetry in the sense "to scan (a verse)"
(Glare, ed. 1982: 1699).[16]

I believe that the very high degree of stability on the semasiological level, despite
the pronounced reshaping on the onomasiological level, can be explained in light of
the conceptual metaphor theory. As we have seen in Section 5.1, the main tenet of
this theory is that the locus of metaphor is not linguistic structure but rather conceptual thought. Hence, I would argue, it is not lexical but rather conceptual stability that is required for the survival of metaphorical patterns from Latin to Romance.
In other words, it does not matter that there is no formal continuity between, say,
Latin CONSCENDERE "to go up" which became obsolete and such Romance lexemes
as French *monter* "to go up", Italian *salire* "to go up", Catalan *pujar* "to go up", and
Romanian *a se ridica* "to go up". Since CONSCENDERE and the corresponding
Romance forms lexicalize the same concept of upward motion, they can share metaphorical functions. For example, in the following five expressions these verbs express social advancement: Latin *ad consulatum conscendere* "to ascend to the Consulate", French *monter au grade de colonel* "to rise to be a colonel", Italian *salire di
grado* "to rise in rank", Catalan *pujar a alcalde* "to attain the mayor's position", and
Romanian *a se ridica la înălţimea cuiva* "to rise to the level of somebody".

The massive continuity of metaphorical patterns that my analysis has uncovered
is consistent with the stability reported in recent studies on Romance like Dworkin
(2006a) for color terms and Gruntova (2007) and Maisak (2007) for the aqua-motion
lexicon. For example, Dworkin (2006a) notes that although the basic Latin term for
"white" was ALBUS, while the basic terms for "white" in a number of the Romance
languages go back to the Germanic root that meant "shiny",[17] the figurative functions

---

16. The fact that Romance motion verbs cannot be used in this sense does not mean, however,
that the Romance languages have undergone semantic loss: cf. such Romance non-motion verbs
as Spanish *escandir*, French *scander*, Italian *scandire*, Portuguese *escandir*, and Romanian *a scan-
da* "to scan (a verse)".

17. E.g., Spanish *blanco*, French *blanc*, Italian *bianco*, Portuguese *branco*, Catalan *blanc*; cf.
Dutch, Swedish *blank* "shiny", German *blank* "shining, bright".

of ALBUS are available for the Romance lexemes as well. For instance, he points out (p. 77) that both Latin ALBUS and Spanish *blanco* can be employed as equivalents of "clear". One of the Old Spanish examples that he offers, based on Duncan (1975: 63), comes from the 13th-century legal text *Setenario* of Alfonso X (1221–1284): *la ley de Dios era blanca e limpia* "the law of God was clear and lucid". A parallel example with Latin ALBUS can be found in the description of Albucius' rhetorical style in Book VII Preface 2 of Seneca the Elder's *Controuersiae*:

(70)   *Sententiae, quas optime Pollio Asinius <u>albas</u> vocabat, simplices, apertae, ni-hil occultum, nihil insperatum adferentes, sed vocales et splendidae.*
                                                                    (Winterbottom, ed. 1974b: 4)
"His epigrams, which Asinius Pollio excellently called 'white',[18] were simple, open, bringing no hidden or unexpected point with them, merely resonant and brilliant." (ibid., p. 5)

Along the same lines, a comparison between Latin (Gruntova 2007) and Portuguese (Maisak 2007) aqua-motion verbs reveals that although Latin NARE, NATARE, FLUITARE, and FLUTARE "to float", on the one hand, and Portuguese *boiar* "to float", on the other hand, are not cognates,[19] they share the ability to figuratively express loose and unstable position or fit. For example, Gruntova (2007: 243) shows that in Book I of his *Ars Amatoria* Ovid employs NATARE in reference to an unstable foot in loosely fitting footwear:

(71)   *Munditie placeant, fuscentur corpora Campo:*
Sit bene conveniens et sine labe toga:
Lingula ne rigeat, careant rubigine dentes,
Nec vagus in laxa pes tibi pelle <u>natet</u>:
Nec male deformet rigidos tonsura capillos:
Sit coma, sit trita barba resecta manu. (Mozley, ed. 1985: 48, verses 513–518)
"Let your person please by cleanliness, and be made swarthy by the Campus; let your toga fit, and be spotless; let your shoe-strep not be too tight, let its buckle be free from rust, and let your feet not float about in shoes too loose; nor let your stubborn locks be spoilt by bad cutting; let hair and beard be dressed by a practised hand." (ibid., p. 49)

---

18.   According to Glare ed. (1982: 93), the adjective ALBUS is used here in the sense "clear, lucid". Because Seneca is writing about Albucius, Winterbottom (1974b: 5, n.4) points out that the use of ALBUS "white, clear" instead of its synonym CANDIDUS "white, clear" may be intended as pun.

19.   Portuguese *boiar* "to float" < Portuguese *bóia* "buoy, beacon" < Old French *boie, boye* < Germanic **baukn* (Maisak 2007: 211). For a discussion of the different theories regarding the meaning, origin, and development of Germanic **baukn*, see Liberman (2008: 3–9).

This Latin passage resonates with the following Portuguese examples with *boiar* provided in Maisak (2007: 214): *Olhe, diz, mostrando como os jeans lhe estão a boiar na cintura* "Look, he says, showing how his jeans fit loosely at his waist", *Estou a boiar na roupa* "This outfit is too big".

As we will see in Chapter 9, the high level of overlap between the figurative meanings of Latin and Romance motion verbs has ramifications for cognitive linguistics, more specifically for the conceptual metaphor theory.

CHAPTER 7

Romance innovative semantic developments

In addition to the figurative meanings shared by Latin and Romance discussed in Chapter 6, the Romance languages acquired a series of new functions not attested in Classical Latin. Some of these novel developments are found across the Romance linguistic area, while others have a more restricted representation.

7.1 Pan-Romance semantic innovations

A good example of an innovation attested widely is the use of motion verbs to encode valid, up-to-date, acceptable, relevant, or fashionable nature of things as part of the VALIDITY IS MOTION mapping. In the majority of the Romance languages the equivalents of "to run" serve as the source domain, as illustrated by Spanish *correr* (72), Italian *correre* (73), Portuguese *correr* (74), Catalan *córrer* (75), and Raeto-Romance *currer* (76):

(72) *Estos bonos ya no corren.*   (Galimberti Jarman & Russell, eds. 1994: 199)
      "These vouchers are no longer valid."

(73) *È una moneta che non corre più.*   (Reynolds, ed. 1981 I: 199)
      "This currency is no longer in use."

(74) *A moeda que corre em nosso país é o real.*   (Geiger, ed. 2008, s.v. *correr*)
      "The currency in use in our country is the real."

(75) *Aquesta moneda ja no corre, pot servir per a la col·lecció.*
                                          (Sagristà i Artigas, ed. 1998: 445)
      "This coin is no longer valid; it can be used for a collection."

(76) *munaida chi nun cuorra pü*   (Planta et al., eds. 1939– IV: 523)
      "currency no longer in official circulation"

This usage has enjoyed a continuous presence in the Romance varieties throughout their history. For instance, the following passage belongs to the 13th-century Spanish legal work *Las siete partidas*:

(77) *Et que lo acojan en ellos [al rey en los castillos] quando hi quisiere entrar, et que corra hi su moneda.*   (quoted in Cuervo 1992–1994 II: 564)
      "And they should let him [the king] in when he wishes to enter them [the castles], and his money should be valid there."

The next example comes from the Italian *Storia fiorentina* by Benedetto Varchi (1503–1565): *Corrono in Firenze monete forestiere di molte ragioni* "In Firenze foreign currencies of different types are in use" (quoted in Battaglia, ed. 1961–2009 III: 823). As example (78) from the Biblical commentary *Exposición del Cantar de los Cantares* by the Spanish Fray Luis de León (1527–1591) illustrates, expressions of the type *moneda que corre* can combine both senses, "currency in general use" and "currency that is legally valid"; cf. French *avoir cours* "(of coinage) to be legal tender, to be current, to be in circulation" (Mansion, ed. 1939 I: 207):

(78)   *O lo que tengo por más cierto, y más conforme al parecer de San Jerónimo [...], es decir, que mirra que <u>corre</u> vale tanto como decir mirra excelentísima y muy fina; porque la palabra hebrea hober quiere decir <u>corriente</u>, y que pasa por buena por todas partes; lo cual según la propiedad de aquella lengua, quiere decir que es muy buena y muy perfecta, aprobada de todos los que la ven, conforme á lo que en nuestra lengua solemos decir de la moneda de ley, que es moneda que <u>corre</u>.* (Fray Luis de León, *Exposición del Cantar de los Cantares*, accessed through Davies 2007)
"Or, what I believe to be true and what conforms better to the view of Saint Jerome [...] is that myrrh that runs means excellent or very fine myrrh; because the Hebrew word *hober* means valid and acceptable everywhere. Based on the property of that language this means that it is very good and of high quality, approved by everyone who sees it. This accords with what we in our own language usually call official coin, which is coin in use."

Along the same lines, earlier texts contain examples in which motion verbs encode validity of items accepted for administrative purposes. For instance, in the passage from a legal work commissioned by the Spanish king Carlos IV (1748–1819), *correr* appears with the meanings "to be valid" and "to be in use" three times – once with *libros* "books", once with *papel sellado* "officially stamped paper", and once with *sello* "official stamp":

(79)   *Que los [libros] que hubiesen de servir para más tiempo de un año, <u>corran</u> hasta que se acabe el papel que se pusiese para su primera formación; y en el año en que se acabasen, se cierren con el sello reservado en fin de las últimas partidas – y se hagan otros del papel sellado que <u>corriese</u> aquel año en que se cerraron; y siendo libros en que no haya inconveniente cesar en cada un año, se cerrarán también en fin del que acaba – formándose otros para el año siguiente con el sello que en él hubiese de <u>correr</u>.* (*Novísima recopilación de las leyes de España, mandada formar por el Señor Don Carlos IV*, quoted in Cuervo 1992–1994 II: 563–564)

"The books that serve for longer than a year should be in use until the paper employed for their creation is used up; and the year they come to their end, they should be closed with a stamp at the end of the last entry; and other books should be made from officially stamped paper that is in use the year that old books were closed. And since it does not cause any inconvenience to bring these books to an end each year, they should also be closed at the end of the year – and new books should be formed for the next year with an official stamp which should be in use that next year."

In addition to the equivalents of "to run", other members of the lexical field of motion can be recruited into the mapping in question. In the case of Romanian, *a merge* "to go" (80) and *a umbla* "to walk" (81) are employed:

(80) *Banii vechi nu mai <u>merg</u>.* (August Scriban, *Dicționaru limbii românești*, 1939, quoted in Pușcariu et al., eds. 1907– VI: 409)
"The old currency is already not valid."

(81) *Într-această vreme <u>au îmblat</u> bani de hârtie.* (Nicolae Iorga, 1871–1940, *Studii și documente cu privire la istoria românilor*, volume XIII, quoted in Pușcariu et al., eds. 1907– XII: A 2-A: 98; this example is from the year 1811)
"During this time paper banknotes were in use."

In the case of Raeto-Romance, *ir* "to go" offers relevant examples, as in *quist franc nu vo pü* "this franc is no longer in use" and *quellas marcas da Pro Juventute von mo sin tiamps* "these Pro Juventute stamps are valid only for a limited time" (Planta et al., eds. 1939– X: 36). Likewise, we find analogous examples with Old Spanish *andar* "to walk": *ii solidos in fossadera de la moneda que andidiere en Castilla* "two gold coins towards the tribute for the military campaign in the type of currency which is in use in Castile" (*Fuero de Ibrillos*, quoted in Cuervo 1992–1994 I: 462).[1] As we will see below, Italian *andare* "to go" also participates in this mapping.

The examples presented above illustrate that one typical context in which motion verbs can appear in the senses "to be valid" and "to be in use" involves currency or similar official items. However, the range of possible collocational patterns is

---

1. The exact date of composition of the *Fuero de Ibrillos* is unknown; presumably it was composed around 1200. It was issued by Alfonso VIII, king of Castile between 1158 and 1214. The original manuscript of the *fuero* is lost, and the extant copy is from the early 13th century (Govantes 1846: 294). Cuervo (1992–1994 I: 462) quotes the *fuero* from the *Diccionario geográfico-histórico de la Rioja* by Ángel Casimiro de Govantes (1846) – in which the place name appears as *in Castella* – and labels it as 'lat[ín] hisp[ánico]' ["Hispanic Latin"]. However, as shown in Wright (1982) and Harris-Northall (2007), *fueros*, which are municipal charters from Medieval Iberia, are often a complex mixture of Latin and Romance. The excerpt quoted above is in Hispano-Romance.

much wider. The up-to-date and valid nature of linguistic norms, for instance, is another possible context. This way, in the Italian sentence from Emilio Cecchi's *Saggi e vagabondaggi* (1962), *correre* "to run" combines with *dialetti* "dialects" and *lingue* "languages", when referring to the dialects and languages in use:

(82)   *I frammenti [...] sono scritti in una lingua che contiene come per incidente alcune voci italiane, ma non è la lingua italiana e nessuno dei dialetti o delle lingue che a quell'epoca correvano in Europa.*

(quoted in Battaglia, ed. 1961–2009 III: 823)

"The fragments [...] are written in a language that contains as if by chance some Italian words, but it is not Italian and it is not any of the dialects or languages that in those times were in use in Europe."

Bernardo de Aldrete's *Del origen y principio de la lengua castellana ó romance que hoy se usa en España* (1606) contains an analogous earlier example with Spanish *correr* "to run": *La lengua vulgar y que más corría en España, era la latina* "The common language and the one that was used the most in Spain was Latin" (quoted in Cuervo 1992–1994 II: 563).

Motion verbs can also encode the legitimate and up-to-date nature of guiding principles such as laws, rules, regulations, and customs. In this way, in the 17th-century passage from Cervantes' *Quijote*, Spanish *correr* is employed with the noun *regla* "rule", making reference to its validity:

(83)   *Digo asimismo que cuando algún pintor quiere salir famoso en su arte pro-cura imitar los originales de los más únicos pintores que sabe, y esta mesma regla corre por todos los más oficios o ejercicios de cuenta que sirven para adorno de las repúblicas [...].*

(Cervantes 1998 I: 274)

"Let me add that when a painter wants to become famous for his art, he tries to copy originals by the finest artists he knows. And this same rule holds good for nearly all the trades and professions of importance that serve to adorn a society [...]."

(Cervantes Saavedra 2001: 207)

Along the same lines, in Spanish *Ya sabes que esas excusas aquí no corren* "You know you can't get away with excuses like that here" (Galimberti Jarman & Russell, eds. 1994: 199), *correr* appears with *excusas* "excuses", thereby marking their level of acceptability. Similarly, in the Italian sentence *In Italia corre l'uso della siesta* "It is the custom to rest in the afternoon in Italy" (Reynolds, ed. 1981 I: 199), *correre* combines with *uso* "custom" to encode a traditional cultural practice. Likewise, Raeto-Romance *currer* can appear with the noun *pretsch* "price", signaling the price's conformity to the established norm: *Dat ün ü jerdi al pretsch chi cuora* "Give half-a-kilo of barley at the current price" (Planta et al., eds. 1939– IV: 523).

Beliefs, opinions, and attitudes deemed adequate is another case in point. In a letter concerning historical matters dated September 3, 1807, addressed to Carlos González de Posada, Gaspar Melchor de Jovellanos (1744–1811) uses Spanish *correr* with the subject *opiniones* "opinions" in reference to their acceptability:

(84)　*La fecha que pone Caro al privilegio, [...], no tiene repugnancia alguna [...]. Por lo demás hallo que Caro copió muy de priesa lo poco que extractó del fuero, Y por lo mismo entendió mal algunas voces, que yo rectifiqué en mi copia [...]. Y porque yo desconfío de la exactitud de las demás, enviaré a usted la mía, [...]. Entonces, y con ella a la vista, podrá usted hacer más sólidas reflexiones sobre lo que dicen los Bolandos, y yo espero que tendrá la bondad de comunicármelas, para que trabajemos de acuerdo en fijar la verdad entre las varias opiniones que <u>corren</u> en este asunto.* (Gaspar Melchor de Jovellanos, *Correspondencia*, accessed through Davies 2007)
"The date that Caro assigns to the document, [...], does not raise any objections [...]. Other than that, I find that Caro copied very fast the little information that he extracted from the charter, and because of this he misunderstood certain words, the ones that I corrected in my own copy [...]. And since I do not trust the accuracy of other copies, I will send you mine, [...]. This way, by taking it into account, you will be able to make a better informed judgment about what the Bollandists had said. And I hope that you will be so kind as to communicate this judgment to me, so that we can work together on establishing the truth among the different opinions that are accepted in the matter."

Motion verbs are equally well suited to express trends that find support among the population. For instance, in the theatre play *La bottega del caffè* (1750) by Carlo Goldoni (1707–1793), the combination of Italian *l'acquavite* "brandy" with *correre* makes reference to the trendy nature of this beverage:

(85)　*Tutti cercan di fare quello che fanno gli altri. Una volta <u>correva</u> l'acquavite, adesso è in voga il caffè.*　　(quoted in Battaglia, ed. 1961–2009 III: 823)
"Everyone wants to do the same thing that others do. At one time brandy was popular, nowadays it is coffee."

As can be seen from the next example, in addition to *correre* "to run", Italian *andare* "to go" is also able to function in this capacity: *Quest'inverno vanno (di moda) i cappotti lunghi* "the fashion is for long coats this winter" (Rubery, ed. 2010: 1492). According to Pfister (1979– II: 618), this use of *andare* is a recent phenomenon. The earliest reference work to gloss *andare* as an equivalent of "avere corso legale (detto di moneta)" ["to be in official circulation (about money)"] is the *Dizionario della lingua italiana* (1865–1879) by Niccolò Tommaseo and Bernardo Bellini, and the first attestation of *andare* as an equivalent of "essere di moda" ["to be in style"] is from 1937 (Pfister 1979– II: 618).

The innovative nature of Romance VALIDITY IS MOTION does not mean that this metaphor bears no connection to the mappings available since Classical Latin. As we have seen in Chapter 6, Latin motion verbs could express dissemination of the subject by appearing with such nouns as MORBUS "sickness", CLAMOR "cry, shout, clamor", FREMOR "noise", TREMOR "shake, shudder, tremble", and RUBOR "blush", as in *rubor cucurrit* "the blush mantled". This association – DIFFUSION IS MOTION – has an experiential basis: e.g., when the visual image spreads as it enlarges it is perceived as moving.[2] In addition, Latin had the VALIDITY IS DIFFUSION mapping which is also grounded in experience: common things have the tendency to be viewed as acceptable, correct, and proper.[3] For instance, we can think of the Latin expression *sensus communis* defined as "perception of what is appropriate" and "feeling for others in the same community (as a guide to conduct)" (Glare, ed. 1982: 370, 1735), which is a combination of SENSUS "sensation, judgment" and COMMUNIS "common, shared". The passage from Book I Section 12 of Cicero's *De Oratore* serves as illustration:

(86) *Quod hoc etiam mirabilius debet videri, quia ceterarum artium studia fere*
      reconditis atque abditis e fontibus hauriuntur; dicendi autem omnis ratio in
      medio posita, communi quodam in usu, atque in hominum more et sermone

---

2.   For instance, in the classic experiment reported in Schiff (1965), seven human subjects (three adult men, three adult women, and a five-year-old girl) repeatedly viewed shadows of two- and three-dimensional forms (e.g., a square, a toy car) projected on the screen. In the course of the experiment, the shadows changed in size: they spread, i.e., "underwent a continuously accelerated magnification" and shrunk, i.e., "underwent a continuously deaccelerated minification" (p. 4). The results revealed that the subjects perceived enlarged shadows as objects moving towards them, and perceived minimized shadows as objects moving away from them: "With only one exception, the adult Ss [subjects] reported all stimulus events as approach and recession of an object (of constant size) in depth" (pp. 9–10). Furthermore, Schiff reported that "The child was also observed to blink and/or withdraw her head abruptly on all magnification trials, but never during minification trials" (p. 10).

3.   See, for instance, the classic experiments reported in Asch (1956) which study the impact of group opinion upon the judgment of the individuals. In one of these experiments, the subjects were asked to compare the relative length of lines. The members of the control group estimated the length of lines individually, and their estimates were virtually free of error. In contrast, the critical subjects estimated the length of lines as part of a group of confederates that unanimously offered the wrong estimate. In other words, the critical subjects were placed "in the position of a *minority of one* against a *wrong and unanimous majority*" (p. 3; original emphasis). The results revealed the following majority effect: "[...] the critical subjects showed a marked movement toward the majority. [...] The action of the majority distorted one-third of the reported estimates, in contrast with errors of less then 1 per cent under control conditions" (pp. 9–10).

versatur: ut in ceteris id maxime excellat, quod longissime sit ab imperito-
rum intellegentia sensuque disiunctum, in dicendo autem vitium vel maxi-
mum sit a vulgari genere orationis, atque a consuetudine <u>communis sensus</u>
abhorrere.   (Sutton & Rackham, eds. 1996: 10)
"And this should seem even more marvellous because the subjects of the
other arts are derived as a rule from hidden and remote sources, while the
whole art of oratory lies open to the view, and is concerned in some mea-
sure with the common practice, custom, and speech of mankind, so that,
whereas in all other arts that is most excellent which is farthest removed
from the understanding and mental capacity of the untrained, in oratory
the very cardinal sin is to depart from the language of everyday life, and
the usage approved by the sense of the community." (ibid., p. 11)

The Romance languages retain the DIFFUSION IS MOTION and the VALIDITY IS DIF-
FUSION mappings. In the case of the former, it is relevant to mention expressions
like Spanish *correrse el maquillaje* "to smudge (about makeup)" (Galimberti
Jarman & Russell, eds. 1994: 199) and Italian *è una voce che corre* "it is a rumor that
is going around" (Rubery, ed. 2010: 1704). In the case of the latter, a good example
is Spanish *costumbre* which means both "habit, custom" and "common law"; cf. the
proverb *La costumbre hace ley* "Custom creates law" (Domingo, ed. 1997: 294). The
Romance mapping VALIDITY IS MOTION can be seen as a combination of DIFFU-
SION IS MOTION and VALIDITY IS DIFFUSION, that is to say, of two projections that
speakers have employed since the Classical Latin stage. In other words, using
Grady's (1997a, 1997b, 2005) terminology, VALIDITY IS MOTION is a complex metaphor which emerged as a combination of two primary ones.[4]

When it comes to the development of new mappings, cognitive motivation
grounded in embodiment often works hand in hand with cultural factors. The
metaphor FUNCTIONING IS MOTION is a good example of this interaction. The association between functioning of a mechanism and movement is experientially
based. As Gries (2006) points out in his discussion of English *to run* in sentences
like *The monitors ran twenty-four hours each day*, "the link to the central sense is
probably that one can often see that machines are functioning because they and/or
their parts move" (p. 68). In fact, in the contexts in which the subject is not the
entire mechanism but rather one of its parts, the idea of motion can be partially
retained. For instance, in the 17th-century passage from Cervantes' *Quijote*,
Spanish *andar* "to walk" that accompanies the noun phrase *piedra del molino*
"grindstone" can be interpreted as either "to function", as in Thomas Shelton's

---

4.   The distinction between primary and complex metaphors will be discussed further in
Chapter 9 (below).

translation of 1969, or "to be in motion", as in John Rutherford's translation of 2001, with a metonymic connection[5] between the two senses:

(87)   *Mire vuestra merced – respondió Sancho, que aquellos que allí se parecen no son gigantes, sino molinos de viento, y lo que en ellos parecen brazos son las aspas, que, volteadas del viento, hacen andar la piedra del molino.*

(Cervantes 1998 I: 95)

"I pray you understand, quoth Sancho Panza, that those which appear there are no giants, but windmills; and that which seems in them to be arms, are their sails, that, swung about by the wind, do also make the mill go."   (Cervantes 1969: 60)

"Look you here, Sancho retorted, those over there aren't giants, they're windmills, and what looks to you like arms are sails – when the wind turns them they make the millstones go round."   (Cervantes Saavedra 2001: 64)

When the grammatical subject is the mechanism as a whole, this ambiguity is reduced, as in the combination of Spanish *andar* "to walk" with *aceña* "water-mill" in (88), and of Romanian *a umbla* "to walk" with *moară* "mill" in (89):

(88)   *Andando gana el aceña, que no estándose queda.* (Hernán Núñez, c.1475– 1553, *Refranes ó proverbios en romance*, quoted in Cuervo 1992–1994 I: 455)

"When the water-mill is working continuously, it achieves what it does not achieve when it remains still [i.e., one can make progress through continuous work]."

(89)   *Această moară va începe a umbla în luna lui martie.* (*Curierul rumânesc*, 1834, quoted in Puşcariu et al., eds. 1907– XII: A 2-A: 99)

"This mill will start working in the month of March."

Technological progress made possible the creation of all sorts of new mechanisms, and as a result contributed to the conventionalization and the elaboration of the metaphor in question. The use of motion verbs to encode functioning of clocks and watches is one of the examples. For instance, in the excerpt from the Spanish adaptation of William Paley's *Natural Theology* (1802) by Joaquín Lorenzo Villanueva (1757–1837), *andar* "to walk" appears with the noun *reloj* "clock":

(90)   *Aun cuando hubiese en el reloj piezas que nos pareciesen superfluas, y se nos demostrase que sin ellas podía andar, la superfluidad de estas piezas no desvanecería el raciocinio que hubiésemos hecho sobre la utilidad de las otras.*

(quoted in Cuervo 1992–1994 I: 455)

---

5.   See Goossens (2003) for the discussion of what he calls "metaphtonymy" of the type "metaphor from metonymy", defined as "metaphors for which there is a link with their metonymic origin" (p. 361).

"Even when there are parts in a clock that might seem unnecessary, and even if it were demonstrated to us that the clock could function without them, the optional nature of these parts would not negate the argument that we have made regarding the usefulness of the other parts."

Romance motion verbs that take on the meaning "to function (of clocks, watches)" also include French *marcher* "to walk" (Mansion, ed. 1939 I: 520), Italian *andare* "to go" (Reynolds, ed. 1981 I: 39), Italian *camminare*[6] "to walk" (Rubery, ed. 2010: 1599), Italian *correre* "to run" (Battaglia, ed. 1961–2009 III: 821), Portuguese *andar* "to walk" (Fernandes 1972: 77), Romanian *a merge* "to go" (Puşcariu et al., eds. 1907– VI: 407), Catalan *anar* "to go" (Alcover & Moll, eds. 1930–1962 I: 627), Occitan *anar* "to go" (Coupier 1995: 55), and Raeto-Romance *ir* "to go" (Planta et al., eds. 1939– X: 29). The fragment from *Pinocchio* by Carlo Collodi (1826–1890) serves as illustration for Italian *correre*:

(91) *E mentre [Pinocchio] camminava con passo frettoloso, il cuore gli batteva forte e gli faceva tic-tac, tic-tac, come un orologio da sala quando *corre* davvero.*   (Collodi 2002: 68)
"His steps were quick and his heart was pounding – tick, tock, tick, tock – like a grandfather clock that's running too fast."   (Collodi 2008: 66)

Different types of transportation such as cars, trains, and their engines provide another relevant context, as in the case of Spanish *andar* "to walk" (92), French *marcher* "to walk" (93), Italian *camminare* "to walk" (94), Portuguese *andar* "to walk" (95), Occitan *marchar* "to walk" (96), and Raeto-Romance *ir* "to go" (97):

(92) *El coche *anda* de maravilla.* (Galimberti Jarman & Russell, eds. 1994: 42)
"The car functions very well."

(93) *[...] il avait une voiture neuve à laquelle il avait appliqué de si nombreux perfectionnements qu'elle ne *marchait* plus du tout.* (André Maurois, 1885–1967, *Bernard Quesnay*, 1926, quoted in Rey, ed. 1989 VI: 250)
"[...] he had a new car to which he had made so many improvements that it was not working at all."

(94) *Cammina* bene questa automobile!*   (Gabrielli 1971: 47)[7]
"This car works great!"

(95) *O carro está tão velho, que já não *anda*.*   (Geiger, ed. 2008: s.v. *andar*)
"The car is so old that it no longer works."

---

6. This usage of Italian *camminare* as an equivalent of *funzionare* is stylistically marked as "colloquiale, lingua parlata" ["colloquial, spoken language"] (Rubery, ed. 2010: 1599).

7. As mentioned in the previous footnote, this usage of Italian *camminare* as an equivalent of *funzionare* is stylistically marked as "colloquiale, lingua parlata" (Rubery, ed. 2010: 1599).

(96) *Uno autò que _marcho_ bèn.*   (Coupier 1995: 858)
      "A car that works well."

(97) *il motor _va_, far _ir_ il motor*   (Planta et al., eds. 1939– X: 29)
      "the engine runs", "to start the engine"

Such transportation-related expressions often specify the source of energy that makes it possible for the mechanism to function, as illustrated by Italian *andare* "to go" (98), Romanian *a umbla* "to walk" (99), and Catalan *anar* "to go" (100):

(98) *_andare_ a benzina, _andare_ a elettricità, _andare_ a pile, _andare_ a vapore*
                         (Rubery, ed. 2010: 1492; Reynolds, ed. 1981 I: 39)
      "to run on petrol", "to run on electricity", "to run on batteries", "to run on steam"

(99) *Trenurile de aici, toate, _umblă_ cu forță electrică.* (*Viața românească*, 1970, quoted in Pușcariu et al., eds. 1907– XII: A 2-A: 99)
      "The trains here, they all work on electricity."

(100) *Aquesta moto _va_ amb gasolina.*   (Torras i Rodergas, eds. 1985: 132)
      "This motorcycle operates on gas."

Other relevant recent technological advances include electronics and office equipment. As an electronics-related example it is appropriate to mention Spanish *andar* "to walk" in *El tocadiscos no anda* "The record player is not working" (Galimberti Jarman & Russell, eds. 1994: 42). In the case of office equipment, *Posada Gurenilor* (1929) by Nicolae Al Lupului (1881–1963) offers a pertinent example with Romanian *a umbla* "to walk": *Se vedea cum umblă mașina de tipărit* "It was possible to see how the typewriter works" (quoted in Pușcariu et al., eds. 1907– XII: A 2-A: 99). In other words, real-world experiences made it possible for speakers to conceptualize the work of a mechanism in terms of motion and socio-cultural changes made it possible for this conceptualization to become conventionalized and to spread to new contexts.

It is reasonable to assume that the use of the equivalents of "to jump" to encode explosion is also a product of conceptualization based on manipulation of objects and a product of culture; more specifically, the introduction of gunpowder from Asia to Europe in the Middle Ages and proliferation of European gunpowder weapons during the Early Modern period discussed in Hall (1997) and Lorge (2011), among others. Such linguistic usage is commonly associated with warfare tactics, as illustrated by Spanish *saltar* (101), French *sauter* (102), Italian *saltare* (103), and Occitan *sautar* (104):

(101)   *Hicieron saltar el edificio con dinamita.*

                    (Galimberti Jarman & Russell, eds. 1994: 685)
        "They blew up the building with dynamite."

(102)   *[Le tank] a sauté sur une mine et s'est mis à brûler.* (Boris Vian, 1920–1959,
        Les Fourmis, 1949, quoted in Imbs, ed. 1971–1994 XV: 111)
        "[The tank] blew up on a mine and started burning."

(103)   *Gli esplosivi sono saltati (in aria).*   (Gabrielli 1971: 185–186)
        "The explosives have exploded."

(104)   *batèu que sauto sus uno mino*   (Coupier 1995: 127)
        "the ship that blows up on a mine"

The projection between jumping and exploding is also available for Portuguese
saltar (Fernandes 1972: 539), Romanian *a sări* (Puşcariu et al., eds. 1907– X: 1:
220), Catalan *saltar* (Torras i Rodergas, ed. 1985: 1167), and Raeto-Romance *siglir*
(Decurtins 2001: 980).

7.2   Language-specific semantic innovations

The novel metaphors discussed in Section 7.1 are widely attested across the Romance linguistic area. However, as mentioned at the very beginning of this chapter, a number of new mappings have a more restricted distribution. For instance,
the use of the equivalents of "to run" in the sense "to embarrass, to shame, to con-
fuse" and of their reflexive counterparts in the sense "to become embarrassed,
ashamed, confused" is limited to Ibero-Romance. In a key work of Spanish 16th-
century linguistic thought entitled *Diálogo de la lengua* (1535), Juan de Valdés
(c.1499–1541) describes this function of Spanish *correr(se)* as follows: "Correr,
demás de su propia significación, que es *currere*, tiene otra y es ésta que dezimos
que se corre uno quando, burlando con él y motejándolo, se enoja" ["*Correr*, in
addition to its own meaning which is 'run', has another one, and we say *se corre uno*
when we are teasing someone and calling them names and they are bothered by
this"] (Valdés 1964: 92). Although in Modern Spanish this usage is rare and is
stylistically marked as colloquial (Schonthal, ed. 2001: 145), it was common in
Classical Spanish, as the passage from Cervantes' *Quijote* illustrates:

(105)   *Haz gala, Sancho de la humildad de tu linaje, y no te desprecies de decir que*
        vienes de labradores, porque viendo que no te corres, ninguno se pondrá a
        correrte, y préciate más de ser humilde virtuoso que pecador soberbio.

                    (Cervantes 1998 I: 970)

"Glory in your humble stock, Sancho, and do not be ashamed to say that you are descended from peasants; because when people see that this does not embarrass you, nobody will try to make you embarrassed about it; and take pride in being a humble and virtuous man rather than a lofty and sinful one."   (Cervantes Saavedra 2001: 768)

As in present-day Spanish, in contemporary Portuguese the use of *correr-se* as an equivalent of "to become ashamed" is rare (Geiger, ed. 2008, s.v. *correr*), but it is found more often in earlier texts such as the novel *Til* (1871) by the Brazilian writer José de Alencar (1829–1877):

(106)   *Tão franca era a fisionomia de Afonso ao proferir estas palavras, e tão cordial afeto ressumbrava de sua voz, que Miguel correu-se de seu injusto ressentimento contra o amigo, e de todo lhe desvaneceram no coração os ressaibos de ciúme, que o pungiam.*   (accessed through Davies & Ferreira 2006)
"Afonso looked so sincere when uttering these words, and such warm affection emanated from his voice, that Miguel became ashamed of his unfair resentment towards his friend, and traces of jealousy that were hurting him completely disappeared from his heart."

Another Ibero-Romance innovative mapping is the association between running and jurisdiction of, administration of, or control over a specific entity or responsibility. In the case of Spanish *correr*, common expressions are *correr por* "to be administered by, to be the responsibility of", as in (107), and *correr con* "to be in charge of, to be responsible for", as in (108):

(107)   *Hecha la elección como conviene, no les impidan el ejercicio y curso ordinario de la justicia: déjenla correr por el magistrado.* (Diego de Saavedra Fajardo, 1584–1648, *Empresas políticas*, quoted in Cuervo 1992–1994 II: 561)
"Once the decision is made, do not impede the course of justice: let it be administered by the supreme judge."

(108)   *Machuca, pintor, escultor y arquitecto, fue el que corrió con la obra del alcázar de Carlos V en aquella ciudad.* (Gaspar Melchor de Jovellanos, 1744–1811, "*Elogio de las bellas artes*", quoted in Cuervo 1992–1994 II: 562)
"Machuca, who was a painter, sculptor, and architect, is the one who was in charge of the residence of Carlos V in that city."

In the case of Portuguese *correr*, equivalent collocations include *correr com a administração da casa* "to be in charge of managing the house" and *correr com as despesas* "to be responsible for the expenses" (Fernandes 1972: 171).

Another mapping with limited Romance representation is the association between running and missing a mandatory event, as in early 20th-century Madrid

Spanish *correr la clase* "to cut class", *correr la escuela* "to skip school", and *correr la oficina* "to not come to work" (Corominas & Pascual 1980–1991 II: 208, based on Pastor y Molina 1908). By the same token, it is relevant to mention the association between running and bothering or annoying represented by French *courir*, as in *tu commences à me courir* "you are starting to bother me" (Rey, ed. 1994 I: 515) and *tu nous cours avec tes histoires* "you annoy us with your stories" (Rey, ed. 1989 II: 1011).[8] Employing the equivalents of "to go down" to encode lodging or staying at a place is also relevant to the discussion of language-specific semantic innovations because while it is available for some Romance lexemes such as French *descendre*, Occitan *descendre*, Italian *scendere*, and Romanian *a coborî*, it is not available for others like Spanish *bajar* or *descender*. Excerpts from letters by Gustave Flaubert (1821–1880) and Giuseppe Mazzini (1805–1872) offer examples with French *descendre* (109) and Italian *scendere* (110):

(109)   *Il me ferait le plus grand plaisir de <u>descendre</u> chez moi. Je l'ai déjà invité et je compte qu'il acceptera.*   (quoted in Imbs, ed. 1971–1994 VI: 1253)
"He would make me very happy by staying at my place. I have already invited him and I assume that he will accept the invitation."

(110)   *Rimane [...] in mani vostre decidere; se decidete, scrivetemi. Il meglio è <u>scendere</u> alla 'Bella Venezia', dove io farò preparare la camera.*
(quoted in Battaglia, ed. 1961–2009 XVII: 934)
"The decision is in your hands. If you decide, write to me. The best choice is to lodge at Bella Venezia where I will ask to prepare a room."

7.3 Semantic innovations through borrowing

It is important to clarify that the emergence of a novel metaphorical function is not always a matter of an independent semantic development. For instance, Italian *montare* "to go up" acquired the transitive usage in the sense "to assemble, to set up, to build", which during the earlier stages of this language was regarded as stylistically marked:

(111)   *'Mettere insieme' è commettere e unire tutte le parti d'un tutto; como, v.g., 'mettere insieme un oriuolo' è accomodare tutte le sue parti al proprio luogo: il che volgarmente si dice '<u>montare</u>'.* (*Note al Malmantile*, 1688–1750, quoted in Battaglia, ed. 1961–2009 X: 849)

---

8.   According to Rey, ed. (1994 I: 515), the use of French *courir* as an equivalent of *importuner* "to bother, to pester, to annoy" is attested for the first time in the early 20th century. It is stylistically marked: Rey, ed. (1989 II: 1011) labels the use of *courir (quelqu'un)* as an equivalent of *ennuyer* "to annoy" as "familier" ["informal"].

"'To put together' is to unite and to join all parts of a whole, as, for example, 'to put together a watch' is to place all its parts in their place: what in the informal/spoken language is expressed as *montare*."

In Modern Italian this function is commonplace, as illustrated by the passage from *Il grande ozio* (1964) by Giovanni Comisso (1895–1969) in (112) and by the passage from *Il taglio del bosco* (1959) by Carlo Cassola (1917–1987) in (113):

(112)   *Dopo alcuni mesi la bicicletta poté essere <u>montata</u> completa.*
                                   (quoted in Battaglia, ed. 1961–2009 X: 849)
      "After several months the bicycle could be completely assembled."

(113)   *L'armatura del capanno era già stata <u>montata</u>.*
                                   (quoted in Battaglia, ed. 1961–2009 X: 849)
      "The armature of the summer house had already been assembled."

This function of Italian *montare* is parallel to the function of French *monter* in sentences like the one from *La maison de Claudine* (1922) by Gabrielle Colette (1873–1954): *Renaud, qui passe quatorze ans, ne songe qu'à monter et démonter des moteurs* "Renaud, who has turned fourteen, thinks of nothing else but assembling and taking apart engines" (quoted in Imbs, ed. 1971–1994 XI: 1045). In fact, the usage in question came into Italian from French (Battisti & Alessio 1950–1957 IV: 2503; Battaglia, ed. 1961–2009 X: 849–850).[9] Catalan *muntar* "to go up" (as well as Catalan *pujar* "to go up") and Occitan *montar* "to go up" have an equivalent transitive usage with both concrete and abstract nouns: *pujar la casa* "to build the house", *muntar una editorial* "to found a publishing house" (Sagristà i Artigas, ed. 1998: 1372, 1130), *mounta un moutour* "to assemble the engine", *mounta uno pèço de tiatre* "to put together a theatre production, to stage a play" (Coupier 1995: 906).[10]

Another semantic extension introduced into Italian from French is the use of Italian *saltare* "to jump" in the sense "to sauté, to stir fry", that is to say, as an equivalent of Italian *rosolare* (Battaglia, ed. 1961–2009 XVII: 437–438):

(114)   *Saltare a fuoco vivo i 30 grammi di burro e i restanti 200 grammi di funghi champignons interi per tre minuti circa.* (*La Stampa*, 24-IV-1986, quoted in Battaglia, ed. 1961–2009 XVII: 437)
      "Sauté on strong fire thirty grams of butter and the remaining two hundred grams of whole champignons for approximately three minutes."

---

9.   The *Dictionnaire historique de la langue française* (Rey, ed. 1994 II: 1268) lists the second part of the 16th century as the time period when French *monter* started being used in the sense "assembler, joindre les différentes parties d'une chose pour permettre de l'utiliser" ["to assemble, to join together different parts of the object in order to be able to use it"].

10.   Cf. Spanish *montar* in *montar el andamiaje* "to build a scaffold" (Domingo, ed. 1997: 685) and Romanian *a ridica* in *a ridica o clădire* "to build a building" (Bantaş et al. 1981: 482).

This function of Italian *saltare* is a calque from French *sauter* used as an equivalent of *cuire à feu vif* "to cook in a brisk oven", as in the following passage from *Physiologie du goût ou Méditations de gastronomie transcendante* (1825) by Jean-Anthelme Brillat-Savarin (1755–1826):

(115) *On les met (la chair d'un coq, et du bœuf) dans une casserole, sur un feu bien vif [...] et on y jette de temps en temps un peu de beurre frais, afin de pouvoir bien sauter ce mélange sans qu'il attache.* (quoted in Rey, ed. 1989 VIII: 604) "Place (chicken and beef) in a pan on strong fire [...] and add from time to time some fresh butter, so that you can stir fry this mixture well without its sticking."

While in Modern French the usage of *sauter* as an equivalent of *cuire à feu vif* is considered archaic (Rey, ed. 1989 VIII: 604), the usage of Catalan *saltar* in gastronomical context as an equivalent of *coure a foc viu* is stylistically unmarked (Sagristà i Artigas, ed. 1998: 501).

French has also exercised influence over the metaphorical extensions of Romanian motion verbs. As we have seen in Chapter 6, French *courir* "to run" can be used with the meaning "to extend", as in *Le chemin court au bord du lac* "The road lies along the lake-side" (Mansion, ed. 1939 I: 206). Although the association between running and extending is available for Latin CURRERE and therefore does not constitute a Romance innovation, it is nevertheless relevant to the discussion of semantic borrowings because from French *courir* it was transferred to Romanian *a alerga* "to run". In this way, in the following example marked as a "franţuzism neobişnuit" ["rarely used Gallicism"] from the poem "*Stepa*" by Alexandru Macedonski (1854–1920), *a alerga* is used in reference to physical extension of the steppe: *Şi de ceruri se izbeşte [stepa] alergând spre răsărit* "[The steppe] clashes with the skies, extending towards the East" (quoted in Macrea & Petrovici, eds. 1955–1957 I: 60).

While the semantic borrowings discussed above are confined to Romance (i.e., from French to Italian and from French to Romanian), it is not unlikely that the inventory of metaphorical meanings of Romance motion verbs has also experienced influence from outside this language family. In Spanish, the verb *salir* "to go out" can be used in the sense "to take after, to resemble by inheriting a certain quality", as in *es gordita, sale a la madre* "she's chubby, she takes after her mother", *¡tiene a quien salir!* "you can see who she takes after!", *en lo tozudo sale a su padre* "he gets his stubbornness from his father" (Galimberti Jarman & Russell, eds. 1994: 684). According to Alonso Pedraz (1986 II: 1569), *salir* is already used as an equivalent of *parecerse* and *asemejarse* "to resemble" in 14th- and 15th-century Old Spanish texts. A passage from the *Libro de Estados* by Juan Manuel (1282–1347) serves as illustration:

(116)   *Otrosi a sus fijos segund el mio entendimiento deue los fazer en esta manera*
        bien en quanto fueren tan ninnos que non saben fablar nin andar deuen los
        catar buenas amas que sean de la mejor sangre & mas alta. & mas linda que
        pudieren aver Ca çierto es que del padre o de la madre en afuera que non ay
        ninguna cosa de que los omnes tanto tomen nin a qui tanto <u>salgan</u> nin a qui
        tanto semejen en sus voluntades & en sus obras commo a las amas cuya
        leche mamaran.   (accessed through Davies 2007)
        "In addition, according to my view, he [the emperor] should raise his chil-
        dren in the following way: when they are so little that they yet do not talk
        or walk, they should be looked after by good nannies of the best lineage
        and pedigree possible. Because it is true that aside from their father and
        mother, there is no other person from whom humans take so much, nor
        who they take after so much, nor who they resemble so much in their in-
        clinations and deeds as the nannies whose milk they nursed on."

Cuervo (1992–1994 VIII: 375) lists a 16th-century example from the *Exposición del Libro de Job* by Fray Luis de León (1527–1591): *Los hijos a los padres salen, y lo vil no puede engendrar fortaleza* "Children take after their parents and evil cannot produce strength". He also makes an observation about the collocational patterns of *salir* in the sense "to resemble by inheriting a certain quality", noting that it is most commonly employed when comparing children to their parents or disciples to their teachers (ibid.).

Several Hispanists have contemplated to what degree the existence of an equivalent usage in Arabic may have played a role in the Spanish semantic development in question. For example, in his *Glosario de voces ibéricas y latinas usadas entre los mozárabes*, Francisco Javier Simonet writes:

> No pocas veces, al registrar los libros arábigos, hemos encontrado frases y giros
> que aún se usan en nuestro idioma, ya culto, ya vulgar; pero en algunos casos es
> difícil juzgar si el orígen del giro pertenece a los Árabes ó á los Españoles, ó si sólo
> se halla en unos y otros por coincidencia casual. Tal nos sucede, por ejemplo, en
> la frase *hárağ li-wíldih*, que se halla en R. Martí[11] bajo *partisare* y que corresponde
> exactamente á la castellana *salió á su padre*. (Simonet 1888: cxxxi, n.2)

---

11.   Schiaparelli, ed. (1871: 513) (*Vocabulista in Arabico*). This work is an anonymous Latin–Arabic, Arabic–Latin dictionary preserved as a 13th-century manuscript and attributed to the 13th-century Catalan theologian, Arabist, and missionary Ramón Martí. The Arabic expressions, which appear in the left column in Arabic script, are glossed in the right column as Latin PATRISARE with one 's'. Latin PATRISSARE (of Greek origin) was used in the sense "to take after or imitate one's father": e.g., *idne tu mirare, si patrissat filius?* "and you are surprised if the son emulates his father?" (Plautus, *Pseudolus*, quoted in Glare, ed. 1982: 1310), *Marsyas cum in artificio patrissaret tibicinii* "although Marsyas followed his father's footsteps in the art of playing the flute" (Apuleius, *Florida*, quoted in Glare, ed. 1982: 1310).

[On many occasions, when consulting Arabic books, we have encountered phrases and expressions that are still in use in our own language, either in the formal register or in the spoken one. However, in some cases it is difficult to judge whether the origin of the expression is Arabic or Spanish, and whether it is just a coincidence that the expression is attested in both languages. This is the case of the phrase *hárağ li-wíldih* which is found in R. Martí under *patrisare* and which is the exact equivalent of Spanish *salió a su padre*.]

The opinion expressed by Joan Corominas in the *Diccionario crítico etimológico castellano e hispánico* (Corominas & Pascual 1980–1991 V: 139) gives an even stronger endorsement to interpreting the Spanish usage as a calque:

> En la locución *salió a su padre, a su madre*, etc. 'nació un niño parecido a su padre, a su madre', no creo [...] que sea parecido semántico casual con su equivalente literal el ár. *hárağ li-wíldih* (ya en R. Martí, como traducción de *patrisare*), sino verdadero calco semántico del árabe por el cast.; el hecho es que una locución así sería imposible con el fr. o cat. *sortir*, con el cat. *eixir* o el it. *uscire*.

> [As far as the expression *salió a su padre, a su madre*, etc. "a child was born who resembles his father or his mother" is concerned, I do not think [...] that its semantic similarity with its literal Arabic equivalent *hárağ li-wíldih* (which appears in R. Martí as the translation of *patrisare*) is random. I think that it is a true semantic calque from Arabic on the part of Spanish: an expression like this one would not be possible either in the case of French and Catalan *sortir*, or in the case of Catalan *eixir*, or in the case of Italian *uscire*.]

According to Lapesa (1991: 154), Arabic influence is also at work in the development of Spanish *correr* with the meaning "to pillage, to devastate, to ravage": "[el árabe] *gawāra*, que valía 'correr' y 'depredar', contagió este segundo sentido al español" ["Arabic *gawāra*, which meant 'to run' and 'to pillage, to devastate, to ravage' passed on the latter meaning to Spanish"]. The excerpt from the 13th-century *Calila é Dymna*[12] serves as illustration: *Dicen que una cibdat que decian Maruca corriéronla enemigos, é mataron muchos homes, é levaron otros cativos* "They say that the enemies pillaged the town called Maruca, and killed many men, and took the other ones as prisoners" (quoted in Cuervo 1992–1994 II: 564).

7.4 Written evidence and the latent state

While making a claim about the innovative nature of the Romance metaphors analyzed in this chapter, it is important to caution that absence of such metaphors

---

12. The Old Spanish *Calila é Dymna* is a translation of the Arabic *Kalila wa-Dimna* which in turn is a translation from Persian. The two extant Old Spanish versions are from the 14th century (Escorial, MS III-h-9) and the 15th century (Escorial, MS III-x-4).

in Latin texts does not necessarily indicate absence of some of these mappings in Latin spoken usage to which we obviously do not have any direct access. This type of concern, of course, is inherent to all diachronic research. For instance, in the historical study of the target concept 'intelligence' carried out within the framework of cognitive linguistics, Allan (2008) expresses her surprise by the lack of certain figurative extensions in earlier English texts. She contrasts the long-standing cultural tradition of employing animals to represent human characteristics in Aesop's *Fables*, the Bible, and the Medieval bestiaries (e.g., sheep as lacking independent thought) with a relatively late attestation date of straightforward metaphorical usage of animals as terms for human beings. For example, according to Allan's analysis, which is based on the database compiled at the University of Glasgow (United Kingdom) for the *Historical Thesaurus of the Oxford English Dictionary* (Kay et al. 2009), the earliest entry for an animal-based intelligence metaphor is the one for *ape* (meaning "a stupid person") which dates from around 1330 (Allan 2008: 134, 175). The next two earliest cases of metaphorical usage of animals are *(blind) buzzard* (meaning "a stupid person") from 1377 and *goosish* (meaning "stupid") from 1374. The earliest entry for *sheepish* (meaning "stupid") dates from 1380, the earliest entry for *sheep* (meaning "a stupid person") is from 1542, and the earliest entries for *sheep's head* are from 1542 (meaning "stupid") and 1624 (meaning "a stupid person") (ibid., pp. 173, 176). Allan logically wonders whether the fact that animals mostly denote lack of intelligence could mean that the metaphors that used animals as their source domain were likely to be associated with colloquial usage or slang, hence their absence from the Old English documents (p. 137). However, based on her data, the earliest attestations of the animal-based metaphors that express cleverness are also from later texts: *owl* (meaning "a clever-wise person" although in a derogatory way) is from 1508, *shrewd* (meaning "clever-sharp and shrewd") derived from *shrew* is from 1589, *shrode* (meaning "clever-sharp and shrewd") derived from *shrew* is from 1594, *eagle-wit* (meaning "a clever-genius person") derived from *eagle wit* is from 1665, *shrewdish* (meaning "clever-shrewd") derived from *shrew* is from 1823, *varment* (meaning "clever-sharp") derived from *vermin* is from 1829, and *sparrow* (meaning "a clever-sharp person") derived from *sparrow* is from 1861 (pp. 172–179). Allan expresses her reaction to the data as follows: "it seems surprising that there is such a long delay between the evidence of folk traditions relating to these animals and the straight metaphorical usage of their names as terms for humans" (pp. 136–137). She goes on to say that one of the factors that could explain the proliferation of animal-based metaphors attested from Early Modern English onward is the enormous expansion undergone by the English lexicon at large (p. 137).

Naturally, the issue of possible discrepancy between actual usage and the language of written documents is not limited to historical semantics; it is a question that cuts across different levels of analysis. Researchers working with Romance historical data are highly attuned to it because of the influential writings of the Spanish philologist Ramón Menéndez Pidal (1869–1968) who in his book *Orígenes del español: Estado lingüístico de la Península Ibérica hasta el siglo XI*, published in 1926, proposed the methodological concept of '*el estado latente*' ["the latent state" or "the latent phase"]. Menéndez Pidal argues that before a linguistic phenomenon establishes itself as part of the written norm, it can remain unnoticed, unattested, or marginalized for centuries. One of his often-cited examples deals with the weakening and eventual loss in Spanish of the word-initial Latin F-: the speakers stopped pronouncing the *f-* in words like *forno* (< Latin FORNUS "furnace") much earlier than the forms *horno* and *orno* became widely attested in writing (Menéndez Pidal 1956 [1926]: 198–233, 533–534). Specialists in historical Romance linguistics have traditionally recognized the pioneering nature of the concept of the 'latent state', highlighting parallels between Menéndez Pidal's ideas on the nature of linguistic change published as early as the the 1920s, and the theoretical findings of sociolinguistics of the second part of the 20th century (Lloyd 1970). Such parallels do not come as a surprise, given that the development of modern sociolinguistics is firmly rooted in dialect geography and historical linguistics studies (Koerner 1995b). In addition to historical Spanish phonology, the concept of the 'latent state' has been applied to the evolution of the Spanish lexicon (Catalán 1989) and morphosyntax (Lapesa 2000 II: 705–729; Girón Alconchel 2004, Stolova 2010b, 2012). Scholars of Classical philology (e.g., García-Jurado & Hualde-Pascual 2002, García-Jurado 2003) have made significant progress in analyzing the Latin texts that allow the colloquial usage to shine through – as in the case of works by Plautus – in light of the conceptual metaphor theory. In case this line of investigation turns to the methodological principle of the 'latent state' and uncovers latent Latin motion-based metaphorical mappings that are not reported in standard reference works such as the *Oxford Latin Dictionary* (Glare, ed. 1982), then future research will be able to compare Latin and Romance with more precision.

7.5 Motion-based semantic innovations within a wider context

The tendency on the part of motion verbs to expand their range of metaphorical functions uncovered throughout this chapter is consistent with the data presented in contemporary studies on other lexical fields in Romance and in other language families. For instance, according to Dworkin (2006a: 76–77), Medieval Spanish color terms do not show as much figurative usage as their Modern Spanish counterparts. Along the same lines, in his study of Germanic spatial metaphors, Swan (2010) shows that while Old English and Old Norse employ the GOOD IS UP mapping in reference to respected social status and spirituality (e.g., Old English *upheah* "noble, upright", Old Norse *uppgangr* "growing power, progress"), Old English *upp*, *up* is rarely used in reference to happiness, cheerfulness, and optimism, and Old Norse *upp* does not seem to have this usage at all. However, with time GOOD IS UP has been extended to positive states of mind: e.g., Modern English *uplifted*, *upbeat* and Modern Norwegian *opp med nebbet* "cheer up" (ibid., pp. 59–62). Likewise, Allan (2008: 134) illustrates that throughout the history of English the number of animal-based intelligence metaphors (e.g., *eagle-wit*) has grown considerably, with less then six percent of the data being pre-1500. To offer another example, while the functions of Latin NAVIGARE "to sail" were limited to the activities related to the sea (Glare, ed. 1982: 1161), Portuguese *navegar* "to sail" has acquired two new usages related to virtual space, "to browse the web" and "to be available on the web":

(117) *Gostaria de poder levar o seu computador para a cama para adormecer enquanto navega na Internet?* (Maisak 2007: 219)
"Would you like to have the opportunity to bring your computer to bed so that you can fall asleep as you are browsing the web?"

(118) *É impossível enumerar todos os livros que ja navegam na Internet, prontos a serem consultados e descarregados.* (ibid.)
"It is impossible to list all the books that already are available on the web ready to be consulted and downloaded."

As we will see in Chapter 9, the innovative nature of Romance verbs of motion reported above has ramifications for cognitive linguistics, more specifically for the conceptual metaphor theory.

CHAPTER 8

Implications for the cognitive typology of motion encoding

8.1 Refining the cognitive typology of motion encoding across languages

Chapters 2 through 4 have explored how the cognitive framework helps us account for patterns of lexical continuity, loss, and innovation in the domain of Latin and Romance motion verbs. The present chapter turns the tables and discusses how my analysis of the lexical developments attested from Latin to Romance contributes to current debates within cognitive linguistics, more specifically to the debates centered on the cognitive typology of motion encoding.

As we have seen in Section 2.2, the cognitive typology of encoding of motion events proposed by Leonard Talmy postulates different lexicalization patterns and associates them with different conceptualization options. According to this typology, all branches of Indo-European – except the Romance languages but including Latin – belong to the satellite-framed type since they place path in the satellite (prefix and/or preposition), while the Romance languages belong to the verb-framed type since they place path in the verb stem. Overall, Talmy's typological classification has been received with great enthusiasm. At the same time, it has been noted that, as often happens with typological studies, it might sometimes paint with a wide brush.

One of the issues raised is that Talmy's classification focuses on the asymmetric strategies, i.e., strategies that rely on a motion verb and a subordinate element that accompanies it. However, in a number of languages path and manner are expressed symmetrically by equivalent grammatical forms. For instance, in the case of serial-verb languages, "two or more verbs, with or without arguments, co-occur in the same clause, apparently expressing the same event" (Zlatev & Yangklang 2004: 160), as in the following Thai example (ibid.):

(119) *chán dəən khâam thanǒn khâw paj naj sǔam*
       I   walk cross road   enter go in   park
       "I walked across the road into the park."

Therefore, Zlatev & Yangklang (2004) classify Thai and other serial-verb languages as 'a third type', i.e., a type distinct from both the verb-framed and the satellite-framed ones.

Linguistic varieties that employ symmetric strategies are quite common. For instance, verb serialization is abundant in such language families as Niger-Congo, Hmong-Mien, Sino-Tibetan, Tai-Kadai, Mon-Khmer, and Austronesian (Zlatev & Yangklang 2004: 160). Thus, in their revision of Talmy's typology, Croft and his collaborators (Croft 2003: 220–224; Croft at al. 2010) propose to distinguish between two main types: (1) asymmetric lexicalization patterns that include satellite-framing and verb-framing and (2) symmetric lexicalization patterns that, in addition to verb serialization discussed above, include compounding attested in such Amerindian languages as Kiowa and Nez Perce, double coding present in Russian and other Slavic languages, and coordination found in Amele (Indo-Pacific language family).

Slobin (2004, 2006) introduces the term "equipollent" for the languages "in which both path and manner receive equal weight" (2006: 59), and proposes the following tripartite classification: (1) verb-framed (e.g., Romance and Semitic families), (2) satellite-framed (e.g., Germanic, Slavic, and Finno-Ugric families), and (3) equipollently-framed. Within the equipollently-framed type Slobin identifies three sub-types: (1) serial-verb languages (e.g., Niger-Congo and Sino-Tibetan families) that he understands as languages "in which it is not always evident which verb in a series, if any, is the 'main' verb"; (2) bipartite verb languages (e.g., Hokan and Penutian families) "in which the verb consists of two morphemes of equal status, one expressing manner and the other path"; and (3) generic verb languages such as Jaminjung (a Jaminjungan language of northern Australia) which encodes motion events by combining one of the "function verbs" ('go', 'come', 'fall', 'hit', 'do') that carries the deictic or the aspectual function "with satellite-like elements, 'coverbs', that encode both path and manner in the same fashion" (2006: 64–65). In addition to introducing the equipollently-framed type, Slobin (2004, 2006) makes another important suggestion: to classify languages based on "the level of attention paid to manner in describing events" (2006: 64). He argues that "it seems possible to place all the languages of the world in a typological categorization of preferred means of encoding motion events, with consequences for the relative salience of manner of motion" (2006: 61). For instance, the satellite-framed languages (e.g., Slavic) have high manner salience, which, among other things, is due to the fact that in these languages the verb root is available to encode manner, as in Russian *vy-letela sova* "an owl flew out", glossed as "out-flew owl" (2006: 62–63). In contrast, the verb-framed languages (e.g., Romance) pay less attention to manner because their verbal slot is taken up by path information, as in Spanish *sale un buho* "exits an owl" (ibid.).

Another tripartite classification was proposed by Wälchli (2001a) who, in a study of forty languages, distinguishes between three types of path encoding: verbal encoding (i.e., by the verb stem), adnominal encoding (i.e., by prepositions, postpositions, or case marking), and adverbal encoding (i.e., by verb affixes or verb particles) (2001a: 301).[1] A language can have "more than one verbal or adnominal or adverbal slot": e.g., "both case and preposition" (ibid.). Wälchli clarifies that these three types are not uniform. For instance, while both French and Mapudungun (an Amerindian language spoken in Chile) use predominantly verbal encoding, they differ significantly in their use of adnominal encoding (2001a: 304). Along the same lines, in his subsequent study of the lexicalization of motion in 109 languages, Wälchli (2006) concludes: "Languages rather than language families must be classified. It can never be taken for granted that related languages behave the same way according to a typology. [...] [L]exicalization patterns are by far not as genealogically stable as is widely believed" (p. 39). Building upon Wälchli's framework, Spreafico (2008a, 2008b, 2009) has investigated the areal typology of the 'Charlemagne Sprachbund' (cf. van der Auwera 1998: 824–825) and has illustrated that the genealogically-related members of the linguistic area in question (German and Dutch; French, Italian, and Bergamasco) exhibit important differences.

The need to pay more attention to intra-typological variation has also been the subject of Ibarretxe-Antuñano (2004, 2009) who has demonstrated that while Basque, Turkish, and Spanish belong to the same verb-framed type, they differ considerably in terms of their degree of description and elaboration of path, with Basque and Turkish showing a higher degree of elaboration and Spanish showing a lower degree. Ibarretxe-Antuñano proposes to compare languages (regardless of their type) by placing them along "a cline of path salience" (2009: 410). She identifies six factors that determine the languages' place on the continuum between the

---

1.   Along the same lines, but independently from Wälchli's classification, Fortis & Vittrant (2011) have proposed an inventory of constructions based on four categories of path-encoding slots which they call *"loci d'expression de la trajectoire"* (p. 83). These four slots, or *loci*, are (1) the head of the sentence (cf. Matsumoto 2003), such as English *left* in *She left the hotel*; (2) the satellite, such as German *hinein* "inside" in *Ich muß hinein* "I must go inside", literally "I must inside"; (3) the adnominal, such as English *to* in *She ran to the hotel*, and (4) the noun, such as Japanese *shuppatsu* "departure" in *eki-o shuppatsu shi-ta* "I left the station", glossed as "station-ACCUSATIVE departure make-PAST" (Fortis & Vittrant 2011: 83). These four path-encoding slots can combine. For instance, in English *She came to the hotel*, the head of the sentence *came* combines with the adnominal *to* (ibid.). Besides the four *loci* listed above, Fortis & Vittrant (2011: 86) propose an additional one, "un *locus* supplémentaire", which constitutes the construction itself. For example, in addition to the satellite *in*, it is the syntactic structure, more specifically the word order, that marks the trajectory of motion in two Dutch sentences: *De jonge loopt het bos in*, glossed as "the boy walks the woods in", translated as "The boy walks into the woods" and *De jonge loopt in het bos*, glossed as "the boy walks in the woods", translated as "The boy walks in the woods" (Fortis & Vittrant 2011: 77, based on Sinha & Kuteva 1995: 173). Fortis & Vittrant (2011: 71, 77–78) propose that in order to establish the language's type it is necessary to establish the sum of the path-encoding constructions that this language employs – a point echoed in Imbert et al. (2011: 113) and Imbert (2012: 253–254).

"high-path-salient" and the "low-path-salient" extremes: (1) "the linguistic devices that these languages provide for encoding different aspects of motion and location", (2) "word order", (3) "tolerance of verb omissions", (4) "existence of dummy [lexically-empty] verbs", (5) "cultural values", and (6) the subdivision of languages, as proposed in Koch & Oesterreicher (1985), into "conceptually oral" and "conceptually written" (2009: 410–412). Bohnemeyer et al. (2007) make a related point regarding the importance of intra-typological variation and the place of path segmentation in it. They demonstrate that some verb-framed languages such as Japanese and Hindi use "double-marking" by placing path functions simultaneously in the verb root and outside of it in the ground phrase, which enables these languages to make reference "to multiple location-change grounds in a single verb phrase" (p. 498). In contrast, Yucatec (an Amerindian language spoken in Mexico across the Yucatán Peninsula) is a "radically verb-framed language" in the sense that it encodes path functions exclusively in the root, thus expressing only one "location-change subevent of departure, passing, or arrival" per verbal phrase (ibid., pp. 524–525).

Another issue that has been raised is that a number of languages belong to the mixed type. That is to say, instead of relying on one characteristic type of motion lexicalization, they routinely employ more than one type.[2] For example, Latvian makes regular use of five slots to mark path: verb stem, preverb, verb particle, preposition, and case marking (Wälchli 2001a: 310–317). The list of mixed linguistic varieties also includes Tswana (a Bantu language of southern Africa) (Schaefer 1985), Emai (an Edoid language of west Africa) (Schaefer 1986), Tsou (an Austronesian language of south-western Taiwan) (Huang & Tanangkingsing 2005), and Lowland Chontal (an Amerindian language of southern Mexico) (O'Connor 2007, 2009). A number of linguistic varieties analyzed in the studies collected in Levinson & Wilkins (2006) do not constitute a pure type either. For instance, Levinson (2006) assesses Yélî Dnye (a language isolate spoken on the Rossel Island, Papua New Guinea) as follows:

> Yélî Dnye does not fall easily into Talmy's (1983) typology of 'verb-framed' languages (with path-encoding verbs) vs. 'satellite-framed' languages (with manner verbs and path encoded in, e.g., particles). [...] although typically the path is partially encoded in the intransitive verb, suggesting a verb-framed strategy, there is also a rich set of manner verbs, including the locally important verbs

---

2.   In his more recent scholarship Talmy (2000 II: 64–67; 2007: 103–105) makes provisions for the mixed languages. More specifically, he draws a distinction between split (or complementary) and parallel systems of conflation. A language that has a split (or complementary) system "can characteristically employ one conflation type for one type of Motion event, and characteristically employ a different conflation type for another type of motion event" (2000 II: 64). A language that has a parallel system "can use different conflation types with roughly comparable colloquiality in representation of the *same* type of Motion event" (2000 II: 66; original emphasis).

glossing 'move by punting', vs. 'move by sail', etc. (A special curiosity is the verb *m:ii* [...], meaning 'move in the characteristic manner for the species', thus swim of fish, walk of mammals, fly of birds.) A further problem is that verbs that seem to encode path, like *kee* 'enter', typically occur with a postpositional phrase too – thus [...], one says in effect 'enter inside the house', the PP repeating some of the information in a way that suggests that the path is not in fact fully specified in the verb. Moreover, manner verbs ('run', 'walk', etc.) can be combined with such path-specifying PPs. (p. 199)

Furthermore, Levinson & Wilkins (2006: 527–537) point out that some languages not only do not fit neatly either the verb-framed type or the satellite-framed type, but also challenge the traditional understanding of such crucial notions as motion and path.

In addition, Talmy's typology has attracted the attention of linguists working within the field of dialectology. For example, Berthele (2004, 2006) has demonstrated that although German is a satellite-framed language while French is a verb-framed one, Swiss German (Moutathal dialect) expresses manner less frequently than Standard German, and in some cases even less frequently than French. Berthele's results have led him to conclude that typological research can achieve a higher level of precision by taking into account the diatopic variation as well as the opposition between orality and literacy. Bernini (2010) has confirmed the importance of the diamesic parameter in the case of such linguistic varieties used mainly for spoken communication as Egyptian Arabic and the Lombard (Northern Italo-Romance) of Bergamo.

Linguists working with Romance linguistic data have also shown great interest in helping to refine Talmy's typology of motion encoding. One of the questions that has been central to this effort is the following: if the Romance languages are classified as verb-framed, how can we account for the satellite-framed phrasal verbs (also known as verb-particle constructions) like Italian *andare fuori* "to exit", characteristic of Italian and of a number of Italian dialects?[3] Earlier ('pre-Talmy')

---

3.   Such constructions were already available in Latin. For examples of combinations of motion verbs with FORIS and FORAS "outside" from different stages of Latin, see Manzelli (1998: 59). For Latin examples of combinations of motion verbs with FORIS and FORAS "outside" as well as with other particles, such as RURSUS and RETRO "back", see Hofmann & Szantyr (1965: 797–799). Cuzzolin (2010) discusses combinations of Latin motion verbs with OBUIAM "towards", ADUERSUS "towards, against", and CONTRA "against". In addition to being abundant in Italian and the Italian dialects, motion verb-particle constructions are also widely attested in Raeto-Romance (e.g., Borodina 1973: 98–100; Berthele 2007, 2009). Other Romance varieties have them as well: e.g., González Fernández (1997) on Old Spanish, Calvo Rigual (2008) on Spanish and Catalan vis-à-vis Italian, Porquier (2001) on Modern French, Schøsler (2008) on different stages in the development of French, Burnett & Tremblay (2009) on Old French. In her study of verb-particle constructions, including the motion ones, in Trentino (Northern Italo-Romance), Cordin

studies that drew attention to this phenomenon (e.g., Ascoli 1880/1883, Rohlfs 1969) maintained the so-called 'Germanic hypothesis': they argued that the structures in question are a calque from German. Later publications (e.g., Simone 1997, Jansen 2004) supported the 'contact hypothesis' by claiming that phrasal verbs first appeared in the Northern Italian dialects and eventually made their way into Standard Italian through dialect contact. More recent studies (e.g., Masini 2005, 2006, Iacobini & Masini 2007a, 2007b, articles collected in Cini 2008, especially Amenta 2008) have shown that these constructions already existed in old Central and Southern Italo-Romance varieties (Old Tuscan, Old Sicilian) and are the result of internal autonomous development. Iacobini & Masini (2007b), for example, identify three internal structural factors that contributed to the development of Italian phrasal verbs: (1) "the passage to a more diagrammatic technique of overt locative marking, due to the morphosemantic bleaching of the Latin prefixed motion verbs in the Romance languages", (2) "the weakening of Italian verbal prefixation to express locative meanings", and (3) "the rise of prepositions in Italian [...] related to the loss of the Latin morphological case for the expression of syntactic relations" (pp. 161–162). In fact, as Iacobini (2009) argues, the issue does not have to be viewed in either/or terms since autonomous Italian developments, dialect contact, and possible Germanic influence can work in tandem. Considering the extensive use of phrasal verbs in Italian, one widely-applied solution has been to classify Italian as a "mixed" language, i.e., a mixture of verb-framed and satellite-framed (e.g., Koch 2001b: 1170), or as a verb-framed language that has "innegabili tendenze di *satellite-framing*" ["undeniable tendencies of satellite-framing"] (Koch 2000a: 109). Hijazo-Gascón & Ibarretxe-Antuñano (2013a: 467; 2013b: 49) view Italian as a verb-framed "high-path salient" language, and Simone (2008: 24) has gone as far as assigning Italian to the satellite-framed type.

Another characteristic of the Romance languages that has presented challenges in view of Talmy's classification of the Romance family as verb-framed is the status of French. Kopecka (2006: 84) calls French "a hybrid system that amalgamates characteristics of both types of language that can encode Path in either a verb or a verbal prefix" due to its retention of earlier Latin and Old French satellite-framed forms (e.g., *accourir* "to run to", *s'envoler* "to fly away") and to the productivity of the 'satellite + root' pattern (e.g., *alunir* "to land on the moon", *apponter* "to land on an aircraft carrier") (ibid., pp. 89, 93). In the comparison of 12th- and

---

(2011: 59) makes the generalization that these structures are more characteristic of the less standardized Romance varieties. While the majority of linguists view Romance verb-particle constructions as exceptions to Talmy's typology, some scholars challenge this view by arguing that these Romance structures are not typologically equivalent to the satellite-framed ones found in Germanic (Mateu & Rigau 2010). Hijazo-Gascón & Ibarretxe-Antuñano (2013b: 49) have referred to Italian directional particles in the constructions in question as "pseudo-satellites".

14th-century *fabliaux* to their modern translations, Kopecka (2009a) provides quantitative data that demonstrate that Medieval French employed the satellite-framed strategies to an even greater degree than the modern language. The Medieval texts in her corpus contain 67 verb-framed tokens and 62 satellite-framed tokens, while their modern equivalents contain 140 verb-framed tokens and 15 satellite-framed tokens (2009a: 419). In addition, the Medieval corpus contains 24 tokens of what Kopecka labels 'verb-/satellite-patterns', which are combinations of path verbs with path satellites (e.g., *trespassee la charier*, glossed as "across-passed the path"), while the Modern French sample contains only one token of this type (2009a: 418). These results mirror the ones reported by Schøsler (2008: 118–122), who points out that the pre-1300 Old French texts make abundant use of prefixed and phrasal motion verbs. In another quantitative study based on French travel narratives and novels written between 1960 and 2000, Kopecka (2009b) analyzes 2293 satellite-framed combinations of nine manner-of-motion verbs with locative prepositions *sur* "on", *dans* "in", and *sous* "under", showing that Modern French can use such combinations not only in reference to atelic change-of-position events, but in reference to telic change-of-place events as well. For instance, in *Je courais dans la sable, m'enfonçant jusqu'aux genoux* "I was running in the sand, sinking in it to knee level" from Jean-Bernard Pouy's *La clef des mensonges* (1988), the motion event is atelic and involves a change of position. In contrast, in *elle [...] souta sur ses pieds, courut sous la douche et ferma le rideau* "she [...] jumped on her feet, ran under the shower, and closed the shower curtain" from Jacques Perry's *Vie d'un païen* (1965), the motion event is telic and involves a change of place (2009b: 58, 60). Kopecka (2009b) also demonstrates that the choice of a specific strategy of encoding motion in French is not just a function of structure, but rather of a series of semantic, aspectual, and pragmatic factors – a point also raised in the analysis reported in Pourcel & Kopecka (2005) of 1800 written and 594 oral elicited motion sentences. For instance, while *nager* "to swim" appears exclusively in the change-of-position context, *grimper* "to climb" and *sauter* "to jump" are more likely to appear in the change-of-place context than in the change-of-position one (Kopecka 2009b: 61).

The extent to which the Romance languages can express reaching the endpoint or goal of motion with the help of the satellite-framed pattern that consists of a manner verb and a prepositional phrase, as in *elle courut sous la douche* "she ran under the shower" quoted in the previous paragraph, has attracted a lot of attention. Some studies have claimed that the Romance languages cannot use this structure to lexicalize telic motion. For example, Aske (1989), who focuses on Spanish but believes that his conclusions may apply to what he calls the 'Spanish-type languages', argues that Spanish cannot replicate word-for-word the English telic motion sentence *Pat swam into the cave* for the same reason that it cannot replicate word-for-word the English resultative sentence *Pat kicked the door open*: "It is easy to see that telic path predicates form a natural semantic class with resultative predicates (they both indicate an end state/location, a 'culmination point', which results from a previous activity), a class which Spanish lacks" (pp. 6–7).[4] At the same time, studies such as Martínez Vázquez (2001) for Spanish, Baciu (2006) for Romanian, Zubizarreta & Oh (2007) for Italian, Spanish, and French, Geuder (2009) for French, and Cardini (2012) for Italian, to name just a few, have presented evidence that challenges this conclusion. To illustrate the point, the following Spanish sentences with *rodar* "to roll", *nadar* "to swim", and *deslizarse* "to slide" are some of the examples that Martínez Vázquez (2001: 48, 50, 51) has retrieved from CREA (*Corpus de Referencia del Español Actual*): *La cabeza de Robespierre rodó en el cesto de la guillotina* "Robespierre's head rolled into the guillotine basket", *La muchacha nadó hasta la roca y se vistió* "The girl swam up to the rock and got dressed", *Con gran facilidad se deslizaba a Cartagena y Mompox a negociar mercancía* "Very easily he would slip into Cartagena and Mompox to negotiate merchandise". In one of the experiments reported in Cardini (2012), twelve out of twelve native speakers of Italian gave the telic boundary-crossing interpretation to the sentence *Il gatto corse dentro la stanza* by matching it with *Il gatto entrò nella stanza di corsa* "The cat entered the room running", rather than with *Il gatto passò del tempo a correre all'interno della stanza* "The cat spent some time running inside the room" (pp. 181, 183). It should be clarified that the studies mentioned above do not imply that speakers of the Romance languages use manner verbs in reference to goal-directed motion as liberally as do speakers of a satellite-framed language like English. For instance, Baciu (2006) illustrates that in Romanian, *a fugi* "to run" can encode directed movement, while this option does not seem to be available for its synonym *a alerga*. However, the evidence that these studies offer does indicate that satellite-framed combinations of the type 'manner-of-motion verb + prepositional phrase' with telic (including boundary-crossing) meaning are not entirely absent from the Romance languages.

In addition, it has been argued that the classification of Latin as satellite-framed requires further investigation. Baldi (2006), who views the status of Latin as "indeterminate" (p. 30), provides examples of Latin sentences that encode manner in a way suggestive of the Romance type. For instance, in *in quas et Indi et Macedones nantes [...] transibant* "which both the Indians and the Macedonians crossed [...] [by] swimming" (Q. Curtius Rufus, *Historiae Alexandri Magni*, 1st century A.D.), the verb TRANSIRE "to go across" is used instead of TRANARE (TRANSNARE) "to swim across" or TRANATARE (TRANSNATARE) "to swim across", and the sentence

---

4.   According to Aske (1989: 5), Spanish *Nadaron (a)dentro de la cueva* can only have the locative interpretation "They swam inside the cave", but not the directional one "They swam into the cave"; see Slobin (1997: 441) on the boundary-crossing constraint.

relies on NANTES to encode manner (Baldi 2006: 23). Although TRANSIRE belongs as much to the satellite-framed category as do TRANARE (TRANSNARE) and TRAN-ATARE (TRANSNATARE), this example is still significant because the use of the participle NANTES is reminiscent of such Romance expressions of manner as Italian and French adverbial phrases *a nuoto* and *à la nage* or the Spanish gerund *nadando* "by swimming" (ibid., pp. 22–23).[5] The encoding of manner as a gerund is already attested in Late Latin, as in the case of DICENDO from *dixit [...] quod [...] sic redirent [...] dicendo psalmos vel antiphonas* "he said [...] that [...] they returned in that way, [...] saying psalms and antiphons" from the *Peregrinatio Aetheriae* (late 4th – early 5th century A.D.), with the gerund DICENDO being used instead of the expected participle DICENTES (ibid., p. 17). Baldi (2006) also compares and contrasts the lexicalization of nine motion concepts ('wiggle', 'float', 'stagger', 'swim', 'wander', 'leap', 'fly', 'flee', and 'dance') in English, German, Dutch, Lithuanian, Italian, French, Spanish, Latin, Greek, and Sanskrit, observing that in a number of cases Latin behaves as verb-framed while Italian, French, or Spanish function as satellite-framed. The results of another comparative study are reported by Schøsler (2008), who analyzes portions from Caesar's *De Bello Gallico* (Classical Latin), *Peregrinatio Aetheriae* (Late Latin), *Chevalier de la charrette* (Old French), Emile Zola's *Germinal* (Modern French), and Villy Sørensen's *Sære Historier* (Modern Dutch). Although Schøsler does not explicitly challenge the status of Classical Latin as satellite-framed, the quantitative findings based on her sample indicate that Classical Latin uses verbs that incorporate manner of motion considerably less frequently than Dutch (a satellite-framed Germanic language) (pp. 126–128).

8.2 Toward a diachrony-inclusive cognitive typology of motion encoding

While the studies mentioned above provide valuable insights, considering the importance of the comparative-historical perspective emphasized in Section 1.4, it becomes evident that in order to understand what Latin and the Romance languages can contribute to Talmy's typology, the approach should be comparative-historical on a more fundamental level. The data presented and analyzed in Chapters 3 and 4 reveal that Romance verbs of motion emerged following several types of patterns:

---

5.   The fact that in order to express "by swimming" Spanish uses the gerund *nadando*, while Italian and French use the adverbial phrases *a nuoto* and *à la nage*, respectively, should not be interpreted as an indication that Spanish lacks adverbial manner-of-motion phrases. As Pharies (1997) details, Spanish, as well as other Hispano-Romance varieties, have a rich inventory of such expressions, including *a cuatro patas, a cuatro pies, a gatas* "on all four", *a rastras* "dragging", *de puntillas* "on tip-toe", *a saltos* "leaping, jumping", and *a tatas* "tottering (of baby's first steps)" (pp. 397–403).

Pattern 1: simple generic motion verb > simple generic motion verb

Latin IRE "to go" > Spanish *ir*, French (part of the paradigm of *aller* < AMBU-LARE) *j'irai* (Future), *j'irais* (Conditional), Old Italian (and some Modern Italian dialects) *gire*, Portuguese *ir*, Occitan (some Old and some Modern dialects) *ir*, Raeto-Romance *ir* "to go"

Italian *andare* "to go" > Sardinian (Logudorese) *andare* "to go"

Pattern 2: simple manner-of-motion verb > simple generic motion verb

Latin AMBULARE[6] "to walk" > French *aller*, Italian *andare*, Catalan *anar*, Occitan *anar*, Sardinian (Campidanese) *andai*, Raeto-Romance (Friulian) *lâ* "to go"

Pattern 3: simple manner-of-motion verb > simple manner-of-motion verb

Latin AMBULARE "to walk" > Spanish *andar*, Portuguese *andar*, Romanian *a umbla* "to walk"

Latin CURRERE "to run" > Spanish *correr*, French *courir*, Italian *correre*, Portuguese *correr*, Old Romanian *a cure*, Catalan *córrer*, Occitan *córrer, corrir*, Sardinian (Campidanese) *curri*, Sardinian (Logudorese) *cùrrere*, Raeto-Romance *currer* "to run"

Latin SALIRE "to jump" > Romanian *a sări*, Raeto-Romance *saglir* "to jump"

Late Latin *JUMPARE "to jump" > Sardinian (Campidanese) *jumpai* "to jump"

Italian *camminare* "to walk" > Raeto-Romance *c(h)aminar* "to walk"

Pattern 4: simple generic motion verb > simple verb of directed motion

Latin CEDERE "to go, i.e., to be in motion, move, walk, go along" > Raeto-Romance *ceder* "to go out"

Latin MOVERE "to move" > Sardinian (Campidanese) *moviri*, Sardinian (Logudorese) *mòvere* "to go away"

Pattern 5: simple manner-of-motion verb > simple verb of directed motion

Latin SALIRE "to jump" > Spanish *salir*, Portuguese *sair*, Occitan *sal(h)ir* "to go out"

Latin SALIRE "to jump" > Italian *salire* "to go up"

French *marcher* "to walk" > Catalan *marxar* "to go away"

---

6.   As we have seen in Chapter 3, although etymologically a compound, AMBULARE was perceived as a simple form already in Classical Latin.

Pattern 6: simple verb of directed motion > simple manner-of-motion verb

Latin FUGERE "to run away" > Romanian *a fugi* "to run"

Pattern 7: simple verb of directed motion > simple verb of directed motion

Latin VENIRE "to come" > Spanish *venir*, French *venir*, Italian *venire*, Portuguese *vir*, Romanian *a veni*, Catalan *venir*, Occitan *venir*, Sardinian (Campidanese) *benni*, Sardinian (Logudorese) *bènnere*, Raeto-Romance *vegnir, gnir* "to come"

Latin INTRARE[7] "to go in" > Spanish *entrar*, French *entrer*, Italian *entrare*, Portuguese *entrar*, Romanian *a intra*, Catalan *entrar*, Occitan *(d)intrar*, Sardinian (Campidanese) *(b)intrai*, Sardinian (Logudorese) *(b)intràre*, Raeto-Romance *entrar* "to enter"

Subjunctive of the aorist of Modern Greek σώνω "I catch up, I reach, I arrive" > Romanian *a sosi* "to come"

Italian *sortire* "to sort, to pick" or French *sortir* "to go out" > Raeto-Romance *sortir* "to go out"

Catalan *pujar* "to go up" > Sardinian (Campidanese) *(a)pujai* "to go up"

Pattern 8: simple non-motion verb > simple generic motion verb

Latin MERGERE "to dip, to plunge" > Romanian *a merge* "to go"

Pattern 9: simple non-motion verb > simple manner-of-motion verb

Latin SALTARE "to dance" > Spanish *saltar*, French *sauter*, Italian *saltare*, Portuguese *saltar*, Romanian *a sălta*, Catalan *saltar*, Occitan *saltar, sautar, sauter*, Sardinian (Campidanese) *sartiai*, Sardinian (Logudorese) *sartiàre* "to jump"

Latin MERGERE "to dip, to plunge" > Romanian *a merge* "to walk"

Pattern 10: simple non-motion verb > simple verb of directed motion

Classical Latin PLICARE (VELAM) "to fold (the sail)" > Late Latin PLICARE > Spanish *llegar*, Portuguese *chegar* "to come"

Latin COMPLERE "to fill up, to fill out, to complete" > Sardinian (Campidanese) *lompi (krompi)*, Sardinian (Logudorese) *lòmpere (cròmpere)* "to come"

Classical Latin PLICARE (TENTORIA) "to fold (the tents)" > Late Latin PLICARE > Romanian *a pleca* "to go away"

---

7.   As we have seen in Chapter 3, although etymologically a compound, INTRARE was perceived as a simple form already in Classical Latin.

Latin PARTIRI/PARTIRE "to divide" > Spanish *partir*, French *partir*, Italian *partire*, Portuguese *partir*, Sardinian (Campidanese) *partiri*, Sardinian (Logudorese) *partìre*, Raeto-Romance *partir* "to go away"

Latin SORTIRI "to throw lots or to choose by a lot" > French *sortir*, Catalan *sortir*, Occitan *sortir* "to go out"

Italian *sortire* "to sort, to pick" or French *sortir* "to go out" > Raeto-Romance *sortir* "to go out"

Classical Latin ORIRI "to rise, to bestir one's self, to get up" > Late Latin *ORICARE > Romanian *a urca* "to go up"

Latin JUNGERE "to join, to unite, to connect" > Italian *giungere* "to come, to arrive"

Pattern 11: simple verb of causative motion > simple verb of directed motion

Classical Greek χαλάω "I lower, I let down" > Late Latin CALARE "to lower, to let down" > Sardinian (Campidanese) *calai*, Sardianin (Logudorese) *calare* "to go down"

Pattern 12: simple noun > simple manner-of-motion verb

Celtic > Late Latin CAMMINUS "way" > Spanish *caminar*, Italian *camminare*, Portuguese *caminhar*, Catalan *caminar*, Sardinian (Campidanese) *caminai*, Sardinian (Logudorese) *caminàre* "to walk"; French *cheminer* "to walk slowly with difficulty"

Pattern 13: simple noun > simple non-motion verb > simple manner-of-motion verb

Frankish **marka* "sign that marks the border" > Frankish **markôn* "to make or imprint a sign" > French *marcher*, Occitan *marchar*, *marcar* "to walk"

Pattern 14: simple noun > simple verb of directed motion

Classical Latin PASSUS "step, pace" > Late Latin PASSARE > Spanish *pasar*, French *passer*, Italian *passare*, Portuguese *passar*, Catalan *passar*, Occitan *passar*, Sardinian (Campidanese) *passai*, Sardinian (Logudorese) *passàre*, Raeto-Romance *passar* "to go along/across, to go in"

Classical Latin PODIUM "elevated place" > Late Latin *PODIARE > Old French *puier*, Catalan *pujar*, Occitan *pujar* (*pojar*) "to go up"

Classical Latin MONS, MONTIS "mountain" > Late Latin *MONTARE > French *monter*, Italian *montare*, Catalan *muntar*, Occitan *montar*, Raeto-Romance *muntar* "to go up"

Classical Latin COLLIS "hill" > Late Latin *COLLARE > Old Sardinian (Campidanese) *koddai*, Old Sardinian (Logudorese) *koddare* "to go up"

Pattern 15: simple adjective > simple verb of directed motion

Classical Latin ALTUS "high" > Late Latin *ALTIARE > Sardinian (Campidanese) *artziai*, Sardinian (Logudorese) *alzare*, *arziàre* "to go up"

Classical Latin BASSUS "low" (or BASSIOR, BASSIUS) > Late Latin *BASSIARE > Spanish *bajar*, Portuguese *baixar*, Catalan *baixar* "to go down"

Pattern 16: compound adverb/noun > simple verb of directed motion

Old Slavic *pogorĭ* "downwards, down, below", *pod gorije* "valley", *pogorije* "mountain range", *gora* "mountain" > Romanian *a coborî*, *a pogorî*, *a scoborî* "to go down"

Pattern 17: compound verb of directed motion > simple verb of directed motion

Latin EXIRE "to go out" > Old Spanish *exir*, Old French *eissir ((s'en) issir)*, Italian *uscire*, Old Portuguese *e(i)xir*, Romanian *a ieşi*, Catalan *eixir*, Valencian *eixir*, Occitan *eissir*, Sardinian (Campidanese) *bessiri*, Sardinian (Logudorese) *bessìre*, Sardinian (Northern Logudorese) *disessire*, *dessessire*, Raeto-Romance (Friulian) *iší* "to go out"

Latin ASCENDERE "to go up" > Spanish *ascender*, Old French *ascendre*, Italian *ascendere*, Portuguese *ascender*, Catalan *ascendir*, Old Occitan *ascendre*, Sardinian (Logudorese) *ašèndere*, Raeto-Romance *ascender* "to go up"

Latin DESCENDERE "to go down" > Spanish *descender*, French *descendre*, Italian *scendere*, Portuguese *descender*, Catalan *descendir*, Old Catalan *dexendre*, Occitan *descendre*, Raeto-Romance *descender* "to go down"

Latin SUBIRE "to move upward" > Spanish *subir*, Portuguese *subir*, Romanian *a sui* "to go up"

Latin DE-/DIS-CEDERE "to depart, to withdraw, to get apart" & DESCENDERE "to go down" > Old Spanish *deçir*, Old Portuguese *deçer*, Portuguese *descer* "to go down"

Pattern 18: satellite + simple noun > compound manner-of-motion verb

Celtic > Late Latin CAMMINUS "way" > AD + CAMMINUS > Old Catalan *acaminar* "to walk"

Pattern 19: compound verb of directed motion > compound verb of directed motion

Latin PERVENIRE "to come" > French *parvenir*, Catalan *parvenir*, Italian *parvenire*, Occitan *parvenir* "to come (with effort/difficulty)"

Latin DESCENDERE "to go down" > Italian *discendere* "to go down"

Pattern 20: satellite + simple noun > simple verb of directed motion

Latin AD "towards" + RIPA "shore" > Late Latin ADRIPARE "to come to shore" > French *arriver*, Italian *arrivare*, Catalan *arribar*, Occitan *arribar*, Sardinian (Campidanese) *arribai*, Sardinian (Logudorese) *arrivare*, Raeto-Romance *arrivar* "to come"

Latin AD "towards" + VALLIS "valley" > Old French *avaler*, Old Catalan *avallar*, Old Occitan *avalar* "to go down"

Latin DE "from" + VALLIS "valley" > French *dévaler* "to go down (swiftly)"

Latin DE "from" + AD "towards" + VALLIS "valley" > Catalan *davallar*, Occitan *davalar* "to go down"

Pattern 21: noun > satellite + simple adnominal verb of directed motion > compound verb of directed motion

a "towards" + Catalan *pujar* "to go up" > Sardinian (Campidanese) *(a)pujai* "to go up"

Pattern 22: simple non-motion verb + satellite > compound verb of directed motion

Latin PARTIRI/PARTIRE "to divide" + SE > Old Spanish *partirse*, Old Italian *partirsi*, Portuguese *partir(-se)* "to go away"

Pattern 23: satellite + simple non-motion verb > compound verb of directed motion

Latin SE + PARTIRI/PARTIRE "to divide" > Old French *se partir* "to go away"

Latin SE + DE "from" + PARTIRI/PARTIRE "to divide" > Romanian *a se depărta* "to go away"

Latin SE + INDE "thence" + PARTIRI/PARTIRE "to divide" > Romanian *a se îndepărta* "to go away"

Pattern 24: simple adjective > satellite + simple deadjectival verb of directed motion > compound verb of directed motion

BASSUS "low' (or BASSIOR, BASSIUS) > AD "towards" + Late Latin *BASSIARE > Old Spanish *(a)baxar*, Portuguese *(a)baixar*, Catalan *(a)baixar* "to go down"

Pattern 25: simple generic motion verb + satellite > compound verb of directed motion

Latin IRE "to go" + SE > Spanish *irse*, Portuguese *ir-se* "to go away"

Pattern 26: satellite + simple generic motion verb > compound verb of directed motion

Latin SE + INDE "thence" + IRE "to go" > Raeto-Romance (Engadine valley) *s'inir* "to go away"

Pattern 27: simple manner-of-motion verb + satellite > compound verb of directed motion

Latin AMBULARE "to walk" + SE + INDE "thence" > Italian *andarsene*, Catalan *anar-se'n* "to go away"

French *marcher* "to walk" + *se* > Spanish *marcharse* "to go away"

Pattern 28: satellite + simple manner-of-motion verb > compound verb of directed motion

Latin SE + INDE "thence" + AMBULARE "to walk" > French *s'en aller*, Occitan *s'enanar* "to go away"

Pattern 29: satellite + compound non-motion verb > compound verb of directed motion

Latin SE + RETRAHERE "to pull back" > Romanian *a se retrage* "to go away"

Latin SE + ERADICARE "to uproot" > Romanian *a se ridica* "to go up"

Pattern 30: simple verb of directed motion + satellite > compound verb of directed motion

Latin INTRARE "to go in" + SE + INDE "thence" > Old Catalan *entrar-se'n* "to go in"

Pattern 31: compound non-motion verb > simple verb of directed motion

Latin ADJUNGERE "to join, to unite, to connect" > Romanian *a ajunge* "to come"

The patterns listed and the lexical instances cited are exhaustive with regard to the data from Chapters 3 and 4. At the same time, as we have seen in Chapter 1 (Section 1.2), a language can have hundreds of verbs that express movement. Therefore, at the level of the lexical field of motion verbs at large, additional instances and patterns could potentially be incorporated into the inventory. For example, Pattern 23 'satellite + simple non-motion verb > compound verb of directed motion' could be expanded by including the combination of Classical Latin RE "back, against" with TORNARE "to round off on a lathe, to mold on the potter's wheel" which in Late Latin produced RETORNARE "to return, to come back";[8] cf. Spanish *retornar*, French *retourner*, Italian *ritornare*, Portuguese *retornar* "to come back, to return". Besides, an additional pattern, which shares a lot in common with Pattern 23, 'satellite + simple non-motion verb + satellite > compound verb of directed motion' may be suggested, as in the case of Classical Latin AD "towards" + BA(T)TUERE "to pound, to beat" + SE, which produced Late Latin ABATTERE "to take down" + SE; cf. Spanish *abatirse*, Italian *abbattersi*, Portuguese *abater-se* "to fall down, to swoop down on (usually of hunting birds)" (Müller 1987– II: 69–72).[9]

The examples provided above demonstrate that the so-called 'mixed' or 'hybrid' characteristics attributed in earlier studies to Italian and French are abundantly found in other Romance varieties as well. In other words, the examples show that the role of satellites in the Romance languages is much more complex and geographically diffused than was originally thought. On the one hand, patterns number 1 through 15 offer examples of simple (monomorphemic) etyma turning into simple (monomorphemic) Romance forms, including simple Romance verbs of directed motion of the verb-framed type presented in patterns number 4, 5, 7, 10, 11, 14, and 15. On the other hand, patterns number 16 through 31 offer examples of compounding either at the level of the etyma, or at the level of the Romance reflexes, or both. More specifically, as illustrated by patterns number 17 and 19, the Romance family retains a series of Latin satellite-framed verbs of directed motion. In addition, as patterns number 18, 20, 21, 22, 23, 24, 25, 26, 27, 28, 29, and 30 demonstrate, members of the Romance family have relied on satellites, i.e., on the old typological pattern characteristic of Latin, to create new Romance forms. What is even more striking is that, as can be inferred from patterns number 22, 23, 25, 26, 27, 28, 29, and 30, the satellites in these new Romance formations do not have to be the preverbs employed in Classical Latin. Instead, two new types of satellites have proliferated in Late Latin: the reflexive particle SE and the deictic adverb INDE "thence".[10] Furthermore, patterns number 18, 19, 21, 22, 23, 24, 25, 26, 27, 28, 29, and 30 present a series of compound Romance formations

---

8.   On Late Latin RETORNARE "to return, to come back", see Niermeyer & Van De Kieft (2002 II: 1197) and Du Cange (1883–1887 VII: 162–163).

9.   Cf. also French *s'abattre*, Romanian *a se abate* "to fall down, to swoop down on (usually of hunting birds)". For examples of Late Latin ABATTERE "to take down", see Niermeyer & Van De Kieft (2002 I: 1).

10.   See Chapter 4 (Section 4.2) for the discussion of the status of SE and INDE and of their reflexes as satellites.

in which a satellite is not only present etymologically but is still identifiable as such, including patterns 19, 21, 22, 23, 24, 25, 26, 27, 28, 29, and 30 that resulted in satellite-framed constructions of directed motion.

Thus, the development from Latin to Romance is not a one-way trajectory away from a system that relies on satellites towards a system that does not employ them. Rather it resembles a street with three parallel threads. The first thread is the inclination to move away from the satellite-framed system towards the verb-framed one through the following five tendencies:

(1) Loss of the compound forms (e.g., Latin ABIRE "to go away").

(2) Retention of the simple forms (e.g., Latin VENIRE "to come" > French *venir* "to come").

(3) Recruitment of simple forms from other lexical fields into the inventory of verbs of directed motion via semantic change (e.g., Latin COMPLERE "to fill up, to fill out, to complete" > Sardinian (Campidanese) *lompi, krompi,* (Logudorese) *lòmpere, cròmpere* "to come").

(4) Creation of new simple verbs of directed motion from nouns and adjectives by mechanisms of word-formation (e.g., Latin BASSUS "low" (or BASSIOR, BASSIUS) > Catalan *baixar* "to go down").

(5) Reanalysis of compound forms as simple ones (e.g., Latin EXIRE "to go out" > Italian *uscire* "to go out").

The second thread is to continue to rely on the satellites by combining prepositions and nouns to produce what eventually became simple verb-framed forms (e.g., Latin AD "towards" + RIPA "shore" > ADRIPARE "to come to shore" > French *arriver* "to come'). The third thread is to preserve the satellite-framed system by retaining the compounds with distinguishable parts (e.g., Latin DESCENDERE "to go down" > Italian *discendere* "to go down") and by creating new compound verbs of directed motion through combination of prepositions, pronouns, and adverbs with the following seven types of lexical items:

(1) Simple non-motion verbs (e.g., Latin SE + PARTIRI/PARTIRE "to divide" > Old French *se partir* "to go away").

(2) Compound non-motion verbs (e.g., Latin SE + ERADICARE "to uproot" > Romanian *a se ridica* "to go up").

(3) Simple generic motion verbs (e.g., Latin SE + INDE "thence" + IRE "to go" > Raeto-Romance *s'inir* "to go away").

(4) Simple manner-of-motion verbs (e.g., Latin AMBULARE "to walk" + SE + INDE "thence" > Italian *andarsene* "to go away").

(5) Simple verbs of directed motion (e.g., Latin INTRARE "to go in" + SE + INDE "thence" > Old Catalan *entrar-se'n* "to go in").

(6) Simple adnominal verbs of directed motion (e.g., PODIUM "elevated place"
     > Late Latin *PODIARE > Catalan *pujar* "to go up" > *a* "towards" + Catalan
     pujar "to go up" > Sardinian (Campidanese) *(a)pujai* "to go up").
(7) Simple deadjectival verbs of directed motion (e.g., Latin BASSUS "low" (or
     BASSIOR, BASSIUS) > AD "towards" + Late Latin *BASSIARE > Old Spanish
     (a)baxar "to go down").

As shown in Chapter 4, these threads reflect the speakers' creativity within the
word-formation patterns available in the lexicon at large.

Studies on Romance typology (e.g., Wanner 2001) stress that the typological
shifts attested on the way from Latin to Romance, such as clitic formation and the
development of the compound tenses, are not a matter of a split but rather of a
combination of "innovative features" and "massive continuity" (Wanner 2001:
1693). Studies on historical Romance linguistics share the view that the analysis of
the evolution of Latin into its daughter languages should focus as much on what
changed as on what did not change. As Wright (2002: 46) aptly warns us in *A Sociophilological Study of Late Latin*, "It is easy to be mesmerized by the differences
and fail to see the great continuities". Likewise, in the introduction to the *Diccionario etimológico de los sufijos españoles (y de otros elementos finales)*, Pharies (2002)
emphasizes that the development of suffixes can only be fully understood when
both the new and the old functions are taken into account. For instance, the ability of the Spanish derivational suffix *-azo* to form adjectives of pertinence (e.g.,
cebada "barley", *cebadazo* "of barley, like barley") is inherited from its Latin etymon -ACEUS (e.g., HEDERA "ivy", HEDERACEUS "of ivy, like ivy"), while its ability to
function as an augmentative suffix (e.g., *sañudo* "angry", *sañudazo* "very angry,
outraged") and to designate blows (e.g., *porra* "club", *porrazo* "blow with a club")
are innovations (Pharies 2002: 14–15). Along the same lines, the editors of the
recent *Cambridge History of the Romance Languages* (Maiden et al., eds. 2010)
state that they regard patterns of inheritance, continuity, and persistence to be as
important as patterns of change and innovation: "[the book] accords persistence
in Romance (and hence inheritance from Latin) a focus in its own right rather
than treating it simply as the background to the study of the changes" (Maiden et
al. 2010: xix). The present evaluation of the place of the Romance family in Talmy's
typology from the comparative-historical perspective and the focus on both nov-
elty and stability offer one more example of the Latin → Romance continuum.

Talmy's typology acknowledges the fact that a particular language can have
items of more than one type, but focuses on the mechanism of lexical borrowing
to explain this phenomenon. For example, while English belongs to the satellite-
framed type, some of its verbs (e.g., *enter, exit, pass*) are of the verb-framed type as
they do not belong to the Germanic stock, but are rather borrowings from Romance

(Talmy 1985: 72; 2000 II: 53–53). Talmy also recognizes that speakers themselves can come up with "constructions that 'push the envelope' of the language's current structure" (2000 II: 119), but does not elaborate on this important point. Romance historical data offer evidence that a language family can make use of both verb-framed and satellite-framed strategies, with both strategies in fact originating within the family, not outside of it. In addition, the data illustrate that a typological shift from a predominantly satellite-framed lexicalization type to a predominantly verb-framed lexicalization type does not necessarily imply a complete loss of productivity on the part of the former. Furthermore, the data suggest that Italian and Raeto-Romance verb-particle satellite-framed constructions, which until now have been regarded (at least implicitly by virtue of the great amount of attention that they have received in the scholarship) as the main counterexample within the verb-framed Romance family, are by far not the only one.

The hybridity of the Romance developments is not unique. It finds a parallel in the evolution of Chinese. Over the course of its history Chinese shifted from a type of language that "conflates motion with path, leaving such notions as manner to be expressed through adjuncts" to a type of language that "conflates manner with motion in the main verb, leaving path to be expressed through satellites" (Li 1997: 237). Examples (120) and (121) quoted from Li (1997: 236–237) illustrate the point:

(120) *Chun Qiu* ["*Spring and Autumn*"], 5th century B.C.   (Classical Chinese)
  Ji hou   da qu   qi guo
  Ji marquis big leave his state
  "The marquis of Ji left his state grandly."

(121) Ba Jin (Li Fei-kan), *Jia* ["*Family*"], 1931   (Contemporary Chinese)
  Ming Feng ma shang   pao chu qu   le
  Ming Feng immediately run exit thither PERF
  "Ming Feng immediately ran out."

In the Classical Chinese verb-framed example (120), the main verb *qu* "leave/go away" encodes the information about the path and the adverbial *da* "in a big way/grandly" encodes manner of motion (Li 1997: 237). In contrast, in the Contemporary Chinese satellite-framed example (121), the main verb *pao* "run" encodes manner of motion and the dual directional complement *chu* "exit/out" *qu* "go/thither" encodes path (ibid., p. 238).[11] In other words, "from its classical to its contemporary

---

11. As we have seen in Section 2.2, Talmy (1985) interprets directional complements in Contemporary Chinese as satellites and therefore classifies Contemporary Chinese as a satellite-framed language. In other words, schematically speaking, *pao + chu* "run out" equals *run + out*, the second part of the construction being a satellite. This interpretation is shared by studies like Li (1997) and Peyraube (2006). However, since we are dealing with morphologically unmarked

form, Chinese appears to have undergone a typological shift in a direction just the reverse of that exhibited by the Romance languages: from a Path-conflation pattern to a Manner/Cause-conflation pattern" (Talmy 2007: 155, based on Li 1993). The Chinese shift from verb-framed to satellite-framed was a gradual process. As Peyraube demonstrates, it proceeded through the following three stages:

> First, Archaic Chinese (Classical Chinese) encoded the path information of the motion events in the main verb of the clause. It was a verb-framed language. [...] Second, at the end of the Wei-Jin-Nan-Bei-Chao period, that is, around the 5th century AD, Chinese started to use directional complements and to undergo a shift from a verb-framed language to a satellite-framed language. Chinese became a mixed language using both strategies. [...] Third, some five centuries later, around the 10th century, the shift from a V-language to a S-language was achieved. (Peyraube 2006: 133)

My evaluation of the developments attested from Latin to Romance as a coexistence over a long period of time of lexicalization patterns that belong to different types and the comparison of this hybridity to the one found in the history of Chinese suggest that the cognitive typology of motion encoding would attain greater precision if it integrated the diachronic dimension into its framework. I share Talmy's opinion that "tracing the route by which a language shifts its typological pattern for the expression of Motion events – or indeed, maintains its pattern while other changes are ongoing – can be a rich research area for diachronic linguistics" (Talmy 2007: 154), and I would suggest that such an exploration (besides belonging to historical linguistics) forms an integral part of cognitive and typological research. In addition to offering a classification of languages according to their predominant type(s), a comprehensive diachrony-inclusive cognitive typology of motion encoding would also concern itself with completed and ongoing shifts between and within types at the level of individual languages and language

---

monosyllabic components and since the second component can function as a verb, *pao + chu* "run out" can also be interpreted as a combination of two verbs *run + exit*. Thus, Slobin (2004) proposes to classify Contemporary Chinese as 'equipollently-framed'. This proposal finds support in studies like Chen (2007), Guo & Chen (2009), and Chen & Guo (2009, 2010). Furthermore, it has been argued that it is not the first (manner-encoding) but rather the second (path-encoding) component that should be treated as the main verb, and that therefore Contemporary Chinese can be viewed "as primarily a verb-framed language and only secondarily a satellite-framed language" (Tai 2003: 311). Talmy (2009, 2012) offers further considerations in favor of classifying Contemporary Chinese as predominantly satellite-framed. In order to not complicate the issue, I follow Talmy's terminology and refer to Contemporary Chinese as satellite-framed because what matters for the purpose of the present discussion is that the first component *pao* "run" encodes manner and that the second component *chu* "exit/out" encodes path (regardless of what the most appropriate term for each one of them might be).

families, with the mixed types as reflections of layers of history, and with the types of shifts attested across the different language families. My suggestion fits well with contemporary interest on the part of scholars working within the framework of Talmy's typology in the mixed languages: e.g., Schaefer (1985) on Tswana, Schaefer (1986) on Emai, Wälchli (2001a) on Latvian, Huang & Tanangkingsing (2005) on Tsou, O'Connor (2007, 2009) on Lowland Chontal, Levinson (2006) on Yélî Dnye. In addition, it is in line with the contemporary outlook on lexical typology which understands the lexicon not as a static closed system but instead as a "dynamic and constantly changing complex structure" (Koptjevskaja-Tamm 2008: 6). It also accords with the contemporary efforts of bridging cognitive linguistics and linguistic typology (Croft 1999, van der Auwera & Nuyts 2007). Besides that, it is in line with contemporary interest in integrating historical and cognitive linguistics (Bybee 2007, Winters 2010). Furthermore, it fits well with the contemporary revival of interest on the part of typology in questions of language variation and change (Croft 2003: 232–279; Bybee 2006); an interest which, as Koerner (1995a) reminds us, goes all the way back to the pioneers of linguistic typology Friedrich Schlegel (1772–1829) and August Wilhelm Schlegel (1767–1845).

CHAPTER 9

Implications for the conceptual metaphor theory

9.1 Conceptual metaphors across language families

Chapters 5 through 7 have focused on how advances within cognitive linguistics can further our understanding of Latin and Romance motion-based metaphors. The present chapter turns the tables and explores how the present analysis of the metaphorical mappings found in Latin and Romance diachronic data informs current discussions within cognitive linguistics, more specifically the discussions centered on the conceptual metaphor theory.

As we have seen in Section 5.1, the conceptual metaphor theory postulates that linguistic metaphors reflect conceptual mappings grounded in human cognition. It also holds that due to this cognitive basis certain metaphors have the potential of being universal[1] or broadly distributed across genetically and areally unrelated languages. Reflecting on Lakoff & Johnson (1980, 1999, 2003), Johnson states: "Our claim was always that there could be a lot of culturally specific development tied to more universally shared kinds of metaphor. [...] I do think that there are some really generic, systematic metaphors which are universal" (Pérez i Brufau 2011: 331). Similar to the case of the typology of motion encoding, linguists have embraced the conceptual metaphor theory with great enthusiasm, while at the same time making an effort to refine it. One of the questions that has required further study has been which metaphors are likely to cut across language families and which ones are not, since in the process of advancing their theory Lakoff and Johnson have focused primarily on English, while at the same time recognizing that there is no reason to expect English to be representative of other linguistic varieties. The metaphor ARGUMENT IS WAR – as in "Your claims are *indefensible*", "He *attacked every weak point* in my argument", "His criticisms were *right on target*", "I *demolished* his argument", "I've never *won* an argument with him", "You disagree? Okay, *shoot!*", "If you use that *strategy*, he'll *wipe you out*", He *shot down* all of my arguments" (Lakoff & Johnson 1980: 4; original emphasis) – is a good illustration of this point:

---

1. I use the term 'linguistic universals' as coterminous with "patterns that occur systematically across languages" (Croft 2003: 1).

Try to imagine a culture where arguments are not viewed in terms of war, where no one wins or loses, where there is no sense of attacking or defending, gaining or losing ground. Imagine a culture where an argument is viewed as a dance, the participants are seen as performers, and the goal is to perform in a balanced and aesthetically pleasing way. In such a culture, people would view arguments differently, experience them differently, carry them out differently, and talk about them differently. But *we* would probably not view them as arguing at all: they would simply be doing something different. It would seem strange even to call what they were doing "arguing." Perhaps the most neutral way of describing this difference between their culture and ours would be to say that we have a discourse form structured in terms of a battle and they have one structured in terms of dance. (ibid., pp. 4–5; original emphasis)

The importance of recruiting data from multiple languages is evident from studies like Lehrer (1990) who observes that "some of the extended senses of *run* as opposed to *walk* are language specific": in order to refer to functioning of machines, English uses *run* (e.g., *the car is not running well*), while Spanish and French employ the equivalent of *walk* (i.e., *andar*, *marcher*) (pp. 226–227). Along the same lines, Radden (1988) draws our attention to the fact that "apparent contradictions between Hungarian *dühbe jön* 'come mad' and English *to go mad* or German *auf den Hund kommen* 'come to the dog' and English *to go to the dogs* make sense within each language and its specific metaphorization principles" (p. 392). Even metaphors based on such orientational universals as 'up-down', 'in-out', 'front-back', 'on-off', 'deep-shallow', and 'central-peripheral' can differ from culture to culture (Lakoff & Johnson 1980: 14). For example, while many languages refer to future events as located in front of the speaker, Aymara (an Amerindian language of western Bolivia, southeastern Peru, and northern Chile) refers to the future as located in the back (Núñez & Sweetser 2006). Besides that, recently it has been reported that the space-to-time mapping, which was earlier considered to be an absolute universal, is not a feature of Amondawa, a Tupi-Guarani language within the Amerindian family spoken in Brazilian Greater Amazonia (Sinha et al. 2011). Furthermore, sometimes differences can be found even between the dialects of one language. For example, in American English *to run* can refer to competing for an elective political office (e.g., *to run for mayor*), while in British English the corresponding verb is *to stand* (Lehrer 1990: 227).

Among the plethora of research initiatives undertaken during the last three and half decades, three programs of study stand out, as they are concerned not just with testing to what degree and in what ways the metaphors proposed by the conceptual metaphor theory are attested cross-linguistically, but more importantly with designing the methodological apparatus that would allow such testing.

One of these research initiatives draws a distinction between primary (or primitive) and complex (or compound) metaphors. Primary metaphors "are motivated by tight correlations in experience" (Grady 2005: 1600). For instance, the primary metaphor IMPORTANT IS BIG (e.g., *Tomorrow is a big day*) is based on the "frequent correlation in our experience between the size of an object and its salience or importance to us" (Grady 2007: 194). In contrast, complex metaphors lack experiential motivation. Instead, they are combinations of primary metaphors. For instance, THEORIES ARE BUILDINGS (e.g., *The theory will stand or fall on the strength of that argument*) is a combination of two primary metaphorical mappings: abstract (i.e., social, political, financial, logical) structure understood as physical part-whole structure (e.g., *The Federal Reserve is the cornerstone of the nation's banking system*), and persistence understood as persisting in an upright position (e.g., *The speed record for the mile still stands*) (Grady 1997b, 2007: 193). Because the recurring correlations in everyday embodied experiences, dubbed as "primary scenes" (Grady & Johnson 2002), are shared by speakers around the world, it is the primary metaphors that tend to be universal or broadly distributed across languages. This way, the metaphorical extension from 'big' to 'important' is attested in Hawaiian *nui*, Malay *besar*, Russian *krupnij*, Turkish *büyük*, and Zulu *-khulu* (Grady 2007: 194). Complex metaphors, on the other hand, have a tendency to be language-specific.

Another methodological trend highlights the need for a systematic fine-grained analysis of metaphors within language pairs. For example, two linguistic varieties can share the same metaphorical mapping, yet exploit it differently. For instance, as discussed in Barcelona (2001: 130–131), DEVIANT COLOR IS DEVIANT SOUND is attested in both English and Spanish. This way, a speaker of English can talk about gaudy colors as excessively intense sounds (e.g., *That's a loud color you are wearing*) or as excessively high-pitched sounds (e.g., *a shrill shade of red*). To express gaudy colors as agents that produce attention-grabbing sounds is less conventional and requires certain poetic license (e.g., *She was wearing a red skirt that cried aloud to heaven*). In contrast, for a Spanish speaker referring to colors as agents is conventional (e.g., *Es un color chillón/llamativo*, literally "It is a screaming/calling color", i.e., "It is a gaudy color"). The TIME IS MONEY metaphorical mapping is another case in point. As shown in Kövecses (2005: 135), it is found in both English and Hungarian: cf. English *That flat tire cost me an hour* and Hungarian *A defekt egy órámba került*, glossed as "The flat tire one hour-POSSESSIVE-LOCATIVE cost-PAST". Yet, the English sentence *How do you spend your time these days?* cannot be rendered into Hungarian using the equivalent of the verb *to spend*. A different metaphorical mapping, namely TIME IS A CONTAINER, is employed instead: *Mivel/hogy(an) töltöd az idődet mostanában?*, glossed as "What-INSTRUMENTAL/how fill-2nd

PERSON the time-POSSESSIVE-ACCUSATIVE present-in". Recent developments in corpus linguistics and the creation of large computerized corpora have opened up new opportunities for conducting the fine-grained research along the principles outlined above (e.g., Deignan & Potter 2004).

Methodological concerns are also at the heart of large-scale panchronic studies like the *Typologie des rapprochements sémantiques* undertaken by Martine Vanhove and her collaborators at the Centre National de la Recherche Scientifique (Paris, France) within the Fédération Typologie et Universaux Linguistiques (Vanhove ed. 2008) and the *Catalogue of Semantic Shifts* carried out by Anna Zalizniak and her collaborators at the Institute of Linguistics of the Russian Academy of Sciences (Moscow, Russia) (Zalizniak 2001, 2008, Gruntov 2007, Zalizniak et al. 2012). The data for the *Typologie des rapprochements sémantiques* project come from "a set of 45 languages belonging to eight genetic stocks, plus one pidgin and one creole, with an average of 25 languages for each semantic association" (Koptjevskaja-Tamm et al. 2007: 163–164). The semantic associations under investigation include hearing and mental perception, breath and soul, as well as meat and animal (Koptjevskaja-Tamm et al. 2007, Vanhove, ed. 2008). The *Catalogue of Semantic Shifts* relies on 162 languages from nine language stocks and includes approximately 500 semantic shifts, while considering for inclusion additional ones (Zalizniak 2001, 2008, Gruntov 2007, Zalizniak et al. 2012). The assumption behind both projects is that synchronic polysemy emerges through diachronic semantic change, as in the case of understanding conceptualized as grasping by polysemous English *grasp*, *get*, Armenian *aŕnel*, Mordvin *fatiams*, and Tibetan *adzin-pa*, as well as by such pairs as German *greifen* "to grasp" → German *begreifen* "to understand", Russian *lovit'* "to grasp" → Russian *ulovit'* "to understand", Russian *sxvatit'* "to grasp" → Russian *sxvatyvat'* "to understand", Old Russian *postiči* "to run down, to catch up" → Russian *postic'* "to understand", Old Russian *pojati* "to grasp" → *ponjat'* "to understand", and Russian *hapat'* "to grasp" → Czech *chápati* "to understand" (Gruntov 2007: 159; Zalizniak 2008: 228).[2] One of the methodological challenges that these large-scale panchronic projects face is that what might look universal at first sight can turn out to be the result of language contact when examined more closely (Gruntov 2007: 158–159).

---

2.   Cf. Latin COMPRAEHENDERE "to take firmly, to seize, to grasp" > French *comprendre*, Italian *comprendere*, Spanish *comprender* "to understand"; French *saisir* "to grasp" > French *saisir* "to understand"; French *piger* "to grasp" > French (colloquial) *piger* "to understand"; Spanish *pillar* "to seize, to grasp" > Spanish (colloquial) *pillar* "to understand"; Latin CAPERE "to grasp" > Italian *capire* "to understand"; Italian *afferrare* "to grasp" > Italian *afferrare* "to quickly achieve a complete understanding" (Koch 1997: 236; Dworkin 2006b: 52; 2010: 588).

9.2 Universal and language-specific conceptual metaphors: Historical Latin and Romance data as testing ground

While the three types of studies mentioned above (i.e., synchronic studies that decompose complex metaphors into primary ones attested cross-linguistically, synchronic studies that compare and contrast metaphors within pairs of unrelated modern languages, and large-scale panchronic studies) offer important insights into the universal nature of some metaphors and the language-specific nature of others, I would argue, based on the data analyzed in Chapters 6 and 7, that a dia-chronic focus on one specific family can be equally instructive. If on the way from Latin to Romance a particular cluster of lexical items X disappears, yet the cluster of new lexical formations Y that emerges in its place is able to encode the very same metaphorical meanings, then we are presented with the metaphorical map-pings proper of the semantic field in question. Conversely, if a particular cluster of lexical item X disappears, and the cluster of new lexical formations Y that emerges in its place is able to encode new metaphorical meanings not associated with the cluster X, or if the cluster of lexical items X is retained while the metaphorical meanings associated with it change, then we are presented with the metaphorical associations that are less fundamental to the field under investigation.

For example, as part of the LINEAR SCALES ARE PATHS metaphor, Classical Latin PERVENIRE "to come" could express reaching a certain amount or quantity. This way in Julius Caesar's *De Bello Ciuili* Book I Section 52 this verb collocates with the noun ANNONA "price of provisions": *iam [...] ad x l in singulos modios annona pervenerat* "the price of provisions had already reached fifty denarii a peck" (quoted in Glare, ed. 1982: 1363). As we have seen in Chapters 3 and 4, PER-VENIRE survived only on the Regional Romance level as a Latinism whose seman-tics excludes it from the inventory of Romance core motion verbs (e.g., French *parvenir* "to arrive with effort"). Yet, in spite of this fact, the metaphorical mapping present in Latin is available in the daughter languages. The Romance equivalents of PERVENIRE that do not derive from this verb but rather go back to different ety-ma exhibit the same metaphorical capacity. In the case of Spanish and Portuguese, the reflexes of Latin PLICARE "to fold", i.e., Spanish *llegar* and Portuguese *chegar*, serve as illustration: *El gasto llegó a diez mil pesetas* "The amount spent reached ten thousand pesetas" (Álvar Ezquerra, ed. 1990: 674), *As despesas não chegam a 200$* "The expenses do not reach two hundred dollars" (Fernandes 1972: 143). French *arriver* and Italian *arrivare* which go back to Late Latin ADRIPARE "to come to the shore" which in turn goes back to the combination of Classical Latin AD "towards" and RIPA "shore" offer similar examples: *Le dollar est arrivé à x francs* "The ex-change rate reached ten francs for one dollar" (Rey, ed. 1989 I: 562), *arriverò fino a 100 sterline* "I'll go [bid] as high as £100" (Rubery, ed. 2010: 1517). In the case of

Romanian, *a sosi* "to come" which goes back to Modern Greek σώνω "I catch up, I reach, I arrive" offers a comparable example:

(122)   *În foamete mare în Țarigrad de sosi chila de grîu cîte un galben.* (*Cronica lui Mihail Moxa,* 17th century, quoted in Pușcariu et al., eds. 1907– X: 4A: 1258)
"During the great famine in Țarigrad the price for a kilo of wheat reached a gold coin."

PURPOSES ARE DESTINATIONS is another case in point because both Latin PERVE-NIRE "to come" and its Romance equivalents that go back not to this verb but rather to Latin PLICARE "to fold" (i.e., Spanish *llegar,* Portuguese *chegar*), to Latin AD "to-wards" + RIPA "shore" (i.e., French *arriver,* Italian *arrivare,* Catalan *arribar,* Sardinian Logudorese *arrivare*), to Latin JUNGERE "to join, to unite, to connect" (i.e., Italian *giungere*), and to Latin ADJUNGERE "to connect" (i.e., Romanian *a ajunge*) can express the completion of one's objective. The following examples with Latin PERVE-NIRE (123), Spanish *llegar* (124), Portuguese *chegar* (125), French *arriver* (126), Italian *arrivare* (127), Catalan *arribar* (128), Sardinian (Logudorese) *arrivare* (129), Italian *giungere* (130), and Rumanian *a ajunge* (131) serve as an illustration:

(123)   *nam melius eodem ratione victus [...] pervenitur* (Spencer, ed. 1989: 216–217)
"for the same result is better attained by dieting"

(124)   *nunca llegó a (ser) director*   (Galimberti Jarman & Russell, eds. 1994: 462)
"He never made it to director."

(125)   *chegou a ministro*   (Fernandes 1972: 143)
"He made it to minister."

(126)   *avec du courage on arrive à tout*   (Mansion, ed. 1939 I: 54)
"With courage one can achieve anything."

(127)   *non arriverò mai a capire la matematica*   (Rubery, ed. 2010: 1517)
"I'll never manage to understand math."

(128)   *després de discutir arribaren a un acord*   (Torras i Rodergas, ed. 1985: 1304)
"After the argument they came to an agreement."

(129)   *arrivare a cumprèndere*   (Espa 1999: 141)
"to achieve understanding"

(130)   *giunse a scoprire il ladro*   (Macchi, ed. 1970 I: 589)
"He succeeded in discovering the thief."

(131)   *a ajunge la perfecțiune*   (Bantaș et al. 1981: 18)
"to attain perfection"

AMOUNT IS VERTICALITY and PROGRESS IS VERTICAL MOVEMENT are equally revealing. For instance, Latin refers to downwards movement with DESCENDERE and DEGREDI, while Romanian refers to it with *a coborî*, *a pogorî*, and *a scoborî* that go back to Slavic *pogorĭ* "downwards, down, below", *pod gorije* "valley", *pogorije* "mountain range", and *gora* "mountain". Yet, both languages are able to recruit their respective lexemes to encode decrease in quantity: e.g., Latin *adfectus qui descendit* "the emotion that decreases in force" and Romanian *a (-și) coborî vocea* "to lower one's voice". Likewise, lack of formal continuity between Latin DESCENDERE and DEGREDI, on the one hand, and Romanian *a coborî*, *a pogorî*, and *a scoborî*, on the other hand, does not preclude the two languages from employing these verbs in reference to lowering the social status: e.g., Latin *descendere regno* "to descend from royalty (abandon the status)" and Romanian *a coborî pe scara socială* "to sink in the social scale".

In other words, in spite of the alteration in form, the metaphorical pairing between arrival and reaching a certain amount, between arrival and reaching one's goal, between verticality and quantity, as well as between vertical movement and progress have remained intact. This is to say that the internal formal reshaping of the lexical inventory has not prevented these metaphorical extensions from living on. Besides that, the fact that Latin and Romance forms are different not just formally but also typologically (e.g., Latin satellite-framed DEGREDI "to go down" vs. Romanian verb-framed *a coborî* "to go down") has had no effect on the continuity of the figurative functions. External changes, i.e., changes in political, social, and cultural life that took place between the Roman times and the modern era, did not preclude the survival of these mappings either. Therefore, such associations are good candidates for being universal or broadly distributed across languages.

Latin CURRERE "to run" – in contrast to Latin PERVENIRE "to come", DESCENDERE, and DEGREDI "to go down" discussed in the previous paragraphs – survived on the Pan-Romance level. Yet, the metaphorical mappings of its Romance reflexes differ from those of the Latin etymon. For instance, Spanish *correr* in (132), Italian *correre* in (133), Portuguese *correr* in (134), Catalan *córrer* in (135), and Raeto-Romance *currer* in (136) refer to the valid and up-to-date nature of the subject, while the Latin equivalent did not function in this capacity:

(132) *Ya sabes que esas excusas aquí no <u>corren</u>.*   (Galimberti Jarman & Russell, eds. 1994: 199)
 "You know you can't get away with excuses like that here."

(133) *In Italia <u>corre</u> l'uso della siesta.*   (Reynolds, ed. 1981 I: 199)
 "It's a custom to rest in the afternoon in Italy."

(134) *A moeda que <u>corre</u> em nosso país é o real.*   (Geiger, ed. 2008, s.v. *correr*)
 "The currency which is in use in our country is the real."

(135)   *Aquesta moneda ja no <u>corre</u>, pot servir per a la col·lecció.*

(Sagristà i Artigas, ed. 1998: 445)

"This coin is no longer valid; it can be used for a collection."

(136)   *munaida chi nun <u>cuorra</u> pü*   (Planta et al., eds. 1939– IV: 523)

"currency no longer in circulation"

In other words, on the way from Latin to Romance the form remained the same, while the range of functions associated with it changed. Therefore, the metaphorical pairing between running and being valid or up-to-date is likely to be less pervasive than the metaphorical pairings discussed in the preceding paragraphs. The association between running and annoying, as in French *Tu nous cours avec tes histoires* "You annoy us with your stories (Rey, ed. 1989 II: 1011), is also likely to be less pervasive: it is a novel Romance usage not available in Latin, it is recent (attested for the first time in the early 20th century), and it is restricted to a particular Romance variety.

The examples provided above suggest that the intra-genetic (i.e., family-internal) diachronic perspective on Romance has the potential to address the issue of universal vs. language-specific metaphors, i.e., the same issue that traditionally has been investigated inter-genetically (i.e., across families). In other words, related linguistic varieties approached historically can serve as the testing ground for what traditionally has been tested on unrelated languages.

CHAPTER 10

Conclusions

The application of the principles of cognitive linguistics to Latin and Romance historical data has allowed me to assess the continuity of Latin verbs of motion and the Romance innovations on both the Pan-Romance and the language-specific levels, to identify the cognitive mechanisms that have served as enabling factors of change, and to uncover ways in which historical Romance linguistics and cognitive linguistics can mutually complement each other. The present concluding chapter summarizes these findings and points towards some possible research directions for the future.

When it comes to lexicalizing motion, the level of continuity between Latin and its descendents depends on the type of motion that is being expressed and on the morphological status of the lexemes. Simple (monomorphemic) generic verbs like 'to go' and manner-of-motion verbs like 'to walk' show the tendency to survive either across the Romance family or at least in a number of its members. For example, Latin IRE "to go" lives on as Spanish *ir*, Portuguese *ir*, and Raeto-Romance *ir*. It also survives in some dialects of Occitan as *ir*, and used to exist in Old Italian as *gire*. Besides, French has retained Latin IRE as part of the paradigm of *aller* "to go" (< AMBULARE "to walk"): future *j'irai*, conditional *j'irais*. At the same time, the relatively high degree of survival on the part of generic and manner-of-motion verbs does not imply that they did not experience any change at all. For instance, while Latin VADERE "to go" is abundantly retained through suppletion as part of the paradigms of the Romance reflexes of Latin IRE "to go" and AMBULARE "to walk" (e.g., Spanish *ir* in the Present Indicative: *voy, vas, va, vamos, vais, van*), its infinitive has disappeared. To offer another example, Latin AMBULARE "to walk" survived on the Pan-Romance level, yet it was able to retain its original meaning only on the periphery: Spanish *andar*, Portuguese *andar*, Romanian *a umbla* "to walk". In the more central Romance varieties, on the other hand, the meaning of the reflexes of AMBULARE has generalized to "to go": French *aller*, Italian *andare*, Catalan *anar*, Occitan *anar*, Sardinian (Campidanese) *andai*, Sardinian (Logudorese) *andare*, Raeto-Romance (Friulian) *lâ*. Even Latin CURRERE "to run" which shows remarkable stability – Spanish *correr*, French *courir*, Italian *correre*, Portuguese *correr*, Old Romanian *a cure*, Catalan *córrer*, Occitan *córrer, corrir*, Sardinian (Campidanese) *curri*, Sardinian (Logudorese) *cùrrere*, Raeto-Romance *currer* "to run" – eventually disappeared from Romanian where *a cure* was replaced by *a fugi* and *a alerga*. In other words, retention of generic and manner-of-motion verbs is high but not absolute.

Another group of verbs that shows a relatively high degree of continuity are simple (monomorphemic) verbs of directed movement, with VENIRE "to come" exemplifying a pattern of such stability: Spanish *venir*, French *venir*, Italian *venire*, Portuguese *vir*, Romanian *a veni*, Catalan *venir*, Occitan *venir*, Sardinian (Campidanese) *benni*, Sardinian (Logudorese) *bènnere*, Raeto-Romance *vegnir*, *gnir* "to come". Etymological compounds that were reanalyzed as simple forms behaved in a similar fashion, with INTRARE "to enter" serving as a *par excellence* case in point: Spanish *entrar*, French *entrer*, Italian *entrare*, Portuguese *entrar*, Romanian *a intra*, Catalan *entrar*, Occitan *(d)intrar*, Sardinian (Campidanese) *(b)intrai*, Sardinian (Logudorese) *(b)intràre*, Raeto-Romance *entrar* "to enter". As in the case of generic and manner-of-motion verbs, such verbs were not exempt from change either. For instance, the deictic value of Spanish *venir* and European Portuguese *vir* does not match that of Latin VENIRE. To offer another example, although the blend of Latin DE-SCENDERE "to go down" (whose prefix seems to have partly lost its value) and DE-/DIS-CEDERE "to depart, to withdraw, to go apart" produced Old Spanish *deçir* "to go down", the latter form eventually became obsolete.

Following the previous research within the fields of morphology and lexicology (e.g., Maiden 2004b, Dworkin 2010), the present study has underscored the role of the internal structural factors, such as excessive phonetic erosion (in the case of Latin IRE), homonymic clash and taboo associations (in the case of the Romanian reflex of Latin CURRERE), and excessive morphological complexity (in the case of Old Spanish *deçir*) as possible triggers of change.

According to my analysis, it is the compound (prefixed, polymorphemic) Latin verbs of directed motion which did not get reanalyzed as simple forms that show the least stability: ADVENIRE "to come", DEVENIRE "to come", ABIRE "to go away", ABSCENDERE "to go away", INIRE "to go in", EVENIRE "to go out", CONSCENDERE "to go up", and ESCENDERE "to go up", as well as the deponent compounds DEGREDI "to go down", INGREDI "to go in", and EGREDI "to go out" disappeared. While the loss of DEGREDI, INGREDI, and EGREDI can be viewed as a part of the more general trend of elimination of the deponent category, we also have seen that not all deponent verbs were necessarily doomed. For instance, Classical Latin ORIRI "to rise, to bestir one's self, to get up" was reanalyzed in Late Latin as *ORICARE and was retained as Romanian *a urca* "to go up". In a similar way, the deponent Classical Latin SORTIRI "to throw lots or to choose by a lot" survived as French *sortir*, Catalan *sortir*, and Occitan *sortir* "to go out". Could it be that the loss of verbs such as DEGREDI, INGREDI, and EGREDI was as much due to their prefixed nature as to their membership in the deponent class? Further research might explore this question.

Building upon the empirically based premise that direction and path are among the most conceptually salient components of the motion event schema, I have proposed to view the contrast between the verbs that exhibit a high degree of continuity and those that tended to disappear in terms of the verbs' ability to maintain their path-encoding function. Generic motion verbs and manner-of-motion verbs never had the ability to convey path, and therefore were affected the least. The monomorphemic verbs of directed motion that contained the information about the path within the stem were also stable. Similar continuity applies to the etymological compounds of directed motion that through reanalysis as simple forms were able to foreground the path-related information by incorporating it into the verbal stem. In contrast, the path-encoding function of the prefixed forms that failed to be reanalyzed could become jeopardized by the opaque nature of the prefix. As a result, such verbs became extinct. I have argued that the connection between speakers' motivation to highlight/foreground the information about path and the lexical changes attested on the way from Latin to Romance may have parallels in other language families. More specifically, I have pointed out that the loss of prefixed motion verbs on the way from Old to Modern English in favor of multi-word constructions (e.g., Old English *in(n)gan* vs. Modern English *go in*) and the use of separate path-encoding words in addition to directional suffixes by polysynthetic native languages of North America (e.g., Karuk *'ú·θ* "toward center of water") may have a similar underlying motive. Extending the cross-linguistic database to test this claim would be highly desirable.

While the prefixed forms were disappearing from the language, their substitutes were being created based on the cognitive relations of conceptual identity, contiguity, metaphorical similarity, taxonomic superordination, and taxonomic subordination. The cognitive relation of contiguity proved to be particularly productive. Based on the cognitive salience of path, a number of nouns and adjectives that referred to landscape or to objects with a certain connotation of direction present within them produced in Late Latin verbs of directed motion that served as the etyma of the Romance forms employed today: e.g., Classical Latin noun MONS, MONTIS "mountain" > Late Latin *MONTARE > French *monter*, Italian *montare*, Catalan *muntar*, Occitan *montar*, Raeto-Romance *muntar* "to go up"; Classical Latin adjective BASSUS "low" (or BASSIOR, BASSIUS) > Late Latin *BASSIARE > Spanish *bajar*, Portuguese *baixar*, Catalan *baixar* "to go down". Nouns and adjectives that encoded important landmarks but did not inherently signal a particular direction used prepositions, but the polymorphemic nature of such etymologically compound items did not retain its transparency: e.g., Latin AD "towards" + RIPA "shore" > Late Latin ADRIPARE "to come to shore" > French *arriver*, Italian *arrivare*, Catalan *arribar*, Occitan *arribar*, Sardinian (Campidanese) *arribai*, Sardinian (Logudorese) *arrivare*, Raeto-Romance *arrivar* "to come".

The new motion verbs that followed the 'noun > verb', 'adjective > verb', 'preposition + noun > verb', and 'preposition + adjective > verb' patterns were part of broader word-formation tendencies that were already present in Classical Latin and were highly productive in Late Latin in a gamut of lexical fields. I have compared the ubiquity of the word-formation mechanisms discussed above with the ubiquity of the word-formation mechanisms that led to the creation of the multi-word verbs in the history of English (e.g., *nod off, frown on*), suggesting that such a comparison can shed light on the difference between Romance and English (Germanic) lexical encoding of movement. A closer examination of this point would be highly desirable.

The overall shift away from polymorphemic towards monomorphemic verbs outlined above does not mean that compounding has been completely eschewed from the Romance lexical field of motion. Some Latin prefixed forms survived and their compound etymology is still transparent: e.g., Latin PER-VENIRE "to come" > French *parvenir*, Catalan *parvenir*, Italian *parvenire*, Occitan *parvenir* "to come (with effort/difficulty)". In addition, some of the new formations that emerged following the 'preposition + noun > verb' and 'preposition + adjective > verb' patterns also retained an identifiable prefix: e.g., PODIUM "elevated place" > Late Latin *PODIARE > *a* "towards" + Catalan *pujar* "to go up" > Sardinian (Campidanese) *(a)pujai* "to go up"; BASSUS "low" (or BASSIUS, BASSIOR) > AD + Late Latin *BASSIARE > Old Spanish *(a)baxar*, Portuguese *(a)baixar*, Catalan *(a)baixar* "to go down". Two other significant sources of Romance motion compounds were the reflexive pronoun SE (e.g., Latin IRE "to go" + SE > Spanish *irse*, Portuguese *ir-se* "to go away"), and the combination of the reflexive pronoun SE with the deictic adverb INDE "thence" (e.g., Latin SE + INDE + IRE "to go" > Raeto-Romance (Engadine) *s'inir* "to go away"). As in the case of new motion verbs that emerged in Late Latin by following the 'noun > verb', 'adjective > verb', 'preposition + noun > verb', and 'preposition + adjective > verb' patterns, the new lexical items that emerged with the help of SE and SE + INDE also form part of broader trends attested in Late Latin: the proliferation of the functions of the reflexive pronoun SE and the recruitment of adverbs into word-formation. In other words, the development of the lexical field of motion verbs is fully entrenched within the evolution of the lexicon at large.

The findings presented above have implications for the cognitive typology of motion encoding established by Leonard Talmy (Talmy 1975, 1983, 1985, 2000, 2007, 2009, 2012). According to this typology, Latin and Romance exhibit two typologically different lexicalization patterns, the former employing a 'Motion + Manner/Cause' satellite-framed pattern, and the latter employing a 'Motion + Path' verb-framed one. My data illustrate that while the shift from satellite-framed Latin to verb-framed Romance does reflect the general tendency, the transition is much more complex then just a substitution of one type by another. While the general drift on the way from Latin to Romance was to become verb-framed, the satellites continued being productive. In fact, the inventory of path satellites expanded beyond the prefixes employed in Classical Latin to include the reflexive pronoun SE and the deictic adverb INDE. Thus, the process of lexical borrowing which is commonly evoked to account for the verbs that do not belong to the dominant type (e.g., verb-framed *to exit* in the predominantly satellite-framed English) is not by any means the only potential source of exceptions. The results also indicate that Italian and Raeto-Romance verb-particle constructions that are often cited as the primary exception within the verb-framed Romance family constitute just one among several other major satellite-framed categories. The coexistence of three trends on the way from Latin to Romance (i.e., the transition away from a satellite-framed system towards a verb-framed one, the ability to retain old satellite-framed items, and the ability to produce new satellite-framed lexemes) suggests that the cognitive typology of motion encoding would benefit from extending its research scope to the diachronic shifts between and within types and from paying special attention to cases of typological hybridity. As we have seen in Chapter 4 (Sections 4.1 and 4.2) and in Chapter 8 (Section 8.2), in addition to the Romance languages, English (Imbert 2008a, b) and Chinese (Li 1997, Peyraube 2006) provide ample relevant empirical data for this kind of inquiry. It should be added that other linguistic varieties can also make a contribution. For instance, the expression of motion in Archaic, Classical, and post-Classical Greek and the transition between these stages (Baldi 2006, Imbert 2008a, 2010, Skopeteas 2008, Nikitina 2013) are equally instructive. The hypothesized typological shift within Ancient Egyptian from a verb-framed to a satellite-framed system between the earlier stages and the Coptic stage (Lincke, in progress) is also significant. The evolution of Latvian path verb particles favored by language contact in the Circum-Baltic region (Wälchli 2001a, b) is relevant as well. In addition, languages that do not have rich historical documentation can offer valuable information by means of comparative evidence and reconstruction (e.g., DeLancey & Golla 1997, DeLancey 1999, 2003 on Klamath; Grinevald 2011 on Jakaltek Popti'). Examples of on-going change, as in the case of semantic bleaching and reduction of productivity on the part of the prefix *vz-* "upwards" in Russian (Ferm 1990: 38, 72) and semantic bleaching on the part of the prefix *uz-* "upwards" in Serbo-Croatian (Slobin 2004: 251; Filipović 2007: 128), are also pertinent. It would be intriguing to see further integration of the historical insights coming from the aforementioned languages, and to observe additional linguistic varieties approached diachronically within the framework of Talmy's typology. In addition, it would be highly desirable to see diachronic linguistic typology and diachronic construction grammar join forces.

While the inventory of motion verbs changed considerably from Latin to Romance, the metaphorical extensions of the field show a much higher level of inheritance. In fact, almost all of the motion-based metaphorical mappings attested in Latin have equivalents in the Romance languages. In other words, neither the fading away of the Latin verb accompanied by the creation of the Romance innovative lexeme in its place, nor the shift from a predominantly satellite-framed type to a predominantly verb-framed type preclude Latin and Romance from sharing the same figurative usage, as in the case of Latin PERVENIRE "to come" and French *arriver* "to come" expressing reaching a certain amount or quantity as part of the LINEAR SCALES ARE PATHS conceptual metaphor. I have proposed that this continuity can be accounted for in cognitive terms: metaphorical linguistic patterns reflect conceptual mappings and therefore are not tied to specific lexical means. In addition to retaining the figurative meanings already attested in Latin, the Romance languages have developed a series of new transferred senses. Some of them have wide representation across the Romance family, as in the case of mechanical functioning or up-to-date validity expressed as motion. Other senses, like the association between running and annoying in French or the projection between running and being embarrassed in Spanish and Portuguese, are more sporadic.

I have argued that the patterns of metaphorical continuity and innovation identified in Romance diachronic data have implications for the conceptual metaphor theory, more specifically for its efforts to establish which mappings are more likely to be universal or broadly attested across languages and which ones are more likely to be language-specific. The extensions found in both Latin and Romance are good candidates for being universal or broadly attested. This is particularly the case in those instances in which the Latin lexical items became obsolete and were replaced by new Romance lexemes. In contrast, the associations that are found in the Romance languages but not in Latin are likely to be less fundamental to the lexical field in question. This is particularly the case in those instances in which the novel metaphors have limited presence within the Romance family, that is to say, are confined to one dialectal variety (e.g., Madrid Spanish), one language (e.g., French), or one sub-group (e.g., Ibero-Romance). In other words, the family-internal historical perspective is as apt to tackle the issue of universal vs. language-specific metaphors as the research carried out across linguistic families. While making this suggestion, however, I have cautioned that lack of written Latin evidence does not necessarily mean inexistence in the spoken language. As scholars of Classical philology have started applying the conceptual metaphor theory to the Latin texts that let the spoken usage shine through (García-Jurado & Hualde-Pascual 2002, García-Jurado 2003), future research might be able to assess the difference between Latin and Romance with more precision.

Another reason to pay close attention to continuity is that novel Romance metaphors can be elaborations of the projections attested since Latin. I have proposed that VALIDITY IS MOTION, as in Spanish *Ya sabes que esas excusas aquí no corren* "You know you can't get away with excuses like that here" (Galimberti Jarman & Russell, eds. 1994: 199), is a compound metaphor that developed in Romance as a combination of two mappings already available in Latin. These two mappings are DIFFUSION IS MOTION (e.g., Latin *rubor cucurrit* "the blush mantled") and VALIDITY IS DIFFUSION (e.g., Latin *sensus communis* "perception of what is appropriate" from SENSUS "sensation, judgment" plus COMMUNIS "common, shared"). This analysis provides support on the level of diachrony for the distinction made by cognitive linguists (Grady 1997a, b, 2005, Lakoff & Johnson 1999) on the synchronic level between primary and complex metaphors.

Recent research on genetically unrelated linguistic varieties has revealed that the place of the language in Talmy's typology can play a role in the way in which this language uses metaphorical pairings. For instance, the motion-based metaphors from the novels written in English (a satellite-framed Germanic language) analyzed in Özçalışkan (2004) show the following distribution: manner verbs such as *to run* – 59%, path verbs such as *to enter* – 34%, neutral verbs such as *to go* – 7%. In contrast, the motion-based metaphors in the novels written in Turkish (a verb-framed language that belongs to the Turkic branch of the Altaic family) employ manner verbs much less often and path verbs much more often: manner verbs – 21%, path verbs – 71%, neutral verbs 8% (Özçalışkan 2004: 79). For instance, in the English sentence from *The French Lieutenant's Woman* (1969) by John Fowles, the occurrence of an unexpected thought is expressed with the manner verb *to spring*: *And as he looked down at the face beside him, it was suddenly, out of nowhere, that Emma Bovary's name sprang into his mind* (Özçalışkan 2004: 79). In contrast, in the Turkish sentence from *Sitem* (1997) by Nihal Yeğinobalı, the same concept is lexicalized with the help of the path verb *gel* "to come": *Sonra o anda çözemediği bir çağrışımla aklına Dalya geldi* "Then Dalya came to her mind with an association that she could not understand" (ibid., pp. 79–80). As we have seen throughout the present study, Latin and Romance exhibit profound differences in the degree to which they rely on satellite-framed and verb-framed patterns. At the same time, we have also seen that Latin and its daughter languages share a great number of motion-based conceptual metaphors. Thus, it would be desirable to find out whether these metaphorical mappings integrate manner to a much greater extent in Latin than in Romance.

Until fairly recently, the conceptual metaphor theory has shown little interest in cultural issues, which is probably due to the effort on the part of the cognitive framework to break away from and to counteract the centuries-long tradition of viewing metaphor as a stylistic or rhetorical device rather than as a matter of thought. The current tendency, however, is to study metaphor both as an aspect of cognition grounded in embodiment and as a product of culture: e.g., Kövecses (1995, 2005, 2008), Gibbs (1999), Sinha et al. (2011). For example, as discussed in

Kövecses (1995, 2005, 2008), the emotion of anger has a number of universal physiological reactions: increase in body temperature and blood pressure, as well as in heart and respiration rates. Since, as we have seen in Section 5.1, conceptual mappings are embodied, we could expect that due to shared somatic experience speakers of different languages would have the same anger metaphors. Yet, this is not the case. Speakers of European languages express anger as heat (e.g., English *They were having a heated argument*) or as a combination of heat and internal pressure (e.g., English *Billy's just blowing off steam*), while speakers of Chinese rely more on internal pressure (Kövecses 1995: 186–191; 2005: 39–43; 2008: 178). In addition, as shown in Gevaert (2005: 199), the conceptualization of anger as heat in the English language has not been a constant: the number of heat-related words employed to refer to anger is very low in the pre-850 documents, is on the rise between 850 and 950, then starts to decrease and keeps decreasing until around 1300, and after that goes up again. By building upon Geeraerts & Grondelaers (1995), Gevaert (2005) demonstrates that it is the cultural element – the importance of the humoral theory of emotions during certain periods of the Western history – that helps to account for such fluctuation.

My findings corroborate that integrating the cognitive and the cultural dimensions strengthens the conceptual metaphor theory's explanatory potential. I have discussed ways in which culture, more specifically technological progress, factors into several Romance motion-based figurative functions. My examples include working of a mechanism expressed as walking, as in French *Ma montre ne marche plus* "My watch no longer works" (Mansion, ed. 1939 I: 520), and exploding expressed as jumping (up into the air), as in Italian *Gli esplosivi sono saltati (in aria)* "The explosives have exploded" (Gabrielli 1971: 185–186). I have also referred to a relevant example reported in Maisak (2007: 219) in his study on aqua-motion: Portuguese *navegar* "to sail" in *navegar na Internet* "to browse the web, to be available on the web". Given the rapid on-going proliferation of new technology in modern society, future research that combines the cognitive and the cultural perspectives might reveal novel types of metaphorical mappings that employ motion verbs as their source domain.

My data also confirm the importance of paying close attention to the origin of metaphorical functions. Recent studies in cognitive semantics have highlighted the fact that an accurate assessment of linguistic universals is contingent upon our knowledge of whether the figurative extensions under investigation developed independently in each language or resulted from language contact. For instance, as discussed in Gruntov (2007: 158–159), the pairing between 'sweet' and 'potable' appears universal at first sight: it is attested in a number of languages, including Classical Greek, Latin, French, Italian, English, German, Swedish, Old Slavonic, Serbo-Croatian, Hungarian, Finnish, Hebrew, Arabic, Turkmen, Turkish, and

Azerbaijani, and could have evolved independently in each one of these linguistic varieties on the experiential basis of non-saline drinking water tasting sweet in comparison to one that contains salt. Yet, it is problematic to identify the association between 'sweet' and 'potable' as a semantic universal because of the role of language contact. For example, Old Slavonic and Serbo-Croatian usage is a borrowing from Greek, since the first instances of Old Slavonic *sladyky* and Serbo-Croatian *sladak* in the sense "potable" are found in translations of Greek religious texts (ibid.). I have touched upon the issue of borrowed metaphorical mappings both within Romance and across language families. More specifically, I have discussed the role of French in the development of Italian *montare* in the sense "to assemble", of Italian *saltare* in the sense "to sauté, to stir fry", and of Romanian *a alerga* in the sense "to extend". I have also addressed the possible role of Arabic in the development of Spanish *salir* in the sense "to resemble by inheriting, to take after" and of Spanish *correr* in the sense "to pillage, to devastate, to ravage". A closer examination of these channels of transmission would be highly desirable.

The present study has focused on the exploration of lexical change through integration of insights from historical Romance linguistics and cognitive linguistics. However, lexical change is only one of many areas that can benefit from combining the diachronic and the cognitive approaches. For instance, the focus on the embodied nature of phonological production has allowed cognitive linguists to gain new insights into the mechanism of articulatorily based and perceptually based sound change (Bybee 2007: 946–957). Also, cognitive linguistics' emphasis on cognitive representation has proven to be relevant to the investigation of morphophonological change, more specifically of analogical change (ibid., pp. 958–964). In addition, our understanding of morphosyntactic change, particularly of grammaticalization, has profited from close attention to such cognitive processes as abstract thought, automatization of neuromotor sequences, categorization, inferencing, and habituation to repeated stimuli (Bybee 2003, 2007: 964–979; Traugott 2003). To give one more example, the concept of the prototype has allowed cognitive linguistics to successfully join forces with historical sociolinguistics in uncovering the mechanisms by which language change is adopted in the community (Grondelaers et al. 2007). In other words, as a partnership between cognitive and diachronic research, historical cognitive linguistics has produced new insights in a range of subfields, including phonology, morphology, syntax, and sociolinguistics. Yet, so far, Romance historical data – in spite of their extraordinary wealth – have been incorporated into these collaborative efforts only to a small degree. It is my hope that in the future more cognitively-oriented studies will focus their attention on the developments attested from Latin to Romance.

References

Adams, J[ames] N[oel]. 1976. *The Text and Language of a Vulgar Latin Chronicle (Anonymus Valesianus II)*. (= *Institute of Classical Studies Bulletin*, Supplement 36). London: University of London.

Adams, J. N. 2007. *The Regional Diversification of Latin 200 B.C. – A.D. 600*. Cambridge: Cambridge University Press. DOI: 10.1017/CBO9780511482977

Adams, J. N. 2011. "Late Latin". *A Companion to the Latin Language* ed. by James Clackson, 257–283. Malden, Mass.: Wiley-Blackwell.

Agualusa, José Eduardo. 1990. *D. Nicolau Água Rosada e outras estórias verdadeiras e inverosímeis*. Lisbon: Vega. [Accessed through COMPARA. See under COMPARA (below) for details.]

Agualusa, José Eduardo. 1995. *The Incredible but True Story of Prince Nicolau Água-Rosada*. Transl. by Alexis Levitin. Madison, Wis.: Farleigh Dickinson University. [Accessed through COMPARA.]

Alarcón Hernández, Paola. 2004. "Esquemas de 'pasar'". *Lenguaje y cognición: Estudios en lingüística cognitiva* ed. by Paola Alarcón Hernández, 279–290. Concepción, Chile: Universidad de Concepción.

Alcover, Antoni Maria & Francesc de B. Moll, eds. 1930–1962. *Diccionari català–valencià–balear: Inventari lexical y etimològich de la llengua que parlen Catalunya espanyola y Catalunya francesa, el Regne de València, les Illes Balears y la ciutat d'Alguer de Sardenya, en totes ses formes literàries y dialectals, antigues y modernes*. 10 vols. Palma de Mallorca: Alcover.

Alibert, Louis. 1965. *Dictionnaire occitan–français d'après les parlers languedociens*. Toulouse: Institut d'Études Occitanes.

Allan, Kathryn. 2008. *Metaphor and Metonymy: A diachronic approach*. (= *Publications of the Philological Society*, 42.) Malden, Mass.: Wiley-Blackwell.

Alonso Pedraz, Martín. 1986. *Diccionario medieval español: Desde las Glosas emilianenses y silenses (s. X) hasta el siglo XV*. 2 vols. Salamanca: Universidad Pontificia de Salamanca.

Álvar Ezquerra, Manuel, ed. 1990. *Diccionario general ilustrado de la lengua española VOX*. Barcelona: Biblograf.

Amenta, Luisa. 2008. "Esistono i verbi sintagmatici nel dialetto e nell'italiano regionale siciliano?". Cini, ed. 2008.159–174.

Anderson, John M. 1971. *The Grammar of Case: Towards a localistic theory*. (= *Cambridge Studies in Linguistics*, 4.) Cambridge: Cambridge University Press.

Asch, Solomon E. 1956. "Studies of Independence and Conformity: I. A minority of one against a unanimous majority". *Psychological Monographs: General and Applied* 70:9.1–70. DOI: 10.1037/h0093718

Ascoli, G[raziadio] I[saia]. 1880/1883. "Saggio di morfologia e lessicologia soprasilvana". *Archivio Glottologico Italiano* 7.406–602.

Aske, Jon. 1989. "Path Predicates in English and Spanish: A closer look". *Proceedings of the Fifteenth Annual Meeting of the Berkeley Linguistics Society, 18–20 February 1989* ed. by Kira Hall, Michael Meachman & Richard Shapiro, 1–14. Berkeley: Berkeley Linguistics Society.

Aski, Janice. 1995. "Verbal Suppletion: An analysis of Italian, French, and Spanish *to go*". *Linguistics* 33:3.403–432. DOI: 10.1515/ling.1995.33.3.403

Aulete, F[rancisco] J[úlio] Caldas, António Lopes dos Santos Valente & José Timóteo da Silva Bastos, eds. 1925. *Diccionario contemporaneo da lingua portugueza*. Feito sobre o plano de F. J. Caldas Aulete. 2nd ed. 2 vols. Lisboa: Antonio Maria Pereira.

Aurnague, Michel, Andrée Borillo, Mario Borillo & Myriam Bras, eds. 1993. *Semantics of Time, Space, Movement, and Spatio-Temporal Reasoning: Proceedings of the 4th International Workshop on Time, Space and Movement (Château de Bonas, 4–8 September 1992)*. Toulouse: CNRS.

Baciu, Ileana. 2006. "Goal of Motion Constructions in English and Romanian: The case of '*a alerga*' and '*a fugi*'". *Revue Roumaine de Linguistique* 51:1.43–54.

Badía Margarit, Antonio M. 1947. *Los complementos pronominalo-adverbiales derivados de IBI e INDE en la Península Ibérica. (= Revista de Filología Española,* Anejo 38.) Madrid: Consejo Superior de Investigaciones Científicas.

Badía Margarit, Antonio. 1952. "Los demostrativos y los verbos de movimiento en iberorománico". *Estudios dedicados a Menéndez Pidal* ed. by Consejo Superior de Investigaciones Científicas, vol. III, 3–31. Madrid: Patronato Marcelino Menéndez y Pelayo.

Baldi, Philip. 1979. "Typology and Indo-European Prepositions". *Indogermanische Forschungen* 84.49–61.

Baldi, Philip. 2006. "Towards a History of the Manner of Motion Parameter in Greek and Indo-European". *Fonologia e tipologia lessicale nella storia della lingua greca: Atti del VI Incontro Internazionale di Linguistica Greca, Bergamo, settembre 2005* ed. by Pierluigi Cuzzolin & Maria Napoli, 13–31. Milano: FrancoAngeli.

Baldinger, Kurt. 1964. "Sémasiologie et onomasiologie". *Revue de Linguistique Romane* 28.249–272.

Baldinger, Kurt. 1980. *Semantic Theory: Towards a modern semantics.* Ed. by Roger Wright. Transl. by William C. Brown. Oxford: Basil Blackwell.

Bally, Charles. 1944. *Linguistique générale et linguistique française.* 2nd ed. Berne: A. Francke.

Bally, Charles. 1951. *Traité de stylistique française.* 2 vols. 3rd ed. Genève: Librairie Georg.

Balzac, Honoré de. 1835. *Le père Goriot.* Bruxelles: A. Wahlen.

Balzac, Honoré de. 1894. *Père Goriot.* Transl. by Katharine Prescott Wormeley. Boston: Roberts Brothers.

Bantaş, Andrei, Andreea Gheorghiţoiu & Leon Leviţchi. 1981. *Dicţionar frazeologic român-englez.* 2nd ed. Bucureşti: Editura Ştiinţifică şi Enciclopedică.

Barcelona, Antonio. 2001. "On the Systematic Contrastive Analysis of Conceptual Metaphors: Case studies and proposed methodology". *Applied Cognitive Linguistics II: Language pedagogy* ed. by Marin Pütz, Susanne Niemeier & René Dirven (= *Cognitive Linguistics Research*, 19), 117–146. Berlin & New York: Mouton de Gruyter.

Barcelona, Antonio & Javier Valenzuela. 2011. "An Overview of Cognitive Linguistics". *Cognitive Linguistics: Convergence and expansion* ed. by Mario Brdar, Stefan Th. Gries & Milena Žic Fuchs (= *Human Cognitive Processing*, 32), 17–44. Amsterdam & Philadelpha: John Benjamins. DOI: 10.1075/hcp.32.05bar

Baroja, Pío. 1904. *La busca.* Madrid: Librería de Fernando Fé.

Baroja, Pío. 1922. *The Quest*. Transl. by Isaac Goldberg. New York: Alfred A. Knopf.

Basore, John W., ed. & transl. 1979. Seneca, *Moral Essays*. Vol. II. (= *Loeb Classical Library*, 254.) Cambridge, Mass.: Harvard University Press; London: William Heinemann.

Bassols de Climent, M[ariano]. 1948. *Sintaxis histórica de la lengua latina. Vol. II.1: Las formas personales del verbo*. (= *Filología Clásica*, 6.) Barcelona: Escuela de Filología.

Bastardas Parera, Juan. 1953. *Particularidades sintácticas del latín medieval: Cartularios españoles de los siglos VIII al XI*. (= *Filología Clásica*, 12.) Barcelona: Escuela de Filología.

Battaglia, Salvatore, ed. 1961–2009. *Grande dizionario della lingua italiana*. 21 vols. Torino: Unione Tipografico-Editrice Torinese.

Battisti, Carlo & Giovanni Alessio. 1950–1957. *Dizionario etimologico italiano*. 5 vols. Firenze: G. Barbèra.

Beavers, John, Beth Levin & Shiao Wei Tham. 2010. "The Typology of Motion Expressions Revisited". *Journal of Linguistics* 46.331–377. DOI: 10.1017/S0022226709990272

Bergh, Lars. 1948. *Moyens d'exprimer en français l'idée de direction: Étude fondée sur une comparaison avec les langues germaniques, en particulier le suédois*. Göteborg: Rundqvists Boktryckeri.

Berlin, Brent & Paul Kay. 1969. *Basic Color Terms: Their universality and evolution*. Berkeley & Los Angeles: University of California Press.

Bernardi, Rut, Alexi Decurtins, Wolfgang Eichenhofer, Ursina Saluz & Moritz Vögeli. 1994. *Handwörterbuch des Rätoromanischen: Wortschatz aller Schriftsprachen, einschliesslich Rumantsch Grischun, mit Angaben zur Verbreitung und Herkunft*. 3 vols. Zürich: Offizin.

Bernini, Giuliano. 2010. "Word Classes and the Coding of Spatial Relations in Motion Events: A contrastive typological approach". *Space in Language: Proceedings of the Pisa International Conference, Pisa, 8–10 October 2009* ed. by Giovanna Marotta, Alessandro Lenci, Linda Meini & Francesco Rovai, 29–52. Firenze: Edizioni ETS.

Berthele, Raphael. 2004. "The Typology of Motion and Posture Verbs: A variationist account". *Dialectology Meets Typology: Dialect grammar from a cross-linguistic perspective* ed. by Bernd Kortmann (= *Trends in Linguistics; Studies and Monographs*, 153), 93–126. Berlin & New York: Mouton de Gruyter.

Berthele, Raphael. 2006. *Ort und Weg: Die sprachliche Raumreferenz in Varietäten des Deutschen, Rätoromanischen und Französischen*. (= *Linguistik – Impulse & Tendenzen*, 16.) Berlin & New York: Mouton de Gruyter. DOI: 10.1515/9783110890464

Berthele, Raphael. 2007. "Contact de langues et conceptualisations spatiales: Aspects de la sémantique et de la grammaire de la référence spatiale en sursilvan, vallader et surmiran". *Vox Romanica* 66.60–71.

Berthele, Raphael. 2009. "The many Ways to Search for a Frog Story: On a fieldworker's troubles collecting spatial language data". *Crosslinguistic Approaches to the Psychology of Language: Research in the tradition of Dan Isaac Slobin* ed. by Jiansheng Guo, Elena Lieven, Nancy Budwig, Susan Ervin-Tripp, Keiko Nakamura & Seyda Özçalýşkan, 163–174. New York & London: Psychology Press.

Bierwisch, Manfred. 1996. "How Much Space Gets into Language?". Bloom et al., eds. 1996.31–76.

Blake, Randolph, Nicholas J. Cepeda & Eric Hiris. 1997. "Memory for Visual Motion". *Journal of Experimental Psychology: Human Perception and Performance* 23:2.353–369. DOI: 10.1037/0096-1523.23.2.353

Blank, Andreas. 1997a. "Les adjectifs temporels du type long/court dans les langues romanes: Un cas de 'métaphoricité étroite'". *L'organisation lexicale et cognitive des dimensions spatiale et temporelle: Actes d'EUROSEM 1996* ed. by Hiltraud Dupuy-Engelhardt & Marie-Jeanne Montibus (= *Recherches en Linguistique et Psychologie Cognitive*, 7), 15–37. Reims: Presses Universitaires de Reims.

Blank, Andreas. 1997b. *Prinzipien des lexikalischen Bedeutungswandels am Beispiel romanischern Sprachen.* (= *Beihefte zur Zeitschrift für Romanische Philologie*, 285.) Tübingen: Max Niemeyer. DOI: 10.1515/9783110931600

Blank, Andreas. 1999. "Why Do New Meanings Occur? A cognitive typology of the motivations for lexical semantic change". Blank & Koch, eds. 1999.61–89.

Blank, Andreas. 2000. "Pour une approche cognitive du changement sémantique lexical: Aspect sémasiologique". *Théories contemporaines du changement sémantique* ed. by Jacques François (= *Mémoire de la Société de Linguistique de Paris, Nouvelle Série*, 9), 59–74. Louvain: Peeters.

Blank, Andreas. 2003. "Words and Concepts in Time: Towards diachronic cognitive onomasiology". *Words in Time: Diachronic semantics from different points of view* ed. by Regine Eckardt, Klaus von Heusinger & Christoph Schwarze (= *Trends in Linguistics; Studies and Monographs*, 143), 37–65. Berlin & New York: Mouton de Gruyter.

Blank, Andreas, Paul Gévaudan & Peter Koch. 2000. "Onomasiologie, sémasiologie et l'étymologie de langues romanes: Esquisse d'un projet". *Actes du XXIIe Congrès International de Linguistique et de Philologie Romanes, Bruxelles, 23–29 juillet 1998* ed. by Annick Englebert, Michel Pierrard, Laurence Rosier & Dan Van Raemdonck, vol. IV: *Des mots aux dictionnaires*, 103–114. Tübingen: Max Niemeyer.

Blank, Andreas & Peter Koch. 1997. "Kognitive romanische Onomasiologie und Semasiologie". *Kognitive romanische Onomasiologie und Semasiologie* ed. by Andreas Blank & Peter Koch (= *Linguistische Arbeiten*, 476), 1–15. Tübingen: Max Niemeyer.

Blank, Andreas & Peter Koch. 1999a. "Introduction: Historical semantics and cognition". Blank & Koch, eds. 1999.1–14.

Blank, Andreas & Peter Koch. 1999b. "Onomasiologie et étymologie cognitive: L'exemple de la tête". *Actas do 1o Encontro de Linguística, Porto, 29–30 May 1998* ed. by Mario Vilela & Fátima Silva, 49–71. Porto: Facultade de Letras do Porto.

Blank, Andreas & Peter Koch, eds. 1999. *Historical Semantics and Cognition.* (= *Cognitive Linguistics Research*, 13.) Berlin & New York: Mouton de Gruyter. DOI: 10.1515/9783110804195

Blank, Andreas & Peter Koch. 2000. "La conceptualization du corps humain et la lexicologie diachronique romane". *La lexicalisation des structures conceptuelles: Actes du Colloque International EUROSEM 1998* ed. by Hitraud Dupuy-Engelhardt & Marie-Jeanne Montibus (= *Recherches en Linguistique et Psychologie Cognitive*, 13), 43–62. Reims: Presses Universitaires de Reims.

Bloch, Oscar & Walther von Wartburg. 1994. *Dictionnaire étymologique de la langue française.* 5th ed. Paris: Presses Universitaires de France.

Blomberg, Johan & Jordan Zlatev. 2009. "Linguistic Relativity, Mediation and the Categorization of Motion". *Studies in Language and Cognition* ed. by Jordan Zlatev, Mats Andrén, Marlene Johansson Falck & Carita Lundmark, 46–61. Newcastle upon Tyne: Cambridge Scholars.

Bloom, Paul, Mary A. Peterson, Lynn Nadel & Merrill F. Garrett, eds. 1996. *Language and Space.* Cambridge, Mass. & London: MIT Press.

Blumenthal, Peter & Jean-Emmanuel Tyvaert, eds. 2003. *La cognition dans le temps: Études cog-nitives dans le champ historique des langues et des texts*. (= *Linguistische Arbeiten, 476*.) Tübingen: Max Niemeyer.

Boggs, R[alph] S[teele], Lloyd Kasten, Hayward Keniston & H[enry] B[rush] Richardson. 1946. *Tentative Dictionary of Medieval Spanish*. 2 vols. Chapel Hill, N.C.: Authorized facsimile.

Bohnemeyer, Jürgen, Nicholas J. Enfield, James Essegbey, Iraide Ibarretxe-Antuñano, Sotaro Kita, Friederike Lüpke & Felix K. Ameka. 2007. "Principles of Event Segmentation in Language: The case of motion events". *Language* 83:3.495–532. DOI: 10.1353/lan.2007.0116

Bonfante, Giuliano. 1963/1964. "E ancora *andare!*". *Studi Linguistici Italiani* 4.160–169.

Booij, Geert. 2010. *Construction Morphology*. Oxford: Oxford University Press.

Bopp, Franz. 1816. *Über das Conjugationssystem der Sanskritsprache in Vergleichung mit jenem der griechischen, lateinischen, persischen und germanischen Sprache*. Frankfurt am Main: Andreäische Buchhandlung.

Borodina, M. A. 1973. *Sravnitel'no-sopostavitel'naja grammatika romanskix jazykov: Retoroman-skaja podgruppa, engadinskie varianty* [*Comparative grammar of the Romance languages: The Raeto-Romance group, the Engadine varieties*]. Leningrad: "Nauka".

Bouchard, Denis. 1995. "Primitives, Metaphor and Grammar". *Contemporary Research in Romance Linguistics: Papers from the 22nd Linguistic Symposium on Romance Languages, El Paso/Ciudad Juárez, February 1992* ed. by Jon Amastae (= *Current Issues in Linguistic Theory*, 123), 205–236. Amsterdam & Philadelphia: John Benjamins. DOI: 10.1075/cilt.123.17bou

Bourciez, Édouard. 1967. *Éléments de linguistique romane*. 5th ed. Paris: Klincksieck.

Bourdin, Philippe. 1992. "Constance et inconstances de la déicticité: La resémantisation des marques andatifs et venitifs". *La deixis: Colloque en Sorbonne, 8–9 juin 1990* ed. by Mary-Annick Morel & Laurent Danon-Boileau, 287–307. Paris: Presses Universitaires de France.

Bréal, Michel. 1897. *Essai de sémantique: Science des significations*. Paris: Hachette.

Brinton, Laurel J. & Elizabeth Closs Traugott. 2005. *Lexicalization and Language Change*. Cambridge: Cambridge University Press. DOI: 10.1017/CBO9780511615962

Brosman, Margaret Cuneo. 1956. *The Verbal Concept of Motion in Old Spanish*. Ph.D. dissertation, University of North Carolina at Chapel Hill.

Brosman, Paul. 1951. *The Verbal Concept of Motion in Old French*. M.A. dissertation, Tulane University.

Buck, Carl Darling. 1949. *A Dictionary of Selected Synonyms in the Principal Indo-European Languages: A contribution to the history of ideas*. Chicago & London: University of Chicago Press.

Budagov, R[uben] A[leksandrovič]. 1963. *Sravnitel'no-semasiologičeskie issledovanija: Romanskie jazyki* [*Comparative semasiological studies: The Romance languages*]. Moscow: Izdatel'stvo Moskovskogo Universiteta.

Buridant, Claude. 1995. "Les préverbes en ancien français". *Les préverbes dans les langues d'Europe: Introduction à l'étude de la préverbation* ed. by André Rousseau, 287–323. Lille: Presses Universitaires du Septentrion.

Burnett, Heather & Mireille Tremblay. 2009. "Variable-Behavior Ps and the Location of PATH in Old French". *Romance Languages and Linguistic Theory: Selected papers from 'Going Romance', Amsterdam 2007* ed. by Enoch O. Aboh, Elisabeth van der Linden, Josep Quer & Petra Sleeman (= *Romance Languages and Linguistic Theory*, 1), 25–50. Amsterdam & Philadelphia: John Benjamins. DOI: 10.1075/rllt.1.02bur

Butler, H[arold] E[dgeworth], ed. & transl. 1969. Quintilian, *Institutio oratoria*. Vol. I. (= *Loeb Classical Library*, 124.) Cambridge, Mass.: Harvard University Press; London: William Heinemann.

Bybee, Joan. 2003. "Cognitive Processes in Grammaticalization". *The New Psychology of Language: Cognitive and functional approaches to language structure* ed. by Michael Tomasello, vol. II, 145–167. Mahwah & London: Lawrence Earlbaum.

Bybee, Joan. 2006. "Language Change and Universals". *Linguistic Universals* ed. by Ricardo Mairal & Juana Gil, 179–194. Cambridge: Cambridge University Press. DOI: 10.1017/CBO9780511618215.009

Bybee, Joan. 2007. "Diachronic Linguistics". *The Oxford Handbook of Cognitive Linguistics* ed. by Dirk Geeraerts & Hubert Cuyckens, 945–987. Oxford: Oxford University Press.

Bybee, Joan, Revere Perkins & William Pagliuca. 1994. *The Evolution of Grammar: Tense, aspect, and modality in the languages of the world*. Chicago & London: University of Chicago Press.

Cadierno, Teresa. 2004. "Expressing Motion Events in a Second Language: A cognitive typological perspective". *Cognitive Linguistics, Second Language Acquisition, and Foreign Language Teaching* ed. by Michel Achard & Susanne Niemeier (= *Studies on Language Acquisition*, 18), 13–49. Berlin & New York: Mouton de Gruyter. DOI: 10.1515/9783110199857.13

Cadiot, Pierre, Franck Lebas & Yves-Marie Visetti. 2004. "Verbes de mouvement, espace et dynamiques de constitution". *Histoire, Epistémologie, Langage* 26:1.7–42. DOI: 10.3406/hel.2004.2185

Cadiot, Pierre, Franck Lebas & Yves-Marie Visetti. 2006. "The Semantics of the Motion Verbs: Action, space, and qualia". Hickmann & Robert, eds. 2006.175–206.

Calvo Rigual, Cesáreo. 2008. "I verbi sintagmatici italiani, con appunti contrastivi con lo spagnolo e il catalano". *Estudios y análisis de fraseología contrastiva: Lexicografía y traducción* ed. by Carmen González Royo & Pedro Mogorrón Huerta, 47–66. Alicante: Universidad de Alicante.

Cardini, Filippo-Enrico. 2008. "Manner of Motion Saliency: An inquiry into Italian". *Cognitive Linguistics* 19:4.533–569. DOI: 10.1515/COGL.2008.021

Cardini, Filippo-Enrico. 2010. "Evidence against Whorfian Effects in Motion Conceptualization". *Journal of Pragmatics* 42.1442–1459. DOI: 10.1016/j.pragma.2009.09.017

Cardini, Filippo-Enrico. 2012. "Grammatical Constraints and Verb-Framed Languages: The case of Italian". *Language and Cognition* 4:3.167–201. DOI: 10.1515/langcog-2012-0010

Casasanto, Daniel. 2010. "Space for Thinking". *Language, Cognition and Space: The state of the art and new directions* ed. by Vyvyan Evans & Paul Chilton, 453–478. London & Oakville: Equinox.

Casasanto, Daniel & Lera Boroditsky. 2008. "Time in the Mind: Using space to think about time". *Cognition* 106.579–593. DOI: 10.1016/j.cognition.2007.03.004

Catalán, Diego. 1989. "De Nájera a Salobreña: Notas lingüísticas e históricas sobre un reino en estado latente". *El español: Orígenes de su diversidad* by Diego Catalán, 296–327. Madrid: Paraninfo.

Cejador y Frauca, Julio. 1971. *Vocabulario medieval castellano*. Hildesheim: Georg Olms.

Cennamo, Michela. 1999. "Late Latin Pleonastic Reflexives and the Unaccusative Hypothesis". *Transactions of the Philological Society* 97:1.103–150. DOI: 10.1111/1467-968X.00046

Cervantes, Miguel de. 1969 [1605]. *The First Part of the Delightful History of the Most Ingenious Knight Don Quixote of the Mancha*. Transl. by Thomas Shelton. New York: P. F. Collier & Son.

Cervantes, Miguel de. 1998 [1605–1615]. *Don Quijote de la Mancha*. Ed. by Francisco Rico. Con la colaboración de Joaquín Forradellas. Estudio preliminar de Fernando Lázaro Carreter. (= *Biblioteca Clásica*, 50.) 2 vols. Barcelona: Instituto Cervantes.

Cervantes Saavedra, Miguel de. 2001. *The Ingenious Hidalgo Don Quixote de la Mancha*. Transl. by John Rutherford. Introduction by Roberto González Echevarría. New York: Penguin Books.

Chalmeta, P. 1981. "Précisions au sujet du monnayage Hispano-Arabe (*dirham qāsimī* et *dirham arba'īnī*)". *Journal of the Economic and Social History of the Orient* 24:3.316–324. DOI: 10.2307/3631911

Chen, Liang. 2007. *The Acquisition and Use of Motion Event Expressions in Chinese*. (= *Studies in Chinese Linguistics*, 3.) Munich: LINCOM Europa.

Chen, Liang & Jiansheng Guo. 2009. "Motion Events in Chinese Novels: Evidence for an equipollently-framed language". *Journal of Pragmatics* 41.1749–1766. DOI: 10.1016/j.pragma. 2008.10.015

Chen, Liang & Jiansheng Guo. 2010. "From Language Structures to Language Use: A case study from Mandarin motion expression classification". *Chinese Language and Discourse* 1:1.31–65. DOI: 10.1075/cld.1.1.02che

Chevalier, Jean-Claude. 1976. "Sur l'idée d''aller' et de 'venir' et sa traduction linguistique en espagnol et en français". *Bulletin Hispanique* 78.254–312. DOI: 10.3406/hispa.1976.4203

Cifuentes-Férez, Paula. 2009. *A Crosslinguistic Study on the Semantics of Motion Verbs in English and Spanish*. (= *LINCOM Studies in Semantics*, 1.) Munich: LINCOM Europa.

Cifuentes Férez, Paula. 2010. "The Semantics of the English and the Spanish Motion Verb Lexicons". *Review of Cognitive Linguistics* 8:2.233–271. DOI: 10.1075/rcl.8.2.01cif

Cifuentes Honrubia, José Luis. 1999. *Sintaxis y semántica del movimiento: Aspectos de gramática cognitiva*. Alicante: Instituto de Cultura Juan Gil-Albert.

Cini, Monica, ed. 2008. *I verbi sintagmatici in italiano e nelle varietà dialettali: Stato dell'arte e prospettive di ricerca. Atti delle giornate di studio (Torino, 19–20 febbraio 2007)*. (= *Spazi Comunicativi/Kommunikative Räume*, 3.) Frankfurt am Main: Peter Lang.

Cioranescu, Alejandro. 1966 [1958–1966]. *Diccionario etimológico rumano*. La Laguna, Canarias: Universidad de La Laguna.

Clackson, James & Geoffrey Horrocks. 2007. *The Blackwell History of the Latin Language*. Malden, Mass.: Blackwell.

Claflin, E. F. 1948. Review of *Syntaktische Forschungen auf dem Gebiete des Spätlateins und des frühen Mittellateins* by Dag Norberg (Leipzig: Otto Harrassowitz, 1943). *The American Journal of Philology* 69:1.109–113. DOI: 10.2307/291327

Collitz, Klara Hechtenberg. 1928/1929. "Propriety in the Light of Linguistics". *Modern Philology* 26.415–426. DOI: 10.1086/387790

Collitz, Klara H. 1931. *Verbs of Motion in their Semantic Divergence*. (= *Linguistic Society of America; Language Monographs*, 8.) Philadelphia: Linguistic Society of America.

Collodi, Carlo. 2002. *Le avventure di Pinocchio: Storia di un burattino*. Introduzione di Stefano Bartezzaghi. Prefazione di Giovanni Jervis. Con un saggio di Italo Calvino. Torino: Einaudi.

Collodi, Carlo. 2008. *The Adventures of Pinocchio*. Transl. by Geoffrey Brock. Introd. by Umberto Eco. Afterword by Rebecca West. New York: New York Review Books.

Colón, Germà. 1993. *El lèxic català dins la Romània*. València: Universitat de València.

COMPARA. 2002. *The Portuguese–English Parallel Corpus*. Lisbon: Linguateca. (http://www. linguateca.pt/COMPARA). Accessed: 2005–2013.

Comrie, Bernard. 1976. *Aspect: An introduction to the study of verbal aspect and related problems.* Cambridge: Cambridge University Press.

Cordin, Patrizia. 2011. *Le costruzioni verbo–locativo in area romanza: Dallo spazio all'aspetto.* (= *Beihefte zur Zeitschrift für Romanische Philologie*, 365.) Berlin: Walter de Gruyter. DOI: 10.1515/9783110261899

Corominas, Joan. 1954–1957. *Diccionario crítico etimológico de la lengua castellana.* 4 vols. Bern: A. Francke.

Corominas, Joan. 1990. *Breve diccionario etimológico de la lengua castellana.* 3rd ed. Madrid: Gredos.

Corominas, Joan & José A. Pascual. 1980–1991. *Diccionario crítico etimológico castellano e hispánico.* 6 vols. 2nd ed. (= *Biblioteca Románica Hispánica; Diccionarios*, 7.) Madrid: Gredos.

Coromines, Joan, Joseph Gulsoy & Max Cahner. 1980–1991. *Diccionari etimològic i complementari de la llengua catalana.* 9 vols. Barcelona: Curial Edicions Catalanes & Caixa de Pensions "La Caixa".

Corpus Inscriptionum Latinarum. 1863–. Berlin: Berlin-Brandenburgische Akademie der Wissenschaften.

Corrà, Loredana. 1981. "Contributo alla bibliografia onomasiologica: Dominio italiano". *La ricerca dialettale III* ed. by Manlio Cortelazzo (= *Centro di Studio per la Dialettologia Italiana*, 12), 393–478. Pisa: Pacini.

Cortelazzo, Manlio & Paolo Zolli. 1979–1988. *Dizionario etimologico della lingua italiana.* 5 vols. Bologna: Zanichelli.

Coseriu, Eugenio. 1964. "Pour une sémantique diachronique structurale". *Travaux de Linguistique et de Littérature* 2:1.139–186.

Coseriu, Eugenio. 1990. "Semántica estructural y semántica 'cognitiva'". *Profesor Francisco Marsá: Jornadas de filología* ed. by Manuel Álvar, 239–282. Barcelona: Universitat de Barcelona.

Coteanu, Ion & Lucreţia Mareş, eds. 1996. *Dicţionarul explicativ al limbii române.* 2nd ed. Bucureşti: Univers Enciclopedic.

Coupier, Jules. 1995. *Dictionnaire Français–Provençal/Diciounàri Francés–Prouvençau.* Marseille: Association Dictionnaire Français–Provençal.

Crocco Galèas, Grazia & Claudio Iacobini. 1993. "Parasintesi e doppio stadio derivativo nella formazione verbale del latino". *Archivio Glottologico Italiano* 78:2.167–199.

Croft, William. 1999. "Some Contributions of Typology to Cognitive Linguistics, and Vice Versa". *Cognitive Linguistics: Foundations, scope, and methodology* ed. by Theo Janssen & Gisela Redeker (= *Cognitive Linguistics Research*, 15), 61–93. Berlin & New York: Mouton de Gruyter. DOI: 10.1515/9783110803464.61

Croft, William. 2000. *Explaining Language Change: An evolutionary approach.* London: Longman.

Croft, William. 2003. *Typology and Universals.* 2nd ed. Cambridge: Cambridge University Press.

Croft, William & D. Alan Cruse. 2004. *Cognitive Linguistics.* Cambridge: Cambridge University Press. DOI: 10.1017/CBO9780511803864

Croft, William, Jóhanna Barðdal, Willem Hollmann, Violeta Sotirova & Chiaki Taoka. 2010. "Revising Talmy's Typological Clasification of Complex Event Constructions". *Contrastive Studies in Construction Grammar* ed. by Hans C. Boas (= *Constructional Approaches to Language*, 10), 201–235. Amsterdam & Philadelphia: John Benjamins. DOI: 10.1075/cal.10. 09cro

Cuartero Otal, Juan. 2006. "¿Cuántas clases de verbos de desplazamiento se distinguen en español?". *Rilce: Revista de filología hispánica* 22:1.13–36.

Cuartero Otal, Juan. 2010. "Estructuras argumentales de los verbos de desplazamiento del sujeto: Una descripción del español frente a una descripción del inglés". *Bulletin of Hispanic Studies* 87:2.149–168. DOI: 10.3828/bhs.2009.9

Cuervo, Rufino José. 1992–1994. *Diccionario de construcción y régimen de la lengua castellana.* Continuado y editado por el Instituto Caro y Cuervo. Nueva edición ordenada por el gobierno de la República de Colombia. 8 vols. Santafé de Bogotá: Instituto Caro y Cuervo. [1st ed. Paris, 1886–1893, 2 vols.]

Cuzzolin, Pierluigi. 2010. "How to Move Towards Somebody in Plautus' Comedies: Some remarks on the adverb *obuiam*". *Studies in Classical Linguistics in Honor of Philip Baldi* ed. by B. Richard Page & Aaron D. Rubin (= *Amsterdam Studies in Classical Philology*, 17), 7–20. Leiden & Boston: Brill. DOI: 10.1163/ej.9789004188662.i-168.10

Darmesteter, Arsène. 1887. *La vie des mots étudiée dans leurs significations.* Paris: Librairie Ch. Delagrave.

Darmesteter, Arsène. 1899. *A Historical French Grammar* ed. by Ernest Muret & Léopold Sudre, transl. by Alphonse Hartog. London: Macmillan.

Darms, Georges, Anna-Alice Dazzi Gross & Manfred Gross. 1989. *Langenscheidts Wörterbuch Rätoromanisch: Rätoromanisch–Deutsch, Deutsch–Rätoromanisch.* 5th ed. Zürich: Langenscheidt.

Dauzat, Albert. 1946. *Études de linguistique française.* 2nd ed. Paris: Éditions d'Artrey.

Dauzat, Albert, Jean Dubois & Henri Mitterand. 1979. *Nouveau dictionnaire étymologique et historique.* 4th ed. Paris: Librairie Larousse.

Davies, Mark. 2007. *Corpus del Español* (100 million words, 1200s–1900s). Completed in 2002, underwent a major revision in 2007. (http://www.corpusdelespanol.org). Accessed: 2007–2013.

Davies, Mark & Michael Ferreira. 2006. *Corpus do Português* (45 million words, 1300s–1900s). (http://www.corpusdoportugues.org). Accessed: July 2013.

de Cihac, A[lexandru]. 1978 [1870–1879]. *Dictionnaire d'étymologie daco-romane. Vol. I [1870]: Éléments latins comparés avec les autres langues romanes. Vol. II [1879]: Éléments slaves, magyars, turcs, grecs-moderne et albanais.* 2 vols. in 1. Osnabrück: Biblio.

Decurtins, Alexi. 2001. *Niev vocabulari romontsch sursilvan-tudestg.* Chur: Legat Anton Cadonau; Societad Retorumantscha; Societad per la Perscrutaziun da la Cultura Grischuna.

de Gorog, Ralph. 1973. "Bibliographie des études de l'onomasiologie dans le domaine du français". *Revue de Linguistique Romane* 37.419–446.

Deignan, Alice & Liz Potter. 2004. "A Corpus Study of Metaphors and Metonyms in English and Italian". *Journal of Pragmatics* 36.1231–1252. DOI: 10.1016/j.pragma.2003.10.010

DeLancey, Scott. 1999. "Lexical Prefixes and the Bipartite Stem Construction in Klamath". *International Journal of American Linguistics* 65:1.56–83. DOI: 10.1086/466376

DeLancey, Scott. 2003. "Location and Direction in Klamath". *Motion, Direction, and Location in Languages: In honor of Zygmunt Frajzyngier* ed. by Erin Shay & Uwe Seibert (= *Typological Studies in Language*, 56), 59–90. Amsterdam & Philadelphia: John Benjamins. DOI: 10.1075/tsl.56.08del

DeLancey, Scott. 2009. "Bipartite Verbs in Languages of Western North America". *Prostranstvo i vremja v jazykax raznoj tipologii: Materialy meždunarodnoj naučnoj konferencii XXV-e "Dul'zonovskie čtenija", Tomsk, 26–29 ijunja, 2008* [*Space and time in languages of various typology: Proceedings of the 25th International Conference "Dulson Readings", Tomsk, 26–29 June 2008*] ed. by Andrej Fil'čenko. Tomsk: Veter.

DeLancey, Scott & Victor Golla. 1997. "The Penutian Hypothesis: Retrospect and prospect". *International Journal of American Linguistics* 63:1.171–202. DOI: 10.1086/466318

De Mauro, Tullio, ed. 1999–2003. *Grande dizionario italiano dell'uso*. 7 vols. Torino: UTET.

Deutschmann, Olaf. 1953. *Untersuchungen zum volkstümlichen Ausdruck der Mengenvorstellung im Romanischen*. Doctoral dissertation, University of Hamburg.

Devoto, Giacomo & Gian Carlo Oli. 1997. *Nuovissimo vocabolario illustrato della lingua italiana*. 2 vols. Firenze: Felice Le Monnier.

Dewell, Robert. 1994. "*Over* again: Image-schema transformations in semantic analysis". *Cognitive Linguistics* 5.351–380. DOI: 10.1515/cogl.1994.5.4.351

Diez, Friedrich. 1836–1844. *Grammatik der romanischen Sprachen*. 3 vols. Bonn: E. Weber.

Diez, Friedrich. 1853. *Etymologisches Wörterbuch der romanischen Sprachen*. Bonn: A. Marcus.

Di Meola, Claudio. 2003. "I verbi deittici di moto in italiano e tedesco". *Intoduzione alla linguisitca cognitiva* ed. by Livio Gaeta & Silvia Luraghi, 181–196. Rome: Carocci.

Dirven, René. 1985. "Metaphor as a Basic Means for Extending the Lexicon". *The Ubiquity of Metaphor: Metaphor in language and thought* ed. by Wolf Paprotté & René Dirven (= *Current Issues in Linguistic Theory*, 29), 85–121. Amsterdam & Philadelphia: John Benjamins. DOI: 10.1075/cilt.29.06dir

Dirven, René. 2005. "Major Strands in Cognitive Linguistics". *Cognitive Linguistics: Internal dynamics and interdisciplinary interaction* ed. by Francisco J. Ruiz de Mendoza Ibáñez & M. Sandra Peña Cervel (= *Cognitive Linguistics Research*, 32), 17–68. Berlin & New York: Mouton de Gruyter.

Dirven, René & Francisco José Ruiz de Mendoza Ibáñez. 2010. "Looking Back at 30 Years of Cognitive Linguistics". *Cognitive Linguistics in Action: From theory to application and back* ed. by Elżbieta Tabakowska, Michał Choiński & Łukasz Wiraszka (= *Applications of Cognitive Linguistics*, 14), 13–70. Berlin: Walter de Gruyter.

Divjak, Dagmar, Laura A. Janda & Agata Kochańska. 2007. "Why Cognitive Linguistics Should Care about the Slavic Languages and Vice Versa". *Cognitive Path into the Slavic Domain* ed. by Dagmar Divjak & Agata Kochańska (= *Cognitive Linguistics Research*, 38), 1–17. Berlin & New York: Mouton de Gruyter. DOI: 10.1515/9783110198799.0.1

Domingo, Ricardo, ed. 1997. *El pequeño Larousse ilustrado*. 3rd ed. Barcelona: Ediciones Larousse.

Du Cange, Charles Du Fresne. 1883–1887. *Glossarium mediae et infimae latinitatis*. 10 vols. Niort: L. Favre. [1st ed. Paris, 1678, 3 vols.]

Ducháček, Otto. 1970. "Sur le problème de la structure du lexique". *Actele celui de-al xii-lea Congres International de Lingvistică şi Filologie Romanică* ed. by Alexandru Rosetti & Sandra Reinheimer-Rîpeanu, vol. I, 864–868. Bucureşti: Editura Academiei Republicii Socialiste România.

Dufresne, Monique, Fernande Dupuis & Mireille Tremblay. 2003. "Preverbs and Particles in Old French". *Yearbook of Morphology* ed. by Geert Booij & Jaap van Marle, 33–60. Dordrecht: Kluwer.

Du Nay, André. 1977. *The Early History of the Rumanian Language*. (= *Edward Sapir Monograph Series in Language, Culture, and Cognition*, 3.) Lake Bluff, Illinois: Jupiter Press.

Duncan, Robert M. 1975. "Color Words in Medieval Spanish". *Studies in Honor of Lloyd A. Kasten* ed. by Theodore Beardsley, 53–71. Madison, Wis.: Hispanic Seminary of Medieval Studies.

Dvoreckij, I. X. 1986. *Latinsko–russkij slovar'* [Latin–Russian dictionary]. 3rd ed. Moscow: Russkij Jazyk.

Dworkin, Steven N. 1977, "Two Etymological Cruxes: Spanish *engreír* and *embaír* (with an afterthought on *desvaído*)". *Romance Philology* 31:2.220–225.

Dworkin, Steven N. 1992a. "La agonía y muerte del esp. ant. *decir* 'bajar'". *Actas del II Congreso Internacional de Historia de la Lengua Española, Sevilla, 5 de marzo de 1990* ed. by M[anuel] Ariza, R[afael] Cano, J[osé] M.ª Mendoza & A[ntonio] Narbona, vol. I, 981–986. Madrid: Pabellón de España.

Dworkin, Steven N. 1992b. "The Demise of Old Spanish *decir*: A case study in lexical loss". *Romance Philology* 45:4.493–502.

Dworkin, Steven N. 1995. "Two Studies in Old Spanish Homonymics". *Hispanic Review* 63.527–542. DOI: 10.2307/474740

Dworkin, Steven N. 1997. "Semantic Change and Lexical Loss: The case of OSp. *luengo*". *La corónica* 26:1.53–65.

Dworkin, Steven N. 1998. "Cambio semántico y pérdida léxica: La suerte del español antiguo *luengo* 'largo'". *Actas del IV Congreso Internacional de Historia de la Lengua Española, La Rioja, 1–5 de abril de 1997* ed. by Claudio García Turza, Fabián González Bachiller & Javier Mangado Martínez, vol. II, 99–107. Logroño: Universidad de la Rioja.

Dworkin, Steven N. 2002. "Pérdida e integración léxicas: *aína* vs. *rápido* en el español premoderno". *Vocabula et vocabularia: Études de lexicologie et de (méta-) léxicographie romanes en l'honneur du 60e anniversaire de Dieter Messner* ed. by Bernhard Pöll & Franz Rainer, 109–118. Frankfurt am Main: Peter Lang.

Dworkin, Steven N., ed. 2003. *Critical Cluster "Historical Romance Linguistics: The death of a discipline?"*. *La corónica* 31:2.1–134. DOI: 10.1353/cor.2003.0019

Dworkin, Steven N., ed. 2005. *Forum: "Historical Romance Linguistics: The death of a discipline?"*. *La corónica* 34:1.125–256. DOI: 10.1353/cor.2005.0024

Dworkin, Steven N. 2006a. "La naturaleza del cambio léxico". *Actas del VI Congreso Internacional de Historia de la Lengua Española, Madrid, 29 de septiembre – 4 de octubre de 2003* ed. by José Jesús de Bustos Tovar & José Luis Girón Alconchel, vol. I, 67–84. Madrid: Arco/Libros.

Dworkin, Steven N. 2006b. "Recent Developments in Spanish (and Romance) Historical Semantics". *Selected Proceedings of the 8th Hispanic Linguistics Symposium* ed. by Timothy L. Face & Carol A. Klee, 50–57. Somerville, Mass.: Cascadilla Proceedings Project.

Dworkin, Steven N. 2010. "Lexical Change". Maiden, Smith & Ledgeway, eds. 2010.585–605.

Dworkin, Steven N. 2012. *A History of the Spanish Lexicon: A linguistic perspective*. Oxford: Oxford University Press. DOI: 10.1093/acprof:oso/9780199541140.001.0001

Dynnikov, A. N. & N. G. Lopatina. 1998. *Narodnaja latyn' [Vulgar Latin]*. 2nd ed. Moscow: Izdatel'stvo Moskovskogo Universiteta.

Edwards, Henry John, ed. & transl. 1919. Caesar, *The Gallic War*. (= *Loeb Classical Library*, 72.) Cambridge, Mass. & London: William Heinemann; New York: G. P. Putnam's Sons.

Eichholz, D. E., ed. & transl. 1962. Pliny, *Natural History*. Vol. X. Libri XXXVI–XXXVII. (= *Loeb Classical Library*, 419.) Cambridge, Mass: Harvard University Press; London: William Heinemann.

Elia, Annibale. 1982. "Une note sur la syntaxe et la sémantique des verbes de mouvement en français". *Quaderni di Semantica* 3/2:6.351–357.

Ernout, A[lfred] & A[ntoine] Meillet. 1985. *Dictionnaire étymologique de la langue latine: Histoire des mots*. 4th ed. rev. by Jacques André. Paris: Klincksieck.

Ernst, Gerhard, Martin-Dietrich Glessgen, Christian Schmitt & Wolfgang Schweickard. 2000. "Une histoire des langues romanes: pourquoi et comment?". *Actes du XXIIe Congrès International de Linguistique et de Philologie Romanes, Bruxelles, 23–29 juillet 1998* ed. by Annick Englebert, Michel Pierrard, Laurence Rosier & Dan Van Raemdonck, vol. II, 185–189. Tübingen: Max Niemeyer.

Espa, Enzo. 1999. *Dizionario sardo italiano dei parlanti la lingua logudorese*. Sassari: Carlo Delfino.

Evans, Vyvyan & Melanie Green. 2006. *Cognitive Linguistics: An introduction*. Edinburgh: Edinburgh University Press.

Evseev, Ivan. 1974. *Semantica verbului: Categoriile de acțiune, devenire și stare*. Timişoara: Facla.

Fanego, Teresa. 2012. "Motion Events in English: The emergence and diachrony of manner salience from Old English to Late Modern English". *Folia Linguistica Historica* 33.29–85.

Feldman, Jerome A. 2006. *From Molecule to Metaphor: A neural theory of language*. Cambridge, Mass. & London: MIT Press.

Feldman, Jerome & Srinivas Narayanan. 2004. "Embodied Meaning in a Neural Theory of Language". *Brain and Language* 89.385–392. DOI: 10.1016/S0093-934X(03)00355-9

Ferm, Ljudmila. 1990. *Vyraženie napravlenija pri pristavočnyx glagolax peremeščenija v sovremennom russkom jazyke: K voprosu prefiksal'no-predložnogo determinizma [Expression of direction with prefixed verbs of motion in modern Russian: A contribution to the study of prefixal-prepositional determinism]*. Doctoral dissertation, Uppsala University.

Fernandes, Francisco. 1972. *Dicionário de verbos e regimes*. 4th ed. Pôrto Alegre: Globo.

Ferrari de Egues, Laura. 1985. "El campo léxico de los verbos de movimiento en español". *Revista Argentina de Lingüística* 1:2.147–174.

Filipović, Luna. 2007. *Talking about Motion: A crosslinguistic investigation of lexicalization patterns*. (= *Studies in Language Companion Series*, 91.) Amsterdam & Philadelphia: John Benjamins. DOI: 10.1075/slcs.91

Fillmore, Charles. 1975. *Santa Cruz Lectures on Deixis 1971*. Bloomington: Indiana University Linguistics Club.

Fillmore, Charles J. 1976. "Frame Semantics and the Nature of Language". *Origins and Evolution of Language and Speech* ed. by Stevan R. Harnad, Horst D. Steklis & Jane Beckman Lancaster (= *Annals of the New York Academy of Sciences*, 280), 20–32. New York: New York Academy of Sciences.

Fillmore, Charles. 1977. "The Case for Case Reopened". *Grammatical Relations* ed. by Peter Cole & Jerrold Sadock (= *Syntax and Semantics*, 8), 59–81. New York: Academic Press.

Fillmore, Charles J. & B.T.S. Atkins. 2000. "Describing Polysemy: The case of 'crawl'". *Polysemy: Theoretical and computational approaches* ed. by Yael Ravin & Claudia Leacock, 91–110. Oxford: Oxford University Press.

Finkbeiner, Matthew, Janet Nicol, Delia Greth & Kumiko Nakamura. 2002. "The Role of Language in Memory for Actions". *Journal of Psycholinguistics Research* 31:5.447–457. DOI: 10.1023/A:1021204802485

Firenzuola, Agnolo. 1848. *Opere* ed. by B[runone] Bianchi. 2 vols. Firenze: Le Monnier.

Firenzuola, Agnolo. 1992. *On the Beauty of Women*. Transl. and ed. by Konrad Eisenbichler & Jacqueline Murray. Philadelphia: University of Pennsylvania Press.

Flaubert, [Gustave]. 1971 [1857]. *Madame Bovary. Mœurs de Province*. Sommaire biographique, introduction, note bibliographique, relevé des variantes et notes par Claudine Gothot-Mersch. Paris: Garnier.

Flaubert, Gustave. 2004. *Madame Bovary; Provincial Manners*. Transl. by Margaret Mauldon. With an introduction by Malcolm Bowie and notes by Mark Overstall. Oxford: Oxford University Press.

Fleischman, Suzanne. 1982. "The Past and the Future: Are they *coming* or *going*?". *Proceedings of the 8th Annual Meeting of the Berkeley Linguistics Society, 13–15 February 1982* ed. by Monica Macaulay, 322–334. Berkeley: Berkeley Linguistics Society.

Floricic, Franck. 2004. "A propos de certaines épenthèses en Sarde". *Cahiers de Grammaire* 29.59–87.

Foerster, Wendelin, ed. 1880/1883. "Antica parafrasi lombarda del 'Neminem laedi nisi a se ipso' di S. Giovanni Grisostomo (Cod. Torin.; N, V, 57), edita e illustrata da W. Foerster". *Archivio Glottologico Italiano* 7.1–120.

Fortis, Jean-Michel & Alice Vittrant. 2011. "L'organisation syntaxique de l'expression de la trajectoire: Vers une typologie des constructions". *Faits de Langues* 3.71–98.

Foster, B[enjamin] O[liver], ed. & transl. 1996. Livy, *History of Rome*. Books XXI–XXII. (= *Loeb Classical Library*, 233.) Cambridge, Mass. & London: Harvard University Press.

Foster, B. O., ed. & transl. 1997. Livy, *History of Rome*. Books III–IV. (= *Loeb Classical Library*, 133.) Cambridge, Mass. & London: Harvard University Press.

Foster, B. O., ed. & transl. 1999. Livy, *History of Rome*. Books VIII–X. (= *Loeb Classical Library*, 191.) Cambridge, Mass. & London: Harvard University Press.

Foster, B. O., ed. & transl. 2002. Livy, *History of Rome*. Books V–VII. (= *Loeb Classical Library*, 172.) Cambridge, Mass. & London: Harvard University Press.

Frauendienst, Margarete. 1935. "Der Ausdruck von Richtungsangaben in losem Zusammenhang mit dem Verb im Deutschen und im Französischen". *Neuphilologische Monatsschrift* 6.26–37.

Frazer, James George, ed. & transl. 1996. Ovid, *Fasti*. Revised by G[eorge] P[atrick] Goold. (= *Loeb Classical Library*, 253.) Cambridge, Mass. & London: Harvard University Press.

Fruyt, Michèle. 2011. "Word-Formation in Classical Latin". *A Companion to the Latin Language* ed. by James Clackson, 157–175. Malden, Mass.: Wiley-Blackwell.

Gabrielli, Aldo. 1971. *Dizionario dei verbi italiani regolari e irregolari*. Milano: Istituto Editoriale Italiano.

Gak, Vladimir G. 1963. "O nekotoryx osobennostjax russkogo jazyka sravnitel'no s francuzskim [On some peculiarities of the Russian language in comparison to French]". *Petit dictionnaire pratique français–russe* ed. by Vladimir G. Gak, 706–709. Moscow: "Nauka".

Gak, Vladimir G. 1966. *Besedy o francuzskom slove: Iz sravnitel'noj leksikologii francuzskogo i russkogo jazykov* [*Essays on French words: Comparative lexicology of French and Russian*]. Moscow: Meždunarodnye Otnošenija.

Galán Rodríguez, Carmen. 1993. "Aproximación al estudio de los verbos de movimiento en alemán y en español: Movimiento real y empleos figurados". *Anuario de Estudios Filológicos* 16.147–158.

Galimberti Jarman, Beatriz & Roy Russell, eds. 1994. *The Oxford Spanish Dictionary*. Oxford, New York & Madrid: Oxford University Press.

Gamillscheg, Ernst. 1969 [1966–1969]. *Etymologisches Wörterbuch der französischen Sprache*. 2nd ed. (= *Sammlung Romanischer Elementar- und Handbücher*, Reihe 3: *Wörterbücher*, 5.) Heidelberg: Carl Winter.

García de Diego, Vicente. 1989. *Diccionario etimológico español e hispánico*. 3rd ed. Madrid: Espasa-Calpe.

García-Hernández, Benjamín. 1978. "Desarrollo polisémico del preverbio *sub*- y su posición en el sistema preverbial". *Helmántica: Revista de filología clásica y hebrea* 29:88/89.41–50.

García-Hernández, Benjamín. 1995a. "Die Evolution des lat. *sub* und die Urbedeutung des idg. **(s)upo*". *Indogermanische Forschungen: Zeitschrift für Indogermanistik und Allgemeine Sprachwissenschaft* 100.163–171.

García-Hernández, Benjamín. 1995b. "Polysémie et signifié fondamental du préverbe *sub*-". *Bulletin de la Société de Linguistique de Paris* 90:1.301–312. DOI: 10.2143/BSL.90.1.2002534

García-Hernández, Benjamín. 1999. "La reinterpretación de *sub(-)*, prefijo y preposición en latín tardío". *Latin vulgaire – latin tardif V: Actes du Ve Colloque International sur le Latin Vulgaire et Tardif, Heidelberg, 5–8 septembre 1997* ed. by Hubert Petersmann & Rudolf Kettemann (= *Bibliothek der Klassischen Altertumswissenschaften*, II:105), 223–233. Heidelberg: Carl Winter.

García-Hernández, Benjamín. 2000. "Los resultados del prefijo latino *sub-* en español". *Latín vulgar y tardío: Homenaje a Veikko Väänänen (1905–1997)* ed. by Benjamín García-Hernández (= *Bibliotheca Linguae Latinae*, 2), 63–96. Madrid: Ediciones Clásicas.

García-Hernández, Benjamín. 2003. "La influencia griega y la renovación del prefijo svb- en el latín tardío". *Latin vulgaire – latin tardif VI: Actes du VIe Colloque International sur le Latin Vulgaire et Tardif, Helsinki, 29 août – 2 septembre 2000* ed. by Heikki Solin, Martti Leiwo & Hilla Halla-aho, 513–523. Hildesheim: Georg Olms; Zürich: Weidmann.

García-Jurado, Francisco. 2003. *Introducción a la semántica latina: De la semántica tradicional al cognitivismo*. (= *Cuadernos de Filología Clásica: Estudios Latinos, Anejos. Serie de Monografías*, 1.) Madrid: Servicio de Publicaciones de la Universidad Complutense.

García-Jurado, Francisco & Pilar Hualde-Pascual. 2002. "Lingüística cognitiva y lenguas clásicas: Aspectos bibliográficos y programáticos". *Actas del II Congreso de la Sociedad Española de Lingüística, Madrid, 11–15 de diciembre de 2000* ed. by Alberto Bernabé, José Antonio Berenguer, Margarita Cantarero & José Carlos de Torres, vol. II, 574–584. Madrid: Sociedad Española de Lingüística.

Geckeler, Horst. 1976. *Semántica estructural y teoría del campo léxico*. Transl. by Marcos Martínez Hernández (= *Biblioteca Románica Hispánica; Estudios y Ensayos*, 241.) Madrid: Gredos.

Geeraerts, Dirk. 1994. "Prototype Semantics". *The Encyclopedia of Language and Linguistics* ed. by R[onald] E. Asher et al., 3384–3386. Oxford: Pergamon.

Geeraerts, Dirk. 2002a. "The Scope of Diachronic Onomasiology". *Das Wort: Seine strukturelle und kulturelle Dimension. Festschrift für Oskar Reichmann zum 65. Geburtstag* ed. by Vilmos Ágel, Andreas Gardt, Ulrike Hass-Zumkehr & Thorsten Roelcke, 29–44. Tübingen: Max Niemeyer.

Geeraerts, Dirk. 2002b. "The Theoretical and Descriptive Development of Lexical Semantics". *The Lexicon in Focus: Competition and convergence in current lexicology* ed. by Leila Behrens & Dietmar Zaefferer, 23–42. Frankfurt am Main: Peter Lang.

Geeraerts, Dirk. 2006a. "Introduction: A rough guide to Cognitive Linguistics". *Cognitive Linguistics: Basic readings* ed. by Dirk Geeraerts (= *Cognitive Linguistics Research*, 34), 1–28. Berlin & New York: Mouton de Gruyter. DOI: 10.1515/9783110199901.1

Geeraerts, Dirk. 2006b. "Prototype Theory: Prospects and problems of prototype theory". *Cognitive Linguistics: Basic readings* ed. by Dirk Geeraerts (= *Cognitive Linguistics Research*, 34), 141–165. Berlin & New York: Mouton de Gruyter. DOI: 10.1515/9783110199901.141

Geeraerts, Dirk. 2006c. *Words and Other Wonders: Papers on lexical and semantic topics*. (= *Cognitive Linguistics Research*, 33.) Berlin & New York: Mouton de Gruyter. DOI: 10.1515/9783110219128

Geeraerts, Dirk. 2007. "Cognitive Sociolinguistics and the Sociology of Cognitive Linguistics". *Annual Review of Cognitive Linguistics* 5.289–305. DOI: 10.1075/arcl.5.13mar

Geeraerts, Dirk. 2010. *Theories of Lexical Semantics*. Oxford: Oxford University Press.

Geeraerts, Dirk & Hubert Cuyckens. 2007 "Introducing Cognitive Linguistics". *The Oxford Handbook of Cognitive Linguistics* ed. by Dirk Geeraerts & Hubert Cuyckens, 3–21. Oxford: Oxford University Press.

Geeraerts, Dirk & Stefan Grondelaers. 1995. "Looking Back at Anger: Cultural traditions and metaphorical patterns". *Language and the Cognitive Construal of the World* ed. by John R. Taylor & Robert E. MacLaury (= *Trends in Linguistics; Studies and Monographs*, 82), 153–179. Berlin & New York: Mouton de Gruyter.

Geiger, Paulo, ed. 2008. *iDicionário Aulete*. Rio de Janeiro: Lexikon Editora Digital. (http://aulete.uol.com.br). Accessed: November 2011.

Gennari, Silvia P., Steven A. Sloman, Barbara C. Malt & W. Tecumseh Fitch. 2002. "Motion Events in Language and Cognition". *Cognition* 83.49–79. DOI: 10.1016/S0010-0277(01)001 66-4

Gentner, Dedre, Mutsumi Imai & Lera Boroditsky. 2002. "As Time Goes by: Evidence for two systems in processing space → time metaphors". *Language and Cognitive Processes* 17:5.537–565. DOI: 10.1080/01690960143000317

Geuder, Wilhelm. 2009. "'Descendre en grimpant': Une étude contrastive de l'interaction entre déplacement et manière de mouvement". *Langages* 175.123–139. DOI: 10.3917/lang.175.0123

Gevaert, Caroline. 2005. "The ANGER IS HEAT Question: Detecting cultural influence on the conceptualization of ANGER through diachronic corpus analysis". *Perspectives on Variation: Sociolinguistic, historical, comparative* ed. by Nicole Delbecque, Johan van der Auwera & Dirk Geeraerts (= *Trends in Linguistics; Studies and Monographs*, 163), 195–208. Berlin & New York: Mouton de Gruyter.

Gévaudan, Paul, Peter Koch & Antonia Neu. 2003. "Hundert Jahre nach Zauner: Die romanischen Namen der Körperteile im DECOLAR". *Romanische Forschungen* 115.1–27.

Gibbs, Raymond W. 1999. "Taking Metaphor out or our Heads and Putting it into the Cultural World". *Metaphor in Cognitive Linguistics: Selected papers from the Fifth International Cognitive Linguistics Conference, Amsterdam, 1997* ed. by Raymond W. Gibbs & Gerard Steen (= *Current Issues in Linguistic Theory*, 175), 145–166. Amsterdam & Philadelphia: John Benjamins.

Gibbs, Raymond W., Jr. 2005a. "Embodied Action in Thought and Language". *Cognitive Linguistics: Internal dynamics and interdisciplinary interaction* ed. by Francisco J. Ruiz de Mendoza Ibáñez & M. Sandra Peña Cervel (= *Cognitive Linguistics Research*, 32), 225–247. Berlin: Walter de Gruyter.

Gibbs, Raymond W., Jr. 2005b. *Embodiment and Cognitive Science*. Cambridge: Cambridge University Press. DOI: 10.1017/CBO9780511805844

Gibbs, Raymond W., Paula Lenz Costa Lima & Edson Francozo. 2004. "Metaphor Is Grounded in Embodied Experience". *Journal of Pragmatics* 36:7.1189–1210. DOI: 10.1016/j.pragma.2003.10.009

Gil Farrés, Octavio. 1978. "Influencia de la moneda árabe en los numerarios de la España cristiana: Dos interesantes documentos". *Boletín de la Asociación Española de Orientalistas* 14:1.137–142.

Girón Alconchel, José Luis. 2004. "Gramaticalización y estado latente". *Dicenda: Cuadernos de filología hispánica* 22.71–88.

Givón, Talmy. 1973. "The Time-Axis Phenomenon". *Language* 49:4.890–925. DOI: 10.2307/412067

Glare, P.G.W., ed. 1982. *Oxford Latin Dictionary*. Oxford: Clarendon Press; New York: Oxford University Press.

Glenberg, A. M. 1997. "What Memory Is for". *Behavioral and Brain Sciences* 20.1–55.

Godefroy, Frédéric. 1969 [1880–1902]. *Dictionnaire de l'ancienne langue française et de tous ses dialectes du IXe au XVe siècle*. 10 vols. Nendeln: Kraus Reprint.

Goldberg, Adele E. & Devin Casenhiser. 2006. "English Constructions". *The Handbook of English Linguistics* ed. by Bas Aarts & April McMahon, 343–355. Malden, Mass.: Blackwell. DOI: 10.1002/9780470753002.ch15

Gómez de Silva, Guido. 1985. *Elsevier's Concise Spanish Etymological Dictionary*. Amsterdam: Elsevier.

González Aranda, Yolanda. 1998. *Forma y estructura de un campo semántico: A propósito de la sustancia de contenido 'moverse' en español*. (= *Colección Humanidades*, 13.) Almería: Universidad de Almería.

González Fernández, María Jesús. 1997. "Sobre la motivación semántica de las expresiones pleonásticas de movimiento: *Subir arriba, bajar abajo, entrar adentro y salir afuera*". *Cambios diacrónicos en el español* ed. by Concepción Company Company (= *Publicaciones Medievalia*, 15), 123–141. México: Universidad Nacional Autónoma de México, Instituto de Investigaciones Filológicas.

González Vázquez, Carmen. 2003. "The Lexical Expression of Stage Movement in Latin Theatre". *Indogermanische Forschungen* 108.248–257.

Goossens, Louis. 2003. "Metaphtonymy: The interaction of metaphor and metonymy in expressions for linguistic action". *Metaphor and Metonymy in Comparison and Contrast* ed. by René Dirven & Ralf Pörings (= *Cognitive Linguistics Research*, 20), 349–377. Berlin & New York: Mouton de Gruyter.

Gordon, W[illiam] Terrence. 2001. "The Origin and Development of the Theory of the Semantic Field". *History of the Language Sciences/Geschichte der Sprachwissenschaften/Histoire des sciences du langue; An international handbook on the evolution of the study of language from the beginnings to the present/Ein internationales Handbuch zur Entwicklung der Sprachforschung von den Anfängen bis zur Gegenwart/Manuel international sur l'évolution de l'étude du langage des origines à nos jours* ed. by Sylvain Auroux, E.F.K. Koerner, Hans-Josef Niederehe & Kees Versteegh (= *Handbücher zur Sprach- und Kommunikationswissenschaft*, 18), vol. II, 1650–1662. Berlin & New York: Walter de Gruyter.

Govantes, Angel Casimiro de. 1846. *Diccionario geográfico-histórico de España, por la Real Academia de la Historia*. Sección II: Comprende La Rioja ó toda la Provincia de Logroño y algunos pueblos de la de Burgos. Madrid: Imprenta de los Señores Viuda de Jordán é Hijos.

Grady, Joseph. 1997a. *Foundations of Meaning: Primary metaphors and primary scenes*. Ph.D. dissertation, University of California at Berkeley.

Grady, Joseph E. 1997b. "THEORIES ARE BUILDINGS Revisited". *Cognitive Linguistics* 8:4.267–290. DOI: 10.1515/cogl.1997.8.4.267

Grady, Joseph. 2005. "Primary Metaphors as Inputs to Conceptual Integration". *Journal of Pragmatics* 37.1595–1614. DOI: 10.1016/j.pragma.2004.03.012

Grady, Joseph E. 2007. "Metaphor". *The Oxford Handbook of Cognitive Linguistics* ed. by Dirk Geeraerts & Hubert Cuyckens, 187–213. Oxford: Oxford University Press.

Grady, Joseph & Christopher Johnson. 2002. "Converging Evidence for the Notions of *Subscene* and *Primary Scene*". *Metaphor and Metonymy in Comparison and Contrast* ed. by René Dirven & Ralf Pörings (= *Cognitive Linguistics Research*, 20), 533–554. Berlin & New York: Mouton de Gruyter.

Grandgent, C[harles] H[all]. 1952. *Introducción al latín vulgar*. Transl. by Francisco de B. Moll. 2nd ed. (= *Publicaciones de la Revista de Filología Española*, 9.) Madrid: Consejo Superior de Investigaciones Científicas & Instituto "Miguel de Cervantes".

Grandgent, C. H. 1962 [1934]. *An Introduction to Vulgar Latin*. New York: Hafner.

Green, John N. 2005. "'Éstas que fueron pompa y alegría': The life cycle of Romance linguistics". *La corónica* 34:1.190–201. DOI: 10.1353/cor.2005.0022

Greenberg, J[oseph]. 1966. *Language Universals with Special Reference to Feature Hierarchies.* (= *Janua Linguarum; Series Minor,* 59.) The Hague: Mouton.

Gries, Stefan Th. 2006. "Corpus-Based Methods and Cognitive Semantics: The many senses of *to run*". *Corpora in Cognitive Linguistics: Corpus-based approaches to syntax and lexis* ed. by Stefan Th. Gries & Anatol Stefanowitsch (= *Trends in Linguistics; Studies and Monographs,* 172), 57–99. Berlin & New York: Mounton de Gruyter. DOI: 10.1515/9783110197709

Grimm, Jacob. 1819–1837. *Deutsche Grammatik.* 4 vols. Göttingen: Dieterich.

Grinevald, Colette. 2011. "On Constructing a Working Typology of the Expression of *path*". *Faits de Langues* 3.43–70.

Grondelaers, Stefan, Dirk Speelman & Dirk Geeraerts. 2007. "Lexical Variation and Change". *The Oxford Handbook of Cognitive Linguistics* ed. by Dirk Geeraerts & Hubert Cuyckens, 988–1011. Oxford: Oxford University Press.

Gruntov, I. A. 2007. "Katalog semantičeskix perexodov: Baza dannyx po tipologii semantičeskix izmenenij [Catalogue of semantic shifts: A database for the typology of semantic evolution]". *Komp'juternaja lingvistika i intellektual'nye texnologii: Trudy meždunaronoj konferencii Dialogue 2007 [Computational linguistics and artificial intellect technologies: Proceedings of the International Conference Dialogue 2007],* 157–161. (http://www.dialog-21.ru/en/dialogue2007/main). Accessed: October 2013.

Gruntova, E. S. 2007. "Latinskaja sistema glagolov plavanija i eë razvitie v romanskix jazykax: Francuzskon, ital'janskom, ispanskom [Latin system of aquamotion verbs and its development in the Romance languages: French, Italian, Spanish]". *Glagoly dviženija v vode: Leksičeskaja tipologija [Aquamotion verbs: Lexical typology]* ed. by Timur Maisak & Ekaterina Rakhilina, 231–266. Moscow: Indrik.

Grzega, Joachim. 2009. "Bibliography of Onomasiological Works". *Onomasiology Online* (http://www1.ku-eichstaett.de/SLF/EngluVglSW/OnOn-7.pdf). Accessed: October 2013.

Guého, Robert. 1979. *Mobilité, rupture, vitesse: Étude des macrostructures d'un groupe de lexèmes verbaux en français moderne.* (= *Romanistik in Geschichte und Gegenwart,* 6.) Hamburg: Helmut Buske.

Guilbert, Louis, René Lagane & Georges Niobey, eds. 1971–1978. *Grand Larousse de la langue française.* 7 vols. Paris: Librairie Larousse.

Guiraud, Pierre. 1982. *Dictionnaire des étymologies obscures.* (= *Histoire et Structure du Lexique Français,* 1.) Paris: Payot.

Guo, Jiansheng & Liang Chen. 2009. "Learning to Express Motion in Narratives by Mandarin-Speaking Children". *Crosslinguistic Approaches to the Psychology of Language: Research in the tradition of Dan Isaac Slobin* ed. by Jiansheng Guo, Elena Lieven, Nancy Budwig, Susan Ervin-Tripp, Keiko Nakamura & Seyda Özçalýşkan, 193–208. New York & London: Psychology Press.

Guryčeva, M[arina] S[ergeevna]. 2008. *Narodnaja latyn' [Vulgar Latin].* 2nd ed. Moscow: URSS.

Hall, Bert S. 1997. *Weapons and Warfare in Renaissance Europe: Gunpowder, technology, and tactics.* Baltimore & London: John Hopkins University Press.

Harris-Northall, Ray. 2007. "Aspects of Official Language Usage in Castile and León: Latin and the vernacular in the early thirteenth century". *Medieval Iberia: Changing societies and cultures in contact and transition* ed. by Ivy A. Corfis & Ray Harris-Northall (= *Colección Támesis; Serie A. Monografías,* 247), 164–174. Woodbridge: Tamesis.

Haspelmath, Martin. 1997. *From Space to Time: Temporal adverbials in the world's languages*. (= *LINCOM Studies in Theoretical Linguistics*, 3.) Munich: LINCOM Europa.

Hawkins, Bruce W. 1984. *The Semantics of English Spatial Prepositions*. Ph.D. dissertation, University of California at San Diego.

Heger, Klaus. 1965. "Les bases méthodologiques de l'onomasiologie et du classement par concepts". *Travaux de Linguistique et de Literatures Romanes* 3:1.7–32.

Heidermanns, Frank. 2005. *Bibliographie zur indogermanischen Wortforschung: Wortbildung, Etymologie, Onomasiologie und Lehnwortschichten der alten und modernen indogermanischen Sprachen in systematischen Publikationen ab 1800*. 3 vols. Tübingen: Max Niemeyer. DOI: 10.1515/9783110929270

Heine, Bernd, Ulrike Claudi & Friederike Hünnemeyer. 1991. *Grammaticalization: A conceptual framework*. Chicago & London: University of Chicago Press.

Hendrickson, G[eorge] L[incoln] & H[arry] M[ortimer] Hubbell, eds. 1999. Cicero, *Brutus*. With an English transl. by G. L. Hendrickson. Cicero, *Orator*. With an English transl. by H. M. Hubbell (= *Loeb Classical Library*, 342.) Cambridge, Mass. & London: Harvard University Press.

Hickmann, Maya & Henriëtte Hendriks. 2006. "Static and Dynamic Location in French and in English". *First Language* 26:1.103–135. DOI: 10.1177/0142723706060743

Hickmann, Maya & Stéphane Robert, eds. 2006. *Space in Languages: Linguistic systems and cognitive categories*. (= *Typological Studies in Language*, 66.) Amsterdam & Philadelphia: John Benjamins. DOI: 10.1075/tsl.66

Hidalgo Rodríguez, Rosa María. 1999. "Verbos de movimiento en español: Una propuesta de clasificación". *Lingüística para el siglo XXI* ed. by Jesús Fernández González (= *Aquilafuente*, 9), 919–926. Salamanca: Ediciones de Universidad de Salamanca.

Hijazo-Gascón, Alberto & Iraide Ibarretxe-Antuñano. 2010. "Tipología, lexicalización y dialectología aragonesa". *Archivo de Filología Aragonesa* 66.245–279.

Hijazo-Gascón, Alberto & Iraide Ibarretxe-Antuñano. 2013a. "Las lenguas románicas y la tipología de los eventos de movimiento". *Romanische Forschungen* 125:4.467–494. DOI: 10.3196/003581213808754483

Hijazo-Gascón, Alberto & Iraide Ibarretxe-Antuñano. 2013b. "Same Family, Different Paths: Intratypological differences in three Romance languages". *Variation and Change in the Encoding of Motion Events* ed. by Juliana Goschler & Anatol Stefanowitsch (= *Human Cognitive Processing*, 41), 39–54. Amsterdam & Philadelphia: John Benjamins. DOI: 10.1075/hcp.41.02hij

Hilferty, Joseph. 2005. "An Interview with Antonio Barcelona and Francisco José Ruiz de Mendoza". *Barcelona English Language and Literature Studies* 14. (http://www.publicacions.ub.edu/revistes/bells14/PDF/metaphor_01.pdf). Accessed: June 2008.

Hiltbrunner, Otto, ed. 1981–1992. *Bibliographie zur lateinischen Wortforschung*. 4 vols. Bern: Francke.

Hiltunen, Risto. 1983. *The Decline of the Prefixes and the Beginnings of the English Phrasal Verb: The evidence from some Old and Early Modern English texts*. (= *Annales Universitatis Turkuensis*, 160.) Turku: Turun Yliopisto.

Hock, Hans Henrich & Brian D. Joseph. 1996. *Language History, Language Change, and Language Relationship: An introduction to historical and comparative linguistics*. (= *Trends in Linguistics; Studies and Monographs*, 93.) Berlin & New York: Mouton de Gruyter.

Hofmann, Johann B. & Anton Szantyr. 1965. *Lateinische Syntax und Stilistik*. (= *Handbuch der Altertumswissenschaft*, II.2.2.) Munich: H. C. Beck.

Hooper, William Davis, ed. & transl. 1999. Marcus Porcius Cato, *On Agriculture*. Marcus Terrentius Varro, *On Agriculture*. Revised by Harrison Boyd Ash. (= *Loeb Classical Library*, 283.) Cambridge, Mass. & London: Harvard University Press.

Hope, T. E. 1971. *Lexical Borrowing in the Romance Languages: A critical study of Italianisms in French and Gallicisms in Italian from 1100 to 1900*. 2 vols. (= *Language and Style Series*, 10.) Oxford: Basil Blackwell.

Hopper, Paul. J. & Elizabeth Closs Traugott. 1993. *Grammaticalization*. Cambridge: Cambridge University Press. (2nd ed., 2003.)

Huang, Xuanfan & Michael Tanangkingsing. 2005. "Reference to Motion Events in Six Western Austronesian Languages: Toward a semantic typology". *Oceanic Linguistics* 44:2.307–340. DOI: 10.1353/ol.2005.0035

Iacobini, Claudio. 2009. "The Role of Dialects in the Emergence of Italian Phrasal Verbs". *Morphology* 19.15–44. DOI: 10.1007/s11525-009-9133-x

Iacobini, Claudio. 2010. "The Number and Use of Manner Verbs as a Cue for Typological Change in the Stratagies of Motion Events Encoding". *Space in Language: Proceedings of the Pisa International Conference 2009* ed. by Giovanna Marotta, Alessandro Lenci, Linda Meini & Francesco Rovai, 495–514. Firenze: Edizioni ETS.

Iacobini, Claudio. 2012. "Grammaticalization and Innovation in the Encoding of Motion Events". *Folia Linguistica* 46:2.359–385. DOI: 10.1515/flin.2012.013

Iacobini, Claudio & Benjamin Fagard. 2011. "A Diachronic Approach to Variation and Change in the Typology of Motion Event Expression. A Case Study: From Latin to Romance". *Cahiers de Faits de Langue* 3.151–172.

Iacobini, Claudio & Francesca Masini. 2007a. "The Emergence of Verb-Particle Constructions in Italian". *Morphology* 16:2.155–188. DOI: 10.1007/s11525-006-9101-7

Iacobini, Claudio & Francesca Masini. 2007b. "Verb-Particle Constructions and Prefixed Verbs in Italian: Typology, diachrony and semantics". *On-line Proceedings of the Fifth Mediterranean Morphology Meeting (MMM5), Fréjus, 15–18 September 2005* ed. by Geert Booij, 157–184. (http://mmm.lingue.unibo.it). Accessed: June 2008.

Iacobini, Claudio & Francesca Masini. 2009. "I verbi sintagmatici dell'italiano fra innovazione e persistenza: Il ruolo dei dialetti". *Italiano, italiani regionali e dialetti* ed. by Anna Cardinaletti & Nicola Munaro, 115–135. Milano: F. Angeli.

Ibáñez, Jorge Edmundo. 1983. *Estudio de la deixis espacial en los verbos españoles* ir *y* venir *con especial consideración del contraste en los verbos de movimiento del francés y del alemán*. Doctoral dissertation, University of Hamburg.

Ibarretxe-Antuñano, Iraide. 2003. "What Translation Tells us about Motion: A contrastive study of typologically different languages". *International Journal of English Studies* 3:2.153–178.

Ibarretxe-Antuñano, Iraide. 2004. "Dicotomías frente a continuos en la lexicalización de los eventos del movimiento". *Revista Española de Lingüística* 34:2.481–510.

Ibarretxe-Antuñano, Iraide. 2005. "Interview: Leonard Talmy. A windowing to conceptual structure and language. Part I: Lexicalization and typology". *Annual Review of Cognitive Linguistics* 3.325–347. DOI: 10.1075/arcl.3.17iba

Ibarretxe-Antuñano, Iraide. 2009. "Path Salience in Motion Events". *Crosslinguistic Approaches to the Psychology of Language: Research in the tradition of Dan Isaac Slobin* ed. by Jiansheng Guo, Elena Lieven, Nancy Budwig, Susan Ervin-Tripp, Keiko Nakamura & Seyda Özçalýşkan, 403–414. New York & London: Psychology Press.

Ibarretxe-Antuñano, Iraide & Alberto Hijazo-Gascón. 2012. "Variation in Motion Events: Theory and applications". *Space and Time in Languages and Cultures: Linguistic diversity* ed. by Luna Filipović & Kasia M. Jaszczolt (= *Human Cognitive Processing*, 36), 349–371. Amsterdam & Philadelphia: John Benjamins. DOI: 10.1075/hcp.36.19iba

Icaza, Francisco A. de. 1916. "Un falso sistema de investigación literaria: 'ir' y 'venir'". *Boletín de la Real Academia Española* 3.73–79.

ICSI. 2012. "Featured ICSI Research: MetaNet". *The ICSI Gazette: The newsletter of the International Computer Science Institute* 10:2.1, 4–6. (http://www.icsi.berkeley.edu). Accessed: July 2013.

Imbert, Caroline. 2008a. *Dynamique des systèmes et motivations fonctionnelles dans l'encodage de la Trajectoire: Description typologique du grec homérique et du vieil-anglais.* Doctoral dissertation, Université Lumière Lyon 2.

Imbert, Caroline. 2008b. "Path Coding in Old English: Functional story of a typological shift". *Historical Englishes in Varieties of Texts and Contexts* ed. by Masachiyo Amano, Michiko Ogura & Masayuki Ohkado (= *Studies in English Medieval Language and Literature*, 22), 17–32. Frankfurt am Main: Peter Lang.

Imbert, Caroline. 2010. "Multiple Preverbation in Homeric Greek: A typological insight". *Cogni-Textes: Revue de l'Association Française de Linguistique Cognitive* 4. (http://cognitextes.revues.org/387). Accessed: July 2012.

Imbert, Caroline. 2012. "Path: Ways typology has walked through it". *Language and Linguistics Compass* 6:4.236–258. DOI: 10.1002/lnc3.329

Imbert, Caroline, Colette Grinevald & Anna Sőrés. 2011. "Pour une catégorie de 'satellite' de Trajectoire dans une approche fonctionnelle-typologique". *Faits de Langues* 3.99–116.

Imbs, Paul, ed. 1971–1994. *Trésor de la langue française: Dictionnaire de la langue du XIXe et du XXe siècle (1789–1960).* 16 vols. Paris: Éditions du Centre National de la Recherche Scientifique.

Iñesta Mena, Eva María & Antonio Pamies Bertrán. 2002. *Fraseología y metáfora: Aspectos tipológicos y cognitivos.* Granada: Método.

Ionescu, Liliana. 1963. "Construcția verbelor de mișcare in limba romînă literară actuală". *Analele Universității București. Seria științe sociale. Filologie* 12.323–337.

Jäkel, Olaf. 2002. "Hypotheses Revisited: The cognitive theory of metaphor applied to religious texts". *Metaphorik.de* 2.20–42. (http://www.metaphorik.de/02/jakel.pdf). Accessed: April 2008.

Janda, Laura A. 2010. "Cognitive Linguistics in the Year 2010". *International Journal of Cognitive Linguistics* 1:1.1–30.

Jansen, Hanne. 2004. "La 'particella spaziale' e il suo combinarsi con verbi di movimento nell'italiano contemporaneo". *Generi, architetture e forme testuali: Atti del VII Convegno SILFI* ed. by Paolo D'Achille, 129–144. Florence: Franco Cesati.

Johnson, Mark. 1987. *The Body in the Mind: The bodily basis of meaning, imagination, and reason.* Chicago: The University of Chicago Press.

Jones, W[illiam] H[enry] S[amuel], ed. & transl. 1951. Pliny, *Natural History.* Vol. VI. Libri XX–XXIII. (= *Loeb Classical Library*, 392.) Cambridge, Mass.: Harvard University Press; London: William Heinemann.

Juge, Matthew L. 2000. "On the Rise of Suppletion in Verbal Paradigms". *Proceedings of the 25th Annual Meeting of the Berkeley Linguistics Society* ed. by Steve S. Chang, Lily Liaw & Josef Ruppenhofer, 183–194. Berkeley: Berkeley Linguisitics Society.

Kalisz, Roman. 1990. "A Cognitive Approach to Spatial Terms Represented by 'in front of' and 'behind' in English, and their Metaphorical Extensions". *Meaning and Lexicography* ed. by Jerzy Tomaszczyk & Barbara Lewandowska-Tomaszczyk (= *Linguistic & Literary Studies in Eastern Europe*, 28), 167–179. Amsterdam: John Benjamins. DOI: 10.1075/llsee.28.17kal

Kasten, Lloyd & Florian J. Cody. 2001. *Tentative Dictionary of Medieval Spanish*. 2nd ed. (= *Spanish Series*, 123.) New York: The Hispanic Seminary of Medieval Studies.

Kay, Christian, Jane Roberts, Michael Samuels & Irené Wotherspoon. 2009. *Historical Thesaurus of the Oxford English Dictionary with Additional Material from A Thesaurus of Old English*. 2 vols. Oxford: Oxford University Press.

Keller, Rudi. 1990. *Sprachwandel: Von der unsichtbaren Hand in der Sprache*. (= *Uni-Taschenbücher*, 1567.) Tübingen: Francke.

Keller, Rudi. 1994. *On Language Change: The invisible hand in language*. Transl. by Brigitte Nerlich. London & New York: Routledge.

Kent, Ronald G., ed. & trans. 1999. Varro, *On the Latin Language*. Books V–VII. (= *Loeb Classical Library*, 333.) Cambridge, Mass & London: Harvard University Press.

Kersten, Alan W., Julia Lechuga, Justin S. Albrechtsen, Christian A. Meissner, Bennett L. Schwartz & Adam Iglesias. 2010. "English Speakers Attend more Strongly than Spanish Speakers to Manner of Motion when Classifying Novel Objects and Events". *Journal of Experimental Psychology: General* 139:4.638–653. DOI: 10.1037/a0020507

Ketterer, Annemarie. 1971. *Semantik der Bewegungsverben: Eine Untersuchung am Wortschatz des französischen Barock*. Zürich: Juris.

Kibrik, A[leksandr] E[vgen'evič]. 1970. "K tipologii prostranstvennyx značenij: Na materiale padežnykh sistem dagestanskix jazykov" [Towards a typology of spatial meanings: Based on the case systems in the languages of Dagestan]". *Jazyk i čelovek: Sbornik statej pamjati professora Petra Savviča Kuznecova (1899–1968)* [*Language and human being: Collection of articles in memoriam of Pëtr Savvič Kuznecov (1899–1968)*] ed. by Vladimir Andreevič Zvegincev, 110–156. Moscow: Izdatel'stvo Moskovskogo Universiteta.

Kibrik, A. E. 2003. *Konstanty i peremennye iazyka* [*Constants and variables of language*]. St. Petersburg: Aletheia.

Kibrik, A. E. 2008. "Lingvističeskaja rekonstrukcija kognitivnoj struktury [Linguistic reconstruction of the cognitive structure]". *Voprosy Jazykoznanija* 2008:4.51–77.

Koch, Peter. 1997. "La diacronia quale campo empirico della semantica cognitiva". *Linguaggio e cognizione: Atti del XXVIII Congresso della Società di Linguistica Italiana, Palermo, 27–29 ottobre 1994* ed. by Marco Carapezza, Daniele Gambarara & Franco Lo Piparo, 225–246. Roma: Bulzoni.

Koch, Peter. 1999. "TREE and FRUIT: A cognitive onomasiological approach". *Studi Italiani di Linguistica Teorica e Applicata* 28:2.331–347.

Koch, Peter. 2000a. "Indirizzi cognitivi per una tipologia lessicale dell'italiano". *Italienische Studien* 21.99–117.

Koch, Peter. 2000b. "Pour une approche cognitive du changement sémantique lexical: Aspect onomasiologique". *Théories contemporaines du changement sémantique* ed. by the Société de Linguistique de Paris (= *Mémoires de la Société de Linguistique de Paris, Nouvelle Série*, IX), 75–95. Leuven: Peeters.

Koch, Peter. 2001a. "Bedeutungswandel und Bezeichnungswandel: Von der kognitiven Semasiologie zur kognitiven Onomasiologie". *Zeitschrift für Literaturwissenschaft und Linguistik* 121.7–36.

Koch, Peter. 2001b. "Lexical Typology from a Cognitive and Linguistic Point of View". *Language Typology and Language Universals /Sprachtypologie und sprachliche Universalien /La typologie des langues et les universaux linguistiques; An international handbook /Ein internationales Handbuch /Manuel international* ed. by Martin Haspelmath, Ekkehard König, Wulf Oesterreicher & Wolfgang Raible (= *Handbücher zur Sprach- und Kommunikationswissenschaft*, 20:2), vol. II, 1142–1178. Berlin & New York: Walter de Gruyter.

Koch, Peter. 2001c. "Onomasiologia cognitiva, geolinguistica e tipologia areale". *La dialettologia oggi fra tradizione e nuove metodologie: Atti del Convegno Internazionale, Pisa 10–12 febbraio 2000* ed. by Alberto Zamboni, Patrizia Del Puente & Maria Teresa Vigolo, 135–165. Pisa: Edizioni ETS.

Koch, Peter. 2002. "Verbe, valence et changement sémantique: Une approche onomasiologique". *Parties du discours: Sémantique, perception, cognition – le domaine de l'audible. Actes d'EUROSEM 2000* ed. by Hiltraud Dupuy-Engelhardt & Marie-Jeanne Montibus (= *Recherches en Linguistique et Psychologie Cognitive*, 17), 151–185. Reims: Presses Universitaires de Reims.

Koch, Peter. 2003a. "Changement sémantique et données linguistiques: Parcours sémasiologique – parcours onomasiologique". *Parcours énonciatifs et parcours interprétatifs: Théories et applications* ed. by Aboubakar Ouattara, 145–170. Paris: Ophrys.

Koch, Peter. 2003b. "Historial Romance Linguistics and the Cognitive Turn". *La corónica* 31:2.41–55. DOI: 10.1353/cor.2003.0063

Koch, Peter. 2003c. "Qu'est-ce que le cognitif?". *La cognition dans le temps: Études cognitives dans le champ historique des langues et des textes* ed. by Peter Blumenthal & Jean-Emmanuel Tyvaert (= *Linguistische Arbeiten*, 476), 85–100. Tübingen: Max Niemeyer.

Koch, Peter. 2004. "Diachronic Onomasiology and Semantic Reconstruction". *Lexical Data and Universals of Semantic Change* ed. by Wiltrud Mihatsch & Reinhild Steinberg (= *Stauffenburg Linguistik*, 35), 79–106. Tübingen: Stauffenburg.

Koch, Peter. 2008. "Cognitive Onomasiology and Lexical Change: Around the eye". Vanhove, ed. 2008.107–137.

Koch, Peter & Daniela Marzo. 2007. "A Two-Dimensional Approach to the Study of Motivation in Lexical Typology and its First Application to French High-Frequency Vocabulary". *Studies in Language* 31:2.259–291. DOI: 10.1075/sl.31.2.02koc

Koch, Peter & Wulf Oesterreicher. 1985. "Sprache der Nähe – Sprache der Distanz: Mündlichkeit und Schriftlichkeit im Spannungsfeld von Sprachtheorie und Sprachgeschichte". *Romanistisches Jahrbuch* 36.15–43.

Koerner, [Ernst Friederyk] Konrad. 1989. "On the Historical Roots of the Philology vs Linguistics Controversy". *Practicing Linguistic Historiography: Selected essays* by Konrad Koerner (= *Studies in the History of the Language Sciences*, 50), 233–244. Amsterdam & Philadelphia: John Benjamins. DOI: 10.1075/sihols.50

Koerner, Konrad. 1995a. "Toward a History of Linguistic Typology". *Professing Linguistic Historiography* by Konrad Koerner (= *Studies in the History of the Language Sciences*, 79), 151–170. Amsterdam & Philadelphia: John Benjamins. DOI: 10.1075/sihols.79

Koerner, Konrad. 1995b. "Toward a History of Modern Sociolinguistics". *Professing Linguistic Historiography* by Konrad Koerner (= *Studies in the History of the Language Sciences*, 79), 117–134. Amsterdam & Philadelphia: John Benjamins. DOI: 10.1075/sihols.79

Kopecka, Anetta. 2006. "The Semantic Structure of Motion Verbs in French: Typological perspectives". Hickmann & Robert, eds. 2006.83–101.

Kopecka, Anetta. 2009a. "Continuity and Change in the Representation of Motion Events in French". *Crosslinguistic Approaches to the Psychology of Language: Research in the tradition of Dan Isaac Slobin* ed. by Jiansheng Guo, Elena Lieven, Nancy Budwig, Susan Ervin-Tripp, Keiko Nakamura & Seyda Özçalýşkan, 415–426. New York & London: Psychology Press.

Kopecka, Anetta. 2009b. "L'expression du déplacement en français: L'interaction des facteurs sémantiques, aspectuels et pragmatiques dans la construction du sens spatial". *Langages* 173.54–75. DOI: 10.3917/lang.173.0054

Kopecka, Anetta. 2013. "Describing motion events in Old and Modern French: Discourse effects of a typological change". *Variation and Change in the Encoding of Motion Events* ed. by Juliana Goschler & Anatol Stefanowitsch (= *Human Cognitive Processing*, 41), 163–184. Amsterdam & Philadelphia: John Benjamins. DOI: 10.1075/hcp.41.07kop

Koptjevskaja-Tamm, Maria. 2008. "Approaching Lexical Typology". Vanhove, ed. 2008.3–52.

Koptjevskaja-Tamm, Maria, Martine Vanhove & Peter Koch. 2007. "Typological Approaches to Lexical Semantics". *Linguistic Typology* 11.159–185. DOI: 10.1515/LINGTY.2007.013

Kövecses, Zoltán. 1995. "Anger: Its language, conceptualization, and physiology in the light of cross-cultural evidence". *Language and the Cognitive Construal of the World* ed. by John R. Taylor & Robert E. MacLaury (= *Trends in Linguistics; Studies and Monographs*, 82), 181–196. Berlin & New York: Mouton de Gruyter.

Kövecses, Zoltán. 2005. *Metaphor in Culture: Universality and variation*. Cambridge: Cambridge Uniersity Press. DOI: 10.1017/CBO9780511614408

Kövecses, Zoltán. 2008. "Conceptual Metaphor Theory: Some criticisms and alternative proposals". *Annual Review of Cognitive Linguistics* 6.168–184. DOI: 10.1075/arcl.6.08kov

Krassin, Gudrun. 1984. *Das Wortfeld der Fortbewegungsverben im modernen Französisch*. Frankfurt am Main: Peter Lang.

Krifka, Manfred. 2001. "Historical Semantics and Grammaticalization". Ms., Institut für Deutsche Sprache und Linguistik, Humboldt-Universität zu Berlin. (http://amor.rz.hu-berlin.de/~h2816i3x/LexSemantik4.pdf). Accessed: October 2013.

Kristol, Andres M. 1978. *Color: Les langues romanes devant le phénomène de la couleur*. (= *Romanica Helvetica*, 88.) Bern: Francke.

Kustova, G. I. 2000. "Kognitivnye modeli v semantičeskoj derivacii i sistema proizvodnyx značenij [Cognitive models in semantic derivation and the system of transferred meanings]". *Voprosy Jazykoznanija* 2000:4.85–109.

Lakoff, George. 1987. *Women, Fire, and Dangerous Things: What categories reveal about the mind*. Chicago: University of Chicago Press. DOI: 10.7208/chicago/9780226471013.001.0001

Lakoff, George. 1990. "The Invariance Hypothesis: Is abstract reason based on image-schemas?". *Cognitive Linguistics* 1:1.39–74. DOI: 10.1515/cogl.1990.1.1.39

Lakoff, George. 1992. "Metaphor". *International Encyclopedia of Linguistics* ed. by William Bright, vol. II, 417–423. New York: Oxford University Press.

Lakoff, George. 2006. "Conceptual Metaphor". *Cognitive Linguistics: Basic readings* ed. by Dirk Geeraerts (= *Cognitive Linguistics Research*, 34), 185–238. Berlin & New York: Mouton de Gruyter. DOI: 10.1515/9783110199901.185

Lakoff, George. 2008. "The Neural Theory of Metaphor". *The Cambridge Handbook of Metaphor and Thought* ed. by Raymond W. Gibbs, 17–38. Cambridge: Cambridge University Press. DOI: 10.1017/CBO9780511816802.003

Lakoff, George. 2012. "Explaining Embodied Cognition Results". *Topics in Cognitive Science* 4.773–785. DOI: 10.1111/j.1756-8765.2012.01222.x

Lakoff, George, Jane Espenson & Alan Schwartz. 1991. "Master Metaphor List". 2nd ed. Ms., Cognitive Linguistics Group. University of California at Berkeley. (http://ulan.mede.uic.edu/~alansz/metaphor/METAPHORLIST.pdf). Accessed: July 2013.

Lakoff, George & Mark Johnson. 1980. *Metaphors we Live by*. Chicago: University of Chicago Press. (2nd ed., 2003.)

Lakoff, George & Mark Johnson. 1999. *Philosophy in the Flesh: The embodied mind and its challenge to Western thought*. New York: Basic Books.

Lamiroy, Béatrice. 1983. *Les verbes de mouvement en français et en espagnol: Étude comparée de leurs infinitives*. (= *Linguisticae Investigationes; Supplementa*, 11.) Amsterdam & Philadelphia: John Benjamins. DOI: 10.1075/lis.11

Lamiroy, Béatrice. 1987. "Les verbes de mouvement: Emplois figurés et extensions métaphoriques". *Langue Française* 76.41–58. DOI: 10.3406/lfr.1987.4730

Landau, Lev D. & Aleksandr I. Kitajgorodskij. 1980. *Physical Bodies*. Transl. by Martin Greendlinger. (= *Physics for Everyone*, 1.) Moscow: Mir.

Langacker, Ronald. 1987, 1991. *Foundations of Cognitive Grammar. Vol. I: Theoretical Prerequisites; Vol. II: Descriptive Application*. Stanford: Stanford University Press.

Langacker, Ronald W. 2010. "Conceptualization, Symbolization, and Grammar". *International Journal of Cognitive Linguistics* 1:1.31–63.

Lanly, André. 1996. *Deux problèmes de linguistique française et romane: I. Le conditionnel en -rais (et le futur en -rai), II. Le verbe* aller *et ses frères romans*. Paris: Honoré Champion.

Lapesa, Rafael. 1991. *Historia de la lengua española*. 9th ed. (= *Biblioteca Románica Hispánica; Manuales*, 45.) Madrid: Gredos.

Lapesa, Rafael. 2000. *Estudios de morfosintáxis histórica del español*. Ed. by Rafael Cano Aguilar & María Teresa Echenique Elizondo, 2 vols. (= *Biblioteca Románica Hispánica; Estudios y Ensayos*, 418.) Madrid: Gredos.

Laur, Dany. 1989. "Sémantique du déplacement à travers une étude de verbes et de prépositions". *Cahiers de Grammaire* 14.65–84.

Lavalade, Yves. 1999. *Dictionnaire occitan/français: Limousin–marche–périgord. Étymologies occitanes*. Limoges: Lucien Souny.

Lebsanft, Franz. 2005. "Historical Romance Linguistics: The future of a discipline". *La corónica* 34:1.202–207. DOI: 10.1353/cor.2005.0027

Lebsanft, Franz & Martin-Dietrich Gleßgen. 2004. "Historische Semantik in den romanischen Sprachen: Kognition, Pragmatik, Geschichte". Lebsanft & Gleßgen, eds. 2004.1–28.

Lebsanft. Franz & Martin-Dietrich Gleßgen, eds. 2004. *Historische Semantik in den romanischen Sprachen*. (= *Linguistische Arbeiten*, 483.) Tübingen: Max Niemeyer.

Lehmann, Christian. 1983. "Latin Preverbs and Cases". *Latin Linguistics and Linguistic Theory: Proceedings of the 1st International Colloquium on Latin Linguistics, Amsterdam, April 1981* ed. by Harm Pinkster (= *Studies in Language Companion Series*, 12), 145–165. Amsterdam & Philadelphia: John Benjamins.

Lehrer, Adrienne. 1990. "Polysemy, Conventionality, and the Structure of the Lexicon". *Cognitive Linguistics* 1:2.207–246. DOI: 10.1515/cogl.1990.1.2.207

Lepetit, Xavier. 2004. *Une classification des verbes de mouvement basée sur leur combinatoire sémantico-syntaxique*. Doctoral dissertation, Københavns Universitet.

Lepori, Antonio. 1988. *Dizionario italiano–sardo: Campidanese*. Cagliari: Edizioni Castello.

Létoublon, Françoise. 1985. *Il allait, pareil à la nuit: Les verbes de mouvement en grec. Supplétisme et aspect verbal*. (= *Études et Commentaires*, 98.) Paris: Klincksieck.

Levinson, Stephen C. 2003. *Space in Language and Cognition: Explorations in cognitive diversity.* (= *Language, Culture, and Cognition,* 5.) Cambridge: Cambridge University Press. DOI: 10.1017/CBO9780511613609

Levinson, Stephen C. 2006. "The Language of Space in Yélî Dnye". Levinson & Wilkins, eds. 2006.157–203.

Levinson, Stephen C., & David P. Wilkins. 2006. "Patterns in the Data: Towards a semantic typology of spatial description". Levinson & Wilkins, eds. 2006.512–552.

Levinson, Stephen C. & David P. Wilkins, eds. 2006. *Grammars of Space: Explorations in cognitive diversity.* (= *Language, Culture, and Cognition,* 6.) Cambridge: Cambridge University Press. DOI: 10.1017/CBO9780511486753

Leviţchi, Leon, ed. 1974. *Dicţionar englez–român.* Bucureşti: Editura Academiei Republicii Socialiste România.

Lewis, Charlton T. & Charles Short. 1966 [1879]. *Latin Dictionary.* Oxford: Clarendon Press.

Li, Fengxiang. 1993. *A Diachronic Study of V-V Compounds in Chinese.* Ph.D. dissertation, State University of New York at Buffalo.

Li, Fengxiang. 1997. "Cross-Linguistic Lexicalization Patterns: Diachronic evidence from verb-complement compounds in Chinese". *Sprachtypologie und Universalienforschung* 50:3.229–252.

Liberman, Anatoly. 2008. *An Analytic Dictionary of English Etymology: An introduction.* With the assistance of J. Lawrence Mitchell. Minneapolis & London: University of Minnesota Press.

Lincke, Eliese-Sophia. In progress. *Verortung in Raum und Zeit im Ägyptischen und Koptischen: Präpositionen, Positions- und Bewegungsverben als Mittel zum Ausdruck spatialer und temporaler Relationen.* Doctoral dissertation, Humboldt-Universität Berlin. Description accessed at (http://www.topoi.org/project/on-the-diachrony-of-spatial-terms-in-egyptian-and-coptic) January 2012.

Linde, Charlotte & William Labov. 1975. "Spatial Networks as a Site for the Study of Language and Thought". *Language* 51:4.924–939. DOI: 10.2307/412701

Llamas Saíz, Carmen. 2005. *Metáfora y creación léxica.* (= *Colección Lingüística,* nueva serie, 2.) Pamplona: Ediciones Universidad de Navarra.

Lloyd, Paul M. 1970. "The Contribution of Menéndez Pidal to Linguistic Theory". *Hispanic Review* 38.14–21.

Lloyd, Paul M. 1987. *From Latin to Spanish. Vol. I: Historical Phonology and Morphology of the Spanish Language.* (= *Memoirs of the American Philosophical Society,* 173.) Philadelphia: The American Philosophical Society.

Lorge, Peter. 2011. "Development and Spread of Firearms in Medieval and Early Modern Eurasia". *History Compass* 9:10.818–826. DOI: 10.1111/j.1478-0542.2011.00802.x

Lüdtke, Helmut. 1999. "Diachronic Semantics: Toward a unified theory of language change?". Blank & Koch, eds. 1999.49–60.

Lüdtke, Helmut. 2004. "El aragonés en el conjunto de las lenguas románicas". *Autas d'a III Trobada d'Estudios e Rechiras arredol d'a Luenga Aragonesa e a suya Literatura, Alquezra, 17–20 d'otubre de 2001* ed. by Francho Nagore Laín, 13–20. Huesca: Instituto de Estudios Altoaragoneses.

Luraghi, Silvia. 2010. "Adverbial Phrases". *New Perspectives on Historical Latin Syntax, vol. II: Constituent Syntax: Adverbial phrases, adverbs, mood, tense* ed. by Philip Baldi & Pierluigi Cuzzolin (= *Trends in Linguistics; Studies and Monographs,* 180), 19–107. Berlin & New York: De Gruyter Mouton.

Lutz, Angelika. 1997. "Sound Change, Word Formation and the Lexicon: The history of the English prefix verbs". *English Studies* 3.258–290. DOI: 10.1080/00138389708599075

Lý, Toàn Thang. 1989. "K voprosu o prostranstvennoj orientacii vo v'etnamskom jazyke v svjazi s kartinoj mira: Ètnopsixolingvističeskie problemy [Towards the question of spatial orientation in Vietnamese based on the picture of the world: Ethno-psycholinguistic issues]". *Voprosy Jazykoznanija* 1989:3.62–73.

Macchi, Vladimiro, ed. 1970. *Dictionary of the Italian and English Languages/Dizionario delle lingue italiana e inglese*. 4 vols. Firenze & Roma: Sansoni Editore.

Machado, José Pedro. 1977. *Dicionário etimológico da língua portuguesa*. 3rd ed. 5 vols. Lisboa: Livros Horizonte.

Machado de Assis, Joaquim. 1984. *Helena*. Transl. by Helen Caldwell. Berkeley: University of California Press. [Accessed through COMPARA.]

Machado de Assis, Joaquim. 2004 [1876]. *Helena*. São Paolo: Companhia Editora Nacional. [Accessed through COMPARA.]

Macrea, Dimitrie, ed. 1958. *Dicționarul limbii romîne moderne*. București: Editura Academiei Republicii Populare Romîne.

Macrea, Dimitrie & Emil Petrovici, eds. 1955–1957. *Dicționarul limbii romîne literare contemporane*. 4 vols. București: Editura Academiei Republicii Populare Romîne.

Maiden, Martin. 1995a. *A Linguistic History of Italian*. London & New York: Longman.

Maiden, Martin. 1995b. "A proposito dell'alternanza *esce/usciva* in italiano". *Lingua Nostra* 56:2/3.37–41.

Maiden, Martin. 2004a. "A Necessary Discipline: Historical Romance linguistics". *La corónica* 32:2.215–221. DOI: 10.1353/cor.2004.0036

Maiden, Martin. 2004b. "Verso una definizione morfologica delle lingue romanze: La nuova fisonomia morfologica del romanzo". *Aemilianense* 1.357–404.

Maiden, Martin. 2004c. "When Lexemes Become Allomorphs – On the genesis of suppletion". *Folia Linguistica* 38:3/4.227–256. DOI: 10.1515/flin.2004.38.3-4.227

Maiden, Martin. 2005. "Morphological Autonomy and Diachrony". *Yearbook of Morphology 2004* ed. by Geert Booij & Jaap van Marle, 137–175. Dordrecht & London: Kluwer. DOI: 10.1007/1-4020-2900-4_6

Maiden, Martin. 2007. "La linguistica romanza alla ricerca dell'arbitrario". *Actes du XXIVe Congrès International de Linguistique et de Philologie Romanes, Aberystwyth, 2004* ed. by David Trotter, vol. III, 505–518. Tübingen: Max Niemeyer.

Maiden, Martin. 2010. "Morphological Innovation". Maiden, Smith & Ledgeway, eds. 2010.216–267.

Maiden, Martin & Cecilia Robustelli. 2007. *A Reference Grammar of Modern Italian*. 2nd ed. New York: McGraw Hill.

Maiden, Martin, John Charles Smith & Adam Ledgeway. 2010. "Introduction". Maiden, Smith & Ledgeway, eds. 2010.xvii-xxii.

Maiden, Martin, John Charles Smith & Adam Ledgeway, eds. 2010. *The Cambridge History of the Romance Languages. Vol. I: Structures*. Cambridge: Cambridge University Press. DOI: 10.1017/CHOL9780521800723

Maisak, Timur. 2005. *Tipologija grammatikalizacii konstrukcij s glagolami dviženija i glagolami pozicii [Grammaticalization paths of motion and posture verbs: A typology]*. Moscow: Jazyki Slavjanskix Kul'tur.

Maisak, Timur. 2007. "Glagoly peremeščenija v vode v portugal'skom jazyke" [Aquamotion verbs in Portuguese]". *Glagoly dviženija v vode: Leksičeskaja tipologija [Aquamotion verbs: Lexical typology]* ed. by Timur Maisak & Ekaterina Rakhilina, 198–230. Moscow: Indrik.

Makkai, Adam. 1978. "Idiomaticity as a Language Universal". *Universals of Human Language* ed. by Joseph H. Greenberg, Charles A. Ferguson & Edith A. Moravcsik, vol. III: *Word Structure*, 401–448. Stanford: Stanford University Press.

Malblanc, Alfred. 1961. *Stylistique comparée du français et de l'allemand: Essai de représentation linguistique comparée et étude de traduction. (= Bibliothèque de Stylistique Comparée, 2.)* Paris: Didier.

Malkiel, Yakov. 1954. "Etymology and the Structure of Word Families". *Word* 10.256–274.

Malkiel, Yakov. 1964. "Distinctive Traits of Romance Linguistics". *Language in Culture and Society: A reader in linguistics and anthropology* ed. by Dell Hymes, 671–688. New York, Evanston & London: Harper & Row.

Malkiel, Yakov. 1984a. "Etimología y trayectoria del verbo ant. esp. *deçir*, port. *descer* 'bajarse'". *Josep Maria Solà-Solé: Homage, homenaje, homenatge: Miscelánea de estudios de amigos y discípulos* ed. by Antonio Torres-Alcalá, Victorio Agüera & Nathaniel B. Smith, vol. I, 341–354. Barcelona: Puvill Libros.

Malkiel, Yakov. 1984b. "The Overlap of CŬRRĔRE, -CŬTERE, and COR-RĪGĔRE in Hispano-Romance". *Romance Philology* 38:2.127–165.

Malkiel, Yakov. 1988/1989. "The Discovery of Lexical Channels of Transmision: From Latin to Romance, with special consideration of Old Spanish". *La corónica* 17:1.8–13.

Malkiel, Yakov. 1989. *Theory and Practice of Romance Etymology: Studies in language, culture and history*. London: Variorum Reprints.

Malkiel, Yakov. 1993. *Etymology*. Cambridge: Cambridge Unversity Press. DOI: 10.1017/CBO9780511611773

Mańczak, Witold. 1974. "Une étymologie romane controversée: *Aller, andar*, etc.". *Revue Roumaine de Linguistique* 19.89–101.

Mańczak, Witold. 1975. "Étymologie de fr. *aller*, esp. *andar*, etc. et calcul des probabilités". *Revue Roumaine de Linguistique* 20.735–739.

Mandler, Jean M. 2004. *The Foundations of Mind: Origins of conceptual thought*. Oxford & New York: Oxord University Press.

Mandler, Jean M. 2008. "On the Birth and Growth of Concepts". *Philosophical Psychology* 21:2.207–230. DOI: 10.1080/09515080801980179

Mandler, Jean M. 2010. "The Spatial Foundations of the Conceptual System". *Language and Cognition* 2:1.21–44. DOI: 10.1515/langcog.2010.002

Mandler, Jean M. 2012. "On the Spatial Foundations of the Conceptual System and its Enrichment". *Cognitive Science* 36.421–451. DOI: 10.1111/j.1551-6709.2012.01241.x

Mansion J. E., ed. 1939. *Heath's Standard French and English Dictionary. Part I: French–English. Part II: English–French*. 2nd ed. Boston: D. C. Heath.

Manzelli, Gianguido. 1998. "Il caso *fuori porta*: Il ruolo del modello ambientale nei processi di grammaticalizzazione". *Sintassi storica: Atti del XXX Congresso Internazionale della Società di Linguistica Italiana. Pavia, 26–28 settembre 1996* ed. by Paolo Ramat & Elisa Roma (= *Pubblicazioni della Società di Linguistica Italiana*, 39), 45–74. Roma: Bulzoni.

Martínez Vázquez, Montserrat. 2001. "Delimited Events in English and Spanish". *Estudios Ingleses de la Universidad Complutense* 9.31–59.

Masini, Francesca. 2005. "Multi-Word Expressions between Syntax and the Lexicon: The case of Italian verb-particle constructions". *SKY Journal of Linguistics* 18.145–173.

Masini, Francesca. 2006. "Diacronia dei verbi sintagmatici in italiano". *Archivio Glottologico Italiano* 91:1.67–105.

Mateu, Jaume & Gemma Rigau. 2010. "Verb-Particle Constructions in Romance: A lexical-syntactic account". *Probus* 22.241–269. DOI: 10.1515/prbs.2010.009

Matisoff, James. A. 1991. "Areal and Universal Dimensions in Grammaticalization in Lahu". *Approaches to Grammaticalization* ed. by Elizabeth Closs Traugott & Bernd Heine, vol. II: *Focus on Types of Grammatical Markers* (= *Typological Studies in Language*, 19:2), 383–453. Amsterdam & Philadelphia: John Benjamins. DOI: 10.1075/tsl.19.2.19mat

Matlock, Teenie. 2004a. "Fictive Motion as Cognitive Simulation". *Memory & Cognition* 32.1389–1400. DOI: 10.3758/BF03206329

Matlock, Teenie. 2004b. "The Conceptual Motivation of Fictive Motion". *Studies in Linguistic Motivation* ed. by Günter Radden & Klaus-Uwe Panther (= *Cognitive Linguistics Research*, 28), 221–248. Berlin & New York: Mouton de Gruyter.

Matlock, Teenie. 2010. "Abstract Motion Is no Longer Abstract". *Language and Cognition* 2:2.243–260. DOI: 10.1515/langcog.2010.010

Matsumoto, Yo. 1996. "Subjective Motion in English and Japanese Verbs". *Cognitive Linguistics* 7:2.183–226. DOI: 10.1515/cogl.1996.7.2.183

Matsumoto, Yo. 2003. "Typologies of Lexicalization Patterns and Event Integration: Clarifications and reformulations". *Empirical and Theoretical Investigations into Language: A Festschrift for Masaru Kajita* ed. by Shuji Chiba, 403–417. Tokyo: Kaitakusha.

Mayer, Mercer. 1969. *Frog, Where Are You?* New York: Dial Press.

McLure, Roger & Paul Reed. 1997. "Making the Most of *vrais amis*: A study in pedagogical economy". *International Review of Applied Linguistics and Language Teaching* 34:4.277–291.

Meini, Giuseppe, ed. 1995. *Il dizionario della lingua italiana De Agostini*. Firenze: Remo Sandron; Novara: Instituto Geografico De Agostini.

Melka, Francine. 2003. "Verbes de mouvement et verbes résultatifs en langues romanes et germaniques". *Actas del XXIII Congreso Internacional de Lingüística y Filología Románicas, Salamanca, 24–30 de septiembre de 2001* ed. by Fernando Sánchez Miret, vol. II:2, 55–63. Tübingen: Max Niemeyer.

Menéndez Pidal, Ramón. 1956 [1926]. *Orígenes del español: Estado lingüístico de la Península Ibérica hasta el siglo XI*. 4th ed. Madrid: Espasa Calpe.

Menovščikova, G. A. 1986. "Vyraženie kategorij prostranstva i vremeni v eskimossko-aleutskix jazykax [Expression of space and time in the Eskimo-Aleut languages]". *Voprosy Jazykoznanija* 1986:2.117–127.

Merlo, Clemente. 1904. *I nomi romanzi delle stagioni e dei mesi studiati particolarmente nei dialetti ladini, italiani, franco-provenzali e provenzali: Saggio di onomasiologia*. Torino: Ermano Loescher.

MetaNet. In progress. *MetaNet: A multilingual metaphor repository*. International Computer Science Institute. University of California at Berkeley. (https://metanet.icsi.berkeley.edu/metanet). Accessed: July 2013.

Meya, Montserrat. 1976. "Modelación del campo semántico de los verbos de movimiento". *Revista Española de Lingüística* 6.145–165.

Meyer, R[ichard] M[oritz]. 1910. "Bedeutungssysteme". *Zeitschrift für vergleichende Sprachforschung auf den Gebiete der indogermanischen Sprachen* 43:4.352–368.

Meyer-Lübke, Wilhelm. 1992 [1911]. *Romanisches etymologisches Wörterbuch*. 6th ed. Heidelberg: Carl Winter.

Migliorini, Bruno & Aldo Duro. 1958. *Prontuario etimologico della lingua italiana*. 3rd ed. Torino: G. B. Paravia.

Mihatsch, Wiltrud & Reinhild Steinberg, eds. 2004. *Lexical Data and Universals of Semantic Change*. (= *Stauffenburg Linguistik*, 35.) Tübingen: Stauffenburg.

Miller, Frank Justus, ed. & transl. 1994. Ovid, *Metamorphoses*. Books I–VIII. Revised by G[eorge] P[atrick] Goold. (= *Loeb Classical Library*, 42.) Cambridge, Mass. & London: Harvard University Press.

Miller, George A. & Philip N. Johnson-Laird. 1977. *Language and Perseption*. Cambridge, Mass.: Harvard University Press.

Milroy, James. 2003. "On the Role of the Speaker in Language Change". *Motives in Language Change* ed. by Raymond Hickey, 143–157. Cambridge & New York: Cambridge University Press.

Milroy, James 2006. "Language Change and the Speaker: On the discourse of historical linguistics". *Variation and Reconstruction* ed. by Thomas D. Cravens (= *Current Issues in Linguistic Theory*, 268), 145–163. Amsterdam & Philadelphia: John Benjamins. DOI: 10.1075/cilt.268.08mil

Mithun, Marianne. 1999. *The Languages of Native North America*. Cambridge & New York: Cambridge University Press.

Monti, Silva. 1981. "L'opposizione *andare/venire* in italiano e spagnolo". *Quaderni di Lingue e Letterature* 6.115–125.

Montibus, Marie-Jeanne. 1996. "Rapide survol au-dessus du champ sémantique des verbes de mouvement en français moderne". *Questions de méthode et de délimitation en sémantique lexicale: Actes d'EUROSEM 1994* ed. by Hiltraud Dupuy-Engelhardt, 137–143. Reims: Presses Universitaires de Reims.

Montserrat, Sandra. 2004. "Evolució semàntica d'*arribar* en català (segles XIII–XVI): Un exemple de canvi de prototipus". *Estudios de Lingüística Universidad de Alicante* 18.421–442.

Montserrat i Buendia, Sandra. 2007. *La semàntica diacrònica cognitiva: Una aplicació a propòsit de* venir, arribar *i* aplegar *(segles XII–XVI)*. (= *Biblioteca Sanchis Guarner*, 68.) Alacant: Institut Interuniversitari de Filologia Valenciana; Barcelona: Publicacions de l'Abadia de Montserrat & Institut d'Estudis Catalans.

Mood, James Raider. 1907. *Some Figurative Usages of* VENIRE *and* IRE. Baltimore: J. H. Furst.

Moore, Clifford H., ed. & transl. 1968. Tacitus, *The Histories*. Vol. II. Books I–III. (= *Loeb Classical Library*, 111.) Cambridge, Mass.: Harvard University Press; London: William Heinemann.

Morimoto, Yuko. 2001. *Los verbos de movimiento*. Madrid: Visor Libros.

Mosca, Monica. 2010. "Un profilo statistico dei verbi di movimento in italiano parlato". *La comunicazione parlata 3: Atti del Terzo Congresso Internazionale del Gruppo di Studio sulla Comunicazione Parlata* ed. by Massimo Pettorino, Antonella Giannini & Francesca M. Dovetto, vol. I, 47–65. Napoli: Università degli Studi di Napoli L'Orientale.

Mosca, Monica. 2012. "Italian Motion Constructions: Different functions of particles". *Space and Time in Languages and Cultures: Linguistic diversity* ed. by Luna Filipović & Kasia M. Jaszczolt (= *Human Cognitive Processing*, 36), 373–393. Amsterdam & Philadelphia: John Benjamins. DOI: 10.1075/hcp.36.20mos

Mozley, J[ohn] H[enry], ed. & transl. 1985. Ovid. *Vol. II: The Art of Love and Other Poems*. 2nd ed. Revised by G[eorge] P[atrick] Goold. (= *Loeb Classical Library*, 232.) Cambridge, Mass.: Harvard University Press; London: William Heinemann.

Müller, Bodo. 1987–. *Diccionario del español medieval*. Heidelberg: Carl Winter.

Nagucka, Ruta. 1980. "Directionality and the Verbs of Motion". *Bulletin de la Société Polonaise de Linguistique* 37.13–27.

Nascentes, Antenor. 1932. *Dicionário etimológico da língua portuguesa.* 2 vols. Rio de Janeiro: Francisco Alves.

Nerlich, Brigitte & David D. Clarke. 2000. "Semantic Fields and Frames: Historical explorations of the interface between language, action, and cognition". *Journal of Pragmatics* 32.125–150. DOI: 10.1016/S0378-2166(99)00042-9

Nerlich, Brigitte & David D. Clarke. 2007. "Cognitive Linguistics and the History of Linguistics". *The Oxford Handbook of Cognitive Linguistics* ed. by Dirk Geeraerts & Hubert Cuyckens, 589–607. Oxford: Oxford University Press.

Newman, John. 1996. *Give: A cognitive linguistic study.* (= *Cognitive Linguistics Research,* 7.) Berlin & New York: Mouton de Gruyter.

Nichols, Johanna. 2010. "Indeterminate Motion Verbs Are Denominal". *New Approaches to Slavic Verbs of Motion* ed. by Victoria Hasko & Renee Perelmutter (= *Studies in Language Companion Series,* 115), 47–65. Amsterdam & Philadelphia: John Benjamins. DOI: 10.1075/slcs.115.05nic

Niermeyer, J[an] F[rederik] & C. Van De Kieft. 2002. *Mediae latinitatis lexicon minus/Lexique latin médiéval/Medieval Latin Dictionary/Mittellateinisches Wörterbuch.* 2 vols. Rev. by J.W.J. Burgers. Leiden & Boston: Brill.

Nikitina, Tatiana. 2013. "Lexical Splits in the Encoding of Motion Events from Archaic to Classical Greek". *Variation and Change in the Encoding of Motion Events* ed. by Juliana Goschler & Anatol Stefanowitsch (= *Human Cognitive Processing,* 41), 185–202. Amsterdam & Philadelphia: John Benjamins. DOI: 10.1075/hcp.41.08nik

Nixon, Paul, ed. & transl. 1966. Plautus. *Vol. I: Amphitryon; The Comedy of Asses; The Pot of Gold; The Two Bacchises; The Captives.* (= *Loeb Classical Library,* 60.) Cambridge, Mass.: Harvard University Press; London: William Heinemann.

Nixon, Paul. ed. & transl. 1988. Plautus. *Vol. II: Casina; The Casket Comedy; Curculio; Epidicus; The Two Menaechmuses.* (= *Loeb Classical Library,* 61.) Cambridge, Mass.: Harvard University Press; London: William Heinemann.

Nixon, Paul. ed. & transl. 1999. Plautus. *Vol. V: Stichus; Trinummus; Truculentus; Tale of a Travelling Bag; Fragments.* (= *Loeb Classical Library,* 328.) Cambridge, Mass. & London: Harvard University Press.

Noblejas Ruiz Escribano, Juan José. 2004. *Itineraria Hierosolymitana (Siglos IV–VI): Estudio lingüístico.* Doctoral dissertation, Universidad Complutense de Madrid.

Núñez, Rafael E. & Eve Sweetser. 2006. "With the Future Behind Them: Convergent evidence from Aymara language and gesture in the crosslinguistic comparison of spatial construals of time". *Cognitive Science* 30.401–450. DOI: 10.1207/s15516709cog0000_62

Nyrop, Kristoffer. 1913. *Grammaire historique de la langue française. Vol. IV: Sémantique.* Kopenhagen: Gyldendalske Boghandel.

O'Connor, Loretta. 2007. *Motion, Transfer and Transformation: The grammar of change in Lowland Chontal.* (= *Studies in Language Companion Series,* 95.) Amsterdam & Philadelphia: John Benjamins. DOI: 10.1075/slcs.95

O'Connor, Loretta. 2009. "All Typologies Leak: Predicates of change in Lowland Chontal of Oaxaca". *New Challenges in Typology: Transcending the borders and refining the distinctions* ed. by Patience Epps & Alexandre Arkhipov (= *Trends in Linguistics; Studies and Monographs,* 217), 343–363. Berlin & New York: Mouton de Gruyter.

Oelschläger, Victor R. B. 1940. *A Medieval Spanish Word-List: A preliminary dated vocabulary of first appearances up to Berceo*. Madison: University of Wisconsin Press.

Ogura, Michiko. 2002. *Verbs of Motion in Medieval English*. Cambridge: D. S. Brewer.

O'Sullivan, Timothy M. 2011. *Walking in Roman Culture*. Cambridge: Cambridge University Press. DOI: 10.1017/CBO9780511733239

Özçalışkan, Şeyda. 2004. "Typological Variation in Encoding the Manner, Path, and Ground Components of a Metaphorical Motion Event". *Annual Review of Cognitive Linguistics* 2.73–102. DOI: 10.1075/arcl.2.03ozc

Pandya, Vishvajit. 1990. "Movement and Space: Andamanese cartography". *American Ethnologist* 17:4.775–797. DOI: 10.1525/ae.1990.17.4.02a00100

Pandya, Vishvajit. 1993. *Above the Forest: A study of Andamanese ethnoanemology, cosmology, and the power of ritual*. Delhi & New York: Oxford University Press.

Panther, Klaus-Uwe. 2012. "Motivation in Language". *Cognition and Motivation: Forging an interdisciplinary perspective* ed. by Shulamith Kreitler, 407–432. Cambridge: Cambridge University Press. DOI: 10.1017/CBO9781139021463.023

Panther, Klaus-Uwe & Günter Radden. 1999. "Introduction". *Metonymy in Language and Thought* ed. by Klaus-Uwe Panther & Günter Radden (= *Human Cognitive Processing*, 4), 1–14. Amsterdam & Philadelphia: John Benjamins. DOI: 10.1075/hcp.4.01pan

Panther, Klaus-Uwe & Günter Radden. 2011. "Introduction: Reflections on motivation revisited". *Motivation in Grammar and the Lexicon* ed. by Klaus-Uwe Panther & Günter Radden (= *Human Cognitive Processing*, 27), 1–26. Amsterdam & Philadelphia: John Benjamins. DOI: 10.1075/hcp.27.02pan

Papafragou, Anna, Christine Massey & Lila Gleitman. 2002. "Shake, Rattle, 'n' Roll: The representation of motion in language and cognition". *Cognition* 84.189–219. DOI: 10.1016/S0010-0277(02)00046-X

Papafragou, Anna, Justin Hulbert & John Trueswell. 2008. "Does Language Guide Event Perception? Evidence from eye movement". *Cognition* 108.155–184. DOI: 10.1016/j.cognition.2008.02.007

Parry, Mair. 1998. "The Reinterpretation of the Reflexive in Piedmontese: 'Impersonal' *se* constructions". *Transactions of the Philological Society* 96:1.63–116. DOI: 10.1111/1467-968X.00024

Pascual Aransáez, Cristina. 1999. A Cognitive Analysis of the Cross-Linguistic Differences between English and Spanish Motion Verbs and the Spanish Translator's Task". *Cuadernos de Investigación Filológica* 25.127–136.

Pastor y Molina, Roberto. 1908. "Vocabulario de madrileñismos". *Revue Hispanique* 18.51–72.

Pause, Peter E., Achim Botz & Markus Egg. 1995. "*Partir* c'est quitter un peu: A two-level approach to polysemy". *Lexical Knowledge in the Organization of Language* ed. by Urs Egli, Peter E. Pause, Christoph Schwarze, Arnim von Stechow & Götz Wienold (= *Current Issues in Linguistic Theory*, 114), 245–282. Amsterdam & Philadelphia: John Benjamins. DOI: 10.1075/cilt.114.12pau

Paz Afonso, Ana. 2009. "Análisis contrastivo y evolución semántica del verbo *pasar*". *Tendencias actuales en la investigación diacrónica de la lengua: Actas del VIII Congreso Nacional de la Asociación de Jóvenes Investigadores de Historiografía e Historia de la Lengua Española (AJIHLE), Barcelona, 2–4 de abril de 2008* ed. by Laura Romero Aguilera & Carolina Julià Luna, 423–432. Barcelona: Publicacions i Edicions de la Universitat de Barcelona.

Pedersen, Bolette Sandford. 1999. "Systematic Verb Polysemy in MT: A study of Danish motion verbs with comparisons with Spanish". *Machine Translation* 14.35–82. DOI: 10.1023/A:1008183205171

Pérez i Brufau, Roger. 2011. "Philosophy and Cognitive Science: Interview with Mark Johnson". *Review of Cognitive Linguistics* 9:1.329–339. DOI: 10.1075/rcl.9.1.16per

Peskett, A[rthur] G[eorge], ed. & transl. 1990. Caesar, *The Civil Wars*. (= *Loeb Classical Library*, 39.) Cambridge, Mass. & London: Harvard University Press.

Petersmann, Hubert. 1999. "Der Einfluß des *sermo militaris* auf das Vulgärlatein: Zur Geschichte von romanisch *andar(e)*". *Latin vulgaire – latin tardif V: Actes du Ve Colloque International sur le Latin Vulgaire et Tardif, Heidelberg, 5–8 septembre 1997* ed. by Hubert Petersmann & Rudolf Kettemann (= *Bibliothek der Klassischen Altertumswissenschaften*, II:105), 529–537. Heidelberg: Carl Winter.

Peyraube, Alain. 2006. "Motion Events in Chinese: A diachronic study of directional complements". Hickmann & Robert, eds. 2006.121–135.

Pfister, Max. 1979–. *Lessico etimologico italiano*. Wiesbaden: Ludwig Reichert.

Pharies, David. 1997. "Adverbial Expressions Signifying Bodily Movements and Postures in Hispano-Romance". *Hispanic Review* 65:4.391–414. DOI: 10.2307/474295

Pharies, David. 2002. *Diccionario etimológico de los sufijos españoles (y de otros elementos finales)*. (= *Biblioteca Románica Hispánica; Diccionarios*, 25.) Madrid: Gredos.

Pharies, David. 2011. "Evolución del prefijo *sub-* en hispanorromance". *Revista de Historia de la Lengua Española* 6.131–155.

Pick, Herbert L., Jr. & Linda P. Acredolo, eds. 1983. *Spatial Orientation: Theory, research, and application*. New York & London: Plenum. DOI: 10.1007/978-1-4615-9325-6

Picoche, Jacqueline. 1986. *Structures sémantiques du lexique français*. Paris: Fernand Nathan.

Picoche, Jacqueline. 1992. *Dictionnaire étymologique du français*. Paris: Dictionnaires Le Robert.

Pinchon, Jacqueline. 1972. *Les pronoms adverbiaux* en et y: *Problèmes généraux de la représentation pronominale*. (= *Publications Romanes et Françaises*, 119). Genève: Droz.

Planta, Robert von, Florian Melcher, Chasper Pult, Andrea Schorta & Alexi Decurtins, eds. 1939–. *Dicziunari Rumantsch Grischun*. Chur: Società Retorumantscha.

Poduska, Donald Miles. 1963. *Synonymous Verbs of Motion in Plautus*. Ph.D. dissertation, The Ohio State University.

Pokorny, Julius. 1959–1969. *Indogermanisches etymologisches Wörterbuch*. 2 vols. Bern & München: Francke.

Porquier, Rémy. 2001. "'Il m'a sauté dessus', 'je lui ai couru après': Un cas de postposition du français". *Journal of French Language Studies* 11:1.123–134. DOI: 10.1017/S0959269501000163

Pott, A[ugust] F[riedrich]. 1852. "Plattlateinisch und romanisch". *Zeitschrift für vergleichende Sprachforschung auf dem Gebiete des Deutschen, Griechischen und Lateinischen* 1:4.309–350.

Pottier Navarro, Huguette. 1991. *La polisemia léxica en español: Teoría y resolución*. Transl. by Segundo Álvarez Pérez. (= *Biblioteca Románica Hispánica; Estudios y Ensayos*, 374.) Madrid: Gredos.

Pountain, Christopher J. 2000a. "Capitalization". *Historical Linguistics 1995: Selected Papers from the 12th International Conference on Historical Linguistics, Manchester, August 1995. Vol. I: General Issues and Non-Germanic Languages* ed. by John Charles Smith & Delia Bentley (= *Current Issues in Linguistic Theory*, 161), 295–309. Amsterdam & Philadelphia: John Benjamins.

Pountain, Christopher J. 2000b. "Pragmatic Factors in the Evolution of the Romance Reflexive (with Special Reference to Spanish)". *Hispanic Research Journal* 1:1.5–25. DOI: 10.1179/hrj.2000.1.1.5

Pourcel, Stéphanie. 2004. "What Makes Path of Motion Salient?". *Proceedings of the Thirtieth Annual Meeting of the Berkeley Linguistics Society, 13–16 February 2004. General Session and Parasession on Conceptual Structure and Cognition in Grammatical Theory* ed. by Marc Ettlinger, Nicholas Fleisher & Mischa Park-Doob, 505–516. Berkeley: Berkeley Linguistics Society.

Pourcel, Stéphanie. 2009. "Motion Scenarios in Cognitive Processes". *New Directions in Cognitive Linguistics* ed. by Vyvyan Evans & Stéphanie Pourcel (= *Human Cognitive Processing*, 24), 371–391. Amsterdam & Philadelphia: John Benjamins. DOI: 10.1075/hcp.24.23pou

Pourcel, Stéphanie. 2010. "Motion: A conceptual typology". *Language, Cognition and Space: The state of the art and new directions* ed. by Vyvyan Evans & Paul Chilton, 419–449. London & Oakville: Equinox.

Pourcel, Stéphanie & Anetta Kopecka. 2005. "Motion Expression in French: Typological diversity". *Durham & Newcastle Working Papers in Linguistics* 11.139–153.

Price, Christy M. & David L. Gilden. 2000. "Representations of Motion and Direction". *Journal of Experimental Psychology: Human Perception and Performance* 26:1.18–30. DOI: 10.1037/0096-1523.26.1.18

Puddu, Mario. 2000. *Ditzionàriu de sa limba e de sa cultura sarda*. Cagliari: Condaghes.

Pușcariu, Sextil. 1973 [1937]. *Études de linguistique roumaine*. Transl. by Yves Auger & Henri Jacquier. Hildesheim: Georg Olms.

Pușcariu, Sextil. 1975 [1905]. *Etymologisches Wörterbuch der rumänischen Sprache: Lateinisches Element mit Berücksichtigung aller romanischen Sprachen*. 2nd ed. (= *Sammlung Romanischer Elementar- und Handbücher*, Reihe 3: *Wörterbücher*, 1.) Heidelberg: Carl Winter.

Pușcariu, Sextil, Iorgu Iordan, Alexandru Graur, Ion Coteanu, Marius Sala & Gheorghe Mihăilă, eds. 1907–. *Dicționarul limbii române*. (*Serie Nouă*). București – Cluj-Napoca – Iași: Editura Academiei Române. [Before 1965 *Dicționarul limbii române*; after 1965 *Dicționarul limbii române. Serie Nouă*.]

Pütz, Martin & René Dirven, eds. 1996. *The Construal of Space in Language and Thought*. (= *Cognitive Linguistics Research*, 8.) Berlin: Mouton de Gruyter. DOI: 10.1515/9783110821611

Quadri, Bruno. 1952. *Aufgaben und Methoden der onomasiologischen Forschung: Eine entwicklungsgeschichtliche Darstellung*. (= *Romanica Helvetica*, 37.) Bern: Francke.

Rackham, H[arris], ed. & transl. 1938. Pliny, *Natural History*. Vol. I: Praefatio, Libri I, II. (= *Loeb Classical Library*, 330.) Cambridge, Mass..: Harvard University Press; London: William Heinemann.

Rackham, H., ed. & transl. 1950. Pliny, *Natural History*. Vol. V: Libri XVII–XIX. (= *Loeb Classical Library*, 371.) Cambridge, Mass.: Harvard University Press; London: William Heinemann.

Rackham, H., ed. & transl. 1967. Cicero, *De finibus bonorum et malorum*. (= *Loeb Classical Library*, 40.) Cambridge, Mass.: Harvard University Press; London: William Heinemann.

Radden, Günter. 1988. "The Concept of Motion". *Understanding the Lexicon: Meaning, sense and world knowledge in lexical semantics* ed. by Werner Hüllen & Rainer Schulze (= *Linguistische Arbeiten*, 210), 380–394. Tübingen: Max Niermeyer.

Radden, Günter. 1996. "Motion Metaphorized: The case of *coming* and *going*". *Cognitive Linguistics in the Redwoods: The expansion of a new paradigm in linguistics* ed. by Eugene H. Casad (= *Cognitive Linguistics Research*, 6), 423–458. Berlin & New York: Mouton de Gruyter.

Radden, Günter & Klaus-Uwe Panther. 2004. "Introduction: Reflections on motivation". *Studies in Linguistic Motivation* ed. by Günter Radden & Klaus-Uwe Panther (= *Cognitive Linguistics Research*, 28), 1–46. Berlin & New York: Mouton de Gruyter.

Rapin, Cristian. 1991–2006. *Diccionari francés–occitan segon lo lengadocian*. 5 vols. Institut d'Estudis Occitans.

Rask, Rasmus. 1818 [1814]. *Undersøgelse om det gamle Nordiske eller Islandske Sprogs Oprindelse*. Kjöbenhavn: Gyldendal. [English transl. by Niels Ege, newly ed. with an Introduction by Frans Gregersen, *Investigation of the Origin of the Old Norse or Icelandic Language* (= *Amsterdam Classics in Linguistics, 1800–1925*, 18.) Amsterdam & Philadelphia: John Benjamins, 2013.]

Raynouard, François. 1816. *Grammaire de la langue romane ou langue des troubadours*. Paris: Firmin Didot.

Reddy, Michael J. 1979. "The Conduit Metaphor – A case of frame conflict in our language about language". *Metaphor and Thought* ed. by Andrew Ortony, 284–324. Cambridge: Cambridge University Press.

Referovskaja, E[lizaveta] A[rturovna]. 1961. "Razvitie predložnyx dopolnenij pri pristavočnyx glagolax udalenija v latinskom jazyke pozdnego perioda [The development of prepositional complements with prefixed verbs that express the concept 'to go away' in Late Latin]". *Issledovanija v oblasti latinskogo i romanskogo jazykoznanija* [*Studies in Latin and Romance linguistics*] ed. by R[uben] A[leksandrovič] Budagov & N[ikolaj] G[rigor'evič] Korletianu, 37–80. Chișinău: "Știința".

Rehfeldt, Gládis Knak. 1980. *Polissemia e campo semântico: estudo aplicado aos verbos de movimento*. Porto Alegre: Editora da Universidade Federal do Rio Grande do Sul.

Reinheimer, Sanda. 1965. "Schiță de descriere structurală a verbelor de mișcare". *Studii și Cercetări Lingvistice* 16:4.519–531.

Rey, Alain, ed. 1989. *Dictionnaire alphabétique et analogique de la langue française de Paul Robert*. 2nd ed. 9 vols. Paris: Le Robert.

Rey, Alain, ed. 1994. *Dictionnaire historique de la langue française*. 2 vols. Paris: Dictionnaires Le Robert.

Rey, Alain, ed. 2001. *Dictionnaire alphabétique et analogique de la langue française de Paul Robert*. 2nd ed. 6 vols. Paris: Dictionnaires Le Robert.

Reynolds, Barbara, ed. 1981. *The Cambridge Italian Dictionary*. 2 vols. Cambridge: Cambridge University Press.

Ricca, Davide. 1991. "*Andare* e *venire* nelle lingue romanze e germaniche: dall'Aktionsart alla deissi". *Archivio Glottologico Italiano* 76.159–192.

Ricca, Davide. 1992. "Le couple de verbes déictiques 'andare'/'venire' en italien: conditions d'emploi et variabilités". *La deixis: Colloque en Sorbonne, 8–9 juin 1990* ed. by Mary-Annick Morel & Laurent Danon-Boileau, 277–286. Paris: Presses Universitaires de France.

Ricca, Davide. 1993. *I verbi deittici di movimento in Europa: Una ricerca interlinguistica*. (= *Pubblicazioni della Facoltà di Lettere e Filosofia dell'Università di Pavia*, 70.) Firenze: La Nuova Italia.

Rini, Joel. 2005. "On the Formation of the Present Indicative Paradigm of Spanish *ir* and the Origin of *vamos* and *vais*". *Studies on Ibero-Romance Lingusitics Dedicated to Ralph Penny* ed. by Roger Wright & Peter Ricketts (= *Juan de la Cuesta Hispanic Monographs; Estudios Lingüísticos*, 7), 59–73. Newark, Del.: Juan de la Cuesta.

Rivano Fischer, Emilio. 1997. *Metáfora y lingüística cognitiva*. Santiago de Chile: Bravo y Allende.

Rohlfs, Gerhard. 1969. *Grammatica storica della lingua italiana e dei suoi dialetti*. Transl. by Salvatore Persichino, Temistocle Franceschi & Maria Caciagli Francelli. 3 vols. Torino: Einaudi.

Rohlfs, Gerhard. 1970. *From Vulgar Latin to Old French: An introduction to the study of the Old French language*. Transl. by Vincent Almazan & Lillian McCarthy. Detroit: Wayne State University Press.

Rohlfs, Gerhard. 1979. *Estudios sobre el léxico románico*. Transl. by Manuel Álvar. (= *Biblioteca Románica Hispánica; Estudios y ensayos*, 294.) Madrid: Gredos.

Rohrer, Tim. 2007. "Embodiment and Experientialism". *The Oxford Handbook of Cognitive Linguistics* ed. by Dirk Geeraerts & Hubert Cuyckens, 25–47. Oxford: Oxford University Press.

Rojo, Ana & Javier Valenzuela. 2003. "Fictive Motion in English and Spanish". *International Journal of English Studies* 3:2.123–149.

Rolfe, J[ohn] C., ed. & transl. 1965. Sallust. (= *Loeb Classical Library*, 116.) Cambridge, Mass.: Harvard University Press; London: William Heinemann.

Rolfe, John C., ed. & transl. 1968. Aulus Gellius, *The Attic Nights*. Vol. II. (= *Loeb Classical Library*, 200.) Cambridge, Mass.: Harvard University Press; London: William Heinemann.

Rosch, Eleanor. 1975. "Cognitive Representations of Semantic Categories". *Journal of Experimental Psychology* 104.192–233. DOI: 10.1037/0096-3445.104.3.192

Rosén, Haim. 1992. "Die Komposita mit *co(n)-* in funktioneller und vergleichender Sicht". *Latein und Indogermanisch: Akten des Kolloquiums der Indogermanischen Gesellschaft, Salzburg, 23–26 September 1986* ed. by Oswald Panagl & Thomas Krisch (= *Innsbrucker Beiträge zur Sprachwissenschaft*, 64), 357–367. Innsbruck: Institut für Sprachwissenschaft der Universität Innsbruck.

Rosén, H[annah]. 2000. "Preclassical and Classical Latin Precursors of Romance Verb-Stem Suppletion". *Indogermanischen Forschungen* 105.270–283.

Rosén, Hannah. 1999. *Latine loqui: Trends and directions in the crystallization of Classical Latin*. München: Wilhelm Fink.

Rosenberg, Sheldon, Paul J. Coyle & Walter L. Porter. 1966. "Recall of Adverbs as a Function of the Frequency of Their Adjective Roots". *Journal of Verbal Learning and Verbal Behavior* 5:1.75–76. DOI: 10.1016/S0022-5371(66)80109-3

Rosselli, Renato & Roberto Eynard. 1996. *Dizionario di base della lingua italiana*. Torino: Società Editrice Internazionale; Firenze: Remo Sàndron.

Rossi, Nathalie. 1999. "Déplacement et mode d'action en français". *French Language Studies* 9.259–281. DOI: 10.1017/S0959269500004713

Rouse, W[illiam] H[enry] D[enham], ed. & transl. 1992. Lucretius, *De rerum natura*. Revised by Martin Ferguson Smith. (= *Loeb Classical Library*, 181.) Cambridge, Mass. & London: Harvard University Press.

Rousseau, André, ed. 1995. *Les préverbes dans les langues d'Europe: Introduction à l'étude de la préverbation*. Lille: Presses Universitaires du Septentrion.

Rubery, Joanna, ed. 2010. *Oxford – Paravia Italian Dictionary: English–Italian/Italian–English*. 3rd ed. Oxford: Oxford University Press.

Ruiz de Mendoza Ibáñez, Francisco José. 1997. "An Interview with George Lakoff". *Cuadernos de Filología Inglesa* 6:2.33–52.

Rushton Fairclough, H., ed. & transl. 1974. Virgil, *Eclogues. Georgics. Aeneid I–VI*. (= *Loeb Classical Library*, 63.) Cambridge, Mass.: Harvard University Press; London: William Heinemann.

Rushton Fairclough, H., ed. & transl. 1996. Virgil, *Aeneid VII–XII. The Minor Poems*. (= *Loeb Classical Library*, 64.) Cambridge, Mass. & London: Harvard University Press.

Rushton Fairclough, H., ed. & transl. 1999. Virgil, *Eclogues. Georgics. Aeneid I–VI*. Revised by G[eorge] P[atrick] Goold. (= *Loeb Classical Library*, 63.) Cambridge, Mass. & London: Harvard University Press.

Russell, Donald A., ed. & transl. 2001a. Quintilian, *The Orator's Education*. Books III–V. (= *Loeb Classical Library*, 125.) Cambridge, Mass. & London: Harvard University Press.

Russell, Donald A., ed. & transl. 2001b. Quintilian, *The Orator's Education*. Books IX–X. (= *Loeb Classical Library*, 127.) Cambridge, Mass. & London: Harvard University Press.

Sablayrolles, Pierre. 1991. "Sémantique spatiotemporelle du déplacement en français: Analyse et réprésentation". *Les Cahiers de Grammaire* 16.119–159.

Sage, Evan T. & Alfred C. Schlesinger, eds. & transl. 2000. Livy, *History of Rome*. Books XL–XLII. (= *Loeb Classical Library*, 332.) Cambridge, Mass. & London: Harvard University Press.

Sagristà i Artigas, Marc, ed. 1998. *Gran diccionari de la llengua catalana*. Barcelona: Enciclopèdia Catalana.

Salarrullana y de Dios, José & Eduardo Ibarra y Rodríguez, eds. 1907, 1913. *Colección de documentos para el estudio de la historia de Aragón: Documentos correspondientes al reinado de Sancio Ramírez, desde MLXIII hasta MLXXXXIIII años. Documentos reales procedentes de la Real Casa y Monasterio de San Juan de la Peña*. Transcripción, prólogo y notas de José Salarrullana y de Dios, Zaragoza, 1907; Transcripción, prólogo y notas de Eduardo Ibarra y Rodríguez, Zaragoza: M. Escar, 1913.

Salomonski, Eva. 1944. *Funciones formativas del prefijo a- estudiadas en el castellano antiguo*. Zurich: Ernesto Lang.

Sánchez-Prieto Borja, Pedro. 1992. "Alternancia entre el lexema con y sin prefijo en castellano medieval (el verbo)". *Actas del II Congreso Internacional de Historia de la Lengua Española, Sevilla, 5 de marzo de 1990* ed. by M[anuel] Ariza, R[afael] Cano, J[osé] M.ª Mendoza & A[ntonio] Narbona, vol. I, 1323–1336. Madrid: Pabellón de España.

Santos Domínguez, Luis Antonio & Rosa María Espinoza Elorza. 1996. *Manual de semántica histórica*. (= *Colección Lingüística*, 21.) Madrid: Síntesis.

Saramago, José. 1989. *A história do cerco de Lisboa*. Lisboa: Caminho. [Accessed through COMPARA.]

Saramago, José. 1996. *The History of the Siege of Lisbon*. Transl. by Giovanni Pontiero. London: Harvill Press. [Accessed through COMPARA.]

Schaefer, Ronald P. 1985. "Motion in Tswana and its Characteristic Lexicalization". *Studies in African Linguistics* 16:1.57–87.

Schaefer, Ronald P. 1986. "Lexicalizing Directional and Nondirectional Motion in Emai". *Studies in African Linguistics* 17:2.177–198.

Schepping, Marie-Theres. 1996. "Un cas de polysémie dans le domaine verbal: *arriver*". *Questions de méthode et de délimitation en sémantique lexicale: Actes d'eurosem 1994* ed. by Hiltraud Dupuy-Engelhardt, 159–174. Reims: Presses Universitaires de Reims.

Schiaparelli, Celestino, ed. 1871. *Vocabulista in Arabico*. Publicato per la prima volta sopra un codice della Biblioteca Riccardiana di Firenze. Firenze: Successori Le Monnier.

Schiff, William. 1965. "Perception of Impending Collision: A study of visually directed avoidant behavior". *Psychological Monographs: General and applied* 79:11.1–26. DOI: 10.1037/h0093887

Schlyter, Suzanne. 1978. "German and French Movement Verbs: Polysemy and equivalence". *Papers from the Fourth Scandinavian Conference of Linguistics, Hindsgavl, 6–8 January 1978* ed. by Kirsten Gregersen, Hans Basbøll & Jacob Mey (= *Odense University Studies in Linguistics*, 3), 349–354. Odense: Odense University Press.

Schlyter, Suzanne. 1979. "Le verbe allemand 'kommen' et ses correspondances en français". *Moderna Språk* 73.251–267.

Schonthal, Hanna, ed. 2001. *The American Heritage Spanish Dictionary: Spanish–English, English–Spanish*. 2nd ed. Boston & New York: Houghton Mifflin.

Schøsler, Lene. 2008. "L'expression des traits *manière* et *direction* des verbes de mouvement: Perspectives diachroniques et typologiques". *Romanische Syntax im Wandel* ed. by Elisabeth Stark, Roland Schmidt-Riese & Eva Stoll, 113–132. Tübingen: Gunter Narr.

Schröpfer, J[ohannes]. 1956. "Wozu ein vergleichendes Wörterbuch des Sinnwandels?". *Proceedings of the Seventh International Congress of Linguists, London, 1–6 September 1952* ed. by Frederick Norman & Peter F. Ganz, 366–371. London: Permanent International Committee of Linguists.

Schwarze, Christoph. 1985. "'Uscire' e 'andare fuori': Struttura sintattica e semantica lessicale". *Sintassi e morfologia della lingua italiana d'uso: Teorie e applicazioni descrittive: Atti del XVII Congresso Internazionale di Studi, Urbino, 11–13 settembre 1983* ed. by Annalisa Franchi De Bellis & Leonardo Maria Savoia, 355–371. Roma: Bulzoni.

Schwarze, Christoph. 1993. "Time, Space and Order in the Lexicon". Aurnague, A. Borillo, M. Borillo & Bras, eds. 1993.3–24.

Schwarze, Christoph & Marie-Theres Schepping. 1995. "Polysemy in a Two-Level Semantics". *Lexical Knowledge in the Organization of Language* ed. by Urs Egli, Peter E. Pause, Christoph Schwarze, Arnim von Stechow & Götz Wienold (= *Current Issues in Linguistic Theory*, 114), 283–300. Amsterdam & Philadelphia: John Benjamins. DOI: 10.1075/cilt.114.13sch

Seco, Manuel, ed. 2003. *Léxico hispánico primitivo (siglos VIII al XII)*. Versión primera del Glosario del primitivo léxico iberorrománico. Proyectado y dirigido inicialmente por Ramón Menéndez Pidal. Redactado por Rafael Lapesa con la colaboración de Constantino García. Madrid: Espasa Calpe.

Seigneuret, Jean-Charles. 1967. "ADULARE > *aller*". *Romance Notes* 9:1.166–169.

Selimis, Stathis. 2002. "Motion Verbs & Manner". *Linguist List* 13:899.1–6. (http://www.linguistlist.org/issues/13/13-899.html). Accessed: January 2003.

Shackleton Bailey, D[avid] R[oy], ed. & transl. 2000. Valerius Maximus, *Memorable Doings and Sayings*. Vol. I. (= *Loeb Classical Library*, 492.) Cambridge, Mass. & London: Harvard University Press.

Shackleton Bailey, D. R., ed. & transl. 2003a. Statius, *Silvae*. (= *Loeb Classical Library*, 206.) Cambridge, Mass. & London: Harvard University Press.

Shackleton Bailey, D. R., ed. & transl. 2003b. Statius, *Thebaid*. Books I–VII. (= *Loeb Classical Library*, 207). Cambridge, Mass. & London: Harvard University Press.

Shay, Erin & Uwe Seibert, eds. 2003. *Motion, Direction and Location in Languages: In honor of Zygmunt Frajzyngier*. (= *Typological Studies in Language*, 56.) Amsterdam & Philadelphia: John Benjamins. DOI: 10.1075/tsl.56

Sikora, Edmund. 1985. "La structure fonctionnelle des verbes de mouvement: Essai d'analyse à partir d'un échantillon français". *Acta Universitatis Wratislaviensis: Romanica Wratislaviensia* 23.71–82.

Simone, Raffaele. 1997. "Essistono verbi sintagmatici in italiano?". *Lessico e grammatica: Teorie linguistiche e applicazioni lessicografiche: Atti del Convegno Interannuale della Società di Linguistica Italiana, Madrid, 21–25 febbraio 1995* ed. by Tullio De Mauro & Vincenzo Lo Cascio (= *Pubblicazioni della Società di Linguistica Italiana*, 36), 155–170. Roma: Bulzoni.

Simone, Raffaele. 2008. "Verbi sintagmatici come categoria e come costruzione". Cini, ed. 2008.13–30.

Simonet, Francisco Javier. 1888. *Glosario de voces ibéricas y latinas usadas entre los mozárabes.* Precedido de un estudio sobre el dialecto hispano-mozárabe por D. Francisco Javier Simonet. Madrid: Establecimiento Tipográfico de Fortanet.

Sinha, Chris & Tania Kuteva. 1995. "Distributed Spatial Semantics". *Nordic Journal of Linguistics* 18.167–199. DOI: 10.1017/S0332586500000159

Sinha, Chris, Vera Da Silva Sinha, Jörg Zinken & Wany Sampaio. 2011. "When Time Is not Space: The social and linguistic construction of time intervals and temporal event relations in an Amazonian culture". *Language and Cognition* 3:1.137–169. DOI: 10.1515/langcog. 2011.006

Skopeteas, Stavros. 2008. "Encoding Spatial Relations: Language typology and diachronic change in Greek". *Sprachtypologie und Universalienforschung* 61:1.54–66.

Slack, Jon & Emile van der Zee. 2003. "The Representation of Direction in Language and Space". *Representing Direction in Language and Space* ed. by Emile van der Zee & Jon Slack (= *Explorations in Language and Space*, 1), 1–17. Oxford: Oxford University Press. DOI: 10.1093/ acprof:oso/9780199260195.003.0001

Slobin, Dan I. 1996. "Two Ways to Travel: Verbs of motion in English and Spanish". *Grammatical Constructions: Their form and meaning* ed. by Masayoshi Shibatani & Sandra A. Thompson, 195–219. Oxford: Clarendon Press.

Slobin, Dan I. 1997. "Mind, Code, and Text". *Essays on Language Function and Language Type Dedicated to T. Givón* ed. by Joan Bybee, John Haiman & Sandra A. Thompson, 437–467. Amsterdam & Philadelphia: John Benjamins.

Slobin, Dan I. 2004. "The Many Ways to Search for a Frog: Linguistic typology and the expression of motion events". *Relating Events in Narrative, vol. II: Typological and Contextual Perspectives* ed. by Sven Strömqvist & Ludo Verhoven, 219–257. Mahwah, N. J.: Lawrence Erlbaum.

Slobin, Dan I. 2006. "What Makes Manner of Motion Salient? Explorations in linguistic typology, discourse, and cognition". Hickmann & Robert, eds. 2006.59–81.

Smith, Colin. 1992. *Collins Spanish–English English–Spanish Dictionary.* Unabridged. In collaboration with Diarmuid Bradley, Teresa de Carlos, Louis Rodrigues & José Ramón Parrondo. 3rd ed. Glasgow & New York: Harper-Collins.

Smith, John Charles & Martin Maiden, eds. 1994. *Linguistic Theory and the Romance Languages.* (= *Current Issues in Linguistic Theory*, 122.) Amsterdam & Philadelphia: John Benjamins.

Soares da Silva, Augusto. 2003. "Image Schemas and Category Coherence: The case of the Portuguese verb *deixar*". *Cognitive Approaches to Lexical Semantics* ed. by Hubert Cuyckens, René Dirven & John R. Taylor (= *Cognitive Linguistics Research*, 23), 281–322. Berlin & New York: Mouton de Gruyter. DOI: 10.1515/9783110219074.281

Sornicola, Rosanna. 2010. "Romance Linguistics and Historical Linguistics: Reflections on synchrony and diachrony" Maiden, Smith & Ledgeway, eds. 2010.1–49.

Soto Andión, Xosé. 2011. "La semántica de *pasar*: Análisis y variación". *Zeitschrift für Romanische Philologie* 127:3.480–513.

Spencer, W[alter] G[eorge], ed. 1989. Celsus, *De Medicina.* Vol. II. Books V–VI. (= *Loeb Classical Library*, 304.) Cambridge, Mass.: Harvard University Press; London: William Heinemann.

Spitzer, Leo. 1967 [1918]. "Über das Futurum *cantare habeo*". *Aufsätze zur romanischen Syntax und Stilistik* by Leo Spitzer, 173–180. 2nd ed. Tübingen: Max Niemeyer.

Spreafico, Lorenzo. 2008a. "Tipologie di lessicalizzazioni adverbali in alcune lingue d'Europa". Cini, ed. 2008.61–81.

Spreafico, Lorenzo. 2008b. "Tipologie di lessicalizzazione degli eventi di moto nelle lingue dell'Area linguistica Carlomagno". *Prospettive nello studio del lessico italiano: Atti del IX Congresso SILFI, Firenze, 14–17 giugno 2006* ed. by Emanuela Cresti, vol. II, 367–372. Firenze: Firenze University Press.

Spreafico, Lorenzo. 2009. *Problemi di tipologia lessicale: I verbi di moto nello Standard Average European.* Roma: Bulzoni.

Stanners, Robert F., James J. Neiser, William P. Hernon & Roger Hall. 1979. "Memory Representation for Morphologically Related Words". *Jounral of Verbal Learning and Verbal Behavior* 18:4.399–412. DOI: 10.1016/S0022-5371(79)90219-6

Stefenelli, Arnulf. 1992. *Das Schicksal des lateinischen Wortschatzes in den romanischen Sprachen.* (= *Passauer Schriften zu Sprache und Literatur*, 6.) Passau: Richard Rothe.

Stefenelli, Arnulf. 2010. "Lexical Stability". Maiden, Smith & Ledgeway, eds. 2010.564–584.

Stein, Achim. 1999. "Describing Verb Semantics in a Type of Hierarchy". *Predicative Forms in Natural Language and in Lexical Knowledge Bases* ed. by Patrick Saint-Dizier (= *Text, Speech and Language Technology*, 6), 111–137. Dordrecht: Kluwer. DOI: 10.1007/978-94-017-2746-4_4

Stengaard, Birte. 1991. *Vida y muerte de un campo semántico: Un estudio de la evolución semántica de los verbos latinos* stare, sedere *e* iacere *del latín al romance del s. XIII.* (= *Beihefte zur Zeitschrift für Romanische Philologie*, 234.) Tübingen: Max Niemeyer.

Stolova, Natalya I. 2003. *Verbs of Motion in the Romance Languages.* Ph.D. dissertation, University of Pennsylvania.

Stolova, Natalya I. 2005a. "Expressing Time through Space: A comparative diachronic perspective on Romance periphrastic past and future". *On Space and Time in Language* ed. by M[artine] Coene & L[iliane] Tasmowski, 193–207. Cluj-Napoca: Clusium.

Stolova, Natalya I. 2005b. "Where Can Working in Tandem Take Us? Romance data meets grammaticalization theory". *La corónica* 34:1.243–252. DOI: 10.1353/cor.2005.0016

Stolova, Natalya I. 2006. "Split Intransitivity in Old Spanish: Irrealis and negation factors". *Revue Roumaine de Linguistique* 51:2.301–320.

Stolova, Natalya I. 2007. "Italian Split Intransitivity and Image Schemas: The cognitive linguistics – neuroscience interface". *Annual Review of Cognitive Linguistics* 5.77–106. DOI: 10.1075/arcl.5.05sto

Stolova, Natalya I. 2008. "From Satellite-Framed Latin to Verb-Framed Romance: Late Latin as an intermediate stage". *Latin vulgaire – latin tardif VIII: Actes du VIIIe Colloque International sur le Latin Vulgaire et Tardif, Oxford, 6–9 septembre 2006* ed. by Roger Wright, 253–262. Hildesheim: Georg Olms; Zürich: Weidmann.

Stolova, Natalya I. 2009a. "Classification of the Romance Languages: Evolution of motion-based periphrases as a new criterion". *Romance Quarterly* 56:2.82–90. DOI: 10.3200/RQTR.56.2.82-90

Stolova, Natalya I. 2009b. "Los corpus diacrónicos al servicio del estudio de los arcaísmos gramaticales". *Diacronía de las lenguas iberorromances: Nuevas perspectivas desde la lingüística de corpus* ed. by Andrés Enrique-Arias (= *Lingüística Iberoamericana*, 37), 387–402. Madrid: Iberoamericana; Frankfurt am Main: Vervuert.

Stolova, Natalya I. 2010a. "La evolución del campo conceptual de movimiento: Una perspectiva cognitiva onomasiológica". *Actes du XXVe Congrès International de Linguistique et de Philologie Romanes, Innsbruck, 3–8 septembre 2007* ed. by Maria Iliescu, Heidi Siller-Rungaldier & Paul Danler, vol. III, 187–195. Berlin & New York: De Gruyter.

Stolova, Natalya I. 2010b. "Ramón Menéndez Pidal's Concept of 'Latent State' and the History of Spanish Aspectual Constructions". *Romance Philology* 64:2.257–267.

Stolova, Natalya I. 2012. "El estado latente y la evolución de las construcciones aspectuales con el verbo 'seguir'". *Actas del VIII Congreso Internacional de Historia de la Lengua Española, Santiago de Compostela, 14–18 de septiembre de 2009* ed. by Emilio Montero Cartelle, vol. I., 1185–1192. Madrid: Meubook.

Stone, Jon R. 2005. *The Routledge Dictionary of Latin Quotations*. New York & London: Routledge.

Strohmeyer, Fritz. 1910. *Der Stil der französischen Sprache*. Berlin: Weidmann.

Sutton, E. W. & H. Rackham, eds. 1996. Cicero, *De Oratore*. Books I–II. With an English transl. by E. W. Sutton. Completed, with an introduction by H. Rackham. (= *Loeb Classical Library*, 348.) Cambridge, Mass. & London: Harvard University Press.

Suxačev, N. L. 1990. "Vyraženie prostranstvennyx otnošenij v reto-romanskom jazyke Švejcarii [Expression of spatial relations in Swiss Raeto-Romance]". *Romanskie Jazyki: Semantika, pragmatika, sociolingvistika [The Romance languages: Semantics, pragmatics, sociolinguistics]* ed. by T. A. Repina, 59–64. Leningrad: Izdatel'stvo Leningradskogo Universiteta.

Svorou, Soteria. 1994. *The Grammar of Space*. (= *Typological Studies in Language*, 25.) Amsterdam & Philadelphia: John Benjamins. DOI: 10.1075/tsl.25

Swan, Toril. 2010. "Spatial Metaphors in the History of English and Norwegian". *Neuphilologische Mitteilungen* 111:1.55–67.

Sweetser, Eve. 1990. *From Etymology to Pragmatics: Metaphorical and cultural aspects of semantic structure*. (= *Cambridge Studies in Linguistics*, 54.) Cambridge: Cambridge University Press. DOI: 10.1017/CBO9780511620904

Swiggers, Pierre. 1998. "Filologia e lingüística: Enlace, divórcio, reconciliação". *Filologia e Lingüística Portuguesa* 2.5–18. DOI: 10.11606/issn.2176-9419.v0i2p5-18

Swiggers, Pierre. 2001. "Les débuts et l'évolution de la philologie romane au XIXe siècle, surtout en Allemagne". *History of the Language Sciences/Geschichte der Sprachwissenschaften/Histoire des sciences du langue; An international handbook on the evolution of the study of language from the beginnings to the present/Ein internationales Handbuch zur Entwicklung der Sprachforschung von den Anfängen bis zur Gegenwart/Manuel international sur l'évolution de l'étude du langage des origines à nos jours* ed. by Sylvain Auroux, E.F.K. Koerner, Hans-Josef Niederehe & Kees Versteegh (= *Handbücher zur Sprach- und Kommunikationswissenschaft*, 18), vol. II, 1272–1285. Berlin & New York: Walter de Gruyter.

Sylvester, Louise. 1994. *Studies in Lexical Field of Expectation*. (= *Costerus*, new series, 90.) Amsterdam & Atlanta: Rodopi.

Šišmarëv, V[ladimir] F[ëdorovič]. 2002 [1941]. *Očerki po istorii jazykov Ispanii [Essays on the history of the languages of Spain]*. 2nd ed. Moscow: URSS.

Taft, Marcus & Sam Ardasinski. 2006. "Obligatory Decomposition in Reading Prefixed Words". *The Mental Lexicon* 1:2.183–199. DOI: 10.1075/ml.1.2.02taf

Tagliavini, Carlo. 1982 [1949]. "Di alcuni denominazioni della 'pupilla' (studio di onomasiologia con speciale riguardo alle lingue camito-semitiche e negro-africane)". *Scritti minori* by Carlo Tagliavini, 529–568. Bologna: Pàtron.

Tagliavini, Carlo. 1952. *Le origini delle lingue neolatine*. 2nd ed. Bologna: Pàtron.

Tai, James H-Y. 2003. "Cognitive Relativism: Resultative construction in Chinese". *Language and Linguistics* 4:2.301–316.

Talmy, Leonard. 1972a. *Semantic Structures in English and Atsugewi*. Ph.D. dissertation, University of California at Berkeley.

Talmy, Leonard. 1972b. "The Basis for a Crosslinguistic Typology of Motion/Location". Part I. *Stanford University Working Papers on Language Universals* 9.41–116.

Talmy, Leonard. 1973. "The Basis for a Crosslinguistic Typology of Motion/Location". Part II. *Stanford University Working Papers on Language Universals* 11.23–83.

Talmy, Leonard. 1975. "Semantics and Syntax of Motion". *Syntax and Semantics* 4.181–238.

Talmy, Leonard. 1983. "How Language Structures Space". Pick & Acredolo, eds. 1983.225–282.

Talmy, Leonard. 1985. "Lexicalization Patterns: Semantic structure in lexical forms". *Language Typology and Syntactic Description* ed. by Timothy Shopen, vol. III: *Grammatical Categories and the Lexicon*, 57–149. Cambridge: Cambridge University Press.

Talmy, Leonard. 2000. *Toward a Cognitive Semantics. Vol. I: Concept Structuring Systems; Vol. II: Typology and Process in Concept Structuring*. Cambridge, Mass. & London: MIT Press.

Talmy, Leonard. 2003. "Concept Structuring Systems in Language". *The New Psychology of Language: Cognitive and functional approaches to language structure* ed. by Michael Tomasello, vol. II, 15–46. Mahwah & London: Lawrence Earlbaum.

Talmy, Leonard. 2007. "Lexical Typologies". *Language Typology and Syntactic Description* ed. by Timothy Shopen, vol. III: *Grammatical Categories and the Lexicon*, 66–168. 2nd ed. Cambridge: Cambridge University Press.

Talmy, Leonard. 2009. "Main Verb Properties and Equipollent Framing". *Crosslinguistic Approaches to the Psychology of Language: Research in the tradition of Dan Isaac Slobin* ed. by Jiansheng Guo, Elena Lieven, Nancy Budwig, Susan Ervin-Tripp, Keiko Nakamura & Seyda Özçalýşkan, 389–402. New York & London: Psychology Press.

Talmy, Leonard. 2012. "Main Verb Properties". *International Journal of Cognitive Linguistics* 3:1.1–23.

Tappolet, Ernst. 1895. *Die romanischen Verwandtschaftsnamen mit besonderer Berücksichtigung der französischen und italienischen Mundarten: Ein Beitrag zur vergleichenden Lexikologie*. Strassburg: Karl J. Trübner.

Taylor, John. 1999. "Cognitive Semantics and Structural Semantics". Blank & Koch, eds. 1999.17–48.

Tekavčic, Pavao. 1972. *Grammatica storica dell'italiano. Vol. III: Lessico*. Bologna: Il Mulino.

Tesnière, Lucien. 1959. *Éléments de syntaxe structurale*. Paris: Librairie C. Klincksieck.

Tiktin, Hariton. 1895–1925. *Rumänisch–deutsches Wörterbuch*. 3 vols. Bucarest: Staatsdruckerei.

Tommaseo, Niccolò & Bernardo Bellini. 1865–1879. *Dizionario della lingua italiana*. 4 vols. Torino: Unione Tipografico-Editrice.

Tornatore, Matthew G. C. 2006. "In Defense of an Endangered Species: Historical Romance linguistics". *Romance Notes* 46:2.243–250.

Torras i Rodergas, Josep, ed. 1985. *Diccionari castellà–català*. Barcelona: Enciclopèdia Catalana.

Traugott, Elizabeth Closs. 1978. "On the Expression of Spatio-Temporal Relations in Language". *Universals of Human Language* ed. by Joseph H. Greenberg, Charles A. Ferguson & Edith A. Moravcsik, vol. III: *Word Structure*, 369–400. Stanford: Stanford University Press.

Traugott, Elizabeth Closs. 1985a. "'Conventional' and 'Dead' Metaphors Revisited". *The Ubiquity of Metaphor: Metaphor in language and thought* ed. by Wolf Paprotté & René Dirven (= *Current Issues in Linguistic Theory*, 29), 17–56. Amsterdam & Philadelphia: John Benjamins. DOI: 10.1075/cilt.29.04clo

Traugott, Elizabeth Closs. 1985b. "On Regularity in Semantic Change". *Journal of Literary Semantics: An international review* 14:3.155–173.

Traugott, Elizabeth Closs. 2000. "Semantic change: An overview". *The First Glot International State-of-the-Article Book: The latest in linguistics* ed. by Lisa Cheng & Rint Sybesma (= *Studies in Generative Grammar*, 48), 385–406. Berlin & New York: Mouton de Gruyter.

Traugott, Elizabeth Closs. 2003. "Constructions in Grammaticalization". *The Handbook of Historical Linguistics* ed. by Brian D. Joseph & Richard D. Janda, 624–647. Malden, Mass.: Blackwell. DOI: 10.1002/9780470756393.ch20

Traugott, Elizabeth Closs & Ekkehard König. 1991. "The Semantics-Pragmatics of Grammaticalization Revisited". *Approaches to Grammaticalization* ed. by Elizabeth Closs Traugott & Bernd Heine, vol. I: *Focus on Theoretical and Methodological Issues* (= *Typological Studies in Language*, 19:1), 189–218. Amsterdam & Philadelphia: John Benjamins. DOI: 10.1075/tsl.19.1.10clo

Traugott, Elizabeth Closs & Graeme Trousdale. 2013. *Constructionalization and Constructional Changes* (= *Oxford Studies in Diachronic and Historical Linguistics*, 6). Oxford: Oxford University Press. DOI: 10.1093/acprof:oso/9780199679898.001.0001

Traugott, Elizabeth Closs & Richard B. Dascher. 2002. *Regularity in Semantic Change.* (= *Cambridge Studies in Linguistics*, 96.) Cambridge: Cambridge University Press.

Trousdale, Graeme. 2008a. "A Constructional Approach to Lexicalization Processes in the History of English: Evidence from possessive constructions". *Word Structure* 1:2.156–177. DOI: 10.3366/E1750124508000202

Trousdale, Graeme. 2008b. "Constructions in Grammaticalization and Lexicalization: Evidence from the history of a composite predicate construction in English". *Constructional Approaches to English Grammar* ed. by Graeme Trousdale & Nikolas Gisborne (= *Topics in English Linguistics*, 57), 33–67. Berlin: Mouton de Gruyter.

Trubačëv, O[leg] N[ikolaevič]. 1964. "'Molčat' i 'tajat": O neobxodimosti semasiologičeskogo slovarja novogo tipa ['To be silent' and 'to melt': On the necessity of a semasiological dictionary of a new kind]". *Problemy indoevropejskogo jazykoznanija: Ètjudy po stavnitel'no-istoričeskoj grammatike indoevropejskix jazykov* [*Issues in Indo-European linguistics: Essays on comparative-historical grammar of the Indo-European languages*] ed. by V[ladimir] N[ikolaevič] Toporov, 100–105. Moscow: "Nauka".

Ullmann, Stephen. 1957. *The Principles of Semantics*. 2nd ed. New York: Philosophical Library.

Ullmann, Stephen. 1972. "Semantics". *Current Trends in Linguistics* ed. by Thomas A. Sebeok, vol. IX: *Linguistics in Western Europe*, 343–394. The Hague & Paris: Mouton.

Väänänen, Veikko. 1990. "PLICARE/APPLICARE 'se diriger vers': Simplex pro composito?" *Latin vulgaire – latin tardif II: Actes du IIème Colloque International sur le Latin Vulgaire et Tardif, Bologne, 29 août – 2 septembre 1988* ed. by Gualtiero Calboli, 239–247. Tübingen: Max Niemeyer.

Väänänen, Veikko. 2003. *Introducción al latín vulgar*. Transl. by Manuel Carrión. 3rd ed. Madrid: Gredos.

Valdés, Juan de. 1964 [1535]. *Diálogo de la lengua*. 4th ed. (= *Colección Austral*, 216.) Madrid: Espasa-Calpe.

Vandeloise, Claude. 1986. *L'espace en français: Sémantique des prépositions spatiales*. Paris: Éditions du Seuil.

van der Auwera, Johan. 1998. "Conclusion". *Adverbial Constructions in the Languages of Europe* ed. by Johan van der Auwera (= *Empirical Approaches to Language Typology*, 20:3), 813–836. Berlin: Mouton de Gruyter. DOI: 10.1515/9783110802610

van der Auwera, Johan & Jan Nuyts. 2007. "Cognitive Linguistics and Linguistic Typology". *The Oxford Handbook of Cognitive Linguistics* ed. by Dirk Geeraerts & Hubert Cuyckens, 1074–1091. Oxford: Oxford University Press.

Vanhove, Martine, ed. 2008. *From Polysemy to Semantic Change: Towards a typology of lexical semantic associations*. (= *Studies in Language Companion Series*, 106.) Amsterdam & Philadelphia: John Benjamins. DOI: 10.1075/slcs.106

Vernay, Henri. 1974. *Essai sur l'organisation de l'espace par divers systèmes linguistiques: contribution à une linguistique de la traduction.* (= *Internationale Bibliothek für Allgemeine Linguistik*, 34.) München: Wilhelm Fink.

Vernay, Henri. 1991–1996. *Dictionnaire onomasiologique des langues romanes.* 6 vols. Tübingen: Max Niemeyer.

Veselinova, Ljuba N. 2006. *Suppletion in Verb Paradigms: Bits and pieces of the puzzle.* (= *Typological Studies in Language*, 67.) Amsterdam & Phildelphia: John Benjamins. DOI: 10.1075/tsl.67

Vicario, Federico. 1997. *I verbi analitici in friulano.* Milano: FrancoAngeli.

Vidos, B[enedetto]. 1963. *Manual de lingüística románica.* Transl. by Francisco de B. Moll. Madrid: Aguilar.

Vinay, Jean-Paul & Jean Darbelnet. 1958. *Stylistique comparée du français et de l'anglais: Méthode de traduction.* (= *Bibliothèque de stylistique comparée*, 1.) Paris: Didier. (Nouvelle éd. revue et corrigée, 1971.)

Vinay, Jean-Paul & Jean Darbelnet. 1995. *Comparative Stylistics of French and English: A methodology for translation.* Transl. and ed. by Juan C. Sager & M.-J. Hamel. (= *Benjamins Translation Library*, 11.) Amsterdam & Philadelphia: John Benjamins. DOI: 10.1075/btl.11

Vincent, Nigel. 1988. "Latin". *The Romance Languages* ed. by Martin Harris & Nigel Vincent, 26–78. New York: Oxford University Press.

Vincent, Nigel. 1999. "The Evolution of C-Structure: Prepositions and PPs from Indo-European to Romance". *Linguistics* 37:6.1111–1153. DOI: 10.1515/ling.37.6.1111

Violi, Patrizia. 1991. "Linguaggio, percesione, esperienza: Il caso della spazialità". *Versus* 59/60.59–105.

Violi, Patrizia. 1996. "La spazialità in moto: Per una semiotica dei verbi di movimento". *Versus* 73/74.83–103.

Wagner, Max Leopold. 1960–1964. *Dizionario etimologico sardo.* 3 vols. (= *Sammlung Romanischer Elementar- und Handbücher*, Reihe 3: *Wörterbücher*, 6.) Heidelberg: Carl Winter. [Vol. III: *Indici delle voci e delle forme dialettali compilati da Raffaele G. Urciolo*.]

Wälchli, Bernhard. 2001a. "A Typology of Displacement (with special reference to Latvian)". *Sprachtypologie und Universalienforschung* 54.298–323.

Wälchli, Bernhard. 2001b. "Lexical Evidence for Parallel Development of the Latvian and Livonian Verb Particles". *The Circum-Baltic Languages: Typology and Contact* ed. by Östen Dahl & Maria Koptjevskaja-Tamm, vol. II: *Grammar and Typology* (= *Studies in Language Companion Series*, 55), 413–441. Amsterdam & Philadelphia: John Benjamins.

Wälchli, Bernhard. 2006. "Lexicalization Patterns in Motion Events Revisited". Ms., University of Konstanz. (http://ling.uni-konstanz.de/pages/home/a20_11/waelchli/waelchli-lexpatt.pdf). Accessed: June 2006.

Wälchli, Bernhard & Michael Cysouw. 2012. "Lexical Typology through Similarity Semantics: Toward a semantic map of motion verbs". *Linguisitcs* 50:3.671–710.

Walde, Alois & J[ohann] B[aptist] Hofmann. 1982. *Lateinisches etymologisches Wörterbuch.* 3 vols. 5th ed. Heidelberg: Carl Winter.

Wanner, Dieter. 2001. "From Latin to the Romance Languages". *Language Typology and Language Universals / Sprachtypologie und sprachliche Universalien / La typologie des langues et les universaux linguistiques; An international handbook / Ein internationales Handbuch / Manuel international* ed. by Martin Haspelmath, Ekkehard König, Wulf Oesterreicher & Wolfgang Raible (= *Handbücher zur Sprach- und Kommunikationswissenschaft*, 20:2), vol. II, 1691–1706. Berlin & New York: Walter de Gruyter.

Wartburg, Walther von. 1936–1970. *Französisches etymologisches Wörterbuch: Eine Darstellung des galloromanischen Sprachschatzes*. 14 vols. Tübingen: J.C.B. Mohr.

Watkins, Calvert. 1993. "Indo-European Roots". *The American Heritage College Dictionary* ed. by Kaethe Ellis, 1584–1625. 3rd ed. Boston & New York: Houghton Mifflin.

Welty, Beat Kaspar. 1974. *Der Bewegungs- und Richtungsausdruck un der italienischen und französischen Gegenwartssprache*. Doctoral dissertation, Universität Zürich.

Wheeler, Arthur Leslie, ed. & transl. 1996. Ovid, *Tristia. Ex Ponto*. 2nd ed. Revised by G[eorge] P[atrick] Goold. (= *Loeb Classical Library*, 151.) Cambridge, Mass. & London: Harvard University Press.

Whorf, Benjamin Lee. 1956 [1939]. "The Relation of Habitual Thought and Behavior to Language". *Language, Thought, and Reality: Selected writings of Benjamin Lee Whorf* ed. by John B. Carroll, 134–159. Cambridge, Mass.: MIT Press.

Wienold, Götz & Christoph Schwarze. 2002. *The Lexicalization of Movement Concepts in French, Italian, Japanese and Korean: Towards a realistic typology*. (= *Arbeitspapiere des Fachbereichs Sprachwissenschaft*, 112.) Universität Konstanz.

Winstedt, E. O., ed. & transl. 1944. Cicero, *Letters to Atticus*. Vol. I. (= *Loeb Classical Library*, 7.) Cambridge, Mass.: Harvard University Press; London: William Heinemann.

Winterbottom, M[ichael], ed. & transl. 1974a. The Elder Seneca, *Declamations. Vol. I: Controversiae*. Books I–VI. (= *Loeb Classical Library*, 463.) Cambridge, Mass.: Harvard University Press; London: William Heinemann.

Winterbottom, M., ed. & transl. 1974b. The Elder Seneca, *Declamations. Vol. II: Controversiae*. Books VII–X. *Suasoriae*. (= *Loeb Classical Library*, 464.) Cambridge, Mass.: Harvard University Press; London: William Heinemann.

Winters, Margaret E. 2010. "Introduction: On the emergence of diachronic cognitive linguistics". *Historical Cognitive Linguistics* ed. by Margaret E. Winters, Heli Tissari & Kathryn Allan (= *Cognitive Linguistics Research*, 47), 3–27. Berlin & New York: Mouton de Gruyter.

Wright, Roger. 1982. *Late Latin and Early Romance in Spain and Carolingian France*. (= *ARCA Classical and Medieval Texts, Papers and Monographs*, 8.) Liverpool: Francis Cairns.

Wright, Roger. 1994. *Early Ibero-Romance: Twenty-one studies on language and texts from the Iberian Peninsula between the Roman Empire and the thirteenth century*. (= *Estudios Lingüísticos*, 5.) Newark, Del.: Juan de la Cuesta.

Wright, Roger. 2002. *A Sociophilological Study of Late Latin*. (= *Utrecht Studies in Medieval Literacy*, 10.) Turnhout: Brepols.

Zaliznjak, Anna A. 2001. "Semantičeskaja derivacija v sinxronii i diaxronii: Proekt 'Kataloga semantičeskix perexodov' [Semantic derivation in synchrony and diachrony: The project 'Catalogue of semantic shifts']". *Voprosy Jazykoznanija* 2001:2.13–25.

Zaliznjak, Anna A. 2008. "A Catalogue of Semantic Shifts: Towards a typology of semantic derivation". Vanhove, ed. 2008.217–232.

Zaliznjak, Anna A., Maria Bulakh, Dmitrij Ganenkov, Ilya Gruntov, Timur Maisak & Maxim Russo. 2012. "The Catalogue of Semantic Shifts as a Database for Lexical Semantic Typology". *Linguistics* 50:3.633–669. DOI: 10.1515/ling-2012-0020

Zauner, Adolf. 1903. "Die romanischen Namen der Körperteile: Eine onomasiologische Studie". *Romanische Forschungen* 14.339–530.

Zlatev, Jordan. 2007. "Spatial Semantics". *The Oxford Handbook of Cognitive Linguistics* ed. by Dirk Geeraerts & Hubert Cuyckens, 318–350. Oxford: Oxford University Press.

Zlatev, Jordan, Johan Blomberg & Caroline David. 2010. "Translocation, Language and the Categorization of Experience". *Language, Cognition and Space: The state of the art and new directions* ed. by Vyvyan Evans & Paul Chilton, 389–418. London & Oakville: Equinox.

Zlatev, Jordan & Peerapat Yangklang. 2004. "A Third Way to Travel: The place of Thai in motion-event typology". *Relating Events in Narrative, vol. II: Typological and Contextual Perspectives* ed. by Sven Strömqvist & Ludo Verhoven, 159–190. Mahwah, N. J.: Lawrence Erlbaum.

Zubizarreta, Maria Luisa & Eunjeong Oh. 2007. *On the Syntactic Composition of Manner and Motion.* (= *Linguistic Inquiry Monographs*, 48.) Cambridge, Mass.: MIT Press.

Index of languages and language families

This index does not include languages and the language family that are discussed in detail in every chapter, such as Catalan, French, Italian, Latin, Occitan, Portuguese, Raeto-Romance, Romanian, Sardinian (Campidanese, Logudorese), Spanish, and Romance.

Index of subjects and terms